THE GLOBAL FINANCIAL CRISIS AND EDUCATIONAL RESTRUCTURING

GLOBAL STUDIES IN EDUCATION

A.C. (Tina) Besley, Michael A. Peters,
Cameron McCarthy, Fazal Rizvi
General Editors

Vol. 31

The Global Studies in Education series is part of the Peter Lang Education list.
Every volume is peer reviewed and meets
the highest quality standards for content and production.

PETER LANG
New York • Bern • Frankfurt • Berlin
Brussels • Vienna • Oxford • Warsaw

THE GLOBAL FINANCIAL CRISIS AND EDUCATIONAL RESTRUCTURING

Edited by Michael A. Peters,
João M. Paraskeva, & Tina Besley

PETER LANG
New York • Bern • Frankfurt • Berlin
Brussels • Vienna • Oxford • Warsaw

Library of Congress Cataloging-in-Publication Data

The global financial crisis and educational restructuring /
edited by Michael A. Peters, João M. Paraskeva, Tina Besley.
pages cm. — (Global studies in education; vol. 31)
Includes bibliographical references and index.
1. Education—Finance. 2. Education—Economic aspects. 3. Education and state.
4. Education—United States—Finance. 5. Education, Higher—United States—
Finance. 6. Global Financial Crisis, 2008–2009. I. Peters, Michael A.
LB2824.G56 371.2'06—dc23 2014048994
ISBN 978-1-4331-2540-9 (hardcover)
ISBN 978-1-4331-2539-3 (paperback)
ISBN 978-1-4539-1492-2 (e-book)
ISSN 2153-330X

Bibliographic information published by **Die Deutsche Nationalbibliothek.**
Die Deutsche Nationalbibliothek lists this publication in the "Deutsche
Nationalbibliografie"; detailed bibliographic data are available
on the Internet at http://dnb.d-nb.de/.

The paper in this book meets the guidelines for permanence and durability
of the Committee on Production Guidelines for Book Longevity
of the Council of Library Resources.

29 Broadway, 18th floor, New York, NY 10006
www.peterlang.com

Printed in the United States of America

Table of Contents

Introduction

Global Financial Crisis and Educational Restructuring

MICHAEL A. PETERS, TINA BESLEY, AND JOÃO PARASKEVA

The worldwide integration and globalization of finance is one of the major developments of this age. This process and its effects have been intensified through a range of factors including economic and trade reforms following the collapse of the Soviet Union in 1991 and China joining the World Trade Organization (WTO) in 2001 and the subsequent development and opening up of Chinese capital markets in 2013.[1] These changes and the establishment of a global finance culture coincided with the rise of a market-oriented neoliberalism that began in the USA and UK and went on to become the dominant politico-economic-social policy system not only in the Western world but also in Asia and Latin America. Neoliberalism established the Washington Consensus free-market ideology of economic structural reforms, macroeconomic stabilization, free trade and foreign investment, market freedom, and the minimal state. As well as nation-states pursuing neoliberal policies, we have seen the neoliberalisation of major world policy agencies promoting free trade and privatization strategies. Education has been at the very core of such strategies and we have been experiencing "an increasing interest in the education of the workforce and the mobilization of financial resources to accomplish this task" (Harvey, 2014, p. 183).

Another vitally crucial parallel process that has highly influenced financial systems and which has intensified especially in the twenty-first century is the acceleration of technological innovation systems. New Internet technologies (IT) have reinforced financial market integration through growth of fibre optics, mobile telephones, new forms of instant messaging, social media, the use of sophisticated algorithms in financial markets, and now high speed trading using lasers and so on. These trends and associated global governance and policy shifts have created and emphasized a form of interconnectedness and interdependence, yet the downside surely has to be a potential fragility in any collapse in just one part of a one-world integrated financial ecosystem that poses new systemic risks and contagion effects. While the world has experienced high levels of technological accomplishments—"the electronic revolution of communications, information, genetics and the biotechnological" (Sousa Santos, 2005, p. vii) serious global contradictions have been exposed.

> It is a time of disquieting regressions, a return of the social evils that appeared to have been or about to be overcome, [a] return of slavery and slavish work [a] return of high vulnerability to old sicknesses that seemed to have been eradicated and appear linked to new pandemics like HIV/AIDS [and now Ebola] [a] return of the revolting social inequalities that gave their name to the social question at the end of the nineteenth century; in sum, the return of the specter of war, perhaps now more than ever a world war, although whether cold or not is as yet undecidable. (ibid, p. vii)

Systemic risk and system failure in global finance can be caused by many different (but interrelated) factors: too much debt (households, corporations, banks, financial institutions, governments), too much borrowing in foreign currency, sovereign debt, asset bubbles, overconfidence, large and complex banking systems, shadow banking systems (non-bank institutions taking on banking functions), financial innovation leading to collateralized debt obligation and securitization, the failure of mathematical models (Klemkosky, 2013). Neoliberalism edifies an economic framework based on the continuing process of subjectification, of a 'subjective economy' that creates a binary creditor-debtor positional continuum (Lazzarato, 2011).

Following the 2007–2008 Global Financial Crisis (GFC) in the USA, the 2010 Dodd-Frank Act instituted a new set of reforms intended to reduce systemic risk and ensure greater system stability through the development of a new regulatory environment intended to supplement the existing Securities Acts of 1933 and 1934. The Consumer Financial Protection Bureau and the Office of Financial Research are supposed to monitor systemic risk for the Federal Reserve Board.[2] These reforms amount to the most massive reform of the US financial system ever with the Act running to hundreds of pages, yet it is clear that the reforms have been incomplete and the regulators have underestimated the systemic risk in destabilizing financial markets. Perhaps even more telling, little thought has gone into the 'risks' of the financialization of everything—the financialization of the economy, society, and culture. Within this financialization matrix, the state plays a key harmonizing role within an interbanking system underpinned by American liberal internationalism and the wilting financial institutions of the Bretton Woods agreement. It is in this context that it is crucial to demystify globalization as it poses challenges that seem to increasingly erode national sovereignty. Quite conversely, Leo Panitch (2011) argues, "The states are crucial, and the power of states are crucial to [the] phenomenon of globalization" (p. 79). While the interstate system is failing, especially with the rise of non-state actors (e.g., massive transnational companies as well as terrorist organizations such as ISIS), there is as yet no alternative.

Education is a central aspect of modern life, seen now not so much as a social good but as an economic good tied in with notions of human capital theory, and as crucial for any state to be competitive and to become fully engaged in the knowledge economy. As such, education entails investment costs both for the state and for individuals engaged in obtaining (or 'consuming') education.

The global picture is complex in terms of what and how much and which education sectors are publicly funded. Globally, we find that the schooling sector comprising primary and secondary education (K–12 in USA) in most countries is generally financed by the state since it is seen as important for advancing social aspects such as equality of opportunity, addressing diversity, and social inclusiveness. Despite this, there is frequent political debate about the extent of that provision and opponents to public education suggest not only voucher systems but also more private or charter schools. Although generally a much smaller sub-sector, alongside publicly funded schools there are also privately funded ones. In contrast to the K–12 sector, the early childhood education sector is predominantly privately funded although parents may receive various levels of state subsidy. Higher education funding in much of the world is publicly funded, but students are required to pay increasingly high fees in many states and there are also an increasing number of private higher education institutions emerging worldwide. Some countries still fund free university education. There is now a considerable discourse about a crisis in publicly funded education.

One of the toughest challenges facing current 'education-state-market' relationships has been examined by Peters and Besley (2006). Drawing on Hardt and Negri's rationale, Peters and Besley warn of the need to frame the interface education-economy within a radically different cultural knowledge economy. One that is at grips with not just new dimensions of labor, such as flexibility and mobility, but also with the intricacies with the immateriality of labor, that concomitantly pushes education for a new dynamics of ideological production. Peters and Besley claim that the postmodernization of production and labor imply unequivocally the postmodernization of the circuits of cultural and economic production and labor unleashing new demands for education and educators.

However, education remains the prime institutional mechanism for the generation and transmission of values, culture, and knowledge. It has long been considered a vehicle for social mobility, social transformation, social cohesiveness, and for social equality leading to a more just and democratic society, but it has been well and truly financialized. This is a multifaceted and as yet incomplete process that has affected source of funding of education at all levels particularly with the rise of private learning institutions and the financialization of student loans. Critical avenues for a serious debate of how public is public education have opened up. Such debate is crucial in a moment when the attempts of a global uniformity at all costs, so visible in most recent conservative educational policies, such as the Common Core in USA, not only mask eugenic claims but also place education at the center of rebooting new processes of humankind's ideological revolution (Paraskeva & Torres Santome, 2012). The concept of public education accordingly has undergone a profound transformation and it unlikely to ever be the same again.

Some six years after the Global Financial Crisis the effects are lingering, and some would argue the structural issues that brought about the crisis have not disappeared but are inherent to the system. The stability and fairness of the world financial system is seen as one of the elements of global order, only recently integrating classical civilizations and regional blocs, especially China, India, and most countries of the Middle East, into a system poised between the old Westphalian order and the relatively new American-styled liberal internationalist democratic order. A stable financial system, along with international rule of law, state sovereignty, and the national-state system would seem to be a condition for peace and prosperity, yet the prevailing world order, if we can call it that, seems to be giving way to regional blocs sometimes based on religious belief rather than a scientific or rational outlook with the rise of movements and non-state actors. In this uncertain climate world financial stability is a prerequisite for world order and such stability implies a fair and neutral set of international controls, standards, and lawful regulation. But, in the present circumstances, the world—educational and life more generally—seems increasingly precarious.

THE ORGANIZATION OF THIS BOOK

This book is a collection of essays that engages systematically with these questions. The collection begins with a number of essays that describe the nature of finance capitalism and the dimensions of the Global Financial Crisis and financialization. These general essays by prominent theorists set the scene for an engagement with the effects of the Global Financial Crisis on education and follows with chapters that more specifically deal with education and often provide exemplars from different countries globally. A strength of the book is that the authors hail from many countries and operate with clear global perspectives. They are also from different academic disciplines and so bring a range of expertise and perspectives, which gives strength to this collection, a first multidisciplinary approach that addresses the issues of financialization and education.

We are fortunate to have world-renowned Slovenian philosopher and scholar Slavoj Žižek providing chapter 1, "A Permanent Economic Emergency." Žižek examines how the current metamorphoses of the last capitalist economy have been produced as a key ideological device to perpetuate a state of permanent emergency. In so doing, Žižek highlights how dynamics and categories such as state and class are more important than ever to understand the intricacies of an unraveled neo-conservative impulse.

Chapter 2, "Finance Capitalism, Financialization, and the Prospects for Public Education," is by Michael A. Peters and Tina Besley. As academics having worked in the UK, USA, and New Zealand, their chapter provides a global perspective, yet acknowledges local effects of financialization, the Global Financial Crisis, and the crisis of finance capitalism. They note the rise of finance culture as an aspect of financialization that impacts individuals and households in creating what can be considered the "financial citizen" or "entrepreneurial self." Peters and Besley use the Libor scandal as just one example of a culture of banking that is endemically fraudulent and has bought off all political opposition. The issue of High Frequency Trading (HFT) and the attempts by countries to regulate following the "Flash Crash" are briefly covered before the chapter addresses the financialization of education and finally the impact of student debt.

Costas Lapavitsas, in chapter 3, "Financialisation, or the Search for Profits in the Sphere of Circulation," points out advanced capitalist economies in the last thirty years represents expansion of the sphere of circulation, while the sphere of production has continued to face difficulties of profitability and productivity growth. In the course of financialization, relations among industrial/commercial capital, banks, and workers have been put on a different footing. The financial sector has become capable of extracting profit directly out of wages and salaries, a process called "financial expropriation." Financial institutions have also become adept at profit-making through mediating transactions in open financial markets, that is, investment banking. The combination of financial expropriation and investment banking were the catalysts for the GFC that began in 2007.

Chapter 4, "The OECD on FIRE: Financialization and Socioeconomic Decline in Advanced Economies," is by Jacob Assa, who lives in New York and is currently a statistician at the UN Department of Economic and Social Affairs (DESA). His perspective uses current data to build his case on the impact of financialization on OECD countries. In particular he notes limited economic growth, which appears to be slowing, financial fragility, and unemployment. He concludes by noting that although some assign blame for the recent economic and financial crises on financialization, the last forty years have seen negative impacts in the developed OECD countries where there is "increasing inequality, slowing down economic growth, and swelling unemployment. It appears that, when financial machinations supersede productive enterprise, to use Krippner's language, both the economy and society suffer."

Stefano Lucarelli and Emanuele Leonardi, from Bergamo, Italy, present chapter 5, "Financial Governmentality: Wealth-Effect as a Practice of Social Control." Lucarelli and Leonardi examine how contemporary capitalism is characterized by an accumulation regime whose main tendency is to incorporate every aspect of individual as well as societal experiences into valorization circuits. The means through which such an internalization occurs include neoliberal economic policies and the wealth-effect, arguably a command device aimed at governing contemporary subjectivity. Hence Lucarelli and Leonardi frame the process of financialization as a practice of social control. They use Michel Foucault's notions of biopolitics and governmentality for reflecting on financialization. In particular, the chapter focuses on one of the unprecedented characters of neoliberal financialization, namely its need for mass participation, its apparent democratic stance.

Chapter 6, "The Embers of Truth in the Ashes of Finance," is by Campbell Jones, Auckland, New Zealand. Jones looks for the immanent possibilities for public education that arise out of the culture of finance as he says "the new publics and new public educations that are summoned by finance in spite of itself." He writes: "I seek to account for the place in finance of logics of division, separation and particularism and at the same time how these unravel in the face of finance, both in the public and in public higher education."

Howard Gibson brings a UK-oriented approach in chapter 7, "Instrumental Reasoning qua Capitalist Rationality: The Embedding of Capitalism within Educational Discourse." The first part of the chapter seeks to explain the philosophical origins and assumptions of the term 'instrumental rationality," a term largely based on Max Horkheimer, by examining some of its philosophical antecedents in the work of David Hume and the sociology of Max Weber. The second part of Gibson's chapter shows how instrumental rationality has inserted itself into three current educational discourses (including managerialism) in England that employ reason instrumentally and becomes normalised. The third part links instrumental rationality with capitalism by showing that many of the secreted purposes contained in these educational discourses are primarily destined to secure a trained and disciplined labour force.

In chapter 8, "Financial Fantasy Documents and Public Learning: The Case of the U.S. Financial Crisis Inquiry Report," James Reveley and John Singleton provocatively examine the interplay between fantasy and financialized capitalism in the USA. While finding Deleuze and Guattari's materialist theory of group fantasy helpful, rather than a psychoanalytic study or a textual or discourse analysis, they draw on work by sociologists and organizational theorists who conceptualize official reports as fantasy documents that fulfill a social function. They use the 2011 report known as the Angelides Commission, issued by the U.S. Financial Crisis Inquiry Commission (FCIC) to illustrate this, treating it as a social fact in its own right rather than merely as a source of information about the crisis. They track the report's engagement with a wider social fantasy about the existence of a new period—immediately prior to the 2008 financial crisis—of finance-driven growth. They supplement the fantasy documents literature with work by economists whose crisis theories have an affinity with an emergent psychoanalytic literature on this topic. After providing a brief overview of the FCIC, Reveley and Singleton introduce the theory of fantasy documents identifying how the FCIC report channels two types of fantasy.

Policy analyst and leading gambling theory scholar Clyde W. Barrow, in chapter 9, "The Rationality Crisis in U.S. Higher Education," dissects how over the course of the last century, many of the stresses and contradictions of advanced capitalism have been displaced onto colleges and universities, which are now directly attached to the state—whether legally, politically, or financially—as an important component of the ideological and economic state apparatuses. As a component of the ideological and economic state apparatuses, the university is implicated in the state's ongoing fiscal crisis as both a cause of the crisis and a solution to the crisis. The author argues that the possibilities for crisis management within the existing corporate model of higher education have been exhausted in a rationality crisis that threatens to implode the administrative apparatus in higher education. The author calls for a radical reconstruction of power relationships within the university and in its relationships to capital and the state.

In chapter 10, "Neoliberal Pedagogy of Debt vs. Debtor Pedagogy: The New Neoliberal Commodities," João M. Paraskeva and Sheila L. Macrine expand on Williams' (2007) notion of debt education to help explicate Macrine's (2012) concept of a neoliberal pedagogy of debt, which she describes as a materialist interpretation of the development of neoliberal capitalism's chief predatory weapon—that of debt subjugation. They argue that in order to reveal the true ideological productive/reproductive practices of a neoliberal pedagogy of debt, it becomes necessary to make the other side of this predatory tool, a 'debtor pedagogy,' explicit, which helps to articulate the citizen/worker responses to such oppression and subjugation. In order to accomplish this, Paraskeva and Macrine (a) define the 'neoliberal pedagogy of debt' and introduce the concept of 'debtor pedagogy,' which is the flip side of the same predatory coin; (b) unmask how such pedagogies have been crucial in feeding the school-to-prison pipeline and force-outs, and; (c) examine how certain pedagogies have been determined by the needs of the current market-based culture of society asphyxiated by austerity policies and practices.

Sharon Rider and Alexandra Waluszewski, from Sweden, present chapter 11, Crowding Out Knowledge: Efficiency, Innovation, and Higher Education. Their chapter examines the monetization and marketization of higher education, research, and scholarship. Following Max Weber, they investigate the "forced marriage" between research and innovation in the modern university and the way in which policies have encouraged a deeper relationship between university research and industry, blurring the boundaries and concepts of different forms of life. Seemingly innocuous policies aimed at encouraging interaction between university research and industry have deeper implications that need exploring.

In chapter 12, "Who's Afraid of Public Financial Literacy?," Shanti Daellenbach considers the widespread enthusiasm for financial literacy programmes, which are supported by governments and financial institutions, suggesting that there are two ways of looking at how the public perceive the GFC. One suggests the public have not yet learnt their lessons, while another that they actually have done so. Globally, people have become increasingly vocal in discussions around the failings of the financial system, on ways to change it, and how it should operate in the future. There have been widespread large-scale protests over government austerity policies, financial sector bailouts, financialization and its social consequences, for example, the Occupy movement, the Icelandic Revolution, anti-austerity movements in Spain and Greece, student-led protests regarding debt and the financialization of education in Chile and Canada, and protests in Brazil and Turkey over government financial expropriation that benefit the few, and so on. Daellenbach notes that despite people becoming increasingly critically financially literate, the growing emphasis on financial literacy education globally operates on the assumption that the public remains financially illiterate.

Chapter 13, by UK–based geographer Sarah Hall, "Financialization and the Production of New Financial Elites through Business Education," considers the intersection between financialization and educational restructuring through a focus on the educational practices of financial elites working in financial services in the City of London in the 2000s. Whilst educational background has been widely recognized as a key determinant of entry into the City historically, processes of financialization in the 2000s increased the demand for financiers significantly, and this greater labour market demand could no longer be met through established recruitment methods. In response, education in the workplace, through business schools and within financial services firms themselves, has become an important way of educating a more diverse group of financiers into legitimate forms of financial practice and the associated cultural norms associated with financial services in the City. By reporting on original empirical research conducted in these forms of education, the chapter examines the distinct spatiality of positional advantage within these graduate labour markets as graduates seek to convert their education credentials obtained in a national context into global positional advantage within international financial labour markets. This argument demonstrates the need to take the spatialities of finance and education seriously as global labor markets continue to contain within them local, national, and regional differences that need to be negotiated by individuals as they seek to maximise their own employability and career progression.

Chapter 14, "Education and the Crisis This Time" is by John Morgan. He notes that despite many commentators predicting that neoliberal capitalist accumulation was in crisis and dying in the aftermath of the GFC, six years later pronouncements about the death of neoliberalism appear to have been premature, with the postcrisis economic landscape populated by 'zombie' economic concepts—ones that are to all intents and purposes dead but that refuse to die. Arguably neoliberalism emerged stronger than ever since 'normal' business resumed remarkably quickly with income and wealth increasingly accumulated by the richest sections of societies as share markets rose rapidly. Alongside this the crisis has seen austerity policies negatively affecting other sections of society. For education the crisis has presented an opportunity to intensify the pace of neoliberal educational reforms, competition, and marketization of education. Apart from opposition from some educational unions and left-oriented politicians, there are few signs of systematic opposition to the dominant discourses of educational growth.

The fifteenth and final chapter, "Finance-subjectivity: Thinking through the Consequences of the Global Financial Crisis in Education," by David R. Cole, develops the concept of 'finance-subjectivity' in relation to the work of Félix Guattari, who furnished a useful notion of semio-capitalism. Semio-capitalism analyzes the ways in which capitalism works on a semiotic level and reveals the codes and axioms that potentially trap and mould subjectivity. The writings of Franco Beradi (Bifo), Christian Marazzi, Maurizio Lazzarato, and others in the autonomous tradition have extended and added to Guattari's sense of semio-capitalism in terms of describing immaterial labor and cognitive capitalism. This chapter will use these ideas to get to the notion of 'finance-subjectivity' and how it now permeates educational practice. A recent (2012–2013) educational research project in the southwest of Sydney with public school teachers illustrates the idea of 'finance-subjectivity."

ACKNOWLEDGMENTS

First, we wish to thank Maggie Lyall, administrator in the Centre for Global Studies in Education at the University of Waikato for her assistance. We are also grateful for the positive and helpful work by the Peter Lang editorial team.

We acknowledge two papers that have been published elsewhere and have been granted permission to appear in this book.

Thank you to *New Left Review* (http://newleftreview.org/) for Slavoj Žižek's 2010 paper "A Permanent Economic Emergency," *New Left Review*, 64, pp. 85–95, which appears as chapter 1.

Thank you to Taylor and Francis for permission to publish "The Rationality Crisis in US Higher Education," by Clyde W. Barrow, published in 2010 in *New Political Science, 32*(3), 317–344. The journal is available online at http://www.tandfonline.com/loi/cnps20#.VD8DfufgBcI. It appears here as chapter 9.

In conclusion, we are grateful to all of the authors who have contributed to this collection.

Michael, Tina, & João

REFERENCES

Harvey, D. (2014). *Seventeen contradictions and the end of capitalism.* Oxford: Oxford University Press.

Klemkosky, R. C. (2013). Financial system fragility. *Business Horizons, 56*, 675–683.

Lazzarato, M. (2011). *The making of the indebt man.* Amsterdam: Semitoext.

Macrine, S. L. (2012). *Neoliberalism's Neoliberal pedagogy of debt.* Paper presented at AERA, 2012.

Panitch, L., & Henwood, D. (2011). Demystifying globalization. In S. Lilley (Ed.), *Capital and its discontents* (pp. 78–89). Oakland, CA: PM Press.

Paraskeva, J., & Torres Santome, J. (2012). Pouring old philosophical wine into new ideological bottles. In J. Paraskeva & J. Torres Santome (Eds.), *Globalisms and power: Iberian educational and curriculum policies* (pp. xvii–xxii). New York: Peter Lang.

Peters, M., & Besley, T. (2006). *Building knowledge cultures. Education and the development in the age of knowledge capitalism.* Lanham, MD: Rowman & Littlefield.

Sousa Santos, B. (2005). *Another knowledge is possible.* London: Verso.

Williams, J. (2006, Summer). Debt education: Bad for the young, bad for America. *Dissent. A Quarterly of Politics and Culture.* Retrieved from http://www.dissentmagazine.org/article/debt-education-bad-for-the-young-bad-for-america

NOTES

1. See "China Opens Capital Markets as U.K. Taps Overseas Yuan Business," http://www.bloomberg.com/news/2013-10-15/china-u-k-agree-on-yuan-pound-direct-trading-investment-quota.html. China pledges to push ahead with capital market reforms, http://www.reuters.com/article/2014/05/09/us-china-markets-reform-idUSBREA4807H20140509
2. See http://www.gpo.gov/fdsys/pkg/PLAW-111publ203/pdf/PLAW-111publ203.pdf

CHAPTER ONE

A Permanent Economic Emergency[1]

SLAVOJ ŽIŽEK

During this year's protests against the Eurozone's austerity measures—in Greece and, on a smaller scale, Ireland, Italy and Spain—two stories have imposed themselves.[2] The predominant, establishment story proposes a de-politicized naturalization of the crisis: the regulatory measures are presented not as decisions grounded in political choices, but as the imperatives of a neutral financial logic—if we want our economies to stabilize, we simply have to swallow the bitter pill. The other story, that of the protesting workers, students and pensioners, would see the austerity measures as yet another attempt by international financial capital to dismantle the last remainders of the welfare state. The IMF thus appears from one perspective as a neutral agent of discipline and order, and from the other as the oppressive agent of global capital.

There is a moment of truth in both perspectives. One cannot miss the superego dimension in the way the IMF treats its client states—while scolding and punishing them for unpaid debts, it simultaneously offers them new loans, which everyone knows they will not be able to return, thus drawing them deeper into the vicious cycle of debt generating more debt. On the other hand, the reason this superego strategy works is that the borrowing state, fully aware that it will never really have to repay the full amount of the debt, hopes to profit from it in the last instance.

Yet while each story contains a grain of truth, both are fundamentally false. The European establishment's story obfuscates the fact that the huge deficits have been run up as a result of massive financial sector bail-outs, as well as by falling government revenues during the recession; the big loan to Athens will be used to repay Greek debt to the great French and German banks. The true aim of the EU guarantees is to help private banks since, if any of the Eurozone states goes bankrupt, they will be heavily hit. On the other hand, the protesters' story bears witness yet again to the misery of today's left: there is no positive programmatic content to its demands, just a generalized refusal to compromise the existing welfare state. The utopia here is not a radical change of the system but the idea that one can maintain a welfare state within the system. Here, again, one should not miss the grain of truth in the countervailing argument: if we remain within the confines of the global capitalist system, then measures to wring further sums from workers, students and pensioners are, effectively, necessary.

One often hears that the true message of the Eurozone crisis is that not only the Euro, but the project of the united Europe itself is dead. But before endorsing this general statement, one should add a Leninist twist to it: Europe is dead—ok, but *which* Europe? The answer is: the post-political Europe of accommodation to the world market, the Europe which was repeatedly rejected at referendums, the Brussels technocratic-expert Europe. The Europe that presents itself as standing for cold European reason against Greek passion and corruption, for mathematics against pathetics. But, utopian as it may appear, the space is still open for another Europe: a re-politicized Europe, founded on a shared emancipatory project; the Europe that gave birth to ancient Greek democracy, to the French and October Revolutions. This is why one should avoid the temptation to react to the ongoing financial crisis with a retreat to fully sovereign nation-states, easy prey for free-floating international capital, which can play one state against the other. More than ever, the reply to every crisis should be *more* internationalist and Universalist than the universality of global capital.

A NEW PERIOD

One thing is clear: after decades of the welfare state, when cutbacks were relatively limited and came with the promise that things would soon return to normal, we are now entering a period in which a kind of economic state of emergency is becoming permanent: turning into a constant, a way of life. It brings with it the threat of far more savage austerity measures, cuts in benefits, diminishing health and education services, and more precarious employment. The left faces the difficult task of emphasizing that we are dealing with *political* economy—that there is nothing 'natural' in such a crisis, that the existing global economic system relies on a series of political decisions—while simultaneously being fully aware that, insofar as we remain within the capitalist system, the violation of its rules effectively causes economic breakdown, since the system obeys a pseudo-natural logic of its own. So, although we are clearly entering a new phase of enhanced exploitation, rendered easier by the conditions of the global market (outsourcing, etc.), we should also bear in mind that this is imposed by the functioning of the system itself, always on the brink of financial collapse.

It would thus be futile merely to hope that the ongoing crisis will be limited and that European capitalism will continue to guarantee a relatively high standard of living for a growing number of people. It would indeed be a strange radical politics, whose main hope is that circumstances will continue to render it inoperative and marginal. It is against such reasoning that one has to read Badiou's motto, *mieux vaut un désastre qu'un désêtre*: better a disaster than a non-being; one has to take the risk of fidelity to an Event, even if the Event ends up in 'obscure disaster'. The best indicator of the left's lack of trust in itself today is its fear of crisis. A true left takes a crisis seriously, without illusions. Its basic insight is that, although crises are painful and dangerous, they are inevitable, and that they are the terrain on which battles have to be waged and won. Which is why today, more than ever, Mao Zedong's old motto is pertinent: 'Everything under heaven is in utter chaos; the situation is excellent.'

There is no lack of anti-capitalists today. We are even witnessing an overload of critiques of capitalism's horrors: newspaper investigations, TV reports, and bestselling books abound on companies polluting our environment, corrupt bankers who continue to get fat bonuses while their firms are saved by public money, sweatshops where children work overtime. There is, however, a catch to all this criticism, ruthless as it may appear: what is as a rule not questioned is the liberal-democratic framework within which these excesses should be fought. The goal, explicit or implied, is to regulate capitalism—through the pressure of the media, parliamentary inquiries, harsher laws, honest police investigations—but never to question the liberal-democratic institutional mechanisms of the bourgeois state of law. This remains the sacred cow, which even the most radical forms of 'ethical anti-capitalism'—the Porto Allegre World Social Forum, the Seattle movement—do not dare to touch.

STATE AND CLASS

It is here that Marx's key insight remains valid, perhaps today more than ever. For Marx, the question of freedom should not be located primarily in the political sphere proper, as with the criteria the global financial institutions apply when they want to pronounce a judgment on a country—does it have free elections? Are the judges independent? Is the press free from hidden pressures? Are human rights respected? The key to actual freedom resides rather in the 'apolitical' network of social relations, from the market to the family, where the change needed for effective improvement is not political reform, but a transformation in the social relations of production. We do not vote about who owns what, or about worker–management relations in a factory; all this is left to processes outside the sphere of the political. It is illusory to expect that one can effectively change things by 'extending' democracy into this sphere, say, by organizing 'democratic' banks under people's control. Radical changes in this domain lie outside the sphere of legal rights. Such democratic procedures can, of course, have a positive role to play. But they remain part of the state apparatus of the bourgeoisie, whose purpose is to guarantee the undisturbed functioning of capitalist reproduction. In this precise sense, Badiou was right in his claim that the name of the ultimate enemy today is not capitalism, empire or exploitation, but democracy. It is the acceptance of 'democratic mechanisms' as the ultimate frame that prevents a radical transformation of capitalist relations.

Closely linked to the necessary de-fetishization of 'democratic institutions' is the de-fetishization of their negative counterpart: violence. For example, Badiou recently proposed exercising 'defensive violence' by means of building free domains at a distance from state power, subtracted from its reign (like the early Solidarnosc in Poland), and only resisting by force state attempts to crush and re-appropriate these 'liberated zones'. The problem with this formula is that it relies on a deeply problematic distinction between the 'normal' functioning of the state apparatus and the 'excessive' exercise of state violence. But the ABC of Marxist notions of class struggle is the thesis that 'peaceful' social life is itself an expression of the (temporary) victory of one class—the ruling one. From the standpoint of the subordinated and oppressed, the very existence of the state, as an apparatus of class domination, is a fact of violence. Similarly, Robespierre argued that regicide is not justified by proving the King had committed any specific crime: the very existence of the King is a crime, an offence against the freedom of the people. In this strict sense, the use of force by the oppressed against the ruling class and its state is always ultimately 'defensive'. If we do not concede this point, we *volens nolens* 'normalize' the state and accept its violence as merely a matter of contingent excesses. The standard liberal motto—that it is sometimes necessary to resort to violence, but it is never legitimate—is not sufficient. From the radical-emancipatory perspective, one should turn it around: for the oppressed, violence is always legitimate—since their very status is the result of violence—but never necessary: it is always a matter of strategic consideration whether to use force against the enemy or not.

In short, the topic of violence should be demystified. What was wrong with 20th-century Communism was not its resort to violence per se—the seizure of state power, the civil war to maintain it—but the larger mode of functioning, which made this kind of resort to violence inevitable and legitimized: the Party as the instrument of historical necessity, and so on. In a note to the CIA, advising them on how to undermine the Allende government, Henry Kissinger wrote succinctly: 'Make the economy scream.' Former US officials are openly admitting today that the same strategy is applied in Venezuela: former US Secretary of State Lawrence Eagleburger said of the Venezuelan economy on Fox News: 'It's the one weapon we have against [Chavez] to begin with, and which we should be using, namely the economic tools of trying to make the economy even worse, so that his appeal in the country and the region goes down'. In the current economic emergency, too, we are clearly not dealing with blind market processes but with highly organized, strategic interventions by states and financial institutions, intent on resolving the crisis on their own terms—and in such conditions, are not defensive counter-measures in order?

These considerations cannot but shatter the comfortable subjective position of radical intellectuals, even as they continue their mental exercises so relished throughout the 20th century: the urge to 'catastrophize' political situations. Adorno and Horkheimer saw catastrophe in the culmination of the 'dialectic of enlightenment' in the 'administered world'; Giorgio Agamben defined the 20th-century concentration camps as the 'truth' of the entire Western political project. But recall the figure of Horkheimer in West Germany of the 1950s. While denouncing the 'eclipse of reason' in the modern Western society of consumption, he simultaneously defended this same society as the sole island of freedom in a sea of totalitarianisms and corrupt dictatorships. What if, in truth, intellectuals lead basically safe and comfortable lives, and in order to justify their livelihoods, construct scenarios of radical catastrophe? For many, no doubt, if a revolution is taking place, it should occur at a safe distance—Cuba, Nicaragua, Venezuela—so that, while their hearts are warmed by thinking about faraway events, they can go on promoting their careers. But with the current collapse of properly functioning welfare states in the advanced-industrial economies, radical intellectuals may be now approaching a moment of truth when they must make such clarifications: they wanted real change—now they can have it.

ECONOMY AS IDEOLOGY

The state of permanent economic emergency does not mean that the left should abandon patient intellectual work, with no immediate 'practical use'. On the contrary: today, more than ever, one should bear in mind that communism begins with what Kant, in the famous passage of his essay, 'What is Enlightenment?', called the 'public use of reason': with the egalitarian universality of thought. Our struggle should thus highlight those aspects of the current 're-structuring' that pose a threat to trans-national open space. One example would be the EU's ongoing 'Bologna Process', which aims to 'harmonize the architecture of the European higher education system', and which is in fact a concerted attack on the public use of reason.

Underlying these reforms is the urge to subordinate higher education to the task of solving society's concrete problems through the production of expert opinions. What disappears here is the true task of thinking: not only to offer solutions to problems posed by 'society'—in reality, state and capital—but to reflect on the very form of these problems; to discern a problem in the very way we perceive a problem. The reduction of higher education to the task of producing socially useful expert knowledge is the paradigmatic form of Kant's 'private use of reason'—that is, constrained by contingent, dogmatic presuppositions—within today's global capitalism. In Kantian terms, it involves our acting as 'immature' individuals, not as free human beings who dwell in the dimension of the universality of reason.

It is crucial to link the push towards streamlining higher education—not only in the guise of direct privatization or links with business, but also in this more general sense of orienting education towards the production of expert knowledge—to the process of enclosing the commons of intellectual products, of privatizing general intellect. This process is itself part of a global transformation in the mode of ideological interpellation. It may be useful here to recall Althusser's notion of 'ideological state apparatuses'. If, in the Middle Ages, the key ISA was the Church, in the sense of religion as institution, the dawn of capitalist modernity imposed the twin hegemony of the school system and legal ideology. Individuals were formed into legal subjects through compulsory universal education, while subjects were interpellated as patriotic free citizens under the legal order. The gap was thus maintained between bourgeois and citizen, between the egotist-utilitarian individual concerned with his private interests and the *citoyen* dedicated to the universal domain of the state. Insofar as, in spontaneous ideological perception, ideology is limited to the universal sphere of citizenship, while the private sphere of egotistical interests is considered 'pre-ideological', the very gap between ideology and non-ideology is thus transposed into ideology.

What has happened in the latest stage of post-68 capitalism is that the economy itself—the logic of market and competition—has progressively imposed itself as the hegemonic ideology. In education, we are witnessing the gradual dismantling of the classical-bourgeois school ISA: the school system is less and less the compulsory network, elevated above the market and organized directly by the state, bearer of enlightened values—liberty, equality, fraternity. On behalf of the sacred formula of 'lower costs, higher efficiency', it is progressively penetrated by different forms of PPP, or public-private partnership. In the organization and legitimization of power, too, the electoral system is increasingly conceived on the model of market competition: elections are like a commercial exchange where voters 'buy' the option that offers to do the job of maintaining social order, prosecuting crime, and so on, most efficiently.

On behalf of the same formula of 'lower costs, higher efficiency', functions once exclusive to the domain of state power, like running prisons, can be privatized; the military is no longer based on universal conscription, but composed of hired mercenaries. Even the state bureaucracy is no longer perceived as the Hegelian universal class, as is becoming evident in the case of Berlusconi. In today's Italy, state power is directly exerted by the base bourgeois who ruthlessly and openly exploits it as a means to protect his personal interests.

Even the process of engaging in emotional relations is increasingly organized along the lines of a market relationship. Such a procedure relies on self-commodification: for internet dating or marriage agencies, prospective partners present themselves as commodities, listing their qualities and posting their photos. What is missing here is what Freud called *der einzige Zug*, that singular pull which instantly makes me like or dislike the other. Love is a choice that is experienced as necessity. At a certain point, one is overwhelmed by the feeling that one already is in love, and that one cannot do otherwise. By definition, therefore, comparing qualities of respective candidates, deciding with whom to fall in love, cannot be love. This is the reason why dating agencies are an anti-love device par excellence.

What kind of shift in the functioning of ideology does this imply? When Althusser claims that ideology interpellates individuals into subjects, 'individuals' stand here for the living beings upon which ideological state apparatuses work, imposing upon them a network of micro-practices. By contrast, 'subject' is not a category of living being, of substance, but the outcome of these living beings being caught in the ISA *dispositif*, or mechanism, in a symbolic order. Quite logically, insofar as the economy is considered the sphere of non-ideology, this brave new world of global commodification considers itself post-ideological. The ISA's are, of course, still here; more than ever. Yet insofar as, in its self-perception, ideology is located in subjects, in contrast to pre-ideological individuals, this hegemony of the economic sphere cannot but appear as the absence of ideology. What this means is not that ideology simply 'reflects' the economy, as superstructure to its base. Rather, the economy functions here as an ideological model itself, so that we are fully justified in saying that it is operative as an ISA—in contrast to 'real' economic life, which definitely does not follow the idealized liberal-market model.

IMPOSSIBLE

Today, however, we are witnessing a radical change in the working of this ideological mechanism. Agamben (2007) defines our contemporary 'post-political' or biopolitical society as one in which the multiple *dispositifs* de-subjectivize individuals, without producing a new subjectivity:

> Hence the eclipse of politics, which supposed real subjects or identities (workers' movement, bourgeoisie, etc.), and the triumph of economy, that is to say, of the pure activity of governing, which pursues only its own reproduction. The right and left which today follow each other in managing power have thus very little to do with the political context from which the terms that designate them originate. Today these terms simply name the two poles—the one that aims at desubjectivation, without any scruples, and the one that wants to cover it with the hypocritical mask of the good citizen of democracy—of the same machine of government. (pp. 46–47)

'Biopolitics' designates the constellation in which *dispositifs* no longer generate subjects ('interpellate individuals into subjects'), but merely administer and regulate individuals' bare life.

In such a constellation, the very idea of a radical social transformation may appear as an impossible dream—yet the term 'impossible' should make us stop and think. Today, possible and impossible are distributed in a strange way, both simultaneously exploding into excess. On the one hand, in the domains of personal freedoms and scientific technology, we are told that 'nothing is impossible': we can enjoy sex in all its perverse versions, entire archives of music, films and TV series are available to download, space travel is available to everyone (at a price). There is the prospect of enhancing our physical and psychic abilities, of manipulating our basic properties through interventions into the genome; even the tech-gnostic dream of achieving immortality by transforming our identity into software that can be downloaded into one or another set of hardware.

On the other hand, in the domain of socio-economic relations, our era perceives itself as the age of maturity in which humanity has abandoned the old millenarian utopian dreams and accepted the constraints of reality—read: capitalist socio-economic reality—with all its impossibilities. The commandment YOU CANNOT is its *mot d'ordre*: you cannot engage in large collective acts, which necessarily end in totalitarian terror; you can not cling to the old welfare state, it makes you non-competitive and leads to economic crisis; you cannot isolate yourself from the global market, without falling prey to the spectre of North Korean *juche*. In its ideological version, ecology also adds its own list of impossibilities, so-called threshold values—no more than two degrees of global warming—based on 'expert opinions'.

It is crucial to distinguish here between two impossibilities: the impossible-real of a social antagonism, and the 'impossibility' on which the predominant ideological field focuses. Impossibility is here redoubled, it serves as a mask of itself: that is, the ideological function of the second impossibility is to obfuscate the real of the first. Today, the ruling ideology endeavors to make us accept the 'impossibility' of radical change, of abolishing capitalism, of a democracy not reduced to a corrupt parliamentary game, in order to render invisible the impossible-real of the antagonism that cuts across capitalist societies. This real is 'impossible' in the sense that it is the impossible of the existing social order, its constitutive antagonism; which is not to imply that this impossible-real cannot be directly dealt with, or radically transformed.

This is why Lacan's formula for overcoming an ideological impossibility is not 'everything is possible', but 'the impossible happens'. The Lacanian impossible-real is not an *a priori* limitation, which needs to be realistically taken into account, but the domain of action. An act is more than an intervention into the domain of the possible—an act changes the very coordinates of what is possible and thus retroactively creates its own conditions of possibility. This is why communism also concerns the real: to act as a communist means to intervene into the real of the basic antagonism which underlies today's global capitalism.

FREEDOMS?

But the question persists: what does such a programmatic statement about doing the impossible amount to, when we are confronted with an empirical impossibility: the fiasco of communism as an idea able to mobilize large masses? Two years before his death, when it became clear that there would be no all-European revolution, and knowing the idea of building socialism in one country to be nonsense, Lenin (1923) wrote:

> What if the complete hopelessness of the situation, by stimulating the efforts of the workers and peasants tenfold, offered us the opportunity to create the fundamental requisites of civilization in a different way from that of the West European countries? (p. 479)

Has this not been the predicament of the Morales government in Bolivia, of the Chavez government in Venezuela, of the Maoist government in Nepal? They came to power through 'fair' democratic elections, not through insurrection. But once in power, they exerted it in a way which is partially, at least, 'non-statal': directly mobilizing their supporters, bypassing the party-state representative network. Their situation is 'objectively' hopeless: the whole drift of history is basically against them, they cannot rely on any 'objective tendencies' pushing in their way, all they can do is to improvise, do what they can in a desperate situation. But, nonetheless, does this not give them a unique freedom? And are we—today's left—not all in exactly the same situation?

Ours is thus the very opposite of the classical early 20th-century situation, in which the left knew what had to be done (establish the dictatorship of the proletariat), but had to wait patiently for the proper moment of execution. Today we do not know what we have to do, but we have to act now, because the consequence of non-action could be disastrous. We will be forced to live 'as if we were free'. We will have to risk taking steps into the abyss, in totally inappropriate situations;

we will have to reinvent aspects of the new, just to keep the machinery going and maintain what was good in the old—education, healthcare, basic social services. In short, our situation is like what Stalin said about the atom bomb: it is not for those with weak nerves. Or as Gramsci said, characterizing the epoch that began with the First World War, 'the old world is dying, and the new world struggles to be born: now is the time of monsters.'

REFERENCES

Agamben, G. (2007). *Qu'est-ce qu'un dispositif?* Paris: Shores.
Lenin, V. I. (1923/1966). 'Our Revolution' in *Collected Works, Vol. 33*. Moscow.

NOTES

1. This chapter has appeared previously as, Slavoj Žižek (2010) 'A Permanent Economic Emergency', *New Left Review,* 64, pp. 85–95. It appears here with permission from *New Left Review.*
2. Thanks to Udi Aloni, Saroi Giri, and Alenka Zupančič.

CHAPTER TWO

Finance Capitalism, Financialization, AND THE Prospects FOR Public Education

MICHAEL A. PETERS AND TINA BESLEY

INTRODUCTION: THE RISE OF FINANCE CULTURE

One of the most significant economic changes of the 1990s in the US and global economy has been the huge growth of finance culture and the responsibilization of households in savings—which is arguably a form of financial citizenship. Households deepened their involvement in the purchase of new financial products including mortgages, mutual funds, stock trading accounts, student loans, car loans, insurance, and various forms of retirement products (e.g., 401k funds[1]), with the consequence that household debt levels blew out enormously and were exacerbated when both the subprime mortgage crisis and the Global Financial Crisis (GFC) and Great Recession (GR) hit in succession from 2008, often with disastrous results for many thousands of households that faced unemployment, eviction, foreclosure, homelessness, and bankruptcy.[2]

This massive change that prefigured the rise of 'the investor' or 'financial citizen' in American households came on the back of the credit card revolution fuelled by developments in Information Technology (IT). Arguably this is the rise of the 'entrepreneurial self,' which has huge ramifications in education (Besley & Peters, 2007; Peters, 2001, 2005). From the issue of the first credit card in 1951, the credit card became wholly adopted by major banks in the 1960s and developed with further innovations in the 1970s and 1980s onwards (reward systems, credit card balance systems, new security signatures, electronic wallets, mobile-payment apps, etc.). By the 1990s credit cards became a standard feature of debit and credit industries. In the preceding decade up to the 2008 recession, credit card debt soared 87% as real wages and the savings rate flatlined. In the late twentieth and more so now in the twenty-first century, Bitcoin and other innovations have led experts to talk of the "cashless society" and many speculate that the credit crisis is over with hundreds of millions of customers using credit cards for more than $50 trillion of consumer spending. The latest innovation in 2014 is Apple Pay, where the iPhone 6 and Apple Watch have introduced a mobile wallet in partnership with Visa, MasterCard, and Amex, major payment networks, banks, and retailers. While credit/debit cards now already have near-field communication chip that enables mobile 'pay and go,' this technology is now included in the latest iPhones, all part of a set of new technologies that include Touch ID fingerprint recognition readers that allow consumers to securely pay for items in a store with the touch of a finger rather than using signatures or PINs.[3] Such technologies are not simply a convenience factor but are highly likely to result in increased personal debt as they simplify consumer purchasing.

Credit and investment are metaphors that now help determine an individual's (and family's) place in society (Davis, 2009). This is in part the basis for the rise of a new finance culture that includes fundamental shifts in attitudes to money, investment, credit, risk, purchasing, mortgages, and the stock market, and in turn it places expectations on individuals in terms of financial literacy and financial education. An important part of the new financial literacy is making 'informed' financial decisions, where the risk economy is widely embraced as a means of preserving family lifestyles in days of static or declining wage opportunities. It has meant also the development of a new mentality that involves greater attunement, calibration, and participation in the finance institutions that have come to dominate culture. The financialization of households includes 'a deepening culture of risk-taking and strategic deployment of assets' while a broad-based process is concentrated within higher income groups (Fligstein & Goldstein, 2012).

In the decades leading up the GFC financial derivatives also arose as an instrument for measuring risk and soon became the dominant form of financial transaction in the world (Bryan & Rafferty, 2006), estimated at between $700 trillion to $1.2 quadrillion.[4] The Dodd-Frank Wall Street Reform and Consumer Protection Act was passed into law in 2010 to promote financial stability

> by improving accountability and transparency in the financial system, to end "too big to fail", to protect the American taxpayer by ending bailouts, to protect consumers from abusive financial services practices, and for other purposes.[5]

Financial derivatives have transformed capitalism leading to the development of finance capitalism through a process of financialization that now affects every aspect of life. Their operation within an unregulated space of international banking and finance utilising new technologies mean that these financial instruments and markets are highly integrated, and the speed of these financial transactions is so rapid that no national or international agency can track or monitor developments, let alone effectively regulate these markets. Their fragility, rapid growth, and dominance, and their pervasiveness pose grave dangers to world financial stability.

THE GLOBAL FINANCIAL CRISIS

In the immediate aftermath of the Global Financial Crisis (GFC) of 2007–2008, the worst financial crisis since the 1930s Great Depression, mainstream economists, financial policy analysts, bankers, and politicians indicated that the crisis, sometimes referred to as the Great Recession, was unprecedented in its global geographical impact, in the nature of its systemic causes and the ongoing challenge it represented to the stability and concept of architecture of the world's financial institutions. The GFC followed on from the huge growth in world financial assets and cross-border capital flows with enormous growth in pension funds and the consequent rapid expansion of the financial sector on the back of a global derivatives market that quickly encouraged high-risk debt levels. Toxic debt levels led to massive write-downs in the USA, UK, and many Western countries as "too big-to-fail" financial institutions bankrupted themselves having swallowed investments and savings of millions of people. World trade and economic growth sharply declined, unemployment rocketed to new highs, and poverty was pushed to new levels especially in developing countries, jeopardising many of the gains of the last decade.

Blankenburg and Palma (2009) note the dimensions and the magnitude of the crisis:

> According to McKinsey's *Mapping Global Financial Markets* (October 2008), global financial assets rose from US$12 trillion in 1980 to US$196 trillion in 2007. The International Monetary Fund's *Global Financial Stability Report* (IMF, 2009a) estimate for the latter figure is considerably higher, at US$241 trillion[6]. Global cross-border capital flows more than doubled between 2002 and 2007, with foreign investors holding one in four debt securities and one in five equities. While in 2000 only 11 countries had financial assets of more than 350% of gross domestic product (GDP), 25 countries had deepened their financial markets to the same extent by 2007. As early as 1990, money managers had increased their control of US corporate equities from 8% in 1950 to 60% (Porter, 1992, p. 6; Whalen, 2002, p. 402). Similarly, pension funds had extended their share of total business equities from less than 1% to just short of 39%, and their fraction of corporate debt from 13% to 50% (Ghilarducci, 1992, p. 117; Whalen, 2002, p. 402). In the period from 1986 to 2006, the US financial sector as a whole increased its share of corporate profits from 10% to 30%, while its outstanding debts grew from 20% of GDP in 1980 to 116% in 2007 (FED, 2009). According to Gillian Tett from the *Financial Times*, outstanding credit defaults swaps

> (CDS) today amount to no less than US$60 trillion, with the risk embodied after discounting mutually off-setting contracts still as high as US$14 trillion. (Tett, 2009, p. 264)

The causes of the GFC are various and different accounts have been offered. In an influential account James Crotty (2009) suggests that the GFC is

> the latest phase of the evolution of financial markets under the radical financial deregulation process that began in the late 1970s "manifested in a series of cycles" in which deregulation accompanied by rapid financial innovation stimulates powerful financial booms that end in crises. (p. 264)

Government bailouts only fund a new round of expansion with the result that financial markets have become even larger and more crisis-prone. Crotty (2009) discusses structural flaws in the very heart of the system of the new financial architecture. By contrast, Pasquale Tridico (2012, p. 17) traces the root cause of the financial crisis and global imbalances to its labour market origins and "the uneven income distribution and inequality caused by the current finance-led model of growth." He begins his account by referencing the process of financialization that began first in the US during the 1980s and later spread to the EU—a process that was anchored in labour flexibility, a contraction of social expenditure, and an end to wage increases, which diminished purchasing power of workers and made them more dependent on a spiralling credit boom.

FINANCIALIZATION

'Financialization' is a term that describes an economic system or process that attempts to reduce all value that is exchanged (whether tangible, intangible, future or present promises) either into a financial instrument or a derivative of a financial instrument. 'Financialization,' like 'globalisation,' is a contestable concept but with a broad and growing interdisciplinary literature. In a general sense it refers to the way in which financial processes are changing relations between and within capital markets, firms, households, and the state. It signals the growth and new global prominence of finance culture with the progressive global integration of capital markets over the last twenty-five years, and the growing reliance on financial systems of calculation in all facets of social and personal life.[7]

The effect of financialization is to be able to reduce any work product or service to an exchangeable financial instrument. It is an aspect of increased symbolization, mathematization, and computerization of financial markets that are trends within knowledge capitalism. Neoliberalism is an expression of the power of finance that has gathered pace with the internationalization of capital and the globalization of markets. Some scholars suggest that neoliberalism and globalization are themselves expressions of finance, closely tied to the development of derivatives markets and the evolution of an international financial system where the international rentiers[8] have managed to significantly increase their share of national income, often on the basis of systematic fraud, corruption, and widespread criminalisation of financial practices. The current financial crisis is a systemic crisis of the entire capitalistic system based on interconnected global financial markets. This is a fundamental shift that represents the financialization of the reproductive sphere of life itself. Under this regime the monopolization and privatization of knowledge and education has proceeded rapidly. One of the effects of financialization and the economic crisis has been to popularize a debate on budget cuts and 'austerity politics' across the board for public services provided at the state level with massive cuts to education in all aspects, attacks on collective bargaining, and the sacking of thousands of teachers. This collection provides an introduction and analysis of 'financialization' and the fate of public education under 'austerity politics.'

THE CRISIS OF FINANCE CAPITALISM

It has now been nearly a decade since the beginnings of the Global Financial Crisis (GFC) first broke in 2007–2008. What has been learned, if anything, by international agencies about the nature of the crisis and how to manage macroeconomic policy? In the wake of the crisis, ongoing problems of the Eurozone, slow and fragile growth in the USA, and a slowdown of emerging economies, governments around the world have been reviewing the risks to insure economies against the systematic failure of banking and insurance systems. The GFC drew attention to market volatility, to knock-on effects of 'too big to fail' entities, the dangers of high levels of public debt, and the risks associated with the massive growth and expansiveness of the finance sector vis-a-vis the real productive economy. Suddenly the role of the state and other extra-state agencies is back on the policy agenda as governments explore the scope of new regulatory tools designed to restructure banks, introduce new capital reserve levels, and monitor professional standards. Greater thought has been given to the threats that the finance sector pose to the economy as a whole, and European governments in particular have sought to deal with these problems by pursuing austerity measures designed to cut levels of unsustainable public debt.

The systematic collapse of global financial institutions is, in part, a result of a number of interrelated problems that indicate the many dimensions of the crisis of finance capitalism and the exhaustion of the neoliberal model of development:

- the failure and subsequent recapitalization, nationalization, or bail-out of major banks, leading to an era of "austerity politics" in Europe;
- the massive growth of the world derivatives market and consequent over-expansion of national banking systems in relation to the "productive economy";

- the growth of unsustainable sovereign and national debt levels, resulting in sequestration and quantitative easing policies in the US;
- the attempted regulation of tax evasion strategies by multinational companies;
- the tax evasion by wealthy individuals in a system of international tax havens and trusts;
- the excessive bonuses and preferential shares given to CEs even in the face of poor performance;
- the way that the EU (acting with the CEB and IMF) has exercised considerable fiscal and economic pressure on democratically elected governments to change policies;
- the rapid growth of new information technologies that produces a new global complexity of high-frequency trading (HFT) at a speed that eludes national and regional agencies to effectively track or regulate;
- the decline of trust and misalignment of incentives at the very heart of the financial culture of equity markets;
- the fraudulent and criminal culture at the highest levels of the finance industry, including the deliberate manipulation of the Libor exchange rate, with few criminal convictions except for Ponzi schemers and insider traders.

The heart of Anglophone finance capitalism is built on the twin pillars of Wall Street and the City of London and the globalization of finance markets has increased this connectivity. In both these dominating poles the culture of the finance sector has come under increasing scrutiny.

The Final Report of the Kay Review of Equity Markets and Long-term Decision-making (Kay, 2012) concludes that "short-termism is a problem in UK equity markets, and that the principal causes are the decline of trust and the misalignment of incentives throughout the equity investment chain" (p. 9). The Kay Review identifies "the systematic nature of the problems" and aims to restore trust and confidence in the investment chain through a variety of measures including "the application of fiduciary standards of care" and "diminish[ing] the current role of trading and transactional cultures" (p. 9). Overall the review focuses on defeating the short-termism of equity market traders and to reintroduce a concept of good stewardship of financial resources based on transparent and trustworthy financial intermediation. The Review is damning of the change in culture that has occurred since the 1970s that has benefitted traders at the expense of users.[9]

The financial system has been transformed since the 1970s by globalization, deregulation, and reregulation. These developments changed the culture of UK financial institutions and the identity and behavior of the leading participants. A culture that had emphasized trust relationships was replaced by one that gave primacy to trading. The trading culture has influenced the behavior of market users—companies and savers—as well as market intermediaries. In the long run, the outcome has benefitted market participants more than market users (p. 88).

John Kay has been a long-time critic of investment banking that has been ruthless in dumping risk on hapless consumers. He suggests, as one commentator summarises it in an interview with Kay, "There is an endemic culture in financial services that makes it incapable of learning from other disciplines," particularly from the study of complex systems that provides sophisticated analysis and understanding of how systems work and the damage that monocultures can inflict on the whole ecosystem.[10] Kay is an advocate of what he calls "narrow banking," the purpose of which is to protect the non-financial economy from financial instability:

> A much needed restructuring of the financial services industry would establish a retail sector focussed on the needs of consumers, rather than on the promotion of products and the remuneration of producers. We could look forward to an industry in which new technologies are used, not just to reduce costs, but to deliver better services. We should establish a market in which customer satisfaction is the measure of success. That would be an outcome very different from our recent experience. But it is an outcome we can—and must—achieve. (p. 5)[11]

Perhaps even more significant is Kay's comment, quoting Simon Johnson's (2009) "The Quiet Coup": "The financial services industry is now the most powerful political force in Britain and the US." He goes on to say:

> If anyone doubted that, the last two years have demonstrated it. The industry has extracted subsidies and guarantees of extraordinary magnitude from the taxpayer without substantial conditions or significant reform. But the central problems that give rise to the crisis have not been addressed, far less resolved. It is therefore inevitable that crisis will recur. (p. 94)

Johnson's (2009) critique is even more devastating and plain. He begins his article with the following paragraph:

> The crash has laid bare many unpleasant truths about the United States. One of the most alarming, says a former chief economist of the International Monetary Fund, is that the finance industry has effectively captured our government—a state of affairs that more typically describes emerging markets, and is at the center of many emerging-market crises. If the IMF's staff could speak freely about the U.S., it would tell us what it tells all countries in this situation: recovery will fail unless we break the financial oligarchy that is blocking essential reform. And if we are to prevent a true depression, we're running out of time.[12]

Sir Mervyn King, the outgoing governor of the Bank of England, in his last public appearance before the Parliament's Treasury select committee complained that top banking officials were interfering with regulatory authority to make banks safer by putting pressure on politicians and government officials to water down new rules to "force lenders to comply with a higher leverage ratio of 3 per cent of capital as a proportion of total assets, years ahead of the Basel III global requirements."[13]

The culture of banking is endemically fraudulent and it has bought off all political opposition. The fact is that fraudulent activity has been at the heart of international banking activities as demonstrated by the systematic manipulation of the Libor[14] rate controlled by the British Bankers Association in the Libor Scandal. The Libor rate is used as the major standard reference for a range of financial products including the US derivatives market, mortgages, and student loans and underpins the world derivatives markets which is worth hundreds of trillions. The Libor scandal involved the manipulation of interest rates based on submissions by selected major banks in London where banks either inflated or deflated submissions, in turn profiting hugely from such manipulation. Given the huge trades of trillions of dollars, small-point manipulated adjusted submissions of less than 1% offered easy and huge returns, sometimes over a trillion dollars. Despite cover-ups and reviews by major banking authorities, including the IMF and the Bank of International Settlements, the story broke in 2008 by the *Wall Street Journal.* Regulatory investigations in 2011 implicated some of the world's largest banks including Barclays, Citibank, JP Morgan, Royal Bank of Scotland (RBS), HSBC, Deutsche Bank, and fifteen others spread over three continents, some of which were later fined for their fraudulent behavior. The accusation of rate-fixing has been leveled at the highest authorities including US Treasury Secretary Tim Geithner. It is becoming apparent this fraudulent practice has been ongoing since the early 1990s, that it was pervasive, involving the world's major banks, and that Libor fixing operated as a cartel.

In June 2012 the Libor Scandal saw "Barclays Bank admit multiple criminal settlements by revealed significant fraud and collusion by member banks connected to the rate submissions." Barclays was fined "$200 million by the Commodity Futures Trading Commission, $160 million by the United States Department of Justice and £59.5 million by the Financial Services Authority for attempted manipulation of the Libor and Euribor rates." However, Barclays are not the only bank implicated: "regulators in at least ten countries on three different continents are investigating the rigging of the Libor and other interest rates. Around 20 major banks have been named in investigations and court cases." It is estimated "that the rate manipulation scandal cost US states, counties, and local governments at least $6 billion in fraudulent interest payments, above $4 billion that state and local governments have already had to spend to unwind their positions exposed to rate manipulation."[15]

Part of the story can be judged by the US Commodity Futures Trading Commission (CFTC)[16] case against the RBS where it is pointed out that the Libor

> rates contributed by the panel banks are supposed to reflect each bank' s honest assessment of the costs of borrowing unsecured funds in the London interbank market, not the profit motives of traders. Over a period of more than four years, RBS violated this fundamental precept and undermined the integrity of LIBOR for Yen and Swiss Franc. (CFTC, 2013, p. 2)

It is alleged that beginning in 2006 the RBS made hundreds of manipulations "to manipulate Yen and Swiss Franc LIBOR and, on numerous occasions, made false LIBOR submissions to benefit its derivatives and money market trading positions. At times, RBS also aided and abetted other panel banks' attempts to manipulate those same rates" (CFTC, p. 2).[17] The true gravity of the situation can be gauged by the following paragraph:

> LIBOR is the most widely used benchmark interest rate in the world. Approximately $350 trillion of notional swaps and $10 trillion of loans are indexed to LIBOR. It is the basis for settlement of interest rate futures and options contracts on many of the world's major futures and options exchanges and is used as a barometer to measure strain in money markets and is often a gauge of the market's expectation of future central bank interest rates. To be sure, LIBOR is fundamentally critical to financial markets and has an enormously widespread impact on global markets and consumers. (CFTC, 2013, p. 4)

The RBS was ordered to desist from the Libor manipulation practices and to pay a fine of $350 million. Other measures were introduced to ensure the integrity of the benchmarking process.

The Parliamentary Commission on Banking Standards was set up in July 2012 in the wake of the Libor scandal to investigate the culture of UK banking and its professional standards. The Final Report was released in June 2013. The Chairman, Andrew Tyrie, confirmed that banking malpractice was widespread and that both taxpayers and customers had lost out and the economy had suffered. The report *Changing Banking for Good* attempts to make bankers personally responsible, to reform bank governance and strengthen the powers of regulators.[18] Some think that if the report's recommendations are implemented, it will destroy London as a global financial centre.[19] Others believe that that the report does not go far enough and are sceptical whether the recommendations can or will be implemented.[20] While proposing new rules and legislation and practical changes to the way in which banks are regulated in the UK designed to enhance individual accountability and standards of governance, the report, rather than taking the opportunity to fully nationalize the RBS, makes practical recommendations of how to return partly state-owned banks to private ownership, naively believing that its recommendations can change banking culture and regulate it, despite its global and increasingly technological nature.

This problem-set concerns an essentially fraudulent culture that is only a symptom of a larger transformation that some commentators call "financialization," where the finance sector overshadows the real productive economy and takes control of it. It is naïve in the extreme to think that a new set of prudential standards can change the finance culture when politicians themselves created it, starting with deregulation policies in the Reagan years, and when financiers hold the highest public office. In one sense, the real power and influence is anchored in a set of beliefs about markets and finance, especially given its immense profits in the 2000s with the invention of new financial products and the new information technologies exploiting the speed of transactions. Under these circumstances the financial moguls hardly needed to buy favours or to exercise pressure: it was done for them by politicians and policymakers. Banks use the latest mathematical modelling to demonstrate risk profiles that popularized the belief that unregulated markets are virtually foolproof. These attitudes still persist today despite the GFC. The greatest stumbling blocks to genuine global financial reform seem to be a lack of will and lack of a global consensus by many politicians, policymakers, and the G20, which in turn raises the spectre and dangers of further crashes.

There is resistance to further taxpayer bailouts of financial institutions deemed 'too big to fail' due to their size, interconnectedness and importance for the economy. Reform solutions that require banks to minimise risks and increase their assets (via two mechanisms of lower leverage ratios and higher capital ratios) that can be easily realised in a crisis have been enacted, for example, in the USA the 2010 Dodd-Frank Act[21] aimed to strengthen regulation of the financial system in the aftermath of the subprime mortgage crisis, which contributed to the GFC and huge distress for so many homeowners.

The suggestion that such large institutions are too big and so should be broken up has largely gone unheeded, no doubt because being so big and important they already hold strong lobbying positions and continue to influence political decisions. Willingly breaking up and forgoing political influence seems an unlikely course. It is only likely to happen if regulated. In the UK at present the emphasis in breaking up large banks now revolves around arguments for opening up banking and competition. The Competition and Markets Authority (CMA), "Britain's new competition watchdog in April, has the power to order a break up of banks considered too dominant, as well as so-called behavioural remedies, such as improving information given to customers."[22]

In the five years since the outbreak of the GFC what progress has been made, especially in rethinking economic policy? This was the theme of the IMF conference "Rethinking Macro Policy II: First Steps and Early Lessons," held April 16–17, 2013.[23] The results are not encouraging. In the panel discussion following the conference, Joseph Stiglitz addressed the issue directly:

> The approximately 100 crises that have occurred during the last 30 years—as liberalization policies became dominant—have given us a wealth of experience and mountains of data …
>
> The big lesson that this crisis forcibly brought home—one we should have long known—is that economies are not necessarily efficient, stable or self-correcting.[24]

Stiglitz draws attention to the need for structural transformation suggesting we may not return to high levels of employment and that reforms have been largely tinkering at the edges. Much of his consideration is devoted to the need for stronger regulation of the global finance industry. The other panel experts were equally pessimistic. George A. Ackerloff, reflecting on the two-day conference proceedings, used the image of a cat up a tree: "My view of the cat is the poor thing is there in the tree; it's going to fall; and we don't know what to do."[25] Olivier Blanchard, IMF chief economist, suggested that there is no consensus on the future global financial architecture:

> Rethinking and reforms are both taking place. But we still do not know the final destination, be it for the redefinition of monetary policy, or the contours of financial regulation, or the role of macroprudential tools. We have a general sense of direction, but we are largely navigating by sight.[26]

David Romer's remarks are perhaps the most sobering. He asks, "Where do we stand in terms of averting another financial and macroeconomic disaster?" and provides the answer:

> The events of the past few years are not an aberration, but just the most extreme manifestation of a broader pattern. And the relatively modest changes of the type discussed at the conference, and that in some cases policymakers are putting into place, are helpful but unlikely to be enough to prevent future financial shocks from inflicting large economic harms.

He concludes:

> After five years of catastrophic macroeconomic performance, "first steps and early lessons"—to quote the conference title—is not what we should be aiming for. Rather, **we should be looking for solutions to the ongoing current crisis and strong measures to minimize the chances of anything similar happening again.** I worry that the reforms we are focusing on are too small to do that, and that what is needed is a more fundamental rethinking of the design of our financial system and of our frameworks for macroeconomic policy. (bold in original)[27]

The consensus is that what is required is fundamental transformation of finance capitalism and that the current neoliberal model is exhausted but there is no new thinking being generated about what alternatives we might pursue or how countries can regain control of their own destinies.

The sophisticated analytics of massive data sets, latest mathematical tools, and rigorous modelling may provide an increasing measure of understanding of what went wrong or what the present dangers are, but these methods and tools of measurement do not provide either imagination or values: the imagination of a new system, a more stable architecture; the values of a system truly redistributive and less damaging to culture, environment, and people. For this possibility to occur we suspect we will need either another crash deeper than the previous one or global revolution: the former seems a lot more likely.

SPEED AND VELOCITY OF FINANCE CAPITALISM

It is clear that speed and velocity are the main aspects of a new finance capitalism that operates at the speed of light based on sophisticated "buy" and "sell" algorithms. Already researchers have demonstrated that data transfer using a single laser can send 26 terabits per second down an optical fibre and there are comparable reports that lasers will make financial "high-frequency" trading even faster.[28]

In 2013, this is how Tyler Falk, blogging for Smartplanet, describes it:

> With high-frequency trading, firms use complex algorithms to exploit price discrepancies in the stock market. All of this trading happens in a flash, microseconds ... Dealing in microseconds means companies need to have the fastest technology to complete their transactions. Superfast fiber-optic networks were the hot technology, then microwave networks came along and now: lasers?[29]

He notes that two companies, Anova and AOptix, are pursuing this vision that looks to a new technology that will shave microseconds off financial trades. As a BBC story explains: "High-frequency trading (HFT) is driven by complex algorithms that allow traders to jump ahead of competitors by exploiting minute discrepancies in price on exchanges in different cities."[30] In such trading, every millisecond counts and the competition to provide ever-faster trading networks is fierce. The first microwave connection between London and Frankfurt was turned on in October 2012 by Perseus Telecom. According to the company, the system cut about 40% off the time taken to complete a trade compared with traditional fibre-optic networks.

Western modernity (and developing global systems) exhibit long-term tendencies of an increasing abstraction described in terms of formalization, mathematicization, aestheticization, and biologization of life. These are characteristic of otherwise seemingly disparate pursuits in the arts and humanities as much as science and technology and are driven in large measure through the development of logic and mathematics especially in digital systems.

Much of this rapid transformation of the properties of systems can be captured in the notion of "bioinformational capitalism" that builds on the literatures on "biocapitalism" and "informationalism" (or "informational capitalism") to develop the concept of "bioinformational capitalism" in order to articulate an emergent form of capitalism that is self-renewing in the sense that it can change and renew the material basis for life and capital as well as program itself. Bioinformational capitalism applies and develops aspects of the new biology to informatics to create new organic forms of computing and self-reproducing memory that in turn have become the basis of bioinformatics.

The notion of "algorithmic capitalism" is an aspect of informationalism (informational capitalism) or "cybernetic capitalism" (Peters, 2012), a term that recognizes more precisely the cybernetic systems similarities among various sectors of the post-industrial capitalist economy in its third phase of development—from mercantilism to industrialism to cybernetics—linking the growth of the multinational info-utilities (e.g., Google, Microsoft, Amazon) and their spectacular growth in the last twenty years, with developments in biocapitalism and the informatization of biology, and fundamental changes taking place with algorithmic trading and the development of so-called 'financialization.'

We use the notion to examine and explain the phenomenon of the May 6, 2010, "Flash Crash," when the Dow Jones Industrial Average lost 1,000 points (some $800 billion)—one of its biggest one-day falls in history—and recovered within minutes. After a five-month investigation, the SEC and CFTC report, "Findings Regarding the Market Events of May 6, 2010," found

> "a market so fragmented and fragile that a single large trade could send stocks into a sudden spiral,"[31] and detailed how a large mutual fund firm selling an unusually large number of E-Mini S&P 500 contracts first exhausted available buyers, and then how high-frequency traders (HFT) started aggressively selling, accelerating the effect of the mutual fund's selling and contributing to the sharp price declines that day.[32]

Following criticisms of this report and further analysis, the CFTC Chief Chief Economist and several academic economists concluded that High Frequency Traders depart from a traditional definition of the market, being aggressive of price but small on trading volume and accumulation of stock, leading to high market volatility and the disguise of liquidity in markets. HFT are not willing to accumulate large positions or absorb large losses. They went on to say:

> Consequently, we believe, that irrespective of technology, markets can become fragile when imbalances arise as a result of large traders seeking to buy or sell quantities larger than intermediaries are willing to temporarily hold, and simultaneously long-term suppliers of liquidity are not forthcoming even if significant price concessions are offered.[33]

Algorithmic trading is sometimes seen as an explanation of market volatility, especially when risk is not transparent or able to be effectively tracked and monitored. Automated buy-sell programs now account for over 80% of all US equity trading. Increasingly, global information systems that operate at the speed of light are now harnessed by HFT (high-frequency trading) firms to create Automated Trading Desks that are capable of trading hundreds of millions of shares daily. So-called 'quant trading programs,' after "quantitative trading programs," are now designed by mathematicians and underlie HFT, where stocks are held often for only microseconds.

With the concerns and criticisms about HFT, by 2014 there are suggestions to regulate HFT. The FCA's CEO Martin Wheatley points out that "regulators have been largely 'technology neutral' … But this doesn't mean it isn't important to analyse whether innovations threaten a fair and efficient market: which is very much in regulated territory."[34] Some countries have already begun to regulate HFT, for example:

> Italy has introduced a tax at two basis points on orders when the order-to-executed trade ratio exceeds a certain threshold. Effectively, requiring HFT users to pay for the additional noise they're creating.
>
> In Germany, similar charges have been introduced but legislators have gone further. Firms engaged in HFT activity are expected to apply for a licence to operate; fees are being charged for excessive system usage; and other tools, like minimum tick sizes and order-to-trade ratios, have also been introduced. (ibid)

Wheatley points out areas of concern related to supervision of firms in the UK on a risk-based approach that provides general oversight that supplements the monitoring of automated trading with the assessment of specific firms. Yet he also acknowledges that algorithmic trading is difficult to assess because of its speed and velocity. The UK approach nevertheless undertakes studies around concepts of market fairness and resilience. Questions remain concerning the appropriate level of regulation, the consistency of the controlling measures, their analytical robustness, and their scope and scale. He acknowledges

> And, perhaps most important, how do we make sure firms, heavily motivated by financial return, accept responsibility for the significant risk they import into the financial markets? (ibid)

He likewise points out difficulties in market surveillance, acknowledging that in face of the volume of trade, the complexity of the market, and the speed of transaction "it is invariably difficult to perform surveillance effectively." The sheer speed and volume of market messages adds complexity defying the monitoring of abuse risk in a cross asset/cross border/cross market world.

The staggering growth of the finance industry, sometimes referred to as "financialization," represents a set of overlapping processes that refer not only to the rapid expansion of the financial sector of the capitalist system—to the growth of financial institutions of all kinds—but also to a qualitative change in the mode of production where banking systems jettison traditional banking practices to become commercial investors and multinational corporations develop as financial institutions able to invest and trade directly in financial markets. Richard Peet (2011), writing for *Monthly Review*, puts it succinctly: "Over the last thirty years, capital has abstracted upwards, from production to finance; its sphere of operations has expanded outwards, to every nook and cranny of the globe; the speed of its movement has increased, to milliseconds; and its control has extended to include 'everything.' We now live in the era of global finance capitalism."

Some critics argue that the rise of neoliberalism is explained by the growing role and power of finance in the political economy of capitalism and that neoliberalism "is the expression of the desire of a class of capitalist owners and the institutions in which their power is concentrated, which we collectively call 'finance,' to restore ... the class's revenues and power" (Duménil & Lévy, 2004, pp. 1–2). Others suggest that financialization is the result of neoliberal restructuring, but it has deeper historical roots. Financialization is not just quantitative expansion but also change in the nature of financial institutions and banks that have jettisoned traditional banking practices to pursue the creation and sale of their own financial instruments. As many theorists suggest, neoliberalism, beginning in 1980 in the US, encouraged a shift from state-regulated capitalism to deregulated neoliberal capitalism. The Glass-Steagall Act, the mainstay of the 1933 Banking Act, up until recently had controlled commercial banks from engaging in securities trading—including the capacity to gamble with depositors' funds through affiliated banks. These controls were finally removed with the repeal of affiliation restrictions (Sections 20 and 32) in 1999 under the Clinton regime—which permitted financial institutions to diversify their products and increase their sources of revenue.

THE FINANCIALIZATION OF EDUCATION

It was with rather astounded looks that we both reacted to a lunchroom question, "What's financialization got to do with education?" Perhaps not surprisingly it has remained under the radar scope in some countries, especially where education remains largely publicly funded and so always politicised. The collection of essays in this book is concerned with an analysis of financialization as the transformation of capitalism and in particular in its effects on education. We provide some general accounts that provide the basis for a better understanding of the phenomenon before focusing on the financialization of education.

One feature of the late twentieth and early twenty-first century has been the increasing number of mergers and acquisitions in publishing and education-based businesses. By 2014, while small independent publishers still exist, the terrain has changed from small publishing houses to publishing being dominated by 'the big six publishers'—Simon and Schuster, HarperCollins, Random House, Macmillan, the Penguin Group, and Hachette. Pearson, a major educational textbook publisher, has acquired two of these to form Penguin Random House. Pearson is much more than a publisher. It is now a multi-billion dollar, multi-national business that along with Thomson Reuters is now one of two dominant global players in educational business (http://thomsonreuters.com/). Here we highlight one of these education-based companies—Pearson, which is listed on two stock exchanges. It was listed in 1969 on London Stock Exchange and later on the New York Stock Exchange (NYSE) where it has been on FTSE 100 since the index began in 1984. Pearson has now have become an enormously dominant player in all levels of education.

Since 2013 it re-organised, combining Pearson International and Pearson North America into one Pearson company, and establishing three main business groupings: Pearson School, Pearson Higher Education, and Pearson Professional, which includes Financial Times Group and Pearson English. Pearson claims to be

> the world's leading learning company, with 40,000 employees in more than 80 countries working to help people of all ages make measurable progress in their lives through learning.
>
> We help to deliver successful learning in a number of ways, including the direct delivery of learning, provision of learning services, assessments, and we collaborate with governments to reform school systems to improve learner outcomes. (http://www.pearson.com)

Pearson has multiple education business interests including publishing and Pearson VUE, which "provides a **full suite of services** from test development to data management, and delivers exams through the **world's most comprehensive** and **secure network** of test centers in 175 countries."[35] (bold in original)

In the USA there are multiple examples of how financialization has permeated education. For-profit education companies that now impact every level of the education system are publicly traded on NYSE (e.g., Kaplan, part of Graham Holding Co, DeVry Education Group; American Public Education; Strayer Education; Capella Education; Grand Canyon Education; American; Bridgepoint Education: ITT Educational Services; Corinthian Colleges; Education Management Corp; Career Education Corp; Apollo Education Group; Lincoln Educational Services).[36] The multiple educational interests that such companies encompass include charter schools, testing systems, online education, school lunch programs, and management of education sector pension funds.

We look now at the university level where Danny Weil comments referring to Sonoma State University (SSU):

> At the college and university level, we see it in the issuance of debt by Wall Street in the form of bonds to finance massive deficits for capital construction projects. In the case of SSU, we also see financialization employing university funds to loan millions of dollars to unsavory real estate moguls for questionable land deals in an effort to seek high-yield returns to pay down debt. SSU also chased high-yield returns and invested in stock that plummeted with the Great Financial Crisis of 2008. The problem, of course, is that the administration used Endowment funds to chase risky investments.[37]

Heather Eggins and Peter West (2010) have analyzed the main global impacts on the financial crisis on developing and developed countries. Countries that have high levels of youth unemployment have experienced a growth in enrollments, especially in the so-called secure professions like teaching and nursing, fueling a growth in student loans and thus greater financialization of education, with some students delaying their graduations because of precarity. Under austerity programs university leaders, while recommending great flexibility of student loan and payments schemes, face the reality of spending cut-backs, especially in the US, that have led to the freezing of academic posts and recruitment and new rounds of redundancies and forced retirements. Some developing countries or newly transitional economies like China have been more immune to the financial crisis and have successfully begun to take up the slack that austerity of Western higher education economies provide, rapidly expanding opportunities in export education.

Inevitably this has led to further reliance of private sector initiatives and a raft of new financial products and services for students as they become yet more in debt. Eggins and West's (2010) review of key measures for coping with the crisis, such as such strengthening stakeholder and local community engagement, with a focus on new governance arrangements, communications, and professional services, seem meager and limited means to address the challenges of the new world economic order.

Lorraine Ling (2012) considers the extent to which the global financial crisis (GFC) has impacted upon teacher education in universities in Australia, a country that has been less affected by the crisis than most. She argues that many of the difficulties faced by the sector are a result of "a highly successful and prolonged period of economic rationalism and policies, which emanate from New Right ideologies," leading to the cumulative underfunding of higher education. She writes:

> While the impact of the GFC in Australia generally was much less severe than in many other countries, the continued starving of teacher education of adequate funding over a long period has taken its toll as reflected in unduly high staff student ratios, an over-reliance on casual staffing, insufficient funds to support the requirements of practicum placements, unrealistic staff workloads, lack of succession planning and inability to innovate. (p. 213)

Yet the global financial crisis has impacted on education in more systematic ways that imperil the nature of public education and its ability to help counter the effects of the crisis through providing the programs necessary for innovation, employment opportunities, and sustainable development. There is no doubt that the system capacity of public education to contribute to the economic and social well-being of citizens has been severely compromised. It is also clear that financialization represents a continued threat to public education and to the very idea of the public.

THE FINANCIALIZATION OF STUDENT LIFE

Perhaps the single most significant form of financialization of education is that of the student debt and the academic and social consequences of further debt loading of students—the endebtification of future generations and also of knowledge workers. Data from the Federal Reserve Bank of New York that was graphed by

Matt Philips in "Everything you need to know about the student borrowing bubble in 17 charts"[38] highlights the rapidity of this change in relation to other forms of debt—home equity credit lines, auto credit, and credit card debt—showing the steady climb of student loans since 2004 and that by 2010 they had outstripped the other three types of debt and continue to climb towards $US 1 trillion.

In *The Nation* George Zornick (2014) reports on the student loan crisis that is spiralling out of control and the campaign, "Higher Education Not Debt," that aims to address it:

> Cumulative student loan debt in the United States has reached an astonishing $1.2 trillion, and it's rising quickly. It shot up 20 percent just from the end of 2011 to May 2013, faster than even the growth of revolving credit products like credit cards. On average, the student loan debt held by 25-year-olds has gone up 91 percent in the past decade. The problem is exacerbated by tough economic times—nearly one-third of borrowers who have begun repayment are seriously delinquent.[39]

The "Higher Education Not Debt" is

> a multi-year campaign of dozens of organizations dedicated to tackling the crippling and ever-growing issue of student loan debt in America. With over $1.2 Trillion in outstanding educational debt, affecting more than 40 million Americans, we have partnered around a simple message and a clear objective: Higher Ed, Not Debt!

The campaign is based on four core principles:

- Providing support to borrowers currently paying off the existing $1.2 trillion of debt;
- Addressing the causes of declining affordability and quality, including changes to state funding and financial aid policies;
- Educating the public about Wall Street's complicity in the creation of the $1.2 trillion student debt crisis; and
- Civic engagement across all geographic, demographic, and political lines. (http://higherednotdebt.org/about/)

The campaign, supported by Senators Elizabeth Warren, Kristen Gillibrand, Tom Udall, and Chuck Schumer, among others, indicates:

> Wall Street is raking in about $44 billion in profits every year from higher education. Students are struggling with rising tuition and skyrocketing student loan debt. Colleges, communities and taxpayers are on the hook for interest payments on loans taken on by colleges. And for-profit institutions divert funds from education programs to shareholder profits. (http://higherednotdebt.org/blog/wall-street-profits-student-opportunity)

Elizabeth Warren has sponsored the Bank on Students Emergency Loan Refinancing Act,[40] which amends Title IV (Student Assistance) of the Higher

Education Act of 1965, to direct the Secretary of Education to establish a program to refinance the unpaid principal, accrued unpaid interest, and late charges on specified student loans. As the Committee on Education and the Workforce puts it:

> College graduates across the country are putting their dreams on hold as they struggle to pay off their student loans. Skyrocketing tuitions have left nearly 40 million Americans working to repay $1.2 trillion in student loans, and a third of all student loan dollars issued through the Federal Direct program are in default, forbearance, or deferment.[41]

The Bank on Students Emergency Loan Refinancing Act would allow more than 25 million people to refinance their student loans to lower interest rates of less than 4%. Warren paid for the bill with the "Buffet Rule"—a minimum 30% income tax payment from people who earn between $1 million and $2 million. The bill would allow all eligible federal student loan borrowers to refinance their loans down to interest rates offered to new 2013–2014 borrowers to take advantage of lower federal rates, as well as benefits and protections offered by the federal student loan program. Only about 10% of borrowers hold private loans eligible for refinancing, allowing an estimated 25 million student loan borrowers to refinance their student loans at lower interest rates and saving the typical borrower $2,000 over the life of his or her loan. According to the Congressional Budget Office it would reduce the deficit by about $14 billion during the 2015–2024 period.[42] But as of early October 2014 Senate Republicans have blocked the bill to allow students to refinance their loans.

Of all the changes that have taken place in the American university during the post-war era, the most significant is the shift toward financing higher education through borrowed money. It is an era that signals the birth of a new capitalist regime that mortgages the futures of students while reducing them to lifelong debt and servitude. In an age of automation it has the effect of putting students under the constraints of permanent indentured elite labour of digital capitalism.

Danny Weil explains:

> Financialization of the student loan debt occurs when student loan debt is transformed into asset-backed securities (ABS). The value and income payments from the ABS's are 'collateralized' ("backed") by a specified pool of underlying assets. None of the ABS can be sold individually. This is why they are sold to large institutional investors.

Student Loan Asset Backed Securities (SLABS) are a major sector of the ABS market with more than $400 billion in assets backing various student loan deals and also massive student default rates.[43]

Finance culture has been promoted as a style of governance through the market. A "new prudentialism" in education rests on the concept of the entrepreneurial self that "responsibilizes" the self to make welfare choices based on an actuarial rationality as a form of social security that insures the individual against risk. This represents a new welfare regime—one that is no longer focused on the rights of the citizen but that is based on the model of the citizen-consumer who makes investments in the self at critical points in the lifecycle (Peters, 2005). 'Responsibilization' is a term that emerges from the Foucauldian approach to governmentality referring to the process

> whereby subjects are rendered individually responsible for a task which previously would have been the duty of another—usually a state agency—or would not have been recognized as a responsibility at all. The process is strongly associated with neo-liberal political discourses, where it takes on the implication that the subject being responsibilized has avoided this duty or the responsibility has been taken away from them in the welfare state era and managed by an expert or government agency.[44]

Claes Belfrage (2009) argues:

> Financialisation is understood as emerging out of conditions which force people to weigh up the market performance of their financial assets when making everyday decisions between saving and consuming (Boyer 2000a, Froud et al. 2002). Financialisation should therefore also be understood in terms of subject-formation. It is, indeed, very much about how financial investment becomes a "life-strategy" (Martin 2002).[45]

Morgan Adamson (2009) advances the following five propositions of student debt and the financialization of student life:

1. The student is no longer a student confined but a student in debt.
2. Students are not simply one among many groups in American society that have been targeted by predatory lending; rather, since the early 1970s, students have been at the center of new experiments in the financial management and control of life through debt.
3. The financialization of student life is an extension of the means of primitive accumulation deployed by contemporary finance capitalism. New technologies of financial control targeted at the student, "Human Capital Contracts," exemplify the unbounded scope of these means in an attempt to control all domains of student life.
4. Student debt is counterrevolution.
5. In opposition to the infinite debt that structures sovereign power, debt in societies of control functions through the production of "the bankrupt," an indefinite form of life. It is on this terrain that struggles over student life must take place.

As he suggests, contrasting the student movement of 1960s with the financially overburdened student of today, "The radical model of the student-worker developed by student movements in the 1960s has been countered with the student overburdened with financial obligation, fully enmeshed in the world outside of the university, and increasingly isolated, over-worked, and resentful" (Adamson, 2009, p. 105). Apparently rather than actually helping students, some financial aid officers are solely focused on helping the university by setting up financing arrangements that ensure a student can get into the college, regardless of any ability to repay loans.[46] Promises of higher paying jobs are no longer as closely related to a degree as they have been in the past. Many recent graduates not only struggle to get high paying jobs commensurate with their qualifications, but they also spend post-university years reducing debt, in effect deleveraging rather than investing in the economy. In turn, over the long run, this hurts students, universities, and lowers economic growth.

In the US recently, senior citizens have been shocked to learn that student loans they took out in the 1970s have still to be repaid even when they are on Social Security. Even if they had other debt forgiven if they had filed for bankruptcy, student loans are usually not included. With reduced Social Security payments many seniors face reduced living standards, even poverty, so are forced to work well into retirement. Figures released in September 2014 by the US Government Accountability Office (GAO) report *OLDER AMERICANS: Inability to Repay Student Loans May Affect Financial Security of a Small Percentage of Retirees* show

> In 2005, older adults owed $2.8bn (£1.61bn) in federal student debt. By 2013, that figure had ballooned to $18.2bn. These seniors account for 706,000 households in the United States—small compared to the 22 million households with non-seniors who hold student load debt, but a growing problem. The number of individuals whose Social Security benefits were offset to pay student loan debt increased from about 31,000 to 155,000 between 2002–13.[47]

Danny Weil argues:

> The university must be understood as turned over to private capital markets and thus is a "borrower", "lender" and "investor". Debt plays a prominent if not central role in the life of the university education, like all institutions, cannot be understood divorced from the economic system that underlies it and which it reflects. When we speak specifically about the "financialization of education", we are addressing how financial motives, markets, specific powerful individuals, corporations and financial institutions impact all of public education.[48]

Particularly worrying is the way that public universities are seen by governments as better investments than private universities because their "credit quality" is steadier.[49] The Campaign for the Public University argues that the financialization of the public university is different from commodification of higher education representing a series of measures designed to open universities to for-profit income streams.[50] The decline in public dollars for higher education and a policy preference for market solutions, among other reasons, has resulted in a growing and heavy involvement of Wall Street in the lending, packaging, buying, servicing, and collection of student loans. With well over $1 trillion of student loans currently outstanding, it is clear to Tamara Draut (2012) that "many of the same problems found in the subprime mortgage market—rapacious and predatory lending practices, sloppy and inefficient customer service and aggressive debt collection practices—are also cropping up in the student loan industrial complex." She remarks that the very same forces that drove subprime mortgages through the roof now fuel Wall Street's seemingly endless appetite for new ways to make profit. "In this case, investor demand for student loan asset backed securities (SLABS) resulted in private student lenders—primarily Sallie Mae, Citi, Wells Fargo, and the other big banks—to relax lending standards and aggressively begin marketing these loans directly to students."[51]

The long-term impact of student loan debt on students has the potential to harm colleges and universities across the country and, in turn, the economy and other social values in democratic civil society.

CONCLUSION

This chapter has highlighted several different vital issues that have resulted from not only the Global Financial Crisis but also from the promotion of financialization itself and how this has impacted individuals and public education in all parts of the education sector.

In late 2014, the impact of GFC, though, is still affecting the global economy with uneven strength and growth in different parts of the world such that some experts worry that global recovery is not currently sustainable. The G20 meeting of Finance Ministers and Central Bank Governors in Washington October 2014 received negative assessments of the global economy by the International Monetary Fund, the Brookings Institution, and the Federal Reserve.[52]

While the US economy seems to be emerging from the GFC with unemployment down to under 6%, stronger than expected GDP growth of 3.5% in the third quarter of 2014, and the Federal Reserve ending its Quantitative Easing (QE) stimulus scheme, which began in November 2008 and bought $3.5 trillion in US government debt and bonds, it is the only major economy showing signs of strength. In contrast, in the EU, South America, Japan, and even China, growth is slow or stalling. There is concern that in Germany, EU's biggest economy, the latest data show such a rapid decline for industrial production, exports, factory orders, and business confidence that there is a risk of falling into recession as "four leading think tanks in Germany have slashed their economic growth forecasts to 1.3 per cent for this year and 1.2 per cent for 2015."[53] Germany currently faces not only weak demand for its goods from the rest of EU and China but also the impact of Russian sanctions due to the ongoing Ukraine crisis. With a strengthened US dollar and weakness for its trading partners, the US Federal Reserve worries that US exports could be depressed. At the G20 meeting officials set a goal of boosting global growth by 2% within five years, a target that would add US$5 trillion to the global economy. Many of the same messages are still being given at G20 meetings:

> The IMF's Christine Lagarde states "bold action was needed to bolster growth … In the face of what we have called the risk of a new mediocre, where growth is low and uneven, we certainly believe that there has to be a new momentum"; US officials said they planned to urge other economies to step up efforts to boost growth and strengthen bank regulations to prevent a recurrence of the 2008 financial crisis; structural economic changes such as deregulation and labour market reforms present serious challenges to political interests; "Europe's weakness has raised pressure on the European Central Bank, which sets interest rate policies for the 18 nations that use the euro currency, to do more to promote growth and fight low inflation."

Moreover, the Ebola crisis threatens West Africa and also the global economy:

> The presidents of three West African nations made urgent pleas Thursday to the finance ministers for money, hospital beds and doctors. World Bank President Jim Kim said the epidemic could have a "catastrophic" impact on the region if it isn't quickly contained and it spreads to other countries.[54]

But the global picture is not simply about GDP or the economy. The October 2014 OECD report, "How was Life? Global Well-being since 1820",[55] by economic historians, is based on ten dimensions: "per capita GDP, real wages, educational attainment, life expectancy, height, personal security, political institutions, environmental quality, income inequality and gender inequality." The report

> presents the first systematic evidence on long-term trends in global well-being since 1820 for 25 major countries and 8 regions in the world covering more than 80% of the world's population. It not only shows the data but also discusses the underlying sources and their limitations, pays attention to country averages and inequality, and pinpoints avenues for further research.

It concludes that

> people's well-being has generally progressed since the early 20th century across a large part of the world.
>
> Life expectancy worldwide has shot up from less than 30 years in 1880 to almost 70 in 2000.
>
> Literacy too has risen dramatically. Less than 20 per cent of people could read in 1820; now the figure is around 80 per cent.

But alarmingly it warns that inequality is now at the same level as in the 1820s. In the West, mid-twentieth-century income inequality dropped sharply from end of nineteenth century to 1970. The rise of communism in Eastern Europe and China reduced inequalities but they increased once the political structure changed. "The global income distribution across all citizens of the world was uni-modal in the 19th century but became increasingly bi-modal between 1910–1970 and suddenly reverted to a uni-modal distribution between 1980–2000."[56] The bi-modal phase seems to coincide with the egalitarian, socialist, and communist revolutionary systems while following globalization processes in the 1980s, and by 2000, global levels of income inequality have increased such that they are at the same levels as in 1820. This report paints a similar picture to French economist Thomas Piketty in his bestselling book *Capital in the Twenty-First Century* (2014) that is witness to the historical fact that capitalism widens rather than diminishes income inequalities. Financial capitalism is a new stage of capital reified in abstract figures that are the basis for a globally integrated economy that favours the rich and wealthy at the expense of the vast majority. It is the scourge of our age and a disaster waiting to happen.

REFERENCES

Ackerloff, G. A. (2013, May 1). The cat in the tree and further observations: Rethinking macroeconomic policy. *iMFdirect*. Retrieved from http://blog-imfdirect.imf.org/2013/05/01/the-cat-in-the-tree-and-further-observations-rethinking-macroeconomic-policy/

Adamson, M. (2009). The financialization of student life: Five propositions on student debt. *Polygraph, 21*, 97–110.

BBC News. (2103, May 2). Financial traders turn to lasers for faster deals. Retrieved from http://www.bbc.com/news/technology-22380611

Belfrage, C. (2008). Towards "universal financialisation" in Sweden? *Contemporary Politics, 14*(3), 277–296. Retrieved from http://www.tandfonline.com/doi/abs/10.1080/13569770802396337#.UeXQho4rTfA

Besley, A. C., & Peters, M. A. (2007). *Subjectivity and truth: Foucault, education, and the culture of self.* New York: Peter Lang.

Blanchard, O. (2013, April 29). Rethinking macroeconomic policy. *iMFdirect*. Retrieved from http://blog-imfdirect.imf.org/2013/04/29/rethinking-macroeconomic-policy/

Blankenburg, S., & Palma, J. G. (2009). Introduction: The Global Financial Crisis. *Cambridge Journal of Economics, 33*, 531–538. Retrieved from http://cje.oxfordjournals.org/content/33/4/531.full.pdf

Boyer, R. (2000a). Is a finance-led growth regime a viable alternative to Fordism? A preliminary analysis. *Economy and Society, 29*, 111–145.

Bryan, D., & Rafferty, M. (2006). *Capitalism with derivatives: A political economy of financial derivatives, capital, and class*. New York: Palgrave.

Crotty, J. R. (2009). Structural causes of the global financial crisis: A critical assessment of the "new financial architecture." *Cambridge Journal of Economics*, 33, 563–580. Retrieved from http://www.peri.umass.edu/fileadmin/pdf/conference_papers/SAFER/Crotty_Structural.pdf

Davis, G. (2009). *Managed by the markets: How finance reshaped America*. New York: Oxford University Press.

Draut, T. (2012, November 16). Subprime students: How Wall Street profits from the college loan mess. *The American Prospect*. Retrieved from http://prospect.org/article/subprime-students-how-wall-street-profits-college-loan-mess

Duménil , G. & Lévy, D. (2004). *Capital resurgent: Roots of the neoliberal revolution*. Cambridge, MA & London, UK: Harvard University Press.

Eggins, H., & West, P. (2010). The global impact of the financial crisis: Main trends in developed and developing countries. *Higher Education Management and Policy, 22*(3), 57–72.

Falk, T. (2013, May 6). How lasers will make financial trading even faster. *Smartplanet, 21*. Retrieved from http://www.smartplanet.com/blog/bulletin/how-lasers-will-make-financial-trading-even-faster/

FED (Federal Reserve Board). (2009). Flow of funds accounts of the United States. Retrieved from http://www.federalreservebank.gov/datadownload

Fligstein, N., & Goldstein, A. (2012). *The Emergence of a Finance Culture in American Households, 1989–2007*. Retrieved from http://sociology.berkeley.edu/sites/default/files/faculty/fligstein/The%20Emergence%20of%20a%20Finance%20Culture%209-04-13.pdf

Froud, J., Johal, S., & Williams, K. (2002). Financialisation and the coupon pool. *Capital and Class, 26*(3), 119–151. Retrieved from http://cnc.sagepub.com/content/26/3/119.refs

Ghilarducci, T. (1992). *Labor's capital: The economics and politics of private pensions*. Cambridge, MA: The MIT Press.

House of Lords, House of Commons. Parliamentary Commission on Banking Standards. (2013). *Changing banking for good*. London: Stationery Office. Retrieved from http://www.parliament.uk/documents/banking-commission/banking-final-report-vol-ii.pdf

IMF. (2009, April). *Global financial stability report. Responding to the financial crisis and measuring systemic risk*. Washington, DC: IMF.

Johnson, S. (2009, May 1). The quiet coup. *The Atlantic*. Retrieved from http://www.theatlantic.com/magazine/archive/2009/05/the-quiet-coup/307364/

Kay, J. (2012, July). *The Final Report of the Kay Review of Equity Markets and Long-Term Decision-making*. Retrieved from https://www.gov.uk/government/uploads/system/uploads/attachment_data/file/253454/bis-12-917-kay-review-of-equity-markets-final-report.pdf

Lauricella, T., Scannell, K., & Strasburg, J. (2010, October 2). How a trading algorithm went awry. *The Wall Street Journal*. Retrieved from http://online.wsj.com/news/articles/SB10001424052748704029304575526390131916792?mg=reno64-wsj&url=http%3A%2F%2Fonline.wsj.com%2Farticle%2FSB10001424052748704029304575526390131916792.html

Libor Scandal. Retrieved from http://en.wikipedia.org/wiki/Libor_scandal

The LIBOR scandal: The rotten heart of finance. (2012, July 7). *The Economist*. Retrieved from http://www.economist.com/node/21558281

Ling, L. (2012). Teacher education, the global financial crisis, frogs and bicycles. *Educational Research, 54*(2), 213–224.

Martin, R. (2002). *Financialization of daily life*. Philadelphia: Temple University Press.

Masters, B., Parker, G., & Giles, C. (2013). King's parting shot at meddling UK banks. *Financial Times*. Retrieved from http://www.ft.com/cms/s/0/14a9d492-ddaf-11e2-892b-00144feab7de.html#axzz2XPHJ2fSY

Mullin, K. (2013, June 20). COMMENT: Changing banking for good? Not from where I sit. *Reuters*. Retrieved from http://www.reuters.com/article/2013/06/20/britain-banking-mullin-ifr-idUSL5N0EW1YN20130620

OECD. (2014, October 2). *How was life? Global well-being since 1820*. Retrieved from http://www.oecd.org/statistics/how-was-life-9789264214262-en.htm

Peet, R. (2011). Contradictions of finance capitalism. *The Monthly Review, 63*(7). http://monthlyreview.org/author/richardpeet/

Peters, M. A. (2001). Education, enterprise culture and the entrepreneurial self: A Foucauldian perspective. *Journal of Educational Enquiry,* 2(2), 59–71. Retrieved from http://www.ojs.unisa.edu.au/index.php/EDEQ/article/view/558/428

Peters, M. A. (2005). The new prudentialism in education: Actuarial rationality and the entrepreneurial self. *Educational Theory, 55*(2), 123–137.

Peters, M. A. (2012). Bioinformational Capitalism. *Thesis Eleven, 110*(1), 98–111.

Piketty, T. (2014). *Capital in the twenty-first century.* Cambridge, MA: Belknap Press of Harvard University Press.

Porter, M. E. (1992). Capital disadvantage: America's failing capital investment system. *Harvard Business Review,* 65–82.

Preston, D. (2012, October 9). Rigged Libor costs states, localities $6 billion. *Bloomberg*. Retrieved from http://www.bloomberg.com/news/2012-10-09/rigged-libor-hits-states-localities-with-6-billion-muni-credit.html

Romer, D. (2013, May 3). Preventing the next catastrophe: Where do we stand? *iMFdirect*. Retrieved from http://blog-imfdirect.imf.org/2013/05/03/preventing-the-next-catastrophe-where-do-we-stand/

Salter, S. (2014, July 18). UK banks face break-up threat as watchdog plans competition probe. *Reuters.* Retrieved from http://uk.reuters.com/article/2014/07/18/uk-banks-britain-competition-idUKKBN0FN0IY20140718

Sheng, A. (2013, June 25). Changing banking for good: Can new regulations really work? *The Nation.* Retrieved from http://www.nationmultimedia.com/opinion/Changing-banking-for-good-Can-new-regulations-real-30208961.html

Sparrow, T. (2014, October 22). US seniors face student loan debt. *BBC News.* Retrieved from http://www.bbc.com/news/magazine-29730227

Stiglitz, J. (2013, May 3). The lessons of the North Atlantic crisis for economic theory and policy. *iMFdirect.* Retrieved from http://blog-imfdirect.imf.org/2013/05/03/the-lessons-of-the-north-atlantic-crisis-for-economic-theory-and-policy/

Tett, G. (2009). *Fool's gold: How unrestrained greed corrupted a dream, shattered global markets and unleashed a catastrophe.* London: Little, Brown.

Trader, T. (2014, August 6). Danes take back fastest data transfer title. *HPC Wire.* Retrieved from http://www.hpcwire.com/2014/08/06/danes-take-back-fastest-data-transfer-title/

Tridico, P. (2012). Financial crisis and global imbalances: Its labour market origins and the aftermath. *Cambridge Journal of Economics, 36*(1), 17–42.

Wakefield, A., & Fleming, J. (2009). *The SAGE dictionary of policing.* Retrieved from http://knowledge.sagepub.com/view/the-sage-dictionary-of-policing/n111.xml

Weil, D. (2012, April 30). The financialization of education and Sonoma State University part II. *Project Censored.* Retrieved from http://www.projectcensored.org/the-financialization-of-education-and-sonoma-state-university-part-ii

Whalen, C. (2002). Money manager capitalism: Still here, but not quite as expected. *Journal of Economic Issues, 36*(2), 401–406.

Wheatley, M. (2014. April 6). Regulating high frequency trading. *Financial Conduct Authority.* Retrieved from http://www.fca.org.uk/news/regulating-high-frequency-trading

Zornick, G. (2014, March 6). Campaign to address the student loan crisis launches. *The Nation.* Retrieved from http://www.thenation.com/blog/178724/campaign-address-student-loan-crisis-launches#

NOTES

1. In the United States, a 401(k) plan is the tax-qualified, defined-contribution pension account defined in subsection 401(k) of the Internal Revenue Code.[1] Under the plan, retirement savings contributions are provided (and sometimes proportionately matched) by an employer, deducted from the employee's paycheck before taxation (therefore tax-deferred until withdrawn after retirement or as otherwise permitted by applicable law), and limited to a maximum pre-tax annual contribution of $17,500 (as of 2014).[2][3] Other employer-provided defined-contribution plans include 403(b) plans, for nonprofit institutions, and 457(b) plans for governmental employers. These plans are all established under section 401(a) of the Internal Revenue Code. 401(a) plans may provide total annual addition of $52,000 (as of 2014) per plan participant, including both employee and employer contributions. (http://en.wikipedia.org/wiki/401k)
2. http://en.wikipedia.org/wiki/Subprime_mortgage_crisis; http://en.wikipedia.org/wiki/Financial_crisis_of_2007%E2%80%9308; http://en.wikipedia.org/wiki/Great_Recession and http://en.wikipedia.org/wiki/Global_financial_system#Reform_efforts
3. https://www.apple.com/apple-pay/
4. http://www.bloomberg.com/news/2014-04-08/global-growth-threatened-in-623-trillion-derivatives-overhaul.html. This unreal growth is also demonstrated in statistics that record that in 2011, the Gross World Product (GWP) totalled approximately $79.39 trillion while the world derivatives market was estimated in excess of $1.2 quadrillion, some twenty times larger than the world's productive economy (http://www.dailyfinance.com/2010/06/09/risk-quadrillion-derivatives-market-gdp/)
5. http://www.gpo.gov/fdsys/pkg/PLAW-111publ203/html/PLAW-111publ203.htm
6. These two sources differ only in their reporting of the bank component of financial stocks.
7. http://awgf.econ.usyd.edu.au/
8. 'Rentier Capitalism' is a term currently used to describe economic practices of parasitic monopolization of access to any (physical, financial, intellectual, etc.) kind of property, and gaining significant amounts of profit without contribution to society. The origins of the term are unclear; it is often said to be used in Marxism, yet the very combination of words 'rentier' and 'capitalism' was never used by Karl Marx himself (http://en.wikipedia.org/wiki/Rentier_capitalism).
9. "In June 2011, the Secretary of State for Business, Innovation and Skills asked me to review activity in UK equity markets and its impact on the long-term performance and governance of UK quoted companies. The Review's principal concern has been to ask how well equity markets are achieving their core purposes: to enhance the performance of UK companies and to enable savers to benefit from the activity of these businesses through returns to direct and indirect ownership of shares in UK companies. More detail on the background to the Review, including its terms of reference and the Interim Report, can be found at www.bis.gov.uk/kayreview." (Kay, 2012, p. 5).
10. http://www.theactuary.com/features/2013/04/the-mild-mannered-prophet-of-doom/
11. http://www.johnkay.com/wp-content/uploads/2009/12/JK-Narrow-Banking.pdf;. See also http://harr123et.files.wordpress.com/2010/07/futureoffinance-chapter81.pdf
12. See http://www.theatlantic.com/magazine/archive/2009/05/the-quiet-coup/307364/
13. See the 2013 story by Brooke Masters, George Parker, and Chris Giles at FT, "King's Parting Shot at Meddling UK Banks." (http://www.ft.com/cms/s/0/14a9d492-ddaf-11e2-892b-00144feab7de.html#axzz2XPHJ2fSY)
14. Libor is the abbreviation for the London Interbank Offered Rate. It is the average interest rate estimated by leading banks in London that the average leading bank would be charged if

borrowing from other banks. It was formerly known as "BBA Libor" (for British Bankers' Association Libor or the trademark "bbalibor") before the responsibility for the administration was transferred to Intercontinental Exchange. It is the primary benchmark, along with the Euribor, for short-term interest rates around the world. (http://en.wikipedia.org/wiki/Libor)

15. http://en.wikipedia.org/wiki/Libor_scandal
16. CFTC Mission: "to protect market participants and the public from fraud, manipulation, abusive practices and systemic risk related to derivatives—both futures and swaps—and to foster transparent, open, competitive and financially sound markets." (http://www.cftc.gov/About/MissionResponsibilities/index.htm)
17. http://www.cftc.gov/ucm/groups/public/@lrenforcementactions/documents/legalpleading/enfrbsorder020613.pdf
18. See the report at http://www.parliament.uk/business/committees/committees-a-z/joint-select/professional-standards-in-the-banking-industry/news/changing-banking-for-good-report/
19. See Keith Mullin's comments at Reuters, http://www.reuters.com/article/2013/06/20/britain-banking-mullin-ifr-idUSL5N0EW1YN20130620
20. See, e.g., http://www.nationmultimedia.com/opinion/Changing-banking-for-good-Can-new-regulations-real-30208961.html
21. The Dodd-Frank Wall Street Reform and Consumer Protection Act (Pub. L. 111–203, H.R. 417).
22. http://uk.reuters.com/article/2014/07/18/uk-banks-britain-competition-idUKKBN0FN0IY20140718
23. http://www.imf.org/external/np/seminars/eng/2013/macro2/index.htm
24. http://blog-imfdirect.imf.org/2013/05/03/the-lessons-of-the-north-atlantic-crisis-for-economic-theory-and-policy/
25. http://blog-imfdirect.imf.org/2013/05/01/the-cat-in-the-tree-and-further-observations-rethinking-macroeconomic-policy/
26. http://blog-imfdirect.imf.org/2013/04/29/rethinking-macroeconomic-policy/
27. http://blog-imfdirect.imf.org/2013/05/03/preventing-the-next-catastrophe-where-do-we-stand/
28. http://www.hpcwire.com/2014/08/06/danes-take-back-fastest-data-transfer-title/
29. Falk, T. (2013, May 6). How lasers will make financial trading even faster. Smartplanet. (http://www.smartplanet.com/blog/bulletin/how-lasers-will-make-financial-trading-even-faster/)
30. BBC News. (2013, May 2). Financial traders turn to lasers for faster deals. (http://www.bbc.com/news/technology-22380611)
31. Lauricella, T., Scannell, K., & Strasburg, J. (2010, October 2). How a Trading Algorithm Went Awry. *The Wall Street Journal.* http://online.wsj.com/news/articles/SB10001424052748704029304575526390131916792?mg=reno64-wsj&url=http%3A%2F%2Fonline.wsj.com%2Farticle%2FSB10001424052748704029304575526390131916792.html
32. Flash Crash (http://en.wikipedia.org/wiki/2010_Flash_Crash)
33. Kirilenko, A., Kyle, A., Samadi, M., & Tuzun, T. (2011). The Flash Crash: The Impact of High Frequency Trading on an Electronic Market. *SSRN.* (http://papers.ssrn.com/sol3/papers.cfm?abstract_id=1686004)
34. Wheatley, M. (2014). Regulating high frequency trading. Financial Control Authority. http://www.fca.org.uk/news/regulating-high-frequency-trading
35. http://www.pearsonvue.com/

36. http://www.kaplan.com/; http://www.devryeducationgroup.com/; http://www.forbes.com/companies/american-public-education/; http://www.forbes.com/companies/strayer-education/; http://www.forbes.com/companies/capella-education/; https://www.google.com/finance?q=NASDAQ%3AAPEI&ei=UtUoVOGsOoSakQXOkYDoBg
37. Weil, D. (2012). The financialization of education and Sonoma State University Part II. *Project Censored.* (http://www.projectcensored.org/the-financialization-of-education-and-sonoma-state-university-part-ii/)
38. http://www.theatlantic.com/business/archive/2013/05/the-whole-truth-about-student-debt-in-17-charts/275466/
39. http://www.thenation.com/blog/178724/campaign-address-student-loan-crisis-launches#
40. http://www.warren.senate.gov/files/documents/BankOnStudentsRefinancingBillText.pdf
41. http://democrats.edworkforce.house.gov/bill/hr-4582-bank-students-emergency-loan-refinancing-act
42. http://elizabethwarren.com/video/senator-elizabeth-warren-bank-on-students-emergency-loan-refinancing-act
43. http://www.dailycensored.com/student-loans-the-financialized-economy-of-indentured-servitude/
44. Wakefield, A., & Fleming, J. (2009). *The SAGE Dictionary of Policing.* (http://knowledge.sagepub.com/view/the-sage-dictionary-of-policing/n111.xml)
45. http://www.tandfonline.com/doi/abs/10.1080/13569770802396337#.UeXQho4rTfA
46. http://www.forbes.com/sites/robertfarrington/2014/09/24/the-long-term-impact-of-student-loan-debt-on-universities/
47. Sparrow, T. (2014). US seniors face student loan debt. BBC News. (http://www.bbc.com/news/magazine-29730227); *OLDER AMERICANS: Inability to Repay Student Loans May Affect Financial Security of a Small Percentage of Retirees*, GAO-14-866T. Published September 10, 2014. Publicly released: September 10, 2014. (http://www.gao.gov/products/GAO-14-866T; http://www.gao.gov/assets/670/665709.pdf)
48. http://www.projectcensored.org/top-stories/articles/the-financialization-of-education-and-sonoma-state-university-part-ii/
49. http://globalhighered.wordpress.com/2009/07/07/moodys-special-comment-report-on-the-global-recession/
50. http://philosophersforchange.org/2013/06/25/student-loans-the-financialized-economy-of-indentured-servitude/
51. http://prospect.org/article/subprime-students-how-wall-street-profits-college-loan-mess
52. http://www.g20.utoronto.ca/2014/2014-1010-finance.html
53. http://www.stuff.co.nz/business/world/10601328/US-okay-but-global-economy-under-threat
54. October 10, 2014, http://www.stuff.co.nz/business/world/10601328/US-okay-but-global-economy-under-threat
55. OECD. (2014). How was Life? Global Well-being since 1820. (http://www.oecd.org/statistics/how-was-life-9789264214262-en.htm)
56. OECD. (2014). http://www.keepeek.com/Digital-Asset-Management/oecd/economics/how-was-life/summary/english_7eeabaee-en#page2

CHAPTER THREE

Financialisation, OR THE Search FOR Profits IN THE Sphere OF Circulation[1]

COSTAS LAPAVITSAS

ANALYZING FINANCIALISATION: APPROACH AND METHOD

Financialisation has attracted much interest among political economists in recent years, and even more since the crisis of 2007–2009. There is no commonly agreed use of the term, though it certainly refers to the extraordinary growth of finance during the last two to three decades. Several analytical approaches to financialisation can be found in the literature, some of which are selectively mentioned below. Despite their differences, these approaches have a common thread, namely to associate financialisation with a change in the balance between the spheres of production and circulation, which is also the point of departure of this article.

Much of the original insight into financialisation came from the Marxist work of the *Monthly Review*, guided by Sweezy and Magdoff, who began to draw theoretical attention to the growth of finance in the 1970s.[2] For Sweezy (1997), financialisation has been caused by the transformation of capitalist accumulation commencing at the end of the nineteenth century. Financialisation is one of three underlying trends of capitalist development in the twentieth century, together with the slowing down of the rate of growth and the rise of monopolistic multinationals. There is a clear rationale for financialisation within the framework developed by Baran and Sweezy in *Monopoly Capital* (1966). Namely, in mature capitalism, the sphere of production is incapable of absorbing as new investment the ever-expanding surplus generated by monopolies. Production therefore stagnates and capital seeks refuge in circulation, particularly in the speculative activities of finance.

Sweezy and Magdoff's observation of the changing balance between production and circulation is particularly prescient in view of the relative neglect of finance in the corpus of the *Monthly Review*'s economic output, including in *Monopoly Capital*. The impact of their argument—direct or indirect—can be discerned among political economists, Marxist and others. For *Monthly Review*'s argument does not ultimately hinge on the theory of the ever-expanding surplus inundating production; rather, it is consistent with several theories that identify persistent malfunctioning in the sphere of production. Thus, it is not surprising that the idea of capital escaping in the sphere of circulation as production stumbled in the mid-1970s has become common currency among heterodox economists.

This notion, for instance, is present—if at times tacitly—in the work of Crotty (1990), Pollin (2007), Epstein (2005), and more broadly for the post-Keynesian current in heterodox economics. Moreover, for these writers financialisation is also associated with the re-emergence of the rentier, which exacerbates the malaise of production. Financial profits have grown at the expense of industrial profits and rentiers are a deadweight on industrial capitalists. Thus, the logic of causation is largely reversed for the post-Keynesian current: financialisation has induced poor performance in investment, output and growth in developed countries in recent years. Financialisation, in turn, has been caused by policy changes and the emergence of liberalization in the realm of finance. Considerable empirical research in this vein has been produced,[3] which overlaps with further economic analysis of the problematic macroeconomic implications of 'finance-led accumulation.'[4]

From a very different Marxist perspective, Brenner (2002) also shares the notion that capital has sought refuge in circulation as production stagnated. Brenner, whilst avoiding financialisation as an organizing category, certainly suggests that financial activities in circulation have grown as a direct response to profitability problems in the sphere of production. The Marxist analysis of Duménil and Lévy (2004), on the other hand, also emphasizes the intensified search for profits in the sphere of finance as profitability in production has remained problematic and neoliberalism took hold.

From a still different, and much broader, historical perspective, the same notion is the basis of Arrighi's (1994) analysis of financialisation. Ranging over centuries, Arrighi essentially argues that finance and circulation thrive when production stagnates. For Arrighi, financialisation represents autumn in the long-term, cyclical alternation of hegemonic capitalist formations in the world market. Arrighi's work is one of the motivations of Krippner's (2005) thorough empirical study of financialisation of the US economy. Krippner established the rising importance of financial profits for non-financial corporations during the last five decades.

In a related way the idea that circulation has expanded and thrived as production has entered a period of trouble is also present in the recent work of the Regulation School.[5] In a nutshell, as Fordism disintegrated, a search for a new regime of accumulation began in the sphere of finance. The new regime gradually took shape focusing on financial markets, particularly the stock exchange. The regulationist approach chimes with the voluminous work on changes in corporate governance since the 1970s. 'Shareholder value' and the associated short-termism of corporate enterprises have been extensively analyzed and documented by political economists, business school writers, and economic sociologists.[6]

The crisis of 2007–2009 has fully justified the emphasis laid by political economists on financialisation since it emanated in the sphere of finance and then spread to production partly through financial mechanisms. But the crisis has also presented unexpected developments shedding fresh light on financialisation and inviting a rethink of the relationship between production and circulation. Thus, its proximate causes were to be found in sub-prime lending in the USA, which was exacerbated by financial engineering within the financial sector. It is unprecedented for a crisis of this magnitude to have sprung out of financial transactions involving the poorest sections of the working class. Moreover, its global spread was due, in the first instance, to securitization associated with the adoption of investment banking functions by commercial banks. In short, financialisation in the 2000s has been closely related to the personal revenue of workers, while entailing a transformation of banking. The combination of the two has proven lethal for both finance and the productive sector.

A Marxist approach that is aware of these aspects of the crisis of 2007–2009 could offer fresh insight into financialisation.[7] As Sweezy and Magdoff note, the balance between production and circulation has shifted in favor of the latter; however, the causes of the shift have to be established in terms of the fundamental relations of accumulation. It is shown below that the deeper roots of financialisation are to be found in the elemental relations among key economic entities of capitalist accumulation, namely industrial (and commercial) enterprises, workers, and financial institutions. In this light, and still more broadly, financialisation is due to changes in the forces and relations of production, combined with the transformation of the institutional and legal framework of capitalist accumulation in recent years.

The approach to financialisation proposed in this chapter is explicitly informed by the classical Marxist debates on imperialism and finance capital at the turn of the twentieth century. At issue was the transformation of capitalism during the last quarter of the nineteenth century. Summarily put, giant monopolistic corporations had emerged, often organized as cartels that operated exclusive trading zones. Global finance, dominated by monopolistic banks, was on the ascendant. At the same time, British predominance in world markets was challenged by Germany and the USA. The political counterpart of these underlying trends was militarism and imperialism among the main powers.

Several Marxist theories contested the explanation of these phenomena, but Hilferding's (1981) analysis stood out. Hilferding, as is well known, argued that the transformation of capitalism was due to the rise of finance capital. This is an amalgam of industrial and banking capital created as monopolistic corporations come increasingly to rely on banks for investment finance. Finance capital is led by banks and 'organizes' the economy to suit its interests, thus resulting in exclusive trading blocs and the export of money capital. Consequently, finance capital seeks to establish empire by mobilizing political and military help from the state. Lenin (1964) took Hilferding's analysis, added 'parasitical rentiers' and greater emphasis on monopoly, and produced the definitive Marxist theory of imperialism in the twentieth century.

It is apparent that Hilferding's theory in its original form fits poorly the phenomena of contemporary capitalism. But for several reasons his theoretical thrust is sound and can be a guide to analysis of financialisation.[8] First, Hilferding seeks the causes of the great transformation of his time in the fundamental relations of accumulation rather than in policy or institutional change. Specifically, he claims that as the size of production grows, monopolies come to depend heavily on investment credit by banks. In his view this entails a closer relationship between banks and industry and, thus, emergence of finance capital. Second, Hilferding is fully aware of the organizational implications of this development. Thus, finance capital rests on dense connections between finance and industry through interlocking appointments, exchange of information, and joint decision making.

Third, despite focusing on the rise of finance, Hilferding never opts for the opposition between 'active' industrialist and 'idle' financier. There is no suggestion in his theory of rentiers pressing on industrial capitalists and lowering investment rates or rates of growth. Rather, finance capital is an amalgam, and hence industrial capital has a direct interest in the profitability of financial operations. Fourth, imperialism is not an arbitrary outcome of political choices but has roots in economic processes. By the same token, imperialism has a specific historical content and is not the result of, say, a human propensity toward aggrandizement and domination of others.

To be sure Hilferding also treats some economic phenomena perfunctorily, while overplaying his hand in other respects. Thus, his view that large monopolies increasingly depend on banks for investment finance is simply incorrect, and probably the result of focusing excessively on the German and Austrian economies of his time. Similarly, the notion that finance capital 'organizes' the economy is far-fetched, and fits badly with the gigantic crises that took place in the 1920s and 1930s. Lenin was more careful on this score. Nonetheless, Hilferding's approach and results were path-breaking and a model for analysis of financialisation.

For financialisation has evident analogies with the transformation of capitalism at the turn of the twentieth century. Multinational corporations currently dominate the world economy; finance is again on the ascendant globally; capital export has grown substantially; a certain type of imperialism has reasserted itself. At the same time, there is no fusion of banks with industry; banks are certainly not dominant over industry; and there are no exclusive trading zones closely related to territorial empires. Nonetheless, the present period is characterized by the interpenetration of finance with industry and, more broadly, of finance with workers' activities, making Hilferding's work an indispensable analytical tool.

In the rest of this article financialisation is discussed on this basis, while drawing on recent theoretical and empirical work.[9] It is shown that financialisation is rooted in changes in the molecular relations between industrial and financial capitals in the first instance. To be specific, large industrial and commercial corporations have become less reliant on banks for finance. Open financial markets have grown and corporations have become 'financialised' in the sense of acquiring financial assets, as well as issuing traded financial liabilities.

Consequently, financial institutions have been forced to change in profound ways during the last three decades. Two among these changes stand out: first, banks have turned toward individual income as a source of profits; and, second, banks have adopted investment banking methods generating profits through fees, commissions, and trading on account. The former is based on the financialisation of workers' revenue in general. Workers have become heavily implicated in the activities of the formal financial system both in terms of borrowing (mortgages and consumption) but also in terms of assets (pensions and insurance). These developments owe much to the withdrawal of public provision across goods and services comprising the real wage: housing, health, education, pensions, and so on. Financial institutions, consequently, have been able to extract profits directly and systematically out of wages and salaries. This process is called 'financial expropriation.'

Financialisation has certainly involved a search for profits in the sphere of circulation. However, this has been a structural and deeply rooted process as is shown in the rest of this article. It should finally be noted here that financialisation has also witnessed changes in the institutions and mechanisms of economic policy making, including the central bank. Moreover, financialisation has entailed a transformation of international finance—typically related to the role of the dollar as world money—which has affected power and surplus transfer relations globally. These developments are beyond the scope of this article, which focuses on the underlying domestic aspects of financialisation.

Section 2 below considers financialisation in terms of the balance between production and circulation. Particular attention is paid to technological change and its impact on productivity. Section 3 then turns to the economic content of financialisation and considers, first, relations between financial institutions and industrial/commercial corporations; second, the turn of financial institutions toward workers' revenue; and, third, the turn of financial institutions toward mediating activities in open financial markets. Section 4 concludes.

FINANCIALISATION AND THE CHANGING BALANCE BETWEEN PRODUCTION AND CIRCULATION

Asymmetry in the Development of Production and Circulation

In some respects the financialisation of major developed countries during the last three decades is apparent to the point of triviality. The financial sector has grown relative to the rest of the economy, including with regard to labour employed; financial assets have become a large part of the assets of non-financial corporations; individual borrowing for housing, consumption, education, and health has grown substantially, as have individual assets held for pensions, insurance, and so on; global financial markets have become increasingly integrated; international money and capital flows have reached unprecedented levels. The list could be easily extended.

Simply and summarily put, the sphere of circulation (particularly the financial sector) has exhibited more dynamism than the sphere of production since the 1970s. There is little doubt that the productive sector of developed countries has performed indifferently during this period, as is manifested in consistently lower rates of growth compared to the pre-1973 period. An asymmetry appears to have advanced within developed capitalist economies between sluggish production and vigorous circulation, particularly booming finance. While the particular characteristics of the asymmetry vary across developed countries (as well as across developed and developing countries), its presence is not in doubt.

This asymmetry is fundamental to financialisation and forms a natural starting point for its analysis. What are the reasons for its emergence? From a Marxist perspective, if the balance between the constituent spheres of the capitalist economy has altered significantly, the deeper causes must be sought in developments in the forces and relations of production. These would account for differential growth patterns in production and circulation, including the appearance of new fields of profitability.

In this light, the roots of financialisation during the last three decades are to be found, on the one hand, in the technological revolution in information and telecommunications and, on the other, in the deregulation of labour and financial markets, with the attendant intensification of labour. These underlying material factors appear to have impacted on the sphere of circulation, including finance, with particular force. Establishing and analyzing their workings in historical detail is, of course, a gigantic task, far beyond the scope of this article. But some insight on the impact of technological change can be gleaned from the trajectory of the growth of the productivity of labour during this period. This is discussed in section 2.2, while the impact of deregulation is briefly considered in section 2.3.

Technological Change and Productivity Growth

Productivity has continued to rise in the USA, Japan, and the other developed countries since the mid-1970s. The point is, however, that the dynamism of capitalist expansion depends on the rate of growth of productivity rather than on its increase alone. In this respect, the asymmetry between production and circulation in recent decades is related to the unstable rate of growth of productivity and, therefore, to the nature of the underlying technological change.

Before discussing this point, there are conceptual problems to confront. Productivity in the sphere of production is a straightforward concept (physical output per worker) and depends on technological progress, labour skills, the organisation of production, and so on. Productivity in the sphere of circulation, on the other hand, is far more problematic. Enterprises that specialize in circulation are often intermediaries (for instance, financial institutions) and hence do not produce output. Furthermore, from a Marxist perspective, they typically do not produce value.

The absence of value creation in circulation is not directly relevant to measuring productivity, since the latter is about physical output per worker. However, lack of value creation limits the economic impact of productivity growth within the sphere of circulation. Productivity growth is ultimately important because it changes the value of output per unit and, therefore, affects costs and profitability across the economy. Nonetheless, intermediaries that engage in circulation have a measurable volume of activities, both on and off the balance sheet. They also employ large numbers of staff that take up the bulk of costs. Hence a measure of the volume of activities relative to workers employed would still be a valuable indication of how intermediaries mobilize resources.

These conceptual problems are compounded by intractable difficulties of measurement, since productivity refers to quantitative aggregates of use values; however, these well-known problems are not a direct concern of this chapter. It suffices for our purposes to refer to mainstream productivity measures, irrespective of the methodology used. In this respect, even Total Factor Productivity, a notoriously problematic, residual measure of productivity, could be of use. If it was systematically applied over time, even Total Factor Productivity would still give a sense of the dynamism of change of productivity.[10]

In this vein, mainstream literature has shown that productivity growth for the economy as a whole has been deficient since the late 1970s across developed countries. Manufacturing productivity growth has been weak but productivity in services has been even weaker. The USA during the short period from the late 1990s to the early 2000s is a partial exception.[11] However, in the course of the bubble of 2001–2007 labour productivity growth appears to have declined again in the USA.[12] It is important to note that productivity growth has also been problematic in finance. Poor productivity growth in finance fits well with the literature that directly examines the costs of banks, which has shown that financial intermediaries have been inefficient in recent years.[13] In short, new technologies and associated labour practices have failed to set the capitalist economy on a path of systematic and rapid productivity growth, including in finance, during the last three decades.

Quite why this should be is unclear but it evidently has to do with the nature of information and telecommunication technologies as well as the work practices that they enforce and encourage. Irrespective of the reasons for it, hesitant productivity growth does not make for dynamic expansion in the sphere of production. In the long term, productivity gains drive down costs, leading to increases in (relative) surplus value and thus expanded capitalist accumulation. Mediocre productivity growth in recent decades is associated with the indifferent performance of the productive sector, including weak profitability. Strengthening profitability in the sphere of production during the last three decades appears to have relied heavily on keeping real wages stagnant while intensifying labour, thus allowing capitalists to reap the benefits of whatever increases in productivity have taken place. Restored profitability has not resulted from dynamic improvements in productivity through technological progress.

At the same time, the impact of new technologies on the sphere of finance has been dramatic. Finance might have become neither more efficient nor more productive in terms of intermediation per worker, but it has become capable of undertaking operations that were previously completely impossible. The changes are apparent in terms of the internal organisation of financial institutions, the speed of transactions, the feasibility of financial engineering, the links between financial markets, the techniques of pricing and risk management, and so on.[14] Not least, finance has become technically capable of dealing with huge numbers of individual borrowers.

These changes lie at the core of the asymmetry between production and circulation. Against a background of hesitant productivity growth, and spurred by new technology and associated labour practices and skills, the sphere of finance has been able to expand faster than production. In doing so, finance has generated new sources of profitability for the capitalist class as a whole. These new avenues of profit making are a vital feature of financialisation, and are particularly important in the context of sluggish productivity growth.

Deregulation

The forces and relations of production do not operate in a vacuum but rather within complex institutional, political, customary, and other mechanisms. These are "external conditions through whose channel capitalist development flows," to use Trotsky's (1923) pithy phrase.[15] For financialisation this "channel" was set by the profound institutional and legal transformations associated with neoliberalism since the late 1970s. Two among these stand out.

The first is the deregulation of labour markets, with an associated shift in the balance of power against organized labour. Deregulation of labour includes reduced protection of employment with parallel use of unemployment as disciplining device. The composition of the labour force has also changed through entry of part-time workers and women, the two often being the same. Flexible employment, invasion of private time by work, unpaid labour, and intensified labour have characterized the period. Real wages, meanwhile, have been relatively stagnant in all advanced capitalist countries. Changes in the labour process and in the institutional and legal framework of employment, together with stagnant real wages, have contributed to a partial recovery of profitability after 1982.[16]

The second is the deregulation of financial markets, a process that commenced in the late 1960s. Financial liberalization initially involved measures to remove controls on interest rates and quantities of credit advanced by financial institutions, mostly banks in developed countries. Deregulation of the price and quantity of credit still remains the core of financial liberalization. However, in the early 1970s the liberalization trend also spread to developing countries, where it gradually assumed the character of a new development paradigm.

Once set in motion, financial liberalization acquired a host of further characteristics, such as establishing and promoting capital markets, removing non-competitive practices among market brokers, channeling private savings to capital markets as pension and insurance funds, removing controls on international flows of loanable capital, promoting cross-border operations of financial institution, and so on. In these complex ways financial deregulation became an integral element of the Washington Consensus that has dominated development thinking and macroeconomic policy since the late 1980s.

In short, and speaking broadly, financialisation is the outcome of developments in the forces and relations of production coupled with changes in the institutional and legal framework of accumulation. It represents a systemic transformation of the capitalist economy and as such it has had profound implications on social life. The full import of this transformation has emerged gradually, partly because the rhetoric and practice of neoliberalism have directed attention to the general freeing of markets. But neoliberalism has acted as midwife of financialised capitalism.

FINANCIALISATION AS ECONOMIC PROCESS

Financialisation, then, represents a shift in the balance between production and circulation that derives from changes in the forces and relations of production as well as in the institutional and legal context of accumulation. This section probes more deeply into the specific economic roots of financialisation, locating them in economic relations among industrial-commercial enterprises, financial institutions, and workers. As was discussed in section 1, the analytical approach adopted here derives from the classical Marxist debates on finance capital and imperialism. In the spirit of Hilferding's analysis, the roots of financialisation are sought in the molecular relations among industry, banks, and workers.

Industrial Capital and Finance

The development of the world market during the last three decades presents two significant trends, which appear contradictory at first sight. On the one hand, competition has intensified across deregulated global markets; on the other, the world economy has come to be dominated by multinational corporations (MNC). Thus, the period of financialisation represents an extremely high concentration of power in the hands of MNC in terms of world trade and foreign direct investment.[17] However, the rise of MNC has not led to emergence of exclusive trading blocs, even though protectionism exists and is often directed against developing countries.

Rather, competition in the world market appears to have intensified without monopolistic control over prices and quantities. New MNC have also emerged in developing countries, including Brazil, China, Korea, Malaysia, and India. They have challenged established MNC from developed countries, often in the very markets of the latter, but also in new markets among developing countries.[18] This phenomenon is symptomatic of the gradual shift of productive capacity away from the established centres of industrial accumulation in the West and mostly toward Asia.

Financialisation has drawn on the changed financial requirements and practices of the dominant corporate enterprises, including MNC. Contrary to what Hilferding had postulated, large industrial corporations have become adept at financing their investment needs while relying less on banks. The primary mechanism is retention of own profits, as Sweezy (1942, p. 267) observed already in the early post-war decades. Several empirical studies bear this out at the aggregate level.[19] The reasons for this phenomenon are not entirely clear, but it probably has to do with the internal organizational structure of MNC, as well as the types of technology that have prevailed in the post-war period.

For external finance, on the other hand, MNC have increasingly turned to open financial markets in bonds, stocks, and related instruments. The evidence of the last four or five decades leaves no room for doubt regarding secular trends across the main developed countries.[20] The most striking example is provided by Japanese corporations, which used to rely heavily on bank finance during the years of the post-war boom but have increasingly diversified their financing toward open markets. The deeper reasons for this shift are again obscure, but they probably have to do with corporations finding themselves in command of temporarily idle funds as their retained earnings have become significant. Inevitably corporations have sought flexible and profitable ways of lending these funds while bypassing financial intermediaries.

The changes in the financing requirements of large corporations have favoured the growth of markets in loanable capital in which corporations could enter as both lenders and borrowers. Flexibility and low cost make such markets attractive relative to banks, thus encouraging corporations to diversify their sources of funding toward markets. As the shift toward open markets has become better established, corporations have been able to develop skills in independent financial trading. Such skills typically include trade credit—in which corporations have always been heavily entangled—but also securities and foreign exchange trading.

Corporate financial skills have been important in the course of the successive waves of mergers and acquisitions during the last three decades. Despite obtaining small amounts of net investment finance from open markets, corporations have become heavily engaged in stock markets, issuing and acquiring equities.[21] Financial assets held by the corporate sector have increased substantially across developed countries. The importance of this phenomenon for financialisation cannot be overemphasized. In spite of greater independence from banks, industrial corporations have become more heavily implicated in financial activities. The modern MNC is 'financialised' in the sense that financial transactions are a substantial part of its activities and profit making.[22]

Finally, the spur given to financial markets by corporate participation has undermined financial regulations. 'Regulatory arbitrage' was prominent already in the 1960s and 1970s as US and other corporations began to hold and trade loanable funds in 'Euromarkets,' that is, off-shore markets beyond the controls on price and quantity that existed at the time. This development prepared the ground for financial deregulation to proceed apace in the 1970s and 1980s. Thus, financial deregulation found ready-made terrain in spontaneous developments among industrial corporations and financial institutions.

To recap, using Hilferding's and Lenin's terminology, during the last three decades monopolistic capitals have become relatively more independent of banks, but also more heavily involved in financial transactions. They have become 'financialised' insofar as they have acquired functions that previously belonged to financial institutions. But they have also become more autonomous relative to the sphere of finance. Monopolistic capital in the era of financialisation is not dominated by banks.

Financial Institutions and Workers' Revenue

These developments have had complex implications for commercial banks in the major developed countries, leading to their gradual transformation. For one thing, profit-making opportunities for banks from lending to large corporations have shrunk as open markets grew. This lies at the core of 'financial disintermediation' that emerged as a major problem for banks in the 1980s and 1990s. Financial deregulation exacerbated pressure on banks by removing controls on interest rates. Bank deposits became more costly and, as open financial markets grew, ceased being a captive source of liquidity. Individual savings found several other outlets, for reasons discussed below. The end result was the end of traditional post-war financial intermediation in developed countries, that is, collecting secure deposits to make loans to industry and elsewhere.

Commercial banks have consequently sought other avenues of profit making and, in the process, re-invented themselves. A variety of activities have been pursued, including mass lending to developing countries in the late 1970s and early 1980s, foreign exchange dealing, money-dealing transactions across the world market, including remittances, and so on. However, two developments stand out and characterize the era of financialisation: first, lending to individuals for mortgages and consumption; second, engaging in financial market mediation to earn fees and commissions as well as on own account (investment banking). Both have been instrumental to the bubble of 2001–2007 and the subsequent crash. The former is briefly considered in this section, the latter in the next.

Credit for individual workers and others is not a new phenomenon, indeed pawnshops (and even formal institutions that lend to individuals) predate industrial capitalism. But in the course of the twentieth century consumer lending and more complex financial operations involving personal income became a permanent fixture of formal finance. Financialisation since the late 1970s has witnessed a profound deepening of these phenomena. The personal revenue of workers and others has been 'financialised.' This refers to borrowing, including loans for housing, general consumption, education, health, and so on. It also refers to financial assets, including (again) housing, pensions, insurance, money market funds, and so on.[23]

The prominence of individual borrowing is due to developments that connect financialisation to changes in production and the economy more generally. Above all, real wages have been effectively stagnant from the late 1970s onwards in several advanced capitalist countries. In that context, consumption has become increasingly mediated through finance. This phenomenon has turned postponement of payment for wage goods into an accepted social practice in several advanced countries. In effect, commodities in the wage basket have been increasingly consumed by discounting future wage earnings. The financial system has inserted itself in this process, extracting profits directly out of wages and salaries.

There is, however, an evident contradiction at the core of this phenomenon: individual debt has been rising while real wages have been stagnant, making the wherewithal to validate expanding personal credit ever more scarce. The implications are also clear. Given that the bulk of such borrowing has been for housing, ideal conditions have been created for real-estate bubbles across the developed (and sometimes the developing) world. Mortgage loans seem validated for short periods of time by rising house prices, but that is mostly due to easy provision of housing loans. The crash inevitably comes when real wages prove incapable of sustaining interest and repayments of rising loans. This is in a nutshell what took place in the USA in 2001–2007, but also in several other countries during the last three decades.

At the same time, and as part of the neoliberal agenda, there has been gradual withdrawal of public provision from several fields that relate directly to the circulation of the income of workers and others. Retreat of public provision has been vital in housing, which forms the large bulk of consumer debt. Meanwhile, private homeownership—as opposed to public housing or renting—has been promoted as a mechanism of social binding in the USA, the UK, and elsewhere. But public provision has also retreated in health, education, transport, and so on. Private arrangements have been put in place to deal with these social needs. Hence, private finance has found new scope to engage in lending. In effect, the circulation of workers' revenue has become more strongly privatized, while being increasingly mediated by private finance. Withdrawal of public provision has fostered the 'financialisation' of the individual, encouraging the emergence of private finance as a mechanism dealing with a range of social needs.

However, worker revenues have also been financialised with regard to assets. To an extent, the growth of individual financial assets is merely an automatic result of turning housing into a financial asset—by far the largest asset possessed by workers. Nonetheless, the financialisation of housing has had deleterious effects on the expenditure of worker income. As liability, housing creates fixed obligations through mortgage debt, but as asset its value varies according to the vagaries of the housing market. This has been a significant aspect of the bubbles characteristic of financialisation. In the course of a housing boom, the net financial wealth of household appears to rise, further boosting consumption; when a housing bubble bursts, the reverse occurs, limiting consumption.

The growth of individual financial assets is also due to developments associated with the retreat of public provision and neoliberal policy in general. Pension provision is the main element of saving for workers and others, particularly as lifespan has lengthened in developed countries. The withdrawal of the state from pension provision has created room for private mediation, primarily through pension funds. Neoliberal policy, furthermore, has actively encouraged the flow of personal savings into pension funds, but also insurance companies and a host of other intermediaries operating in open financial markets. Thus, regulation 401K in the USA and a range of similar measures in the UK has actively diverted personal savings into the realm of private financial capital. For commercial and investment banks, this presented further opportunities for profit making through mediating open market transactions. In short, investment banking functions were encouraged, as is shown in more detail below.

The rising importance of worker revenue in the operations of banks signifies major changes in profit making that are characteristic of financialisation. In line with classical political economy, Marxist theory analyses bank profits as deriving typically from handling the monetary transactions of enterprises (earning the average rate of profit) as well as from lending to enterprises (earning interest, a part of surplus value). Bank profits that derive from mediating the circuits of worker revenues (whether as liabilities or assets) constitute a new source of profits. Such financial profits are rooted in the sphere of circulation and derive directly from wages and salaries. This process has elsewhere been called financial expropriation.[24]

Financial expropriation has exploitative aspects deriving from systematic differences between financial institutions and workers in terms of information availability, economic and social power, and alternatives in undertaking transactions. On the one hand, workers have been increasingly forced into the arms of private finance as public provision of key wage goods has retreated. Financial profits have been generated out of wage income in ways reminiscent of the practice of trucking, except that this now happens on a social scale and the profits accrue to financial institutions, not to the providers of wage goods. On the other hand, financial profits have also been generated out of wage income through predatory lending and other forms of over-charging through fees and commissions. These practices are reminiscent of the age-old tradition of usury, but they are now performed by the formal financial system.

Financial expropriation represents the generalization on a social scale of financial practices that resemble trucking and usury. It has allowed financial institutions to boost their profits independently of surplus value generated by the indifferently performing sphere of production. This is a constituent element of financialisation.

Financial Market Mediation and the Growth of Investment Banking

The second trend characteristic of the transformation of banks in the course of financialisation is the turn toward financial market mediation. Banks have aimed at earning fees and commissions but also at making profits through trading on own account. These are essentially investment banking functions. Combined with the turn of banks toward workers' revenue, they have been a prime cause of the crisis of 2007–2009. Lending to individuals, even for housing, could never have generated a global capitalist crisis by itself, as is apparent from the relatively small size of the US subprime market compared to the mortgage market as a whole, and even more compared to the US financial system. But when lending to individuals was combined with the growth of investment banking, it proved capable of triggering a major recession.

The acquisition of investment banking practices is partly a reaction of banks to the growth of open financial markets. Such markets are the natural terrain of investment banking, that is, banking that borrows short in wholesale money markets to invest in securities, thus earning profits through fees, commissions, and proprietary trading.[25] Profits from these sources, above all, proprietary trading, were instrumental to bank profitability during the bubble of 2001–2007. The rise of these banking activities has been notable since the late 1970s; it accelerated in the 1980s; and it was given formal status with the abolition of the Glass-Steagall Act in the USA in 1999 and similar legislation elsewhere.

The turn of banks toward financial market mediation is related to broader developments, discussed above. First, the rise of monopolistic capitals in the form of MNC has encouraged repeated bouts of mergers and acquisitions. Monopoly capital might not have sought significant finance for investment in capital markets, but it has certainly turned to them to foster the centralization of capital. The ideology of 'shareholder value' also seems to have affected the behavior of industrial/commercial corporations, forcing them to organize activities with an eye of stock market returns. The proliferation of leveraged buy-outs, takeovers, share buy-backs, and the like has provided natural terrain for growth of investment banking. Second, the channeling of personal savings toward capital markets (as public provision has retreated) created scope for investment banks to intervene in transactions associated with pension funds, insurance companies, and so on. Third, floating exchange rates and volatile interest rates have contributed to expansion of derivative markets. Investment banking has found room for proprietary trading in these markets, including financial engineering.

Securitization of mortgages and other assets represents a combination of commercial with investment banking. In a nutshell, long-term assets are transformed into (presumably) liquid securities that are then taken off the balance sheet. Meanwhile, liabilities are shifted toward borrowing in wholesale money markets, diluting the importance of deposits. Capital adequacy is effectively reduced—despite regulations—through 'churning' capital to create off-balance sheet items, the final responsibility for which still lies with the bank. US and UK banks took the lead in expanding this process, while continuing to engage in standard commercial banking activities of deposit collection and lending to a variety of borrowers. Thus, commercial banks have continued to act as financial intermediaries but acquired a strong admixture of the investment banker. The combination eventually resulted in the effective bankruptcy of a broad swathe of commercial banks across developed countries.

One reason for the eventual disaster was that, as commercial and investment banking functions were combined, tensions were generated between solvency and liquidity. All banks are obliged to walk a tightrope between liquidity and solvency, since they borrow short to lend long. However, things differ significantly between commercial and investment banks. Commercial bank liquidity typically originates in deposits and is held as secure, tradable assets to meet withdrawal pressure on money-like deposits. In contrast, investment bank liquidity originates in wholesale markets and is not subject to demands from money-like deposits. Solvency, on the other hand, requires all banks to hold sufficient own capital. This is typically lower for investment banks, partly because they act as brokers, and partly because commercial bank capital adequacy is closely regulated to protect their monetary functions.

When commercial banks engage in securities trading—be that to earn fees or on own account—they typically seek wholesale liquidity to finance their operations. If the securities acquired prove problematic (as was the case with mortgage-backed securities) wholesale liquidity could dry up, potentially creating shortages in meeting deposit withdrawal requirements. The spectre of a bank run is always present. If, at the same time, banks have effectively reduced capital adequacy along investment banking lines (by moving assets off-balance sheet but still having ultimate responsibility for them), liquidity shortages due to poor securities could become a solvency problem. For those commercial banks that cannot easily recapitalize and obtain fresh liquidity the outcome is bankruptcy. This was, in short, the predicament of a host of large commercial banks across developed countries in 2008–2009.

A further reason why combining commercial and investment functions has proven so damaging in the crisis of 2007–2009 is the impact of the information-gathering practices of commercial banks, leading to changes in risk management. The information costs of lending to large numbers of individuals are of a different order of magnitude to those of lending to enterprises. Consequently, the turn toward personal income on a mass scale would have been impossible without the technological revolution in information and telecommunications. Thus, banks have acquired ways of managing the risks attached to housing and consumer loan through 'credit scoring' and the associated statistical manipulation of its results.[26] This is a clear instance of the development of the forces of production favoring the asymmetric growth of finance in recent years.

But technological change has had further profound effects as investment banking activities spread, for commercial banks have gradually adopted essentially investment banking techniques in managing credit risk as well as their balance sheets in general. Computationally intensive, statistically based techniques have come to dominate the management of Value at Risk. These are necessarily related to mark-to-market accounting. And they have been fostered through the global imposition of BIS requirements on capital adequacy.

The overall outcome has been that commercial banks have become even more 'arms-length' from corporations and borrowers in general. Banks appear to have lost some ability to collect information through personal visits, by placing bank employees within corporation structures, by managing corporate accounts and monetary transactions, and so on. These 'relational' methods have traditionally been fundamental to banks' ability to assess borrower risk. But banks have gradually replaced them with 'hard' techniques of information collection and risk management that draw on computationally intensive statistical methods.

The result has been far from happy as the crisis of 2007–2009 testifies. As 'relational' risk management declined, the banking system as a whole seems to have experienced a net loss of capacity to assess risk altogether. This has been exacerbated by the subcontracting of due diligence on loans to other institutions within the financial system, with the final result that mortgage-backed securities were not properly assessed by anyone. These developments pose profound questions regarding the future of banking in financialised capitalist economies. If commercial banks are less important to large corporations as providers of funds, if they grossly mishandle and exploit lending to individuals, and if they are bad at managing risk, what is their future role?

CONCLUSION

Financialisation is a complex social and economic process that has emerged gradually in the course of the last three decades. The sphere of circulation has shown considerably more dynamism than the sphere of production. At one remove, this reflects the continuing difficulties that production has faced during the period, resulting in uncertain productivity growth and problematic profitability. At a further remove, it is the outcome of deregulation across the financial sector and the labour market. Consequently, new sources of profitability have been sought in the sphere of circulation, above all, in finance. This is a distinguishing feature of financialisation as a period of capitalist development.

Using a political economy framework based on Hilferding's Marxist analysis, this chapter has further shown that financialisation has originated in changing relations among industrial/commercial capital, banks, and workers. Specifically, industrial and commercial corporate enterprises have become less reliant on banks for loans, while engaging in independent financial transactions in open markets. As a result, banks were forced to alter their operations, above all, by turning toward individual income as a source of profits, and by adopting investment banking practices in open markets. Meanwhile, workers have been forced into the arms of the financial system through withdrawal of public provision across a range of wage goods as well as through legislative change over pensions and other forms of saving. The result has been financial expropriation, that is, the extraction of financial profit directly out of wages and salaries. The combination of financial expropriation and investment banking lent particular destructiveness to the crisis of 2007–2009.

REFERENCES

Aglietta, M. (2000). Shareholder value and corporate governance: some tricky questions. *Economy and Society, 29*(1), 146–159.

Aglietta, M., & Breton, R. (2001). Financial systems, corporate control and capital accumulation. *Economy and Society, 30*(4), 433–466.

Arrighi, G. (1994). *The long twentieth century: Money, power, and the origins of our times*. London & New York: Verso.

Baran, P., & Sweezy, P. (1966). *Monopoly capital*. New York: Monthly Review.

Bellamy Foster, J. (2007). The Financialization of Capitalism. *Monthly Review, 58*(11). Retrieved from http://www.monthlyreview.org

Bellamy Foster, J. (2008). The financialization of capital and the crisis. *Monthly Review, 59*(11). Retrieved from http://www.monthlyreview.org

Berger, A., & Mester, L. (1997). Inside the black box: What explains differences in the efficiencies of financial institutions? *Journal of Banking and Finance, 21*, 895–947.

Berger, A., & Mester, L. (2003). Explaining the dramatic changes in performance of US banks: Technological change, deregulation, and dynamic changes in competition. *Journal of Financial Intermediation, 12*, 57–95.

Boyer, R. (2000). Is a finance-led growth regime a viable alternative to Fordism? A preliminary analysis. *Economy and Society, 29*(1), 111–145.

Brenner, R. (2002). *The boom and the bubble: The US in the world economy*. London: Verso.

Corbett, J., & Jenkinson, T. (1997). How is investment financed? A study of Germany, Japan, the United Kingdom and the United States. Papers in Money, Macroeconomics and Finance. *The Manchester School Supplement, 65*, 69–93.

Crotty, J. (1990). Owner-manager conflict and financial theory of investment stability: A critical assessment of Keynes, Tobin, and Minsky. *Journal of Post Keynesian Economics, 12*(4), 519–542.

Dos Santos, P. (2009). On the Content of Banking in Contemporary Capitalism. *Historical Materialism, 17*(2), 31–56.

Duménil, G., & Lévy, D. (2004). *Capital resurgent: Roots of the neoliberal revolution*. Cambridge, MA: Harvard University Press.

Duménil, G., & Lévy, D. (2005). The Profit Rate: Where and How Much Did It Fall? Did It Recover? (USA 1948–1997). CEPREMAP-ENS, http://www.jourdan.ens.fr/levy/dle2002f.pdf

Dymski, G. (2009). Racial Exclusion and the Political Economy of the Sub-Prime Crisis. *Historical Materialism, 17*(2), 149–179.

Epstein, J. (Ed.). (2005). *Financialization and the world economy*, Northampton, MA: Edward Elgar.

Gordon, R. (1999). *Has the "New Economy" Rendered the Productivity Slow-Down Obsolete?* Working Paper, Northwestern University, mimeo.

Grahl, J., & Teague, P. (2000). The *Régulation* School, the employment relation and financialization. *Economy and Society, 29*(1), 160–178.

Hein, E., Niechoj, T., Spahn, P., & Truger, A. (Eds.). (2008). *Finance-led capitalism?* Marburg: Metropolis Verlag.

Hilferding, R. (1981/1910). *Finance Capital.* London: Routledge & Kegan Paul.

Jorgenson, D., & Stiroh, D. (2000). Raising the speed limit: US economic growth in the Information Age. *Brookings Papers on Economic Activity, 1*, 125–211.

Krippner, G. (2005). The financialization of the American Economy. *Socio-Economic Review, 3*, 173–208.

Lapavitsas, C. (2009). Financialised capitalism: Crisis and financial expropriation. *Historical Materialism, 17*(2), 114–148.

Lapavitsas, C. (2013). *Profiting without producing.* London & New York: Verso.

Lapavitsas, C., & Dos Santos, P. (2008). Globalization and contemporary banking: On the impact of new technology. *Contributions to Political Economy, 27*, 31–56.

Lazonick, W., & O'Sullivan, M. (2000). Maximizing shareholder value: A new ideology for corporate governance. *Economy and Society, 29*(1), 13–35.

Lenin, V. (1964/1916). *Imperialism, the highest stage of capitalism, Collected Works, Vol. 22.* Moscow: Progress.

Magdoff, H., & Sweezy, P. (1987). *Stagnation and the financial explosion.* New York: Monthly Review.

Morera, C., & Rojas, J. A. (2009). *The globalization of financial capital, 1997–2008.* RMF Discussion Paper No. 6. Retrieved from http://www.researchonmoneyandfinance.org/index.php/component/finder/search?q=The%20globalization%20of%20financial%20capital,%201997%E2%80%932008

Oliner, S., & Sichel, D. (2000). The resurgence of growth in the late 1990s: Is information technology the story? *Journal of Economic Perspectives, 14*(4), 3–22.

Orhangazi, O. (2008). Financialization and capital accumulation in the non-financial corporate sector: A theoretical and empirical investigation of the US economy, 1973–2004. *Cambridge Journal of Economics, 32*, 863–886.

Pollin, R. (2007, July August). The Resurrection of the Rentier. *New Left Review, 46*, 140–153.

Savage, M., & Williams, K. (Eds.). (2008). *Remembering elites.* London: John Wiley & Sons.

Stockhammer, E. (2004). Financialization and the slowdown of accumulation. *Cambridge Journal of Economics, 28*, 719–741.

Sweezy, P. (1942). *The theory of capitalist development.* New York & London: Monthly Review.

Sweezy, P. (1997). More (or less) on globalization. *Monthly Review, 49*(4). Retrieved from monthlyreview.org/1997/09/01/more-or-less-on-globalization/

Triplett, J., & Bosworth, B. (2003, September). *"Baumol's Disease" has been cured: IT and multifactor productivity in the U.S. services industries.* Prepared for the Texas A&M Conference, The New Economy: How New? How Resilient? April 19, 2002. Brookings Economics Papers.

Trotsky, L. (1923). *The Curve of Capitalist Development.* Retrieved from http://www.trotsky.net/trotsky_year/curve_of_development.html

UNCTAD. (2006). *World Investment Report. FDI from Developing and Transition Economies: Implications for Development.* New York & Geneva: United Nations.

NOTES

1. This is an edited version of an article that appeared in Spanish in *Economiaz*, 2009, *72*(3), 98–119.
2. See Magdoff and Sweezy (1987). Bellamy Foster (2007, 2008) offers a clear account of the use and meaning of the term for *Monthly Review*. Pollin (2004) has lauded Sweezy's early awareness of financialisation, acknowledging his own debt to it.
3. Notably Stockhammer (2004) and Orhangazi (2008).
4. See Hein, Niechoj, Spahn, and Truger (2008).
5. See Aglietta (2000), Boyer (2000), and Aglietta and Breton (2001). See also Grahl and Teague (2000).
6. Lazonick and O'Sullivan (2000) are particularly insightful. Shareholder value has been extremely prominent in the work of the CRESC group on financialisation; see Savage and Williams (2008) for recent work on financialisation and elites.
7. This approach has been discussed in depth in Lapavitsas (2013).
8. Always bearing in mind that Hilferding's brief analysis of the sphere of production is grounded on inadequate empirical evidence.
9. See, above all, Lapavitsas (2013) but also the special issue of *Historical Materialism* on financialisation, namely Lapavitsas (2009), Dymski (2009), and Dos Santos (2009).
10. The methodology of measuring productivity has changed significantly in the USA during the last two decades with the adoption of 'hedonic indices,' which are deeply unsatisfactory. But that again does not matter for the purposes of this article.
11. The literature is extensive. See, very selectively, Gordon (1999), Jorgenson and Stiroh (2000), Oliner and Sichel (2000), Triplett and Bosworth (2003).
12. The US Bureau of Labor Statistics (various) has reported a consistently declining rate of growth of labour productivity since 2002.
13. See Berger and Mester (1997, 2003).
14. Discussed in Lapavitsas and Dos Santos (2008).
15. While concisely criticising Kondratieff's long wave theory.
16. For the path of profitability and the factors affecting it, see Duménil and Lévy (2005).
17. See Morera and Rojas (2009).
18. Recent trends are summarized in UNCTAD (2006).
19. See, for instance, Corbett and Jenkinson (1997).
20. For some relevant data see Lapavitsas (2009).
21. The trend is particularly clear in the USA, see Dos Santos (2009).
22. As was established for US corporations in the previously mentioned work by Krippner (2005).
23. Relevant evidence for these trends can be found in the above-mentioned special issue of *Historical Materialism.*
24. See Lapavitsas (2009). See also Dymski (2009) and Dos Santos (2009) for further analysis of the exploitative content of individual lending.
25. Investment banking profits are a theoretical problem for Marxist political economy. Hilferding (1981) argued that they originate in 'founder's profit,' which is future profit of enterprise accruing as lump sum. This is not persuasive and it is better to treat 'founder's profit' as a share of the loanable capital traded.
26. See Lapavitsas and Dos Santos (2008).

CHAPTER FOUR

The OECD ON FIRE

Financialization and Socioeconomic Decline in Advanced Economies

JACOB ASSA

INTRODUCTION

Some of the most advanced economies in the world are members of the Organization for Economic Cooperation and Development (OECD)—often referred to as a 'club of rich countries'—which was established in 1961. It is the successor of the Organization for European Economic Cooperation (OEEC), created in 1948 to administer the Marshall Plan for the reconstruction of Europe. The OECD's mission is "to promote policies that will improve the economic and social well-being of people around the world."[1] As of 2013, there were 34 countries that were members of the OECD, with a combined Gross National Income (GNI) of $46.5 trillion for the year 2012, or 65% of total world income. In terms of per capita income, the OECD average in 2012 was $37,062 a year, compared to $10,012 for the world as a whole. Even more impressively, the 20 countries with the highest per capita income in the world (in 2011) included 18 OECD members.

The current membership of the OECD includes Australia, Austria, Belgium, Canada, Chile, Czech Republic, Denmark, Estonia, Finland, France, Germany, Greece, Hungary, Iceland, Ireland, Israel, Italy, Japan, Korea, Luxembourg, Mexico, Netherlands, New Zealand, Norway, Poland, Portugal, Slovak Republic, Slovenia, Spain, Sweden, Switzerland, Turkey, United Kingdom, and the United States. In terms of geographic coverage, the OECD membership spans Asia, Europe, the Americas, and Oceania. Furthermore, of these 34 countries, 21 are members of the European Union, 15 use the Euro as their currency, and 6 were formerly socialist economies (the Czech Republic, Estonia, Hungary, Poland, the Slovak Republic, and Slovenia). All but three are considered High Income countries according to the World Bank classification[2] (the exceptions are Hungary, Mexico, and Turkey, which are in the Upper Middle Income group).

These highly developed countries boast a strong record of industrialization and economic growth, as described on the organization's website:

> OECD member countries worldwide regularly turn to one another to identify problems, discuss and analyze them, and promote policies to solve them. The track record is striking. The US has seen its national wealth almost triple in the five decades since the OECD was created, calculated in terms of gross domestic product per head of population. Other OECD countries have seen similar, and in some cases even more spectacular, progress.[3]

Notwithstanding this overall progress, however, in the past three decades there has been a worsening of several socio-economic conditions in the countries of the OECD. The pace of economic growth has slowed down from its levels in the 1960s and 1970s; unemployment has risen; and inequality has dramatically increased. Starting with unemployment, table 4.1 shows averages (per decade) of unemployment as a percentage of the civilian labor force for all OECD countries for which data were available. The data are sorted by the column before last, change in percentage points, in descending order.

Several things stand out from the data in table 4.1. First, all but four of the countries shown have seen increases in unemployment. Of the four countries with decreases, only Korea and Mexico have a long time series (Slovenia and Hungary's data start in the 1990s). Second, the nine countries at the top of the table saw their unemployment rate increase by more than 5 percentage points, as shown in the penultimate column. These countries had an average unemployment rate in the 1970s ranging from 0.55% in New Zealand to 4.72% in Portugal, but by the period 2000–2012 their unemployment rates averaged near or above 10%. Third, and most dramatically, the last column in table 4.1 shows the increase as a relative (percent) change rather than in percentage points. This is calculated by deducting the unemployment rate in the first period available from that in the last period available, and dividing the result by the first period data. Thus, a 100% increase means the unemployment rate has doubled; a 200% increase means it has tripled, and so forth. Seen this way, five countries (Estonia, Luxembourg, New Zealand, Spain, and Switzerland) had a relative increase of over 1,000% in their unemployment rate (that is, unemployment has increased by a factor of more than 10). Spain, for example, went from an admittedly very low 0.80% unemployment in the late 1950s (and a reasonable 4.28% in the 1970s) to double-digit rates of unemployment in the period 1980–2002. Likewise, New Zealand's rate increased from 0.06% in the late 1950s to 5.18% in 1980–2002.

Turning to inequality, one first confronts the question of which measure to use. A common indicator of inequality is the ratio of the disposable income of the top 10% of earners to that of the bottom 10% (technically known as the P90/P10

Table 4.1. Average rates (per decade) of unemployment in OECD countries.

							Change	
	1955–1959	1960s	1970s	1980s	1990s	2000–2012	Percentage Points	Percent
Spain	0.80	1.52	4.28	17.91	19.83	13.93	13.12	1636%
Estonia				0.56	7.15	10.30	10.30	1844%
France	1.09	1.55	3.48	8.34	9.66	8.36	7.27	669%
Portugal	1.97	2.51	4.72	7.45	5.58	8.15	6.18	314%
Finland	2.14	1.96	3.61	4.89	11.90	8.28	6.13	286%
Germany	2.86	0.85	2.43	6.17	7.84	8.32	5.46	191%
Greece	5.80	5.28	2.30	6.63	9.59	11.19	5.39	93%
New Zealand	0.06	0.18	0.55	4.60	8.16	5.18	5.12	8653%
Sweden	1.70	1.69	2.12	2.77	7.52	6.81	5.10	300%
United Kingdom	1.40	1.62	3.57	9.75	8.08	5.92	4.52	323%
Belgium	3.18	2.24	4.36	11.37	11.26	7.68	4.49	141%
Australia	1.60	1.87	3.91	7.58	8.81	5.41	3.81	237%
Switzerland	0.10	0.02	0.21	0.61	2.88	3.55	3.45	3318%
Iceland		0.98	0.52	0.79	3.64	4.07	3.08	314%
Luxembourg		0.06	0.25	1.33	1.94	2.92	2.86	4668%
Czech Republic					4.49	7.17	2.68	60%
Netherlands	1.08	0.83	3.70	9.95	6.12	3.67	2.60	241%
Japan	2.19	1.29	1.67	2.50	3.04	4.65	2.46	113%
Norway	1.35	1.02	1.56	2.80	4.88	3.58	2.23	165%
Slovak Republic					13.15	15.10	1.95	15%
Canada	5.26	5.02	6.69	9.40	9.55	7.13	1.87	36%
Poland					12.20	13.75	1.55	13%
Ireland	6.18	5.27	7.24	14.15	12.20	7.54	1.36	22%
United States	5.01	4.79	6.21	7.27	5.76	6.31	1.30	26%
Chile					7.15	8.35	1.20	17%
Austria	3.40	1.93	1.56	3.30	3.84	4.34	0.94	28%
Israel					7.71	8.33	0.61	8%
Turkey	9.70	10.10	7.75	7.80	7.78	10.28	0.58	6%
Denmark	4.72	1.54	4.05	8.16	7.46	5.23	0.52	11%
Italy	8.32	5.17	6.41	10.19	11.32	8.43	0.11	1%
Mexico			3.76	3.05	3.78	3.74	(0.02)	0%
Slovenia					7.07	6.37	(0.70)	-10%
Hungary					9.69	7.96	(1.72)	-18%
Korea		6.58	4.00	3.78	3.27	3.58	(3.00)	-46%

disposable income decile ratio). While this is a useful overall measure of disparity in income, the fact that it uses *disposable* income (that it, *after* taxes and transfers such as social security and unemployment benefits) means that it captures the effects of redistributive policy and hides the *ex-ante*, pre-tax, and pre-transfer inequality emerging from the economy. Another possibility is to use the GINI index. Below is the definition of the measure from the World Bank:

> [The] Gini index measures the extent to which the distribution of income or consumption expenditure among individuals or households within an economy deviates from a perfectly equal distribution. A Lorenz curve plots the cumulative percentages of total income received against the cumulative number of recipients, starting with the poorest individual or household. The Gini index measures the area between the Lorenz curve and a hypothetical line of absolute equality, expressed as a percentage of the maximum area under the line. Thus a Gini index of 0 represents perfect equality, while an index of 100 implies perfect inequality.[4]

Instead of ranging from 0 to 100, GINI data is often divided by 100 and shown as values between 0 and 1. For example, a GINI index of 0.6 indicates a highly unequal income distribution, whereas 0.3 indicates a relatively equal one. The closer the GINI index is to 1, therefore, the higher the inequality in that country.

Similar to the problem with the P90/P10 ratio, however, the GINI index *post*-tax and transfers is equally biased. For example, Sweden's 2010 GINI is 0.441 before tax and transfers, but 0.269 after redistribution. The United States has a less general welfare policy, and so its pre-and post-tax-and-transfer GINI data for 2010 are 0.499 and 0.380, respectively, much closer together than Sweden's. We will thus use the pre-tax-and-transfer GINI index in order to capture ex-ante rather than ex-post income inequality.

While GINI data is far sparser than unemployment numbers, it is still quite telling. Table 4.2 shows the available GINI data for OECD countries for all available years:

The data are sorted by the last column, percentage change, in descending order. Thus Japan is on top with the largest relative increase in inequality, 41%, from 1985 to 2009. Besides Australia and the Netherlands, which experienced only insignificant changes in inequality, all other OECD countries for which data before 2000 were available for the earlier data point saw an increase in disposable income inequality (before taxes and transfers). Of these countries, the United Kingdom had the highest inequality in 2010, at 0.523, compared with its 0.378 in 1975. To put these figures in perspective, Brazil—one of the most unequal countries in the world—had a GINI index of 0.547 in 2009. Belarus, a relatively more equal country, had a GINI index of 0.277 in the same year.

Finally, economic growth has slowed down considerably in most OECD countries since the 1960s. Table 4.3 shows the average (per decade) growth rates of Gross Domestic Product (GDP) for OECD countries (for which data were available at least from the 1990s).

Table 4.2. Inequality (GINI index before tax and transfer) in OECD countries with available data.

	Earliest Data		Latest Data		
	GINI	Year	GINI	Year	Change
Japan	0.345	1985	0.488	2009	41%
United Kingdom	0.378	1975	0.523	2010	38%
Italy	0.386	1984	0.503	2010	30%
Finland	0.387	1986	0.479	2010	24%
United States	0.406	1974	0.499	2010	23%
Norway	0.351	1986	0.423	2010	21%
Canada	0.385	1976	0.447	2010	16%
Denmark	0.373	1985	0.429	2010	15%
Sweden	0.389	1975	0.441	2010	13%
Germany	0.439	1985	0.492	2010	12%
New Zealand	0.408	1985	0.454	2009	11%
France	0.473	1996	0.505	2010	7%
Israel	0.472	1985	0.501	2010	6%
Czech Republic	0.442	1996	0.449	2010	2%
Australia	0.467	1995	0.469	2010	0%
Netherlands	0.426	1977	0.424	2010	0%

The table is sorted by the change in percentage points (last column) from the earliest period for which data are available to the latest. Thus the countries with the biggest slowdown in economic growth show up on top. Korea, which grew at around 10% annually for most of the 1980s and 1990s, suffered the biggest drop in growth rates, a decline of 5.9 percentage points overall in the average growth rate per decade. The United States had an average growth rate of 4.5% a year in the 1960s, but slowed down to a mere 1.9% since 2000. The six countries at the bottom of the table saw some gains in average growth, albeit the data are only from the 1990s (with the exception of New Zealand, which improved its performance from 0.5% a year in the 1980s to 2.6% since then).

FINANCIALIZATION

These three trends—rising unemployment, worsening inequality, and the slowdown in economic growth rates—coincide with the processes of both globalization and financialization. While a lot has been written about the former and its discontents, the latter is a relatively newer topic. Over the past decade, however, a growing literature has focused on the causes, patterns, and consequences of financialization, drawing on the contributions of scholars from different disciplines

Table 4.3. Average rates (per decade) of GDP growth in OECD countries.

Period	1960s	1970s	1980s	1990s	2000–2012	Change (percentage points)
Korea		10.3	8.6	6.7	4.3	-5.9
Italy	5.8	4.0	2.6	1.5	0.4	-5.3
France	5.6	3.7	2.3	1.9	1.3	-4.3
Mexico	6.5	6.4	2.2	3.4	2.4	-4.1
Portugal				4.3	0.5	-3.8
Canada	5.6	4.1	2.9	2.4	2.2	-3.4
Netherlands			4.4	3.2	1.3	-3.1
Iceland				5.2	2.4	-2.8
Luxembourg				5.6	2.8	-2.8
Norway		4.4	2.8	3.6	1.7	-2.6
United States	4.5	3.2	3.1	3.2	1.9	-2.6
Austria			3.9	2.8	1.7	-2.2
Slovenia				4.4	2.3	-2.1
Poland				5.7	3.8	-1.9
Australia	4.9	3.3	3.4	3.3	3.1	-1.8
United Kingdom	3.5	2.6	2.7	2.5	1.7	-1.8
Denmark				2.5	0.8	-1.7
Estonia				6.0	4.7	-1.4
Sweden				3.5	2.3	-1.2
Hungary				2.6	1.9	-0.8
Switzerland			2.1	1.1	1.8	-0.2
Germany				1.4	1.3	-0.1
Israel				4.0	4.0	-0.1
Japan				0.8	0.9	0.1
Finland				1.8	1.9	0.2
Belgium				2.7	1.5	1.5
Slovak Republic				2.2	4.2	2.0
New Zealand			0.5	2.6	2.6	2.1
Czech Republic				0.2	3.0	2.8

in the social sciences. Greta Krippner, a historical sociologist, highlights recent corporate scandals as dramatizing "the degree to which financial machinations have superseded productive enterprise in the US economy" (Krippner, 2005). Her work reveals that accumulation in the US economy was "occurring increasingly through financial channels" (p. 199) rather than through production of goods and services, and that "financial institutions sit at the center of the corporate network" (p. 201). In the wake of the recent financial and economic crises, some have argued that financialization was a contributing factor to the meltdown. Labor economist Richard Freeman documents "the huge costs to the real economy of the finance-induced 'Great Recession', in terms of lost employment and likely reductions in public goods and economic growth as countries re-stabilize their fiscal budgets following costly bailouts and stimulus packages" (2010, p. 164). Entrepreneurship researchers Kedrosky and Stangler (2011) specifically mention the financialization of the US economy as leading, "in part, to the financial crisis of 2008/2009" (p. 2) and conclude that financialization has increased distortions in capital allocation.

These authors focus on financialization in the US economy. However, as Palley (2007) points out, "Judging by the increase in rentier income shares, financialization appears to have infected all industrialized economies" (p. 3). This claim is supported by Power, Epstein, and Abrena (2003) as well as Jayadev and Epstein (2007) and Assa (2012) for OECD countries.

The literature on financialization points out the negative impacts of financialization on both the real and financial sides of the economy. Palley (2007) notes that "the era of financialization has been associated with tepid real economic growth, and growth also appears to show a slowing trend ... [as well as] ... increased financial fragility" (p. 3). Epstein (2001) finds financialization to be "associated with substantial economic costs: increased income inequality; increased shares of GDP going to owners of financial assets, who tend to be among the very rich in most countries" (PERI). Stockhammer (2004) builds a model to show how financialization slows down economic growth, explained by a shift of corporate power from managers to shareholders who prefer a higher profit rate to a faster growth rate (assuming an explicit growth-profit trade-off built into the model).

Yeldan (2000) conducts a detailed case study of Turkey (one of the 20 founding OECD members), where the process of deregulation and financialization caused a widening of the income distribution. Yeldan is able to

> associate the rising income inequality with the broad tendency towards the marginalization of labor due to informal industrial relations, advances in new technologies which favor skill-intensive production patterns, and an unequivocal trend towards the disassociation of the financial sector from the productive sphere of the economy and the concomitant expansion of financial rents. (p. 8)

The same paper observes not only the adverse effect of financialization on inequality but also its negative impact on economic growth:

> With the complete deregulation of financial transactions [in Turkey] and the consequent ascendancy of finance over industry, international finance capital was able to assume a dominant role so as to act as the sole arbiter, aiming at immediate financial gains rather than at long-term economic development and sustainable growth. (p. 15)

The mechanisms suggested by Yeldan are globalization, deregulation, and financialization, all severing "the links between the processes of savings generation and the productive use of these funds in the enhancement of capital accumulation ...

[the] unbalanced structure failed to generate the necessary accumulation patterns to achieve sustained growth" (p. 16).

Finally, financialization appears to negatively impact unemployment as well, as found by both Stockhammer (2004) and Freeman (2010), either through the channel of financial crises or through slower accumulation of (real) capital. The increasing automation of financial trading could be another contributing factor to reductions in employment as the economy becomes more financialized.

Our analysis below uses the latest available panel data and several models to examine both the extent and the consequences of financialization in the 34 member countries of the OECD. The following four hypotheses are tested:

- Hypothesis 1: Most OECD countries have experienced a significant financialization of their economies since around 1970.
- Hypothesis 2: Financialization in OECD countries has been associated with increased inequality.
- Hypothesis 3: Financialization in OECD countries has been associated with slower growth rates of GDP.
- Hypothesis 4: Financialization in OECD countries has been associated with higher rates of unemployment.

Based on the literature surveyed above we expect to find strong evidence for accepting all four of these hypotheses. The rest of the chapter proceeds as follows. Section 3 discusses alternative definitions and measures used in the literature on financialization. Section 4 examines the extent to which financialization has taken place in OECD countries since 1970, using two indicators. Section 5 looks at data and models used to test the impacts of financialization, section 6 describes the results of the estimation, and section 7 concludes.

DEFINITIONS AND MEASUREMENT

There are several definitions of financialization. Epstein (2001) defines it as "the increasing importance of financial markets, financial motives, financial institutions, and financial elites in the operation of the economy and its governing institutions, both at the national and international level" (quoted in Palley, 2007, p. 3). Krippner (2005) defines financialization "as a pattern of accumulation in which profits accrue primarily through financial channels rather than through trade and commodity production" (p. 174). Stockhammer (2004) defines it as "the increased activity of non-financial businesses on financial markets" (p. 720).

Associated with this variety of definitions is a plethora of indicators used to measure the extent of financialization. Kedrosky and Stangler (2011) measure it using the size of the financial sector as a percentage of GDP. Stockhammer (2004) uses interest and dividend income ('rentiers' income') of non-financial businesses as a proxy for financialization. Freeman (2010) looks at the financial sector's share of profits, the ratio of financial-sector profits to the wages and salaries of all private-sector workers, and the ratio of financial assets divided by GDP. Krippner (2005) uses portfolio income of non-financial firms and profits of financial vs. non-financial firms. Krippner's choice is motivated by her preference for an 'accumulation-centered' view rather than an 'activity centered' one, given that "the financial sector is not employment-intensive and its 'products' do not show up in transparent ways in national economic statistics" (p. 175). This claim is supported by recent research by Basu and Foley (2013) who find that output growth has a lower effect on employment growth in the services sector (especially in the so-called FIRE sectors—finance, insurance, and real estate), and that standard national accounts data overestimate real output in these sectors since they are imputed from income data rather than measured directly. Christophers (2011) describes this latter point in detail, demonstrating how finance only came to be seen as a productive activity through changes in the international standard, the System of National Accounts (SNA).

In this chapter, however, we will use output and employment data since our concern is not merely with documenting financialization, but more important, with examining its relationship to other macroeconomic variables—unemployment, growth, and inequality. Profit data would thus be less comparable to data on the other variables of interest to us than aggregate employment and output statistics. The analysis below measures the extent of financialization in OECD countries using two aggregate indicators:

- Finance as a percentage of total economic activity (as measured by value added)
- Employment in finance as a percentage of total employment

This approach thus looks at financialization from both the output and input sides of the economic process, since value-added measures net economic output (that is, output minus intermediate consumption), while employment is the labor input into these industries. As far as defining 'finance' to include the FIRE sectors (financial intermediation, real estate, renting, and business activities) instead of just financial intermediation, we follow Krippner who writes that "real estate markets share many characteristics of financial markets, including their speculative nature" (p. 179, n. 7). The choice of sectoral unit is complicated by the fact that the 'financialization' looks different based on whether one looks just at financial intermediation or FIRE in general. For example, figure 4.1 shows the extent of financialization in the US from 1970 to 2008 using both measures:
If financial intermediation alone is used, the share of finance in the US economy doubled from 4.2% to 8.3%, but if FIRE is used instead, its share has risen from 19.6% to 33.8%, respectively. Relatively speaking the change is almost the same—both finance and FIRE roughly doubled in size—but in terms of overall weight in the economy, FIRE now represents a third of all economic activity in the United States, while financial intermediation accounts for less than 10%. Given

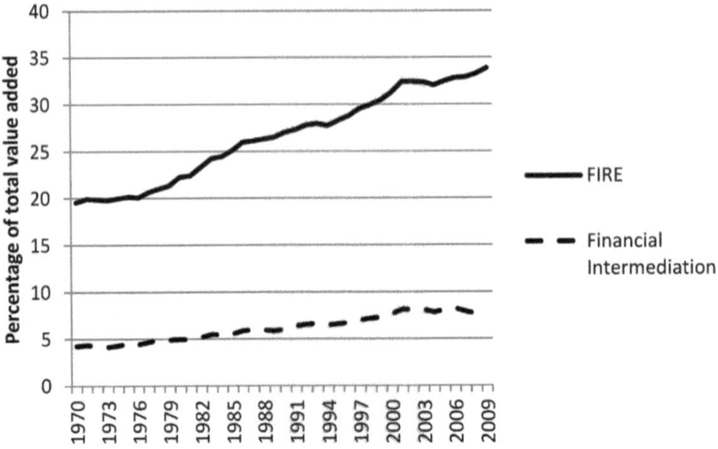

Figure 4.1. FIRE vs. financial intermediation sectors as % of economic activity in the US.
Source: OECD Stat, http://stats.oecd.org, accessed 27 November 2013.

these magnitudes, as well as Krippner's point about the speculative nature of real estate, we will use the broader FIRE measure in this chapter.

The example in figure 4.1 above has already demonstrated the extent of financialization in the US in terms of our first indicator, the share FIRE in total economic activity. Using the second indicator, employment in FIRE as a percentage of total employment, we see a similar trend—the change in employment in financial intermediation is negligible, supporting our decision to look at the larger category of FIRE.

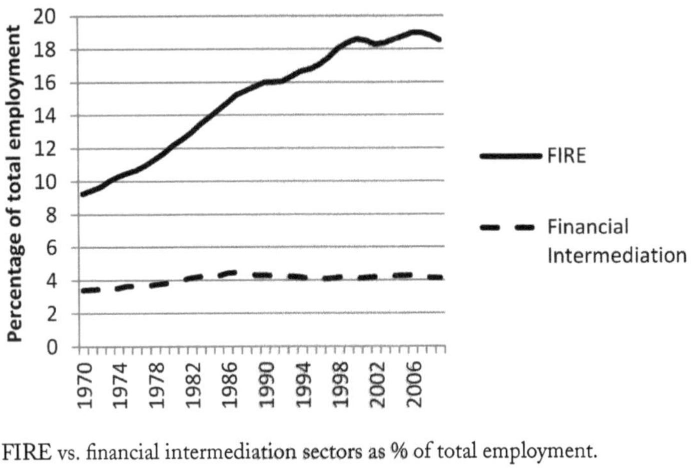

Figure 4.2. FIRE vs. financial intermediation sectors as % of total employment.
Source: OECD Stat, http://stats.oecd.org, accessed 27 November 2013.

THE EXTENT OF FINANCIALIZATION IN OECD COUNTRIES

In 1970, the first year for which OECD data on FIRE as percentage of the total economy are available, only three countries—France, the United States, and Greece—had FIRE sectors around a fifth of the size of their economies (at 21.3%, 19.6%, and 19.3%, respectively). By 2009 a majority (28 of the 34 OECD members) had FIRE shares of over 20% (see table 4.A1 in the appendix for complete data). In seven countries, the FIRE sectors accounted for more than 30% of all economic activity as shown below:

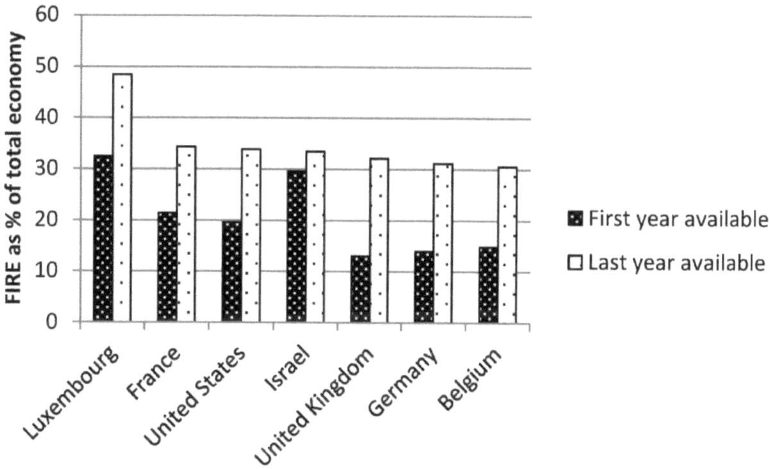

Figure 4.3. Change in FIRE as % of total economy, first to last year of data available.
Source: OECD Stat, accessed 27 November 2013.
Note: First year available is 1970 except for Luxembourg (1985) and Israel (2000). Last year available is 2009 except for Israel and the United Kingdom (2008).

Luxembourg is clearly an outlier, being a small and specialized financial center, but the other six countries in the chart have traditionally had strong industrial economies. Another way to look at the drastic changes to economic structures is the relative (percentage) increase in the size of the FIRE sector, which more than doubled in nine countries.

While Italy doubled its FIRE sector from 1970 to 2009 (an increase of 100%), Korea nearly tripled it (an increase of 192%), from 7.3% of the economy in 1970 to 21.3% in 2009. Thus we see that the extent of financialization was different across countries. Greece had not experienced financialization by this measure, with only a 2% increase in the relative size of its FIRE sector (from 19.3% in 1970 to 19.7% in 2009).

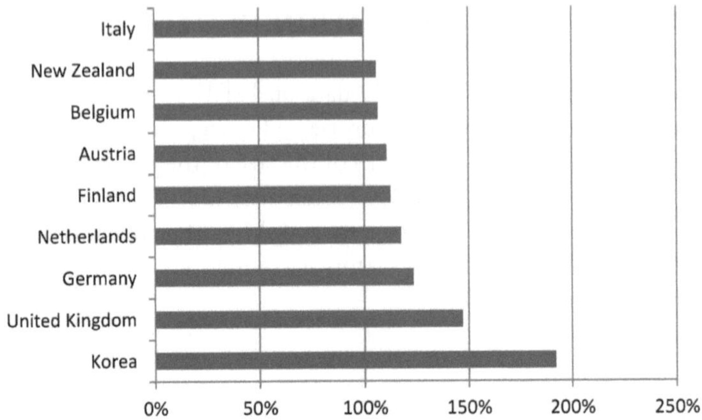

Figure 4.4. Percentage change in share of FIRE sector in total economy.
Source: OECD Stat, http://stats.oecd.org, accessed 27 November 2013.

The other measure of financialization, employment in finance as a percentage of total employment, tells a similar story. In 1970 no OECD countries had 10% or more of their workforce employed in finance (widely defined as above to include all FIRE sectors). Only seven countries had more than 5% in that year (the United States with 9.3%, the Netherlands with 8.5%, Belgium with 8.1% in 1988, France with 7.6%, Canada with 7.3%, Denmark with 6.6%, Germany with 6.1%, and Sweden with 5.8%). By 2008–2009, a majority of OECD members—29 countries—had more than 10% employed in finance (see table 4.A2 in the Appendix for complete data). Even if we exclude the special case of Luxembourg (with 28.9% employed in finance in 2009), 15 countries had more than 15% of their employment in finance by 2008–2009, and five countries had around 20% of their total labor force employed in finance: Netherlands, Belgium, United Kingdom, France, and the United States.

In relative terms financialization has gone even further, with 15 countries doubling their ratio of employment in finance to total employment, three countries tripling it, and three going much farther (Ireland and Italy saw their ratios increase fourfold, and Korea increased its share of finance in total employment by a factor of 9, from 1.3% of total employment in 1970 to 13% in 2009).

DATA AND MODELS

Having established the clear presence of financialization in the OECD, we can now examine the relationships between financialization and our three variables of interest—inequality, growth, and unemployment—using the latest annual data from the OECD. The independent or explanatory variable—financialization—is measured using data on two different measures as mentioned above, both from the OECDStat database:

FIRE_size = finance as a % of total economic activity (value added)

FIRE_empl = employment in finance as a % of total employment

For all three dependent variables—inequality, unemployment, and growth—an updated panel dataset from the OECD is available as well. As mentioned in the previous section, data on GINI coefficients exist for income inequality before and after taxes. The before-tax GINI was selected for the present analysis, since tax and transfer policies tend to reduce inequality and would thus make it hard to see the impact of financialization on the income distribution. These data as well as those for annual growth rates of GDP and unemployment are available from 1970 (in most countries) to 2009 or 2010. However, only data up to 2007 were used to avoid capturing the effects of the financial crisis and muddling the analysis. The dependent variables are as follows:

GiniAnte = GINI coefficient for income inequality (before taxes and transfers)

Growth = annual growth rates of real gross domestic product

Unemployment = annual rate of unemployment

Correlation Analysis

Table 4.4 below presents the matrix of correlation coefficients between the five variables used in this chapter (two independent variables and three dependent variables). As predicted by the literature, our first measure of financialization—the share of finance in total economic activity—is positively correlated with inequality (before taxes and transfers). It also has a negative relationship with growth and a positive relationship with unemployment. There is also a strong positive correlation between the two explanatory variables (the two measures of financialization), as would be expected.

Table 4.4. Correlation coefficients (missing values were skipped).

FIRE_size	FIRE_empl	Unemployment	GiniAnte	Growth	
1.0000	0.8644	0.0422	0.3546	-0.2086	FIRE_size
	1.0000	-0.0335	0.2615	-0.2269	FIRE_empl
		1.0000	0.2461	-0.0908	Unemployment
			1.0000	0.0398	Inequality
				1.0000	Growth

Our second measure of financialization—employment in finance as a percentage of total employment—also has a positive relationship with inequality and a negative relationship with growth, but a negative rather than positive correlation with unemployment. This could be due to Luxembourg's outlier position (28.9% of its total employment is in finance as mentioned above). Indeed, looking at the correlation *excluding* Luxembourg's data resolves the problem and gives the expected signs as in table 4.5 below—a negative relationship between employment in finance and growth, and a positive relationship with unemployment and inequality.

Table 4.5. Correlation coefficients excluding Luxembourg (missing values were skipped)

FIRE_size	FIRE_empl	Unemployment	GiniAnte	Growth	
1.0000	0.8385	0.1387	0.4268	-0.2860	FIRE_size
	1.0000	0.0388	0.2799	-0.2955	FIRE_empl
		1.0000	0.2610	-0.0771	Unemployment
			1.0000	0.0364	Inequality
				1.0000	Growth

Regression Analysis

Moving beyond correlations to regression analysis, the following models have been estimated, using both the FIRE_size and the FIRE_empl measures of financialization. The models also include a control for per capita income[5] to account for the various levels of development of different OECD countries. The following three models in four variants are estimated using random-effects panel regression:

Financialization and Inequality

1. GiniAnte = α + β1 FIRE_size + ε
2. GiniAnte = α + β1 FIRE_size + β2 Per_Capita + ε
3. GiniAnte = α + β1 FIRE_empl + ε
4. GiniAnte = α + β1 FIRE_empl + β2 Per_Capita + ε

Financialization and Growth

1. GDP_growth = α + β1 FIRE_size + ε
2. GDP_growth = α + β1 FIRE_size + β2 Per_Capita + ε
3. GDP_growth = α + β1 FIRE_empl + ε
4. GDP_growth = α + β1 FIRE_empl + β2 Per_Capita + ε

Financialization and Unemployment

1. Unemployment = α + β1 FIRE_size + ε
2. Unemployment = α + β1 FIRE_size + β2 Per_Capita + ε
3. Unemployment = α + β1 FIRE_empl + ε
4. Unemployment = α + β1 FIRE_empl + β2 Per_Capita + ε

EMPIRICAL RESULTS

Financialization and Inequality

The literature describes a negative effect of financialization on inequality. This impact works through several channels, including an increase in financial rents at the expense of wages from productive work, a breakdown of formal labor relations including long-term contracts, benefits and company loyalty, and an increasing polarization between the top and bottom of the income distribution as middle-class industrial jobs disappear.

Table 4.6 below shows the random-effects regression results where the dependent variable is inequality before taxes and transfers. The relationship between finance as a share of economic activity and inequality is strong and positive, with a coefficient of 0.52 in column 1 (significant at the 1% level). Controlling for per capita income yields a similarly strong parameter, 0.65 (column 2). The share of finance in employment is also significant (at 0.65 without and 0.87 with a control for per capita income in columns 3 and 4 respectively). Financialization is therefore strongly related to higher inequality. Each percentage increase in the share of finance in the economy is associated with up to 0.65% more inequality, while each percentage increase in the share of finance in total employment is associated with up to 0.87% more inequality (holding per capita income constant).

Table 4.6. Financialization and inequality (before taxes and transfers).

Random-effects (GLS). Dependent variable: Gini_Ante.				
Sample Size	N = 29	N = 29	N = 29	N = 29
	(1)	(2)	(3)	(4)
Constant	32.73***	32.85***	36.70***	37.46***
	(22.03)	(22.39)	(29.58)	(27.93)
FIRE_size	0.52***	0.65***		
	(9.96)	(6.58)		
FIRE_empl			0.65***	0.87***
			(9.12)	(5.33)
Per_Capita		0.00		0.00
		(-1.59)		(-1.48)

t-statistics are in parentheses. ***denotes significance at the 1% level; **denotes significance at the 5% level; *denotes significance at the 10% level.

Financialization and Growth

The literature on financialization links it to a slowdown in accumulation and economic growth. This effect works through increased financial fragility and an increased tendency for financial crises, a shift in corporate preference from long-term growth to short-term profits, and the weakening links between savings and investment as the financial sector diverts ever more funds to speculative purposes.

Table 4.7 below shows the random-effects regression results where the dependent variable is GDP growth rate. The share of finance in the overall economy has a small but negative relationship (and significant at the 1% level) with GDP growth (column 1), as predicted by the literature. Controlling for per capita income (column 2) results in a somewhat larger coefficient, still negative and significant. Employment in finance also has a significant coefficient and a strong negative relationship with the growth rate of GDP (column 3), which again increases once we control for per capita income (column 4). Financialization is thus clearly related to slower GDP growth. Each percentage increase in the share of finance in the total economic activity is associated with up to 0.12% slower growth, while each percentage increase in the share of finance in total employment is associated with up to 0.19% slower growth (holding per capita income constant).

Table 4.7. Financialization and GDP growth rate.

Random-effects (GLS). Dependent variable: Growth.				
Sample Size	N = 33	N = 33	N = 33	N = 33
	(1)	(2)	(3)	(4)
Constant	5.11***	5.15***	4.42***	4.11***
	(8.9)	(9.0)	(10.22)	(8.85)
FIRE_size	-0.07***	-0.12***		
	(-3.2)	(-3.08)		
FIRE_empl			-0.08***	-0.19***
			(-2.67)	(-2.89)
Per_Capita		0.00		0.00*
		(1.45)		(1.87)

t-statistics are in parentheses. ***denotes significance at the 1% level; **denotes significance at the 5% level; *denotes significance at the 10% level.

Financialization and Unemployment

The negative impact of financialization on unemployment described in the literature works through multiple channels, including more frequent crises, slower growth, and increased automation.

Table 4.8 shows the random-effects regression results where the dependent variable is the rate of unemployment. Once again, the share of finance in total economic activity has a strong positive relationship with the dependent variable, in this case the rate of unemployment. The coefficient is even larger with a control for per capita income (column 2). Employment in finance also has a significant positive relationship with unemployment, especially when controlling for income (column 4). Each percentage increase in the share of finance in total economic activity is associated with up to 0.36% more unemployment, while each percentage

Table 4.8. Financialization and the rate of unemployment.

Random-effects (GLS). Dependent variable: Unemployment.				
Sample Size	N = 33	N = 33	N = 33	N = 33
	(1)	(2)	(3)	(4)
Constant	3.50***	3.13***	5.46***	6.98***
	(4.72)	(4.45)	(8.27)	(11.04)
FIRE_size	0.16***	0.36***		
	(8.32)	(10.05)		
FIRE_empl			0.16***	0.81***
			(5.70)	(11.78)
Per_Capita		0.00***		0.00***
		(-6.51)		(-10.37)

t-statistics are in parentheses. ***denotes significance at the 1% level; **denotes significance at the 5% level; *denotes significance at the 10% level.

increase in the share of finance in total employment is associated with up to 0.81% more unemployment (holding per capita income constant).

CONCLUSION

The empirical evidence provided above confirms all four hypotheses presented at the beginning of the chapter. First, financialization has definitely taken place on a large scale in most countries of the OECD, whether measured by the increase in the share of economic activity taking place in the FIRE sector or by growing employment in that sector as a percentage of total employment.

Second, and more important, this strengthening of finance vis-à-vis the rest of the economy did not come without a price. The empirical evidence clearly confirms the relationships discussed in the literature on financialization, in particular its negative effects on equality, growth, and employment. Each percentage increase in financialization is associated with between 0.52% and 0.87% more inequality (depending on which indicator of financialization is used). A similar increase in financialization is related up to 0.19% slower growth of GDP, and between 0.16% and 0.81% higher unemployment.

This casts a doubt on the OECD quote above regarding spectacular progress. It is true that the overall size of OECD economies has increased from $12.6 trillion in 1970 to $39 trillion in 2012, and it is also true that average per capita income in the OECD as a whole has also risen from $14,252 to $31,353 over the same period (both measures in PPPs, adjusted for inflation). However, the growth of the size of the economy and the rise of *average* income mask, as we have seen, a deterioration of socio-economic conditions affecting the majority of the population in the OECD. While the economic pie has gotten larger, the pace of growth has slowed considerably, the fruits of growth have not been distributed equally, and many are excluded from sharing in them as they lack gainful employment.

Some blame the process of financialization for the recent economic and financial crises. Whether or not it served as one of the key factors leading up to the meltdown, financialization over the past four decades certainly seems to have negatively impacted the economies and societies in the developed countries of the OECD by increasing inequality, slowing down economic growth, and swelling unemployment. It appears that, when financial machinations supersede productive enterprise, to use Krippner's language, both the economy and society suffer.

APPENDIX

Table 4.A1. Share of FIRE sector in total value added—first and last year available and changes.

	First data point available	Year	Last data point available	Year	Change (percentage points)	Relative change (%)
Australia	15.6	1970	29.8	2007	14.2	91%
Austria	11.2	1976	23.7	2009	12.4	111%
Belgium	14.8	1970	30.5	2009	15.8	107%
Canada	16.8	1970	25.4	2006	8.6	52%
Czech Republic	18.8	1993	18.3	2009	(0.5)	-3%
Denmark	15.5	1970	27.5	2009	12.0	77%
Estonia	16.0	1993	24.8	2009	8.8	55%
Finland	11.8	1970	25.0	2009	13.2	113%
France	21.3	1970	34.3	2009	13.0	61%
Germany	13.9	1970	31.1	2009	17.2	124%
Greece	19.3	1970	19.7	2009	0.4	2%
Hungary	14.5	1991	23.5	2009	9.0	62%
Iceland	13.0	1973	25.6	2009	12.7	98%
Ireland	18.5	1986	27.2	2009	8.7	47%
Israel	29.6	2000	33.4	2008	3.9	13%
Italy	14.4	1970	28.8	2009	14.4	100%
Japan	14.3	1970	27.9	2009	13.6	95%
Korea	7.3	1970	21.3	2009	14.0	192%
Luxembourg	32.5	1985	48.4	2009	16.0	49%
Mexico	13.9	1970	20.9	2009	7.0	50%
Netherlands	12.9	1970	28.2	2009	15.2	118%
New Zealand	14.5	1971	29.9	2006	15.4	106%
Norway	13.2	1970	19.5	2009	6.3	48%
Poland	12.7	1994	19.1	2008	6.5	51%
Portugal	15.7	1977	22.0	2006	6.3	40%
Slovak Republic	14.8	1993	19.1	2009	4.4	30%

	First data point available	Year	Last data point available	Year	Change (percentage points)	Relative change (%)
Slovenia	19.9	1995	23.3	2009	3.4	17%
Spain	15.3	1980	23.6	2009	8.2	54%
Sweden	15.7	1970	26.4	2009	10.7	68%
Switzerland	22.4	1990	29.5	2008	7.1	32%
Turkey	14.5	1970	21.1	2008	6.5	45%
United Kingdom	13.0	1970	32.1	2008	19.1	147%
United States	19.6	1970	33.8	2009	14.3	73%

Source: OECD.Stat, accessed 27 Nov 2013.

Table 4.A2. Employment in FIRE sector as a % of total employment—first and last year available and changes.

	First data point available	Year	Last data point available	Year	Change (percentage points)	Relative change (%)
Australia	7.8	1971	16.5	2007	8.7	111%
Austria	6.5	1976	14.9	2009	8.4	130%
Belgium	8.1	1970	20.9	2009	12.9	159%
Canada	7.3	1970	17.9	2008	10.6	145%
Czech Republic	9.2	1995	13.3	2009	4.1	45%
Denmark	6.6	1970	16.0	2009	9.4	143%
Estonia	4.5	1989	10.7	2009	6.2	139%
Finland	4.3	1970	13.9	2009	9.6	222%
France	7.6	1970	19.1	2007	11.5	151%
Germany	6.1	1970	17.3	2009	11.2	183%
Greece	5.9	1993	10.1	2009	4.2	71%
Hungary	4.8	1992	10.4	2009	5.5	114%
Iceland	9.6	1991	15.4	2008	5.8	61%
Ireland	3.4	1971	14.7	2009	11.3	331%
Israel	12.1	1995	17.7	2008	5.5	46%
Italy	3.6	1970	14.9	2009	11.4	320%
Japan	5.0	1970	15.2	2008	10.2	203%
Korea	1.3	1970	13.0	2009	11.6	867%
Luxembourg	12.1	1985	28.9	2009	16.8	139%
Mexico	3.9	1995	6.4	2009	2.5	63%
Netherlands	8.5	1970	21.4	2009	12.9	151%
New Zealand	12.9	1989	16.3	2008	3.5	27%
Norway	4.8	1970	14.1	2009	9.3	196%
Poland	4.3	1994	8.6	2008	4.2	98%
Portugal	2.6	1977	8.0	2006	5.4	203%
Slovak Republic	6.8	1995	11.3	2009	4.5	65%
Slovenia	8.2	1995	14.6	2009	6.4	78%

Continued

	First data point available	Year	Last data point available	Year	Change (percentage points)	Relative change (%)
Spain	6.3	1980	12.4	2009	6.0	96%
Sweden	5.8	1970	16.5	2009	10.7	183%
Switzerland	13.6	1991	17.8	2008	4.2	31%
Turkey	3.7	2000	5.5	2008	1.8	49%
United Kingdom	9.3	1971	20.9	2008	11.7	126%
United States	9.3	1970	18.5	2009	9.3	100%

Source: OECD.Stat, accessed 27 Nov 2013.

NOTES

1. OECD website, http://www.oecd.org/about/
2. The 2012 threshold for the high-income group was per capita GNI income of at least $12,616.
3. OECD website, http://www.oecd.org/about/history/
4. World Bank website, http://data.worldbank.org/indicator/SI.POV.GINI
5. GDP per head, US$, constant prices, current PPPs, OECD base year.

REFERENCES

Assa, J. (2012, January). Financialization and its consequences: The OECD experience. *Finance Research, 1*(1), 35–39.

Basu, D., & Foley, D. K. (2013). Dynamics of output and employment in the US economy. *Cambridge Journal of Economics, 37*, 1077–1106.

Christophers, B. (2011). Making finance productive. *Economy and Society, 40*(1), 112–140.

Epstein, G. (2001). *Financialization, rentier interests, and central bank policy*. Paper prepared for PERI Conference on Financialization of the World Economy, December 7–8, 2001, University of Massachusetts, Amherst.

Freeman, R. (2010). It's financialization! *International Labor Review, 149*(2), 163–183.

Jayadev, A., & Epstein, G. (2007, January). *The correlates of rentier returns in the OECD countries*. Unpublished manuscript, Department of Economics, University of Massachusetts, Amherst.

Kedrosky, P., & Stangler, D. (2011, March). *Financialization and its entrepreneurial consequences*. Kauffman Foundation Research Series: Firm Formation and Economic Growth.

Krippner, G. (2005, May). The financialization of the American economy. *Socio-Economic Review, 3*, 2.

Palley, T. (2007, December). *Financialization: What it is and why it matters*. Levy Economics Institute, Washington, D.C., Working Paper No. 525.

Power, D., Epstein, G. & Abrena, M. (2003, April). *Trends in the rentier income share in OECD countries, 1960–2000*. Department of Economics, University of Massachusetts, Amherst.

Political Economy Research Institute (PERI). Interview with Gerald Epstein. http://www.peri.umass.edu/341

Stockhammer, E. (2004). *Financialization and the slowdown of accumulation. Cambridge Journal of Economics, 28*(5), 719–741.

Yeldan, A. (2000, November). *The impact of financial liberalization and the rise of financial rents on income inequality: The case of Turkey*. UNU/WIDER Working Paper No. 206.

CHAPTER FIVE

Financial Governmentality

Wealth-Effect as a Practice of Social Control

STEFANO LUCARELLI AND EMANUELE LEONARDI

INTRODUCTION

In the last few years the term *financialization* has entered the realm of everyday language. Above all, it is used to evoke the semantic field of financial speculation, which undoubtedly constitutes a reoccurring risk in free market economic systems. Although this is far from being untrue, the crucial element to be investigated in the context of the financial vertical motion on which contemporary capitalism appears to be grounded is—according to us—the *political dimension of financialization*.

Some post-Keynesian scholars[1] have argued that the main aspect of the process of financialization is to be located in the influence gained by financial markets, institutions, and elites both on decision-making regarding economic policies and on real variables concerning productive activities. On the one hand, such an influence takes the shape of an increase of households' rate of indebtedness. On the other hand, it leads to an increase of corporations' debt/equity ratio, since financial markets tend to prefer that corporations use debt to finance their activities owing to the higher rates of return on equity that leverage allows. Moreover, that same influence contributes to wage stagnation. This is an important analytical perspective that should be deepened by reflecting on the links among financial conventions, subjective behaviors, and economic policies.

We are convinced that Nobel Laureate in Economics Robert Shiller's concerned focus on this issue is highly relevant. Shiller is extremely critical toward the theory of efficient financial markets and believes that an alternative interpretative paradigm—based on experiments that are potentially able to assess the actual conducts of financial operators (so-called behavioral finance)—is necessary. He argues that financial operators must pursue the efficiency of financial tools by making reference to innovation. Thus, they should constantly try to think otherwise, to embrace change through planned elaborations of new psychological frameworks. Conversely, they should be patient and proactively wait—at times for long—for new ideas to be grasped by the general public and to penetrate the common sense (Shiller, 2003). In so doing, Shiller perfectly expresses the pervasiveness of finance and sheds decisive light on the necessity—felt especially by financial operators—for a kind of strategic planning that proves effective in influencing both individual and institutional selection/decision criteria. In this sense, what is at stake in financialization is no longer the immediate application of sovereign power; rather, it is the channeling of human behaviors as a whole in such a way that sovereignty ends up being coherent with the command performed by financial markets (Lucarelli, 2010).

The 2007 global crisis has entailed the diffusion of a suspicious attitude toward everything related to the financial sphere—from banks to pension funds, from consumer credit to securitization. Yet such a broad discontent did not translate into a radical overcoming of a system whose growth is predicated on financial markets. In other words, we witness the ultimate recognition that the great transformation of economic systems—whose inceptive element is represented precisely by the process of financialization—has impacted so profoundly on corporate strategies and governmental policies (as well as consumption habits and saving attitudes) that it has become a *reality* that proved resilient even when struck by an epochal crisis. It is our conviction that, in order to properly grasp the new character of contemporary capitalism, such a speculative activity needs to be analyzed through historically specific lenses: this crisis should be understood starting from the peculiarities that characterize the current accumulation regime. In other words, an accumulation regime allows and guarantees the re-absorption of imbalances arising in the course of the process of accumulation.[2]

Our central argument is twofold: (1) contemporary capitalism is characterized by an accumulation regime that tends to internalize every specific moment of individual and social experience back within the process of valorization; (2) the means through which such an absorption occurs do not only include economic policies of neoliberal inspiration, but also command devices such as the *wealth-effect*, whose very intelligibility is to be found in the hybrid zone where political economy meets other social sciences. Otherwise put: an accumulation regime is not only composed by internal economic elements; it also discloses a broader governmental horizon, a political rationality whose main target is *subjectivity*.

To properly frame this argument we will analyze financialization as a historically determinate practice of social control. Our premise—in line with Lucarelli (2010)—is that the new configuration of capitalism requires a form of social control that is compatible with democratic societies whose procedures imply the formalized participation of large masses. This is why we need to begin our analysis by highlighting that financialization envelops us in its mechanisms of mass participation, in its formal democratic feature. In order to shed light on this line of reasoning, we shall borrow a few categories from Michel Foucault, in particular *biopolitics* and *governmentality* (§2).[3] We suggest that already in Foucault's oeuvre a few useful elements for reflecting on financialization as a governmental device are detectable; furthermore, such elements are of primary relevance from the perspective of monetary policy (§3). Subsequently, we shall adapt Foucauldian categories to our object of analysis, concentrating on the role that the wealth-effect assumes in the financialization process (§4). We shall then illustrate the role played by monetary policy within the circuits of the current accumulation regime (§5). Finally, we shall advance our reading of the successive shifts from the New Economy to the contemporary Great Recession (§6).

BIOPOLITICAL GOVERNMENTALITY

The reason why a reference to Foucault's categorical apparatus is pivotal to us relies on the fact that the rise of a new regime of accumulation immediately discloses the emergence of a new society. From this perspective, the twin notions of *biopolitics* and *governmentality* are extremely useful since they point to the non-sufficiency of sectorial investigations: political subjectivities are constitutively means of production as well as outcomes of economic activities, just as these latter necessarily configure instances of social control. In fact, the concept of biopolitical governmentality reveals the profound closeness that links the *economic field* to the *political field*. Refusing simultaneously a *formal isomorphism*, which would imply the possibility to conceive of power as a "sellable good" on the basis of its conformity to a contractual exchange, and a *functional subordination*, which would conceptualize power as the trustee of the status quo, Foucault finds himself in a suitable position to re-articulate the relation between the two fields. Such a link could be defined as *a-symmetrical complementarity*, since the first term implies the second (and vice-versa) without a possible harmonic and peaceful configuration. The two elements must be thought as *distinct but inseparable*. They are not the same thing, but outside of their relation they lose their meaning as theoretical categories. This conceptual linkage allows Foucault to use the transformations of the triadic structure power-market-political economy as a theoretical compass to analyze the historical shifts occurred to governmental power within the biopolitical horizon.

Although Foucault did not coin the term, his fundamental contribution to the field of studies related to biopolitics cannot be overestimated. Moreover, the fragmented nature of his reflection about this issue might be considered responsible for the profound richness (but also, to a certain extent, for possible confusions) of biopolitics as a specific theoretical tool. In fact, Foucault undertook this research project in the mid-1970s and carried it until 1980 in a variety of different forms: official publications (*The History of Sexuality, Vol. 1*, 1976), academic conferences (*La naissance de la médicine sociale*, 1974; *Les mailles du pouvoir*, 1976), and four series of lectures at the Collège de France (*Society Must Be Defended*, 1975–1976; *Security, Territory, Population*, 1977–1978; *Birth of Biopolitics*, 1978–1979; *On the Government of Living Beings*, 1979–1980), whose definitive publication was not complete until very recently.[4] As a starting point, from an empirical, micro-physical perspective, it is possible to situate the emergence of biopolitics in the progressive implementation of governmental technologies of power whose specific goal is the simultaneous empowerment of individual and collective bodies. With the term *governmentality*, Foucault articulates three aspects: (1) the *ensemble* of institutions, tactics, and analyses that allow a specific kind of power to be exercised over the population (through a knowledge apparatus defined by political economy and a set of technical devices oriented toward security); (2) the historical tendency of this new kind of power to become prominent over older forms of power (namely, sovereignty); (3) the process through which, from the Middle Ages onwards, the state shifts progressively from being juridically based to being thought of in terms of administrative procedures and, finally, to being entirely governmentalized (Foucault, 2007). This set of practices, initially proposed in the second half of the eighteenth century, was organized around four main fields of intervention: *natality*, *morbidity*, *ability*, *environment* (Foucault, 2003). As a consequence of this, biopolitics is deployed through four different types of social control. First, this form of power is exercised over phenomena such as fecundity and longevity by means of demographic regulation and statistical analysis. Second, it refers to health variables such as endemic and epidemic diseases through a conception of death as a decreasing factor of individual and collective performances, whose inevitable outcomes involve an increase regarding the administrative costs of treatments and, more generally, a reduction of efficiency in the medical regulation of society. Third, biopower intervenes on aleatory events that imply a more or less severe reduction of social abilities (such as accidents, infirmities, anomalies, and old age) by means of the development of a pervasive system of governmental insurance. Finally, biopolitics implies the political creation of an intermediate space between natural environment and artificial urbanization, investing in particular the process of shaping natural systems (both at the climatic and hydrographical level) according to governmental expansive necessities.

One point is of particular significance here: when Foucault insists that Western society, in the course of the second half of the eighteenth century, crossed a "threshold of biological modernity" and consequently "wagered the life of the species on its own political strategies" (Foucault, 1978, p. 143), he intends to establish a line not of *homology* but rather of *convergence* among the theoretical triad of *biopolitics*, *governmentality*, and *capitalism*. Those concepts, in other words, do not by any means identify the same set of phenomena. On the contrary, their specificity should be jealously preserved (the risk here is that of a linearization of the historical process, potentially at the service of yet another grand narrative). Simply, they converge not primarily in their chronological simultaneity (which is, after all, far from perfectly congruent) but, more important, in the unprecedented *political intelligibility* that their integration provides.

Although the biopolitical hypothesis is initially based on a new micro-physical understanding of the second half of the eighteenth century, it cannot be reduced to that. On the contrary, its core resides in a novel formulation of a classical theoretical element that refers to the relationship between *life* and *politics*. To put it crudely, we might say that before the emergence of biopolitics, the relation between life and politics was *extrinsic*, in the sense that the two poles defined different fields of intervention and development, which, although often overlapping each other, used to be conceived autonomously, as irreducibly distinct. On the contrary, after the "threshold of biological modernity" was crossed, the two fields merged into one set of phenomena within the context of which their respective identities became indistinguishable.[5] This zone of indistinction represents the privileged terrain of deployment for the political rationalities that compose the category of governmentality.

Within the context of the above-sketched framework, we need to emphasize the *twofold nature of governmentality*. As Thomas Lemke has aptly noted, the shapes of power and their underlying rationalities should be simultaneously investigated. As a consequence, governmentality can be developed along two different—albeit closely interrelated—lines of research: on the one hand, "the term pin-points a specific form of *representation*; government defines a discursive field in which exercising power is 'rationalized'"; on the other hand, "it also structures specific forms of *intervention*. For a political rationality is not pure, neutral knowledge which simply 're-presents' the governing reality; instead, it itself constitutes the intellectual processing of the reality which political technologies can then tackle" (Lemke, 2001, p. 191).

We are now in the position to address the internal split that marks the development of biopolitical governmentality. In fact, its historical horizon is not flatly linear but, rather, contested and traversed by social transformations. Simplifying a little, at least two different phases of governmentality can be detected. The first is *liberalism*: in the lectures delivered at the Collège de France at the end of the 1970s, Foucault reads the emergence of liberalism, conceived of in terms of a political rationality rather than of an economic theory, as a shift from the centrality of external legal limits to the absolute power of the sovereign (disciplinary mechanisms) to the increasing importance of an art of government based on political economy (security apparatuses). From this perspective, liberalism—and the natural traits it attributes to market-laws—are justified in that they play a *veridical limiting role* with regard to sovereign power: being unable to fully grasp the opaque totality represented by the economic process, the sovereign must limit its interventions to possible market failures. Those incidental failures, however, do not put into question the spontaneous deployment of the invisible hand that, in connecting individual pursuit of profit to the general interest, naturally leads to the best allocation of social wealth.

The second phase of governmentality, whose inception dates back to the early 1970s, is labelled as *neoliberalism*, and it is interesting to note how profoundly its emergence is connected to the processes of financialization and to the kind of subjectivity it requires. To make a long story short, what *does not change* in the shift from liberalism to neoliberalism is the function of the market as a site of veridiction. Thus, also neoliberalism is concerned with the construction of an economic naturalness that is enacted by a biopolitical regime of truth based on the market. In other words, the formal invariance of governmentality is the *production of limits to power exercise*.[6] What, on the contrary, *does change* is the specific modality of that production, its historical contingency. In liberalism the naturalness of the market is centered on the notion of *exchange* and, as such, it is still clearly distinguished from the artificiality of fluxes of money, commodities, and individuals it is supposed to rationally channel. By contrast, in neoliberalism the naturalness of the market is directly created in accordance to the artificial principle of formalization represented by *competition*. To put it crudely, naturality has to be artificially constructed in order to practically allow the formal structure of economic competition to work. This is why the first wave of neoliberal thinkers considered by Foucault (German *ordoliberalism* of the 1940s and 1950s)[7] could accuse their liberal predecessors of "naturalistic naïveté." According to the Ordoliberals, the market is not a primary *datum* whose spontaneous structure would be revealed by competitive logic. The order of the factors must be reversed: for the market to function properly, competition is to be first established and then continually enforced at a subjective level—broadly conceived. The very *status* of competition as an economic category is radically and originally displaced. According to Pierre Dardot and Christian Laval, such a displacement entails a crucial transformation with regard to capitalist neo-management strategies:

> [Their] major novelty consists in the molding whereby individuals are rendered more capable of tolerating the new conditions created for them—and this even though they help to make these conditions increasingly harsh and abiding through their own conduct. The novelty consists in triggering a "chain reaction" by producing "enterprising subjects"

> who in turn will reproduce, expand, and reinforce competitive relations between themselves. In accordance with the logic of the self-fulfilling prophecy, this requires them to adapt subjectively to ever harsher conditions which they have themselves created. (2014, p. 307)

At this point, two further relevant effects of the shift of emphasis from exchange to competition must be acknowledged. The first concerns the necessity of a constant intervention on the part of the state not *on* the market (to fix negative outcomes), but rather *within* its conditions of possibility (to structure reality according to its needs). Rather than a passive referee supposed to supervise the rules of the market-game, what is needed is now an *interventionist governmentality*, a proactive political entity whose task is to incessantly re-create the material conditions of a given society according to competition, which is to say a flexible principle of formalization.[8] As Foucault brilliantly summarizes, in neoliberalism "one governs *for* the market, not *because of* the market" (Foucault, 2008, p. 121—our emphases). The analysis carried out by the Ordoliberals perfectly exemplifies such transformation. For them, in fact, the main problem is to create "a state under the supervision of the market rather than a market under the supervision of the state" (Foucault, 2008, p. 116). Otherwise put, what needs to be tested is the capacity of a market economy based on competition to shape the state and re-form society. Competition, therefore, becomes a social model centered on inequality (as opposed to the crucial role of equivalence in a system structured around contractual exchange). This perfect inversion of roles between market and sovereignty "displaces the naturalist idea of *laissez-faire*, which needs an essence, whereas competition is a principle of formalization, and as such is produced by an effort, by a tendency" (Zanini, 2010, p. 95). What in classical liberalism was a spatial, indirect separation between political sphere (state) and economic sphere (market), in neoliberalism is substituted by a mutual interference.[9] In passing, it is important to underline that contemporary financialization, to be conceived of as a specific neoliberal feature, can be configured as the sectorial answer to this newly discovered governmental need to intervene in/for the economic field to create proper solutions for profit.

The second effect to be highlighted concerns the profound *ambivalence* that marks governmental devices in the neoliberal era. In fact, the specific modalities of social control they enact—or, the subjective *homo oeconomicus* they ceaselessly mold—are characterized by the reliance on a paradoxical *production of coercive liberty*. In order for competition to become the uncontested principle of formalization of society as a whole, the subject must be free to choose among different options. Such options, however, must never escape the entrepreneurial matrix that defines neoliberal subjectivity. This fragile and always reversible composition between freedom and constraint should be addressed as a complex terrain of struggle rather than a given condition for political analysis.[10] Also in this regard financialization is configured as a fitting case in point: as we shall see in the next section, its pervasiveness needs the active support of the population. To anticipate a point we shall develop later, the wealth-effect represents precisely the contested battlefield on which neoliberal conventions have fought their struggles for social legitimation.

WEALTH, MONEY, AND MONETARY POLICY: A FOUCAULDIAN APPROACH

We believe that a brief investigation of a few Foucault's references to economic thought can be relevant to our purposes. More specifically, we would like to focus on passages where his reflection concerns some of the crucial issues—for instance, wealth, money, and monetary policy—which are necessary to understand how something like a *process of financialization* could appear in the course of human history. In *The Order of Things*, originally published in 1966, the French philosopher describes the Mercantilists analysis of wealth: this kind of analysis drives the discussion on prices and currency towards a universal taxonomy, namely the representation of a certain order among money, prices, and values. What results is a system of signs related to a specific, functional mode of exchange. We are not yet facing a biopolitical governmentality, but what counts the most is that Foucault is already isolating the political specificity of Mercantilist elaborations on commodity prices. Even more important, he highlights the fact that precious metals are a mere representation of value: gold is precious exactly because it is money, not the other way around. Mercantilism, thus, is analyzed as a radical reversal of the previous perspective according to which the value of money is supposed to depend on the prince's image and seal. In other words, Mercantilism inaugurates a new order in which the relationships between wealth and money are established *within* the process of exchange.

Although—as we just saw—the triadic issue of wealth-money-value is addressed by Foucault already in the 1960s, his philosophical trajectory will not develop towards a financial and monetary history. Yet, a comprehensive understanding of *biopolitical governmentality* cannot easily set it aside: the importance of financial and monetary apparatuses as they emerged in the eighteenth century cannot be underestimated. As many seminal studies on the history of money have unmistakably shown, this century represents an incredibly significant moment for such a historical parable in Europe: it is the moment in which European money frees itself from the traditional configuration, namely that of guaranteeing account correctness and payment stability in the whole empire. For example, the monetary policy that characterized the Italian States in the course of the seventeenth century presupposed a stable international currency to which national currencies had to be solidly linked. The stability of the currency employed in international trade directly implied the stability of the domestic currency. Such a situation could occur only through the State's commitment to control the national monetary spaces—through the transformation of imaginary money into national coin of account. In turn, this goal could be pursued only by means of monetary reform whose outcome was the substitution of eroded currency with good currency, and a cautions policy of tariffs carried out through the use of imaginary money and aimed at maintaining the equivalence relationships among currencies as constant for the longest time possible. As Massimo Amato compellingly argues:

> The Prince's duty is to maintain a treasure from which it is possible to draw if the need arises—namely in case the community requires it; its regulatory function is limited to this ... The "nature" of money is exhausted in its distributive capacity and is naturally delimited by the quantity/measure of goods (which is to say their actual presence). With regard to such quantity/measure, money is constantly able to account for the presence of things, but can never solicit their coming into presence: it is measure of abundance as well as scarcity, given their natural alternation in time. (Amato, 1999, p. 20—our translation)

In modernity—from the eighteenth century onward—the need to strengthen the territorial states shattered the imperial political-administrative balance we briefly described. The dominant exigency was to allow money to modify value in relation to the changing needs that arose within nation-states; in a word, the main problem became the valorization of money. Money's 'nature' is no longer delimited by the quantity/measure of goods but resides instead in the urge to get rich. In this context, grasping the link between this function of money and the incremental regulation of populations might clarify the concrete meaning of *biopolitical governmentality*. In order to expand this fundamental Foucauldian concept into a political category that is able to shed new interpretative light on the current process of financialization, we suggest it is necessary to simultaneously incorporate in it the dimension of *money self-valorization*. If the most rapid way to produce abstract wealth—that is, money—is to realize it by minimizing the risks and conflicts that emerge when commodity production gets organized, then it is rational from a governmental perspective to minimize the costs of production—including state and bank control over economic activities—thus maximizing the possibility of autonomously disposing of money itself. In such a way, a new power of control over the population is exerted. The risk distribution inherent to the production of money by means of money becomes a new strategy to manage economic activities.

The modality of power that is exercised within an accumulation regime dominated by finance is profoundly different from the kind of power exercised by a sovereign state over its citizens. The *governmental freedom* markets incessantly claim goes right along with the management of the populations that nation-states take responsibility for. In order for the population to produce wealth within money's valorization cycle, a new form of social control is necessary. Such an unprecedented form is irreducible to both the lord-bondsman dialectic and the relationship between state and citizens. Let us note, in passing, that although Foucault in his lectures never directly addresses the issues of money and finance, we can implicitly derive an important reference to them in the lecture delivered on February 14, 1979. Discussing Eucken's thought, Foucault realizes that for the Ordoliberals political interventions must target not so much the mechanisms of the market economy but rather the very conditions of their possibility (their performative feature resides precisely in this element). As we read in the text:

> The main objective of regulatory action will necessarily be price stability, understood not as fixed prices but as control of inflation ... In particular, the primary objectives must not be the maintenance purchasing power, the maintenance of full employment, or even balancing the balance of payments ... What does this mean for the instruments to be used? It means first of all using the policy of credit, that is to say, establishing the discount rate. It means using foreign trade by reducing the credit balance when you want to contain the rise in foreign prices. Shifts in taxation will also be employed, but always moderate ones, when seeking to act on saving or investment. (Foucault, 2008, pp. 138–139)

All this means that an expansive monetary policy is impossible. The Ordoliberals conceive of money in such a way that the emphasis is placed on its function as a value-reserve. The resulting ethical dimension privileges those who, by accumulating wealth, can maintain their position as creditors and demand the payment of debts. As a consequence, foreign trade is to be managed according to Mercantilist practices. Following this line of reasoning it is possible to articulate—as Foucault does—a reflection on the social policy promoted by German neoliberals, which require the formalization of society on the model of competitive enterprises. It is our conviction that here we can find the roots of the process through which collective risk management is transferred to financial markets. Thus, even though Foucault does not make explicit references to financialization, he still proves illuminating with regard to it. For instance, let us consider the following passage: "Social policy will have to be a policy which, instead of transferring one part of income to another part, will use as its instrument the most generalized capitalization possible for all the social classes, the instrument of individual and mutual insurance, and, in short, the instrument of private property" (Foucault, 2008, p. 144). Financialization appears as a form of socialization (of risk but also of the perspectives of enrichment that are complementary to it) that leads to a revolution in the concept of sovereignty. As Lucarelli (2010) argues, what is at stake in financialization is no longer the immediate application of sovereign power, but the channeling of human behaviors in such a way that sovereignty ends up being coherent with financialization itself.

FINANCIALIZATION AND THE WEALTH-EFFECT

Having assembled a Foucauldian analytical toolbox, we are now in the position to investigate the rise of financial mechanisms as pervasive *governmental devices*. As we argued in the previous section, it seems doubtless to us that the contemporary process of financialization and the rise of neoliberal governmentality must be read in close connection. In this context, by *financialization* we mean the differentiated practices through which companies, institutions, and individuals alike become completely embedded in financial transactions. The outcome is an unprecedented dependence on unstable markets and volatile money for everything from food supplies[11] to services, from education to income. Obviously, we are aware of the fact that finance has always been a feature of the capitalist mode of production since even before it appeared in its mature form; nonetheless, we contend that the current configuration of finance—namely, its neoliberal form—is qualitatively and quantitatively unique. From a quantitative perspective, it suffices to recall that in 1973 financial returns accounted for 16% of all US profits, whereas in 2007 they made up a stunning 41% (McNally, 2011). Such an increase is even more evident if we consider the changing amount of daily turnover in foreign exchange from 1973 (when the de-linking of money from gold first showed its effects) to 2007: $15 billion versus $3.2 trillion (McNally, 2011). On a different level, but still from a quantity-based standpoint, we need to refer to the radical pervasiveness that characterizes contemporary finance. It is actually difficult to think of a single productive activity that is not, in one way or another, captured in global financial flows: the coercive expansion of pension funds; the inclusion of the planet's poor in financial markets through micro-credit; the inscription of real-estate mortgages in the very core of economic growth; the increasing political power of rating agencies; the privatization of Keynesian deficit spending; the explosion of consumer debt to cover the gap between diminishing real wages and spiking costs of living; and the list might continue for long (Haiven, 2013).

Contemporary finance is unprecedented, however, also from a qualitative perspective. In other words, it is a new, specifically neoliberal governmental device. To grasp this novelty we need to focus on the inceptive event of financialization, its structural foundation. We are referring to the collapse of the Bretton Woods system, agreed upon in 1945, whose main feature was the creation of a dollar/gold standard ($35 per ounce) and the establishment of a fixed rate of exchange to tie all other currencies to the US dollar. This agreement guaranteed a considerable degree of monetary stability from 1945 to 1971: in that year, in fact, Nixon suspended the dollar/gold convertibility. There are complex and controversial political and economic reasons for this move on the part of the US administration, but for our purposes what is pivotal to highlight is that "for the first time in history capital operated with officially de-commodified money, a global currency regime lacking any tie to past labor embodied in a commodity" (McNally, 2011, p. 92). This peculiar de-commodification gave rise to a head-spinning proliferation of financial tools: derivatives that appear as nothing else than immensely complicated—and rapidly multiplying—attempts to make profit out of the financialization of every human economic activity.[12] As Christian Marazzi brilliantly argues:

> *Financialization is not an unproductive/parasitic deviation of growing quotas of surplus-value and collective savings, but rather the form of capital accumulation symmetrical with new processes of value production* ... Beyond the role of finance in the sphere of consumption, what has happened in these last 30 years is a veritable metamorphosis of production processes of this very surplus-value. There has been a transformation of valorization processes that witnesses the extraction of value no longer being circumscribed to the place dedicated to the production of goods and services, but that extending beyond the factory gates so to speak, in the sense that it enters directly into the sphere of *circulation* of capital, that is in the sphere of the exchange of goods and services. (Marazzi, 2011, p. 48)

Endless expansion led eventually to abstract self-reflexivity. Marazzi himself, by referring to the dot-com bubble of 2000, significantly talks about a crisis of *overproduction of self-referentiality* (Marazzi, 2008). Moreover, a new form of accumulation/valorization requires an institutional, governmental counterpart. And it is in this conjuncture that finance shows itself as a neoliberal device. In fact, financialization fundamentally transformed managerial practices in at least three central areas: (1) in business strategy, it privileged the logic of shareholders' activism; (2) in wage relations, it internalized workers by turning them into powerless micro-shareholders; (3) in monetary policy, it modified the decision-making criteria followed by nation-states (as we shall see in more detail in the next sections). In general we are witnessing the deployment of a veritable *government through instability*,[13] an expansion of financial reason to society as a whole. In particular, from our perspective, such an expansion is clearly visible by referring to the *wealth-effect*.

Ever since the 1980s, the US economy has been characterized by the process of financial markets, liberalization and by the consequent explosion of new financial tools. As a consequence, the passage from a Keynesianism built on a pact between producers within a monetary system that binds currency fluctuations[14] to a financial Keynesianism based on private deficit spending, in which massive deregulations are accompanied by savage reductions of welfare programs. Again: what we see in this conjuncture is the emergence of a neoliberal governmentality. This latter's economic face, in other words, is nothing else than financial Keynesianism. Shareholder value becomes the fundamental macroeconomic index, the compass that guides both investment and consumption through the wealth-effect. As French Regulationist Michel Aglietta (2008) appropriately argues:

> The radical change in monetary policy in the late 1970s and early 1980s triggered financial liberalization. Not only was there a shift from intermediate to market financing that

> redistributed risk-taking from banks to institutional investors; there was also a dramatic change in the ownership structure of corporations, that has shifted business strategy from "insider productivity-sharing" to "shareholder value-optimizing." The norm of profitability has changed altogether. Market-value accounting has replaced reproduction-cost accounting as the yardstick of corporate performance. Furthermore, achieving shareholder value in practice means extracting a rent on behalf of shareholders. This rent is the positive difference between the actual rate of return on equity and the equilibrium stock-market rate of return of the corporation, given by the capital asset pricing model (CAPM), multiplied by the capital of the firm. Combined with the long ascending wave in the stock market, the imperative of shareholder value gave rise to a much higher required rate of return than in the heyday of post-war growth. Most business strategies—downsizing, spin-offs and the like, but also external growth via mergers and acquisitions and share buybacks—were driven by the lucrative adjustment of corporate executives to the principle of shareholder value. The US adopted shareholder value on a large scale in the early 1990s, at a time when Europe was crippled by extravagantly high real interest rates. Shareholder value does not hamper innovative investment spurred by private-equity funds, especially venture-capital funds; it has had a large impact on productivity growth—the IT revolution was largely financed by such investment funds. (p. 69)

For wealth effect, usually, is meant an increase in consumer spending based on the perceived wealth created by the escalating value of stock market portfolios. According to Guttmann and Plihon (2010), consumption expenditures in the Anglo-Saxon countries are determined by changes in asset prices rather than by income. Evidence for the early 2000s suggests that the falling savings rate and the increasing debt burden did not solely occur in the top income groups—who benefitted the most from the increase in financial wealth—but have grown rapidly also for middle-class households (Wolff, 2009). In other words, the falling saving rates and the increasing debt burden may be explained by a wealth-effect due to the rise in the value of financial assets because of the stock exchange boom.[15] The wealth-effect is precisely that psychological condition that is necessary in order for a finance-led growth regime to prove durable. As shown by Fumagalli and Lucarelli (2007; 2011), when the productivity of the economic system significantly depends on learning economies and network economies (an aspect that, in the case of the US, is indicated by the increasing intangibles), it is possible to witness a cumulative growth if and only if the sum total of capital gains–dependent investment propensity and consumption propensity is higher than the salary-dependent consumption propensity.

Quite obviously, the model is highly risky, constantly on the verge of instability. The repetitive and frequent nature of recent financial crises is just further proof of this. From a neoliberal, governmental standpoint this form of specific command over individual behaviors is to be reintroduced each and every time: the consolidated rule consists in shifting from one bubble to the next,[16] forcing individuals to believe that their wealth depends more on financial markets than on wages (and conflicts over them) or on other forms of income (and struggles over them). From this standpoint, *the wealth-effect represents the form of command which is typical of financial Keynesianism*, here understood as a specific device of neoliberal governmentality. The dynamic that goes from profit to financial market—and vice-versa—replaces the pivots of political decision-making in the Fordist-Keynesian paradigm, namely the productivity/wage connection, and the production/mass consumption nexus.

The impact of financial returns on patrimonial decisions becomes the key factor in investment plannings; these must take into account not only the variations of demand, but also—and crucially—the expected financial returns. Although consumption still depends on the accumulation of traditional income from labor (i.e., wages), a new variable aimed at measuring the value of households' owned financial tools appears and directly intervenes on consumption behaviors. If financialization is highly developed—which is to say: if households' wealth depends more on the share of income coming from financial markets than on salaries—wage moderation produces a twofold effect: on the one hand, it favors companies' profitability; on the other one, it increases financial returns. Thus an economic dynamic founded on the wealth-effect can be triggered: it could spur private consumption even in a situation marked by a decrease of real wages. As a consequence, *the level of production mostly depends on financial valuation*. We witness an inversion of the relations between the real sphere and the financial sphere that prevailed under Fordism: market dynamics replace wages as the main source of cumulative growth. Moreover, such a reversal also revolutionizes the regime of social control, both at the individual and the collective level. In other words, *the wealth-effect is configured as the fundamental device of financial governmentality*: it rests not only on the subsumption of labor under capital—as Marx had already correctly understood—but also on the subsumption of life itself under finance—here lies the contemporary link between capitalism and biopower.

In macroeconomic terms, this form of subsumption expresses itself in the growing liquidity attracted by financial markets, starting with private savings that were previously invested in state bonds. Yet, this growing liquidity is not sufficient to sustain such a process. Thus, a second explanatory variable is necessary in order for the wealth-effect to gain persistence: this variable is nothing less than a sort of Durkheimian *collective conscience* (or common sense, or socially shared beliefs), in both its economic dimensions. On the one hand, collective conscience concerns a shared view about the production of money by means of money; on the other, it refers to a mutual agreement on the hierarchy of needs whose satisfaction defines an acceptable social status. Through its penetration in the deep layers of common sense, the logic of valorization profoundly transforms social relations. More precisely, this means that financialization is the form of socialization that characterizes neoliberal governmentality. Moreover, it is worth noting that such a socialization is accompanied by a corresponding production of *financial subjectivity*.

This is why the analysis of financialization cannot be limited to a focus on the conditions of the system's macroeconomic sustainability. Much more is at stake: the analysis also requires a particular attention to the social codes through which human relations are framed, managed, exploited—and, at times, subverted. We must thus understand the *conventions* that regulate the population's mindset, starting from the recognition that their contemporary source/*milieu* is to be found in the business world. A convention provides an *a priori* valuation system and defines the *ensemble* of social rules that governmentally homogenize individuals' differentiated behaviors. Constantly traversed by a systemic uncertainty, a convention provides an *a priori* set of criteria for valuation. Thus, it indicates the *ensemble* of social rules that introduce a significant degree of homogeneity into subjective behaviors. The adherence of conventions to reality should not be taken for granted: it is definitely possible that they rely on incorrect epistemic models. However, what is crucial is that the convention irradiates a valuation system whose impact on social reality is profoundly transformative and subjectively performative. In fact, it actually fostered a sort of collective blindness that unified the community of financial operators and guaranteed a certain stability to its system of valuation.

To emphasize—somewhat crudely—the very kernel of our argument, we might say the following: *macroeconomic stability is directly dependent on prevailing conventions*. As soon as conventions lose their cogency, fear and panic spread, easily leading to the disintegration of the community. Therefore, financial markets can be understood as institutions that financial operators establish in order for titles transaction to take place through valuation. Needless to say, such transactions aim at increasing the economic system's level of liquidity. In other words, stock exchange markets represent a space in which a new rule for valuation—based on a collective judgment on the part of financial operators—actually occurs. In Foucauldian terms, financial markets are the centerpiece of the specific regime of truth that sustains governmentality in its neoliberal phase.

Elaborating on Keynes's teaching (especially 1936, chap. 12), French economist André Orléan argues that financial markets, by their very nature, function on the basis of investors' gregarious behaviors. This is due to their massive adhesion to symbols and signs, which everybody recognizes as a legitimate expression of wealth. For this crucial reason, the analysis of conventions cannot be limited to the business world. The state of confidence defined by conventional valuation is in fact legitimated by public opinion (or collective conscience, or prevailing form of subjectivity). Although it originally spurts from the business world, it subsequently involves the population as a whole and becomes a fully political object. Once again, it is fairly evident how profoundly these conventional elements cross the Foucauldian issue of neoliberal governmentality (Orléan, 1999).

MONETARY POLICY FACING WEALTH-EFFECTS

As we just argued, the wealth-effect is the collective psychological attitude that guarantees the existence and legitimation of a particular regime of accumulation: *the finance-led growth regime.* Inasmuch as financial markets, through capital gains, keep constant or even increase the level of liquidity, a sort of self-propulsive mechanism is set in motion. In turn, such a self-feeding device generates an ever-increasing shareholder value, thus producing more capital gains. It is a classical self-referential structure that explains speculation as a result of financial markets' internal workings. Such self-referentiality implies a cognitive constraint that refers to all investors since it derives from the supremacy of "market psychology," namely the primacy of financial collective beliefs over individual opinions.[17]

The dominant accumulation system in contemporary capitalism imposes a series of transformations to the political sphere. First of all, growth conditions depend on the acceptance of a new productive model in which labor assumes an unprecedented role. This new role is not only defined by the de-structuration of the Fordist union; nor is it merely linked to the reduced importance of wages as the fundamental macroeconomic variable for accumulation—which in turn indicates the annihilation of the conflictual dynamics that characterizes wage claims. Actually, this new role is predicated on a valorization process in which the very core of wealth-production changes: *valorization itself now depends on conventions that are primarily asserted in the financial community.* In a similar fashion, macroeconomic stability depends largely on the interventions of the Central Banks that, when facing a scarcity of liquidity in financial markets, must promptly react inasmuch as another financial crisis is to be prevented. This Central Banks' prompt reaction is consciously sustained through the wealth-effect upon which—in Foucauldian terms—the security of the population (in turn delimited by financial markets) is endured.

The levers of power are no longer to be located in the distribution of banking credit nor in deficit spending. The current independent variable is neither wages nor profit; rather, it is the *accumulation rate from financial capital gains.* The money supply is freed by the *quantum* of currency held by the Central Bank and is tied to the reorganization of the division of labor, and to the redefinition of social relations in the circulation-reproduction sphere. In other words, money supply is linked to the dynamic of capital (living) labor: as the journal *Primo Maggio* workgroup on money argues, monetary policy directly represents a modality of capitalist command. Nowadays such a task is no longer accomplished through the control of the quantity of circulating money, nor is it merely justified by inflationary pressures. Both at the level of Central Banks and within the academic world, an important principle got established in the 1990s: the credibility of monetary policy must rely either on a *pegging* of the exchange rate or on the delegation of monetary policy to a foreign Central Bank with a renowned inflation aversion. First of all, this *New Consensus* rejects Friedmanian monetary theory: the main instrument for monetary policy control is interest rate rather than money supply. Moreover—at least in theory—the role of the Central Bank consists in ensuring the equivalence between the monetary interest rate and the real interest rate that regulates the balance between loanable and investment funds. When market rates (in real terms) are below the natural rate, inflation emerges. Supposedly, a restrictive monetary policy would have no negative effects and would contribute to inflation control. In actuality, however, in order to sustain the rate of accumulation of capital gains, monetary policy institutions were not afraid to differ: Alan Greenspan, for example, did not hesitate to cut Federal Fund rates *eleven* times in one year, bringing it to the lowest nominal level of the last forty years. And the ECB willingly followed his example! Even in Europe, the maximalism of the ECB statute was strongly mitigated by most managers' commonsensical wisdom.

Monetary policy in a finance-led growth regime must follow a convention-based process of valorization. The money-creation performed by financialization sets in motion a recovery process of capital profitability that incorporates the population as a whole—people's lives, expectations, relations—within the realm of financial risk. In other words, financialization articulates the temporalities of capitalist reorganization and, thus, facilitates the subsumption of *circulation* under the valorization process—here understood as an abstract totality. This last element is what connects the four phases undertook by the process of financialization from 1993 onwards: the boom of the New Economy (1993–2000), the reaction to its crisis (2000–2003), the real-estate bubble (2003–2007), and finally the shift from the subprime slump to the so-called Eurozone crisis (2008–2014). All four phases belong to the same technological paradigm. For this reason, the *conventions* that regulate financial valuation were not subjected to radical changes over the last three decades. The valuation logics that dominate the financial community are, for the most part, the same.

THE DYNAMICS OF FINANCIAL GOVERNMENTALITY: FROM THE NEW ECONOMY TO THE GREAT RECESSION

In the course of the 1990s, financialization—in this case as investment of collective savings in the stock market—generated additional incomes. These incomes were created in the financial markets through business indebtedness to the banking system.[18] In the period between 1993 and 2000, the New York Stock Exchange upwardly exploded (the Dow Jones from 4,000 to 11,700, Standard & Poor's from 450 to 1,530). Financial capital gains fostered real growth due to the exploitation of knowledge and labor productivity—especially in the high-tech sector. The valuation of financial markets began to depend on the organizational change aimed at supporting innovative cooperation among relatively autonomous workers. *The dynamism of organizational change eventually became*—given the attention paid to it by financial markets—*a new modality of valorization of productive capital.*

Thus a new finance-led regime of accumulation emerged: its specific governmental rationality rested on the promise of a new world. Correspondingly, the second half of the 1990s saw the affirmation of a new convention: that of a digitalized society with liberating effects on work and life alike. Be it true or false, there can be no doubt that this convention entailed a process of *real* transformation. Even Joseph Stiglitz's lucid critique of the roaring 1990s confirms this point:

> Modern American-style capitalism was pivoted around what would later be called the New Economy, symbolized by the so-called dot-coms that were revolutionizing the way that America—and the rest of the world—did business, modifying the rhythms of the very technological shifts and increasing the growth rate of productivity to extraordinary levels, that had not been seen for over 25 years ... Halfway through the 1990s, the manufacturing sector had slipped to a scarce 14% of total production, with a percentage of employees even lower in respect to the active population. (Stiglitz, 2004, p. 4)

As a matter of fact, the lever of innovation shifted from R&D laboratories to the workforce's living bodies, while capitals from the rest of the world flowed into the stocks and businesses bonds listed on the US financial markets. In such an accumulation system, new forms of remuneration arose—mostly tied to the overall business performance. A fitting case in point are the stock options for managers, but also pension or investment funds show how financial growth is predicated on waged laborers involvement. These forms of remuneration increased financial market liquidity but, in the absence of an adequate redistribution rule, they also compressed salaries since the main capitalist drive cannot but be that of commanding living labor. Quite obviously, such a wage compression leads to systemic instability. Nothing else than this is what happened in the crisis of March 2000: on the one hand, newly generated incomes had been unequally distributed; on the other, their production entailed the destruction of wage and employment stability. A new common sense—more precisely: a new subjective dynamics of neoliberal governmentality—had just imposed itself: to create stock value in financial markets everything is acceptable, even extreme organizational "innovations." Just think of the innumerable processes of downsizing, reengineering, outsourcing, and mergers and acquisitions. Hence, finance fosters, translates, and betrays real innovative processes by devaluing living labor. To attract investors to the stock markets, companies offer ever-increasing returns precisely through merger and acquisition operations. They even acquire their own shares, they even rig their accounts. The necessary capital for this restructuring—whose goal is the control of technological development—was actually obtained by reducing labor-power remuneration.

The March 2000 crisis brought the process of financialization to a further level of generalization: a new phase characterized by a marked decline—with losses of 40% in the Dow Jones, 50% in Standard & Poor's, and 80% in the NASDAQ. In the meantime, we saw a consolidation of wage deflation under the double pressure of the Asian (mainly Indian and Chinese) industrial reserve army and of widespread outsourcing. The markets finally recovered in 2003. The fact that the New Economy did not precipitate into a depression equivalent to that of the 1930s depends both on the monetary policy of the FED and on precise financial innovations. In the two-year period following the March 2000 crisis (2001–2002), the FED drastically lowered the interest rate from 6% to 1%. That pushed economic agents into an utterly unreasonable rate of indebtedness: in fact, they hoped to benefit from the discrepancy between their own capital returns and the interest rate. This incentive to accumulate debt means that the wealth-effect was articulated in different ways than during the roaring years of the New Economy. In particular, the prices on real-estate markets rose and the FED's monetary policy supported the purchasing power of American consumers. American families could thus obtain practically unlimited credit from the banking system, acquiring a significant real-estate patrimony with increasing value as a guarantee. The expected earnings were high—sustained as they were by a negative real interest rate. Stock prices newly rose in March 2003 (just before the American intervention in Iraq). It is possible to find a precise description of this kind of financialization as a practice of social control in the words of Stiglitz:

> The story goes back to the recession of 2001. With the support of Federal Reserve Chairman Alan Greenspan, President George W. Bush pushed through a tax cut designed to benefit the richest Americans but not to lift the economy out of the recession that followed the collapse of the Internet bubble. Given that mistake, the FED had little choice if it was to fulfill its mandate to maintain growth and employment: it had to lower interest rates, which it did in an unprecedented way—all the way down to 1%.
>
> It worked, but in a way fundamentally different from how monetary policy normally works. Usually, low interest rates lead firms to borrow more to invest more, and greater indebtedness is matched by more productive assets.
>
> But, given that over-investment in the 1990's was part of the problem underpinning the recession, lower interest rates did not stimulate much investment. The economy grew, but mainly because *American families were persuaded to take on more debt, refinancing their mortgages and spending some of the proceeds*. And, as long as housing prices rose as a result of lower interest rates, Americans could ignore their growing indebtedness. (Stiglitz, 2007—our emphasis)

In other words, the population was involved in the production of (financial) wealth in two main ways: first, through the construction of the New Economy, and second—after the diffusion of unbundled innovative instincts that initially fed financial euphoria but eventually turned into positional rents to be solely appropriated by the most aggressive businesses—by repositioning the financial level onto the real-estate sector. All this, it must be remembered, implied the active regulation of a 'euphoric' society by means of massive outsourcing of productive activity toward developing countries that highly exploit labor as well as the environment. Monetary policy facilitates this process without governing it: from spring 2003 to January 2007 the FED extraordinarily increased the liquidity available to the markets. Although badly hit by wage deflation,[19] 97% of Americans maintained their standard of living through the rise of real-estate prices, the generosity of American credit markets, and the low price of imported goods. Nevertheless, this financial lever sustained financial earnings without any relation with the capacity to generate profits in the 'real' economy: the risk proved tragically high. Similar credits were grouped and converted into bonds and derivatives to be placed on financial markets. Thus risk was transferred to the operators of these financial activities: this transfer increased bank solidity in the short run but eventually led to an even more severe crisis. As Boyer, Dehove, and Plihon warned in a 2005 study, the fact that a reduced number of actors (insurance companies, non-financial corporations, etc.) can assume a large share of risk may be dangerous for the financial system if the level of market liquidity abruptly decreases:

> The severity and thus the outcome of the crises depend on the degree of concentration/dispersion of risks and the banking system's degree of resiliency. Indeed, we find that financial crises are all the more serious because the risks tend to be concentrated on the banks, which are essential to the continuity of the payments and credit-relations system. (Boyer, Dehove, & Plihon, 2005, p. 2)[20]

The real-estate market boom moves parallel to wage deflation: after having exhausted wage prospectives and aspirations by selling market dreams, the selling of another dream begins: a house that can be paid for by credit—an infinite credit with a high insolvency risk. This is where subprime loans are brought to the foreground: high risk mortgages for buying houses conceded to families with few income guarantees. The goal once again was to foster the wealth-effect by compressing real wages. The main economic agents, beginning with the chief economists of financial institutions, cannot but realize that the American crisis is so profound precisely because it started from a real-estate bubble that touched the most crucial of the US economy, namely housing property. The cases of Fannie Mae and Freddie Mac perfectly represent the twilight of the American dream: a house at all cost, no matter what. The two institutions, equipped with a $83.2 million capital, managed to sustain—with a little help from the FED—mortgages for $5.2 billion, half of the overall existing mortgages, in an unsustainable relation of 1 to 65.

While the subsumption of life under finance sharpened, the transformation of social relations proved conducive to the concentration of financial risk in the weakest sectors of the population. The August 2007 crisis hit after many years of strong expansion of real-estate credit that followed the Internet bubble. In order to properly function, the financialization of the economy requires the inclusion a growing number of domestic economies within the process of value creation. On the one hand, the securitization of subprime loans represents a formidable lever for the creation of credit. On the other hand, however, the distribution of risk to the share portfolios of a large number of investors on a global scale—through the credit bond markets—makes the internal relationships among monetary institutions even more fragile.

The formal principle of competition—upon which neoliberal governmentality is grounded—once applied to finance provokes the madness of markets according to a perfectly reasonable logic. At a first sight such a madness could be attributed to market operators: after all, they are those who more readily follow the conventions that for a certain period of time act as unbreakable laws—both during euphoric phases and in situations of widespread panic. At a closer look, however, this is not the main issue: in fact, the deepest madness is to be located in what results from the interaction among the institutions that operate on financial markets—including traditional credit institutes, Central Banks, and even states. The outcome of such interaction is a *state of exception* that imposes the necessity of public interventions. It is highly relevant that the call for public help came exactly from those who—in a not so distant past—had so tenaciously affirmed the desirability of a lean state: banks and markets now make pleas for governmental intervention so that its impact on aggregate demand might contribute to give a price to financial activities. If properly understood, both the Paulson Plan and the Geithner Plan are centered on this logic. As Paul Krugman noted in March 2009: "In essence, the Geithner plan is the same as the Paulson plan from six months ago: buy up the toxic assets, and hope that this unfreezes the markets. Do not be fooled by the apparent role of private enterprise: more than 90 percent of the funds will come from taxpayers. And the way the funds are structured provides a strong incentive for investors to overpay for assets." All this is meant to give a new impulse to financial markets and to securitization, which is to say the process by means of which bank credits are transformed into titles that are negotiable on secondary markets. Thus, public policies are shaped according to a state of exception whose ultimate core is a sort of *destructuring power*: in order to artificially keep alive an institution (i.e., financial markets) that is legitimated by unstable conventions, the durable conventions on which nation-states are founded are consciously demolished. In so doing, the compatibility between accumulation and regulation—upon which a viable growth regime can be established—is further undermined.

The European debt crisis, as well as the apparent "return of the sovereign state" in which banks directly implement public policies, is perfectly congruent with the new financial (dis)order we just described. The public governance of the crisis, in fact, entirely depends on the state capability to borrow capitals from financial markets. The explosion of public debt in Europe is mainly due to the finance and banks bailouts that took place after the 2008 crisis. The Eurozone average public deficit was merely 0.6% of the GDP in 2007 (66% public deficit/GDP ratio), whereas in 2010 it skyrocketed to 7% (84% public deficit/GDP ratio). All this occurs while the public spending/GDP ratio is stable or even declining since the early 1990s—also due to fiscal competition among European states (Lucarelli & Vercellone, 2011).

The possibility of a state sovereignty governed by financial markets—which is to say: structured around the specific rationality of financial governmentality—is from the very beginning inscribed in European Union DNA. European treaties forbid national Central Banks to directly lend to states, so that they must sell their titles on financial markets. Moreover, the European Central Bank is not entitled to subscribe directly to public bonds issued by European states as it has been conceived of as a body that is independent from the member states governments and, thus, it does not act as an issuing bank. It must be noted that this institutional setting—grounded as it is on economic theories that are as widely accepted as rationally disputable[21]—has actually favored the second phase of the crisis, notwithstanding the BCE's exceptional interventions.

First Jean-Claude Trichet, then Mario Draghi (as ECB presidents) implemented their policies without European political leaders—Angela Merkel *in primis*—protecting the stability of the monetary area. The opposition to the aids to Greece, the idea of two European monetary areas, the call for private investors' participation in the rescue of troubled European countries, the creation of an all-but-transparent—even unclear—European Financial Stability Facility (EFSF) devoid of the liquidity which is necessary—to actually safeguard financial stability: all these are signals of the institutional weakness that has fostered financial speculation. The political chaos that still characterizes the EU has diffused—and continues to do so—the legitimate worry of a potential insolvency. Moreover, it has actively encouraged the selling of titles emitted by troubled countries. Such processes have pushed the interest rates on public debt to a very high level and, in so doing, have increased the so-called spread between, for example, Italian and German titles. Furthermore, the non-sustainability of Greek, Irish, Spanish, Portuguese, and Italian (so-called PIIGS) public debts has been nourished in similar ways, although such non-sustainability has revealed itself in different moments since the Eurozone crisis is marked by a discordance among national impacts and, as a consequence, by a discrepancy among the temporalities of its recognition. Finally, international investors who had in their share portfolio PIIGS public titles started to sell these or to ensure themselves through a specific kind of derivatives, namely *credit default swaps* (CDS).

From 2008 onwards, the largest capital gains attained by institutional investors come from the exchange of CDS, in particular those concerning the risk of public default, through the following mechanism: some influential financial corporations start to sell state titles of those countries that rating agencies consider "risky"; as a consequence, the value of these titles decreases; such decrease gives rise to negative expectations with regard to their future performance; a negative expected future value induces an increase in the interest rates related to the emission of new titles, so that the *spread* augments. This tendency is self-feeding and necessarily leads to an emergency that forces the ECB to intervene in two main, simultaneous ways: buying states titles for new monetary liquidity, and proposing/imposing to national governments to drastically cut public spending in order to reduce public deficit, at the same time, CDS value hugely increase—proportionally to the *spread* augmentation; finally, this augmented value allows CDS owners to speculate and obtain colossal capital gains (Fumagalli, 2011).

Through the *debt trap*, in an institutional context in which monetary sovereignty is de facto subordinated to financial (dis)order, governments enact new policies whose declared aim is the downsizing of the welfare state: social security and public health get reduced, public utilities are privatized. Here we can appreciate how profoundly neoliberal governmentality is creating new markets for financial penetration: pension funds, health insurances, service companies—mainly specialized in care giving—as well as energy and hydric big players (mostly concentrated in Germany, France, and England) can now access unprecedented markets characterized by primary needs once satisfied by the welfare state.

The 'return' to state sovereignty—in the specific form of *austerity* imposed by supranational entities—is thus an outcome of the process of financialization. Its goal is to guarantee monetary liquidity and to sustain those conventions that result dominant in the market arena. The necessity for governments to place their state titles on financial markets and the impossibility for the ECB to act as lender of last resort represent nothing less than the *end of state money*, that is to say the imposition of a monetary policy that is configured as directly governed by financial operators.

CONCLUSIONS

The main point the present work aimed at emphasizing was that financial governmentality does not solely refer to transformations occurring in a narrowly defined economic realm. Rather, it involves the production of a specific subjectivity whose adaptive model is to be found in competitive financial markets. We also intended to show how the crucial tool through which a sort of *financialized reality* is socially enacted is the wealth-effect, namely the belief—theoretically indisputable but empirically indemonstrable—that individual as well as collective well-being relies more on financial markets' performances than on conflict-dependent wage levels. This is precisely what we mean by the expression *political dimension of financialization*.

Although it is true that this particular modality of governance—that we tried to grasp through Foucault's categorical apparatus—leads to specific differences that need to be read in their singularity (just think of the current divergence between US and EU monetary policies), it seems to us that such differences need to be addressed by an interpretative framework that goes beyond the traditional critique of imperialism. An interesting line for further research is delineated by an author whose work Foucault openly and deeply appreciated, namely Pierre Klossowski. In *Living Currency* (2012), an important book, he argues that "money, while representing and guaranteeing that which exists, becomes all the more a signifier for *what does not exist*—i.e., for the fantasy—as, in the world of integral monstrosity, the transgression of norms presents itself as the progressive conquest of the non-existent: that is of the possible" (p. 25). In contemporary capitalism what we name *money* assumes precisely such features of conquest of the nonexistent, and it does so by grounding its effectiveness on the influence exercised by financial conventions. The biopolitical nature of financial devices, to which money is in constant reference, is configured as a form of law making whose 'normal' functioning is based on a ceaseless transgression of established norms. Here we newly encounter the crucial issue of ambivalence: neoliberal transgression, in fact, is simultaneously a democratizing element (no *Grundnorm* is definitively imposed on social subjects) and a direct form of social control (every difference, every singularity must be translatable in monetary terms).

To analytically assume such an ambivalence, we consider the broadly discussed *theory of common/s* to be another significant line of further research. The conceptual history of the notion of commons has a very long tradition, but it also shows unprecedented characters in the current phase of capitalist development. Thus, our hypothesis is that, although capital has attempted to pillage the commons ever since its inception—that is, primitive accumulation—its contemporary configuration diverges from the preceding ones in that *the commons play the role of crucial element of production*, not just an aspect among many. After all, in order for the wealth-effect to work, large masses of population must be participating in its communal production. It is this historical novelty that suggests to use the expression *common/s* instead of commons. As Sandro Mezzadra and Brett Neilson appropriately argue, the difference between the singular and the plural (common versus common*s*) is important: in fact, "the former signals a process of production, both entirely immanent and material, by which instances of the latter acquire extension in time and space. At the same time it gives to these plural instances an intensive quality that brings them into relation in contingent but also constitutive ways." In other words, there is a "moment of excess that characterizes the common with regard to the commons" (2013, pp. 278, 297). It is precisely such a moment of excess that is at play in recent—and very promising—reflections on the issue of the *money of the common/s* (Baronian & Vercellone, 2013).

To be sure, our reference to potential developments to come is just a preliminary one. However, what both living currency and money of the common/s share is a particular understanding of the process of financialization—and of its peculiar ambivalence. If the wealth-effect is a productive, neoliberal source of commonwealth, it is now time for the class of producers to re-appropriate the products of its labor. This means, first and foremost, to directly challenge the governmental hegemony of financial markets, as *Occupy* in North America, the *Indignados* in Europe, and many other radical movements around the world have been doing in recent years. Financial systems, however, should not be carelessly destroyed or merely decommissioned: they express the power of the general intellect and this power must be retained in order to foster the common/s growth. Rather, it is the common/s corruption that should be pitilessly targeted by activists. Following an intuition of Italian philosopher Carlo Sini (2012), we would like to conclude this work on a provocative note: what if financial markets themselves are nothing else than the most amazing common/s waiting to be saved from itself, from its own privatistic disease?

REFERENCES

Aglietta, M. (2007, 5 September). "Le capitalisme de bulle enbulle." *Le Monde*, http://www.lemonde.fr/economie/article/2007/09/01/le-capitalisme-de-bulle-en-bulle_950165_3234.html

Aglietta, M. (2008, November–December). Into a new growth regime. *New Left Review, 54*, 61–74.

Amato, M. (1999). *Il bivio della moneta. Problemi monetari e pensiero del denaro nel Settecento italiano.* Milano: Egea.

Baronian, L., & Vercellone, C. (2013). *Moneta del comune e reddito sociale garantito*. Retrieved from http://www.uninomade.org/moneta-del-comune-e-reddito-sociale-garantito/

Boyer, R. (2002). The Origins of Regulation Theory, in R. Boyer & Y. Saillard (Eds.). (2002). *Regulation theory: The state of the art*. pp. 13–20. London & New York: Routledge.

Boyer, R. (2004). *The future of economic growth: As new becomes old.* Cheltenham, UK & Northhampton, MA: Edward Elgar.

Boyer, R., Dehove, M., & Plihon, D. (2005, April). Contemporary financial crises: Between newness and repetition. *Issues in Regulation Theory,* 1–6. Retrieved from http://webcom.upmf-grenoble.fr/regulation/Issue_Regulation_theory/LR52english.pdf

Brown, W. (2006). American nightmare: Neoliberalism, neoconservatism, and de-democratization. *Political Theory, 34*(6), 690–714.

Dardot, P., & Laval, C. (2014). *The new way of the world.* London: Verso.

De Cecco, M. (1999). The lender of last resort. *Economic Notes, 28*(1), 1–14.

De Grauwe, P. (2011, August). Only a more active ECB can solve the euro crisis. *CEPS Policy Briefing, 250*, 1–8.

Dyer-Withford, N. (2005). Cyber-Negri: General intellect and immaterial labor. In T. Murphy & A. Mustapha (Eds.), *The philosophy of Antonio Negri.* pp. 136–163. London: Pluto.

Flew, T. (2012, February). Michel Foucault's *The Birth of Biopolitics* and contemporary neoliberal debates. *Thesis Eleven, 108*(1), 44–65.

Foucault, M. (1978). *The history of sexuality, Vol. I: An introduction.* New York: Pantheon.

Foucault, M. (2002). *The order of things.* London: Routledge.

Foucault, M. (2003). *Society Must Be Defended.* Lectures at the Collège de France 1976. New York: Picador.

Foucault, M. (2007). *Security, Territory, Population.* Lectures at the Collège de France 1977/1978. New York: Palgrave Macmillan.

Foucault, M. (2008). *Birth of Biopolitcs.* Lectures at the Collège de France 1978/1979. New York: Palgrave Macmillan.

Fumagalli, A. (2011, 10 August). *Il default come contropotere alla speculazione finanziaria.* Retrieved from http://www.uninomade.org/il-default-come-contropotere-alla-speculazione-finanziaria/

Fumagalli, A. & Lucarelli, S. (2007). A model of cognitive capitalism: A preliminary analysis. *European Journal of Economic and Social Systems, 21*(1), 117–133.

Fumagalli, A. & Lucarelli, S. (2011). A financialized monetary economy of production. *International Journal of Political Economy, 40*(48–69).

Galbraith, J. K. (1994). *A short history of financial euphoria.* London: Penguin.

Guttmann, R. & Plihon, D. (2010). Consumer debt and financial fragility. *International Review of Applied Economics, 24*(3), 269–283.

Haiven, M. (2014). *Crises of imagination, crises of power.* New York: Zed.

Hardt, M., & Negri, A. (2000). *Empire.* Cambridge, MA: Harvard University Press.

Hardt, M., & Negri, A. (2004). *Multitude.* New York: Penguin.

Hardt, M., & Negri, A. (2009). *Commonwealth.* Cambridge, MA: Harvard University Press.

Holmes, B. (2010). Is it written in the stars? Global finance, prevarious destinies. *Ephemera: Theory & Politics in Organization, 10*(3–4), 222–233.

Jessop, B. (1990). *State theory.* Cambridge: Polity.

Keynes, J. M. (1936). *General theory of employment, interest and money.* Cambridge: Macmillan Cambridge University Press, for Royal Economic Society.

Klossowski, P. (2012). *Living Currency.* English translation available online at http://monoskop.org/images/b/b0/Klossowski_Pierre_Living_Currency.pdf

Krugman, P. (2009). *Will the Geithner Plan Work?* Retrieved from http://roomfordebate.blogs.nytimes.com/2009/03/24/will-the-geithner-plan-work/_php=true&_type=blogs&_php=true&_type=blogs&_r=1

Lazzarato, M. (2013). *La fabbrica dell'uomo indebitato.* Roma: DeriveApprodi.

Lebert, D., & Vercellone, C. (2004). L'économie de la connaissance et de l'immatériel, entre théorie et histoire: du capitalisme industriel au capitalisme cognitif. *L'économie industrielle en mutation.* Paris: Cahiers Lillois d'économie et sociologie, L'Harmattan.

Lemke, T. (2001). *The Birth of Biopolitics*: Michel Foucault's Lectures at the Collège de France on Neoliberal Governmentality. *Economy & Society, 30*(2), 190–207.

Leonardi, E. (2012). *Biopolitics of Climate Change*, PhD Dissertation, University of Western Ontario.

Leonardi, E. (2013). Back to the land: Which return? To what land? Notes on the financialization of food. *Scienze del Territorio, 1*(225–230).

Lucarelli, S. (2010). Financialization as biopower. In A. Fumagalli & S. Mezzadra (Eds.), *Crisis in the global economy: Financial markets, social struggles and new political scenarios*. Cambridge, MA: MIT Press, Series Semiotext(e)/Active Agents.

Lucarelli, S. (2013). The 1973–1978 workgroup on money of the journal *Primo Maggio*: An example of pluralist critique of political economy. *International Journal of Pluralism and Economics Education, 4*(1), 30–50.

Lucarelli, S., & Vercellone, C. (2011). Welfare systems and social services during the systemic crisis of cognitive capitalism. *European Journal of Economic and Social Systems, 24*(1/2) 77–97.

Marazzi, C. (1977–1978, Winter). Commento a Convenevole. *Primo Maggio, 11*(28–34).

Marazzi, C. (1978). Alcune proposte per un lavoro su 'denaro e composizione di classe. *Primo Maggio*, Supplement to no. 12, 75–80.

Marazzi, C. (2007, Hiver). Amortissement du corps-machine. *Moltitudes, 27*(27–36).

Marazzi, C. (2008). *Capital and Language*. New York: Semiotext(e).

Marazzi, C. (2010). *Il comunismo del capitale*. Verona: Ombre corte.

Marazzi, C. (2011). *The violence of financial capitalism*. New York: Semiotext(e).

McNally, D. (2011). *Global slump: The economics and politics of crisis and resistance*. Oakland, CA: PM.

Mezzadra, S., & Neilson, B. (2013). *Border as method, or, the multiplication of labor*. Durham, NC: Duke University Press.

Negri, A. (2008). *The porcelain workshop: For a new grammar of politics*. Los Angeles: Semiotext(e).

Orléan, A. (1999). *Le pouvoir de la finance*. Paris: Odile Jacob.

Orléan, A. (2008). Knowledge in finance: Objective value versus convention. In R. Arena & A. Festré (Eds.), *Handbook of knowledge and economics* (pp. 313–336). Cheltenham, UK: Edward Elgar.

Palley, T. (2007). *Financialization: What It Is and Why It Matters*. Working Paper No. 525, The Levy Economics Institute.

Pellizzoni, L. (2011). Governing through disorder. *Global Environmental Change, 21*, 795–803.

Revel, J. (2010). *Foucault, une pensé du discontinu*. Paris: Editions Mille et une nuits.

Senellart, M. (2012). Situation du cours. In M. Foucault, *Du gouvernment des vivants*. Paris: Gaillmard/Seuil.

Shiller, R. J. (2003). *The New Financial Order*. Princeton, NJ: Princeton University Press.

Sini, C. (2012, 14 September). La vita catturata dentro un segno? *Il Manifesto*, 10.

Stiglitz, J. (2004). *The roaring nineties: A new history of the world's most prosperous decade*. New York: W. W. Norton.

Stiglitz, J. (2007, August). *America's Day of Reckoning*. Retrieved from http://www.project-syndicate.org/commentary/stiglitz90

Stockhammer, E. (2010). Income distribution, the finance-dominated accumulation regime and the present crisis. In S. Dullien, E. Hein, A. Truger, & T. van Treeck (Eds.), *The world economy in crisis: The return of Keynesianism?* (pp. 63–85). Marburg: Metropolis.

Vercellone, C. (2007). From Formal Subsumption to General Intellect: Elements for a Marxist Reading of the Thesis of Cognitive Capitalism. *Historical Materialism, 15*(1), 13–36.

Wolff, E. (2009). *Recent trends in household wealth in the United States. Rising debt and the middle class squeeze—An update to 2007*. Working Paper 589, Levy Economics Institute.

Wright, S. (2008, 7–9 November). *Revolution from above? Money and Class composition in Italian operaismo*. Presented at the 5th annual Historical Materialism Conference, School of Oriental and African Studies, London.

Zanini, A. (2006). Invarianza neoliberale. In S. Chignola (Ed.), *Governare la vita. Un seminario sui Corsi di Michel Foucault al Collège de France (1977–1979)* (pp. 117–152). Verona: Ombre corte.

Zanini, A. (2010). *L'ordine del discorso economico*. Verona: Ombre corte.

NOTES

1. See, for example, Thomas Palley, *Financialization: What It Is and Why It Matters*, The Levy Economic Institute of Bard College, Working Paper No. 525, December 2007.
2. As a preliminary definition, we might say that an accumulation regime delineates a long-term growth model. This term, introduced by the scholars of the so-called French Regulation School, refers to the set of regularities that insure a general and relatively coherent progression in the accumulation of capital (Boyer, 2002). In the UK, the main contribution to the Regulation Approach has been provided by Bob Jessop: "The key concepts initially offered by the Parisian Regulationists were 'regime of accumulation' and 'mode of regulation'. An accumulation regime is defined as a particular combination of production and consumption which can be reproduced over time despite conflictual tendencies; and a mode of regulation comprises an institutional *ensemble* and complex of norms which can secure capitalist reproduction *pro tempore* despite the antagonistic character of capitalist social relations" (Jessop, 1990, p. 308).
3. The choice of referring to Foucauldian categories depends first of all on the desire to re-elaborate one of the directions traced by the journal *Primo Maggio* workgroup on money. We refer in particular to a passage where Christian Marazzi stresses how the critique of the political economy needed to hybridize its toolkit with the critique of power developed by Foucault. As Marazzi writes: "It is simple to see the simultaneous presence of the knowledge-power relation and the exchange-wealth relation" (Marazzi, 1977–1978, p. 34—our translation). About the *Primo Maggio* workgroup on money, the English reader can refer to Wright (2008) and to Lucarelli (2014).
4. It is important to recall the vertical motion in which Foucault's thought was kept during the second half of the 1970s, even though in the context of the present work our limited aim is to briefly present Foucault's argument in order to highlight a historical point and a novel theoretical articulation.
5. In other words, life became a specific target of political power and, as a consequence, their relationship was configured as *intrinsic*. To put it differently: neither scientific reductionism nor cultural determinism can properly represent the new internal and qualitative connection between life and politics. As Foucault famously stated: "For millennia, man remained what he was for Aristotle: a living animal with the additional capacity for political existence; modern man is an animal whose politics calls his existence as a living being into question" (1978, p. 143).
6. There is, of course, also a substantial invariance: it is nothing else than the utter *violence* which, according to Marx, characterizes—in different ways—both primitive accumulation and the 'normal' functioning of labor markets.
7. This group of German economists, also known as the Freiburg School of political economy, includes Walter Eucken, Franz Bohm, Müller-Armack, Wilhelm Ropke, and, in general, those who were involved in the journal *Ordo* (founded in 1936) and later became advisors of Chancellor Ludwig Ehrard. The latter, in 1948, declared that "the priorities of Germany during the reconstruction period would be the removal of price controls, and the setting of clear boundaries between individuals and the state. Erhard was aiming not only to differentiate the new Germany from the National Socialist state of the recent past; this reconstitution of state powers also reflected the challenge facing the new German state, which could draw upon neither historical rights nor the continuity of its juridical institutions as bases for its own legitimacy. What instead emerged was a performative basis for legitimacy, where the economic freedom of citizens can in itself constitute the basis for political legitimacy" (Flew, 2012, p. 53).

8. With regard to our contemporary situation, Wendy Brown (2006) has poignantly underlined, as a consequence of this radically interventionist governmentality, the silent process of de-democratisation that has been under way for decades. As she writes: "Neo-liberalism casts the political and social spheres both as appropriately dominated by market concerns and as themselves organised by market rationality [...] The state itself must construct and construe itself in market terms, as well as develop policies and promulgate a political culture that figures citizens exhaustively as rational economic actors in every sphere of life" (Brown, 2006, p. 694).
9. Thomas Lemke (2001) has correctly noted how, from this perspective, it is possible to read the process of so-called withdrawal of the state as a governmental technique.
10. This is why we are sceptical toward Michael Hardt and Antonio Negri's claim that the current phase of capitalist development is defined by a radical separation between *biopower* (the parasitical apparatus through which capital ensures exploitation) and *biopolitical production* (the level at which the potentiality of social cooperation is autonomously and fully actualized). In the authors' view (see, for example, Hardt & Negri, 2004, pp. 94–95), biopolitical production names the creative side of social ontology and is conceived of as an extension of class struggle in the Post-Fordist era of capitalist development. Conversely, biopower is the purely exploitative element that performs a sort of domination without social guidance. Hardt and Negri concede that in the first biopolitical period (liberalism) the rule of capital was managerially progressive (although absolutely damaging and finally parasitical). However, with the shift from Fordism to post-Fordism (neoliberalism) the new level of autonomy gained by social cooperation makes the rule of capital *completely* parasitical, without any positive role whatsoever. On the contrary, our analysis of neoliberal financialization assumes the simultaneous presence—with regard to subjective behaviours—of violent coercion, passive acceptance, and enthusiast support. It seems to us that a deep ambivalence pervades financial markets. Moreover, the sharp opposition between biopolitics and biopower is not to be found in Foucault's late-1970s lectures. Although we find extremely interesting Judith Revel's work on Foucauldian sources, it is difficult for us to deny what Michel Senellart (2012) has accurately remarked, namely that Foucault employs the concepts of biopolitics and biopower basically as synonymous.
11. On the financialization of food, see Leonardi (2013).
12. The best critical definition of a derivative is to be found in Brian Holmes: "The idea was that all risks, including collective ones, should be made into sellable products, formatted for the market by private actors in search of a profit. Yet although it is sellable, the derivative cannot be understood as an ordinary commodity of the industrial era. Marx described the commodity as that product of human labour whose exchange-value, seemingly animated with a life of its own, acts to render invisible the social relations that produced it. Derivatives, however, have nothing directly to do with production; instead they are conceived to manage the environmental risks that weigh on the future of speculative activity. In this sense they are *meta-commodities* that govern the unfolding of the contemporary economic model" (2010, p. 230).
13. Our perspective is here very similar to what Italian sociologist Luigi Pellizzoni refers to as *governing through disorder*: "Uncertainty [in neoliberalism] is seen no more as a circumscribed situation on which to build a few strategic decisions, but as an empowering everyday condition ... Contingency means lack of limits rather than lack of order. Better: disorder, as a positive, enabling systems condition, can be handled by carving out provisional room for purposeful *manouvre*. The more unstable the world, the more manageable" (2011, p. 797).

We prefer the term *instability* over *disorder* because it more clearly indicates the constant but differentiated alternation of ordered and disordered states as the specific terrain upon which contemporary neoliberal governmentality deploys itself.

14. It is worth noting that such Keynesianism had already been weakened by President Nixon's declaration of the dollar/gold inconvertibility in 1971.
15. While there is substantial evidence supporting this argument for the US, the evidence on European economies has always been much thinner. See Stockhammer (2010).
16. This brilliant expression is Michel Aglietta's (2007). Aglietta argues that the system shifts from one bubble to the next because it is not equipped with any internal brakes. Even when prices have completely lost any relation with fundamental value, the short-term logic prevails. Fund managers, intermediaries, and business managers have built a mechanism of remuneration and incentives that is consistent with this logic. So the next bubble is caused exactly by the same financial organization that caused the previous in the first place!
17. Although we agree with Maurizio Lazzarato (2013) that there are frequent situations in which the Foucauldian self-entrepreneur gets transfigured into an endlessly indebted man, we would also like to note that, in strictly logical terms, the indebted man can not represent a generalized social figure. In fact, when there is a debt there must also be a corresponding credit. It seems to us that the common ground upon which both debtors and creditors become eminently governable subjects is provided by the wealth-effect, conceived of as a neoliberal financial device.
18. It is worth noting that the disinvestment in fiscal capital that freed liquidity from productive processes should be taken into account. This liquidity was used to increase the market value of capital: "If in addition to the increase in liquidity—due to the reduction of investments in fixed capital—we consider the increase of business debt to the banking system, then we can understand why the financialization of economy (payment of dividends, interests, Merger & Acquisitions, the buyback of already exposed stocks) was an extraordinary transfer of wealth to the class of stock investors and to those managers who were responsible for financialization processes" (Marazzi, 2007, p. 79—our translation).
19. It is important to recall that wage deflation expresses in the clearest way the process of devaluation of living labour, which has so far accompanied the diffusion of financial governmentality.
20. As Marazzi (2010) notes, the profound crisis we are experiencing was partially triggered by the declassification of titles emitted on credit by rating agencies in August 2007, just a year after the inversion of the business cycle!
21. A convincing critique—among others—of BCE's independence is formulated by Paul De Grauwe (2011). The weaknesses affecting a Central Bank that does not act as a lender of last resort have been accurately described by Marcello De Cecco (1999).

CHAPTER SIX

The Embers OF Truth IN THE Ashes OF Finance[1]

CAMPBELL JONES

To register only the suffering that so demonstrably follows the process of financialisation and its most recent crisis would run the risk of underplaying the radically transformative possibilities that arise in the wake of finance ascendant. This is certainly the case in relation to public education, in the context of a breach of many of the previously existing boundaries within educational institutions and of the spaces between education and its publics. This breach has been opened in significant part by financialisation, and above all by the new and increasingly extensive forms of circulation and association that accompany the rise of finance in the economy, politics, and culture.

If finance is something that everyone must learn today even if only to learn disobedience, finance is also opening up immense new spaces in common and with this new struggle over these commons. These spaces call into question a number of divisions, separations, and particularisms within the university: first of all the division of the disciplines, but also the division between the university and its outside and divisions outside the university. Equally, the universalising tendencies of finance, even if in their present form are merely 'abstract universals,' they invite new forms of universalism premised on but simultaneously exceeding the very real differences between our bodies.

Much could be said about the difficulties that finance presents for the idea of the public. Indeed, the financial crisis of 2008 precipitated a series of radical revisions and withdrawals resulting in waves of dispossessions of public obligations justified as necessary austerity in a time of crisis and an increasingly confident belligerence on the part of business elites who assert with moral, if not religious, fervour the righteousness of their path and the justifiability of the suffering of others. In a way none of this is new, as the history of austerity demonstrates (see Blyth, 2013). But the fact that finance capital is so deeply implicated in the creation and maintenance of avoidable suffering has led many to lament, with good reason. Of course fortunes can and have been made in times of crisis, but there is also less than fine news in the reality today of widespread rent gouging; the evisceration of livelihoods; the racialised impact of exclusion; the catastrophic and irreversible environmental decisions made today for financial reasons; the continued compromise of the livelihoods of youth, ever-expanding cycles of debt that extend indenture into the foreseeable future, effectively unrestrained and rampant banking, insurance, and real estate sectors; and a smirking, callous self-justified elite unwilling to enter into serious deliberation about its actions and their consequences (for detail see Engelen et al., 2011; Lapavitsas, 2012).

Much could also be said about the sorry state of public education in the face of finance, and much of it prepares for sobering reading. The financial transformations it has entailed have been well documented, in a process that goes well beyond rising fees, student debt, and the imposition of market logic, extending to a thorough retooling of the university in financial terms and with this a transformation of the relationship between the university and its publics (McGettigan, 2013). There now exists an oppressively comprehensive critical catalogue of the university ruined beyond recognition, with economic machinations, and above all finance explicitly or implicitly central to a widely sung lament. One critic, for instance, writes that the impact of neoliberal market fundamentalism has weakened if not nearly destroyed those institutions that enable the production of a formative culture in which individuals learn to think critically, imagine other ways of being and doing, and connect their personal troubles with public concerns. Matters of justice, ethics, and equality have once again been exiled to the margins of politics. Never has this assault on the democratic polity been more obvious, if not more dangerous, than at the current moment, when a battle is being waged under the rubric of neoliberal austerity measures on the autonomy of academic labour, the classroom as a site of critical pedagogy, the rights of students to high quality education, the democratic vitality of the university as a public sphere and the role played by the liberal arts and humanities in fostering an educational culture that is about the practice of freedom and mutual empowerment (Giroux, 2011, pp. 145–146).

I have dealt with some of these issues before, in terms of the place of finance in the university, the impact of student debt, rankings and ratings agencies, and the implications of the current state of the publishing industry (Jones, 2014). With this move of finance into the university the central and probably most troubling dynamic is not that this happens but that it goes unnoticed. It goes unnoticed because finance transforms not only economic reality but also the ways in which that reality is experienced. Finance involves a financialisation of the senses that transforms the capacities for seeing, reasoning and judgement. In this process of financialisation in which the concepts, techniques, and metaphors of finance come to increasingly order life, finance goes unseen and unregistered as it becomes the basis for seeing and registering what is.

Being occupied with tracking financialisation and its devastation of what was previously imagined as the university, it is possible to lose sight of the fact that many of the ways out of this situation are already right here in our midst. I propose here that what is so clearly the name of a problem—that is, finance—is also the grounds for momentous upheavals that invite radically different progressive visions of the future of public education. At the same time, these prospects are not restricted to the university. Indeed, the cultures of circulation and modes of association within finance exceed containment and forge new interconnections and relations between bodies both inside and outside the university. Throughout this chapter I will seek to show that especially after finance, bodies are nowhere near so separate or distinct as is often thought.

What is therefore needed is not another description in ever more detail of the incomprehensibly miserable pit into which we are led by finance. A barely legible logic of finance certainly is putting in place a world for which we must not fail to account. To describe this reality is a vital part in accounting for what Alain Badiou (2005) calls the 'situation.' Badiou highlights, however, that restricting oneself to an account of the situation in however rigorous a fashion recounts the situation as it is already counted. Although this might be the starting point for any action, what is required above all is an account of what is not accounted for in a situation. Those elements that barely appear within any situation, these elements that 'inexist' or only have a minimal capacity of appearing (Badiou, 2009), can be found in the situation, at its edge or limit, and because they are neither entirely inside nor outside they have the capacity to puncture a hole in the situation. From a description of the state of the situation we can attain knowledge about that situation. This is a vital first step. But from what inexists in the situation, in the rubble or ashes typically counted as nothing, it is also possible to discern truths that can set the situation alight.

This chapter therefore seeks to indicate specific immanent possibilities for public education at the present moment out of finance both within the university and outside it, paying particular attention to the logics of division, separation, and particularism. The point is to ask what can arise out of what is, and as such can be neither naively utopian nor nostalgic for what in the university never existed.

I will need to make some theoretical provisions, although it should be stressed that my motivation here is practical and is grounded in the concrete material conditions that are directly or indirectly encountered. Finance reshuffles the theoretical and the practical, insofar as it is both a form of knowledge that is monumentally abstract and technical and also has the most palpable physical manifestation as is evident in the historically unprecedented capacity it has for modification of nature and the mobilisation of productive effort. Thus it is important to recall Max Haiven's important injunction that finance requires undertaking a considerable act of 'theoretical heavy lifting' (2011, p. 118).

Clearly this theoretical heavy lifting will not take place in a single clean and jerk. What is presented here draws on the work of many others and in detail on the work of Randy Martin. I seek to account for the place in finance of logics of division, separation, and particularism and at the same time how these unravel in the face of finance, both in the public and in public higher education. This work intersects with my parallel work on the place in finance of trading on difference, a dynamic that is clearly identifiable in finance in the identification and exploitation of the arbitrage opportunities that result from existing or manufactured pricing differentials at the intersection of two or more markets (Jones, 2015). I will therefore leave some of the technical elements of arbitrage and further elaboration of separation and difference aside. I begin by identifying the embers before turning to the ashes and then returning to the new publics and new public educations that are summoned by finance in spite of itself.

EMBERS

The most significant effort to think through the interwoven social, cultural, and political consequences of finance appears in the work of Randy Martin. His books on finance have scrutinised in turn the financialisation of daily life (Martin, 2002a), the application of derivative logic and risk management to warfare (Martin, 2007), the rendering of administrative labour under finance in the university (Martin, 2011b), and the forms and prospects of knowledge after finance (Martin, forthcoming). In doing so Martin has elaborated a nuanced yet biting analysis of the meaning and consequences of what he later calls the "social logic of the derivative" (Martin, 2012; 2013; 2014; forthcoming).

It is clear that finance is something that affects us all today. This was noticed with the most recent financial crisis, but is even more present in the everyday life of finance (see Martin, 2002a). This can be seen in the impact of finance on economic lives, from the real-estate market to the precaritisation of work but above all in a financial hegemony that is exercised well beyond the financial sector (see Duménil & Lévy, 2011; Lapavitsas, 2013). In this process of the financialisation of the economy, "finance escapes from particular banking sites and institutions to become a general aspect of commercial production and transaction"

(Martin, 2011b, p. 14). Finance ranges far and wide across the economy. "Finance will not return to its vault, its promiscuity ranges from rarified precincts of expertise to the most quotidian quarters" (Martin, 2010b, p. 428).

Martin's work articulates a broad process of the drift of finance, in which not simply the economic but a range of practices previously considered outside of economy come to be ordered according to finance. This and related work (see, for instance, Baucom, 2005; de Goede, 2005) demonstrate how financial logics draw from and spread often imperceptibly into a range of other practices and modes of interpretation. They are imperceptible precisely because, as I have intimated, financialisation involves above all a financialisation of the senses, in which not only the world but the ways in which the world is registered in terms of finance. This is because, as Martin puts it, financialisation stands "simultaneously as subject and object of analysis—something to be explained and a way of making sense out of what is going on around us" (2002a, p. 8).

Admitting the reality of this process—that is, acknowledging that subjects as much as objects are transformed in their everyday practices of producing, living and imagining—is a vital step toward understanding the very real transformations in the categories of thought that have been and are still underway today. Nevertheless, noticing a social dynamic that plays out behind the back of others always runs the risk that the assumed completeness of this process might overshadow the equally real emancipatory possibilities that are contained within that process. The risk of overstating the effectiveness and above all the consistency of ideology continues to dog the social sciences. There is always the risk that an invisible process taken to shape consciousnesses in a way that goes unchallenged and is, hence, one-sided, always seeming to work out in the interests of the already dominant.

What this means for social analysis is that there are processes that are not visible to social actors but that these processes are not one-sided in either the sense that their domination is complete or that their result is always domination. To formalise, following Jacques Lacan: we are speaking beings that exist in the symbolic order, but that being is not one of simple victimhood. Lacan's maxim "the big Other does not exist" means precisely that, yes, we live in ideology but also that ideology is incomplete, inconsistent, fractured, broken, pathetic. Too often social critics seek to explain the defeats of the small by imagining that the weak have been defeated because of the immense powers of ideological persuasion of the dominant. In what could be called a sycophancy of the dominant, elites are imagined to wield a mighty power of ideological command. The thing is that, fortunately, both ideology and its victims often operate otherwise than imagined.

Such a formalisation might help to clarify Martin's subtle ongoing effort to expose both the intricate web of ideological effort behind finance and, even more importantly, the way that even at what today appears its zenith, finance brings with it its own gravediggers. In this sense Martin is classically grounded in the critique of political economy when he emphasises "the other that capitalism produces in its midst" (Martin, 2002b, p. xx) and when he stresses that "capital can never sleep in the bed it makes" (Martin, 2010c, p. 191).

Here Martin builds on the emphasis that Marx places on the fact that with capitalism proper, "not only do we have here an increase in the productive power of the individual, by means of co-operation, but the creation of a new productive power, which is intrinsically a collective one" (Marx, 1867, p. 443). While Marx is in this context faithful to the classical tradition of Smith and others in emphasising the constant search by capital for increased productivity of labour, Martin follows Marx's account of socialisation as one of the key practical measures to achieve this increased productivity, alongside yet beyond extension of the working day, intensification of labour, and the use of technology (see also Martin, 2002b; 2010c). He therefore stresses the way that "the incessant search for new avenues of accumulation forces human activity into productive interdependence" (Martin, 2010c, p. 188).

Under finance, this socialisation considerably exceeds the concentration of workers "working together, at the same time, or in one place" that is the starting point of the account of cooperation that appears in chapter 13 of volume 1 of *Capital* (Marx, 1967, p. 439). Ranging more broadly across Marx's work (see Martin, 2002b) makes it possible to see how finance much more profoundly creates new modes of association and relations of mutual indebtedness. Capitalism is "a beast that forces people into complex association and feeds on the novelties of social life they yield" (Martin, 2011a, p. 157). Thus financialisation is a two-sided process: "Financialization then, is ultimately not simply more finance everywhere, but also more socialization, more interdependence, more mutual debt" (Martin, 2014, p. 197). Martin insists that "indeed finance persistently cuts the social fabric, sundering connections and dividing populations and resources unequally. But it also reassembles, bundles, and imposes interdependence, and shared predicaments amongst what were once disparate situations and circumstances" (Martin, forthcoming).

Hence the emergence of an association of producers at the heart of the relentless search for relative surplus value that finance mobilises in radical new directions. Pricing in order to coordinate and work the apparently incommensurable into new productive combinations, finance operates not only a conspiracy of capital through the stock, bond, and futures markets but moreover brings into its orbit a vast network of interconnections both present and future. As Martin argues, "Financial operations have made far-flung values commensurable in the global economy as well as in the ordering of our lives, where the connections between us are at once deeper and more volatile, distant and mutually entangled" (2011b, p. xii). Thus the importance of Martin's emphasis on the aspect of finance that is so often underplayed, but is an equally real part of the work of finance: "The world we live in is more interdependent than ever, even if the contributions of many considered too poor, marginal, or difficult are disavowed, and denied a claim on available resources. Further, our world is saturated with languages of mutual indebtedness to an unprecedented degree" (forthcoming).

Being a modality of capital, finance must also divide, separate, particularise. Thus these new relations of trust-based indebtedness encounter their insurmountable limit of participation that is concomitant with an economy in which a few live off the labour of others. As Martin explains, capital "generates an expertise it cannot abide" (2009b, p. 345) while at the same time it must partition "expertise" in order to denigrate shared or collective intelligence and mastery (see Martin, forthcoming; Daellenbach, 2015). Thus the double bind that finance faces as it "picks up the potent thrust of mutual association that capital has always depended on but cannot abide" (Martin, 2009a, p. 109). This unendurable limit appears in symbolic non-disclosure, in the fact that the relations of interdependence on which finance feeds are unsymbolisable in the immediate terms of finance while they remain the matter that finance constantly seeks to represent in order to harvest. Thus the crucial importance of the efforts of Martin to track "the powers of incorporation and interdependence that finance bears but does not disclose" (2012, p. 63).

Among so many other merits, what is perhaps most important in Martin's work on finance is his identification of the real possibilities that arise out of finance and financial crisis. As he asks of the massive public interventions following the crisis: "If the norms that underwrite economy no longer compel, what else is brewing in our midst?" (2013, p. 84). Martin draws to hand a practical politics that returns to centre stage questions about the production and distribution of common wealth. The ongoing Global Financial Bailout is one thing, but it exposes another reality: "When the news arrives that there is $700 billion of social wealth that can be used to save the day, a very different vigilance rears its head" (Martin, 2010b, p. 422). In such a context "trillions of dollars could suddenly be considered up for grabs, and the excesses of an age could be redeployed as the source of a very tangible abundance" (Martin, 2010c, p. 193).

Martin thus sets the stage for thinking the politics of our age in a different key, departing from the positions of the dominant and also from so many critical imaginings of what alternatives might look like and how they might be expressed. This is a concrete politics grounded in the prospects opened by finance. "The money is there, the mutuality exists, the means to make what is desired are at hand—this is the new political imaginary that derivatives potentially augur" (Martin, forthcoming). This is both concrete economic possibility but also the nascent recognition of desire on the part of various publics: "The present regime of finance has aggregated great sums of wealth, has produced a popular utterance of trillions wasted without use or reference, accountability or governance, which could be said to yield both a desire and a prospect for excess well put" (Martin, 2010a, p. 362). Rather than calling for minor local responses or cancelling particular debts, Martin calls for "a consideration of what it means to be able to suddenly muster trillions of dollars and to undertake a public deliberation over what might be done with a social surplus that was never acknowledged as such to be one" (2014, p. 207).

ASHES

Martin's analysis presents important ways of rethinking the possibilities for new public spaces and for demands on the common wealth. With respect to public education it presents direct possibilities regarding the question of funding and ways of formulating the demand for public education. This is certainly one battle to be fought. But while a fully funded public education system with universal access is an immanent possibility and a practical demand in the light of current social wealth, it does not go even nearly far enough. The present forms of division, separation, and particularism that characterise public higher education are themselves radically destabilised by the new forms of circulation and association that are otherwise channelled elsewhere by finance. It is not just the material existence of institutions such as the universities that is at stake, as if continuation in whatever debased form is a good in itself. It is not just that public education needs to be preserved but that there is a need to think very carefully about the relations between bodies therein and the dynamics of their circulation.

Central to this dynamic is the ongoing dialectic of association and dissociation that Martin's analysis of finance so importantly clarifies. The new forms of circulation and association and relations of interconnection and mutual indebtedness call into question a number of assumed divisions and separations both within the university and the public and their relation to one another. The results of this exceed the bounds of the otherwise vital analysis of the institution of public education outlined by Martin (1999; 2011a; 2011b). Above all it calls for reconsideration of the generally assumed notions of division and separation that institutions of public education have inherited from classical liberal political thought and classical political economy. If finance is today recoding the relations presumed of capital, labour, and the public, then, equally, classical conceptions of division and separation, which have always been contested, are again threatened with extinction.

In classical liberal political thought John Locke is indispensable not only for the place that, as Etienne Balibar (2013) shows, he played in the elaboration of the idea of individual consciousness. Equally important is Locke's understanding of the dynamics of distinction and separation, which operate in his thought on registers that are at once epistemological, ontological, political, and moral. While these are firmly embedded in the mercantile, financial, political, and global context in which he was writing, at the same time they consolidate and refine the ideology of his time and propels it forward into a great project of division and separation that runs through subsequent history to the present day. While documentation of this project and its contradictions is ongoing, the following brief specifications regarding Locke might provide some points of orientation.

Regarding knowledge and human understanding, Locke specifies the importance that ideas "which are, as it were, pictures of things" be "clear and distinct," which involves stressing the importance that we "keep things distinct that in themselves are different" (1690a, pp, 329, 327). The faculties of knowing are for him also distinct, holding as he does that knowledge of things, knowledge of action and the use of signs for attaining knowledge and conveying it to others, are "toto cœo different," they are "wholly separate and distinct from one another" (Locke, 1690a, p. 635). The same logic of separation is equally the grounds of Locke's defence of the idea that it is the labour of each distinct and separate individual that "put a distinction between them and common" (Locke, 1690b, p. 288). Again, we find this dynamic of division in the renowned distinction and separation of the legislative and executive functions of government stressed by Locke and taken up in the constitution of the United States (Locke, 1690b, chap. 12). Such separation of spheres equally entitles the same Locke to criticise what he calls "slavery" while receiving dividends from his shareholding in the Royal African Company (see Losurdo, 2011). It also entitles Locke's proposals for the solution to poverty by keeping the poor away from "superfluous brandy shops and unnecessary alehouses" and the separation of children from their parents from the age of three so that children will "from their infancy be inured to work" (1697, pp. 447, 453).

Freedom in this liberal tradition means freedom from contagion, that is to say, freedom means distinction and separation, a retreat into the particularities of the consciousness of the individual, the thing that is for Locke each person's own most possession. Locke seeks to find ontological security for his principle of individuation, his *principium individuationis*, in the nature of being itself. The grounds of this principle "is existence itself, which determines a being of any sort to a particular time and place incommunicable to two beings of the same kind" (1690a, p. 297). This separation of bodies is taken as at once naturally grounded in being, but moreover to issue ultimately from God. Division and separation are thus, for Locke, doubly beyond reproach, grounded in reality and divine providence.

In the classical political economy of the eighteenth century such principles of division and separation are further credited with being the basis of social progress through productivity and expansion of the common wealth. Adam Smith is clear about the stultifying effects of divisions between people and the way that class stratifications arise from the most minimal differences in ability or character (see, for instance, Smith, 1776a, p. 120; 1776b, p. 368). Division is for Smith a necessary evil in the face of progress, for which the solution is a healthy dose of Christian morality and good character (Smith, 1759). Above all Smith discovers in the division of labour the answer to the alchemists' dream of drawing out the bright from the dull, which in economic terms manifests itself in the "improvement of the productive powers of labour" (Smith, 1776a, p. 109).

Romantic concerns about division and separation that echo through the nineteenth century are strictly continuous with Smith and others of his stamp, even if they lack his spirit of resignation. In the middle of the nineteenth century John Ruskin would write that with the division of labour "it is not, truly speaking, the labour that is divided; but the men:—Divided into mere segments of men—broken into fragments and crumbs of life; so that all the little intelligence that is left in a man is not enough to make a pin, or a nail, but exhausts itself in making the point of a pin or the head of a nail" (1853, p. 43).

Romantic refusal of division and separation begs the question of the existence of such a community of men and the question of to whom such community was available. Most important, this romantic critique fails to account for the concrete social practices by which unity and division are produced and eroded. These practices are brought to centre stage by focusing on the new forms of circulation and association arising in the political economy in general and finance in particular. The point is that association is too often assumed to be present but is ascribed a role as secondary or supplementary to division. Alternatively it is given a mystical presence in the form of an invisible hand that inexplicably integrates what has been separated.

Such conceptual contortions persist when ideas regarding the division of society and labour are imported directly into the disciplinary architecture of the modern university and its division into disciplines. Such practical political and economic entailments frame the rise of the modern German university system, most famously associated with Wilhelm von Humboldt. In the preface to his *Groundwork of the Metaphysic of Morals*, published in 1785, just nine years after the *Wealth of Nations*, Immanuel Kant writes:

> All trades, crafts and arts have gained by the division of labor, namely when one person does not do everything but each limits himself to a certain task that differs markedly from others in the way it is to be handled, so as to be able to perform it most perfectly and with greater facility. Where work is not so differentiated and divided, where everyone is a jack-of-all-trades, there trades remain in the greatest barbarism. (1785, p. 44)

The shallow optimism found in Kant reproduces, almost word for word, the ideology of the rising European capitalist class of his time. It is also mirrored in his later framing of the division of the disciplines in *The Conflict of the Faculties*, drafted in the decade following Groundwork and ultimately published in 1798. Here we read:

> Whoever it was that first hit on the notion of a university and proposed that a public institution of this kind be established, it was not a bad idea to handle the entire content of

> learning (really, the thinkers devoted to it) by mass production, so to speak—by a division of labor, so that for every branch of the sciences would be a public teacher or professor appointed as its trustee, and all of these together would form a kind of learned community called a university (or higher school). (Kant, 1798, p. 23)

In Kant we find a mystification of both the origins of division but equally and more importantly of the mechanism by which the faculties so separated will then form a learned community. The agent of this unification is as invisible and ineffable in Kant as it is in Smith, but also is equally chaotic and unreliable. This learned community would either already exist or somehow emerge, based in a shared connection to what Kant calls the "lower faculty," that is, philosophy, but this presupposed universal interest in admission or even interest in this faculty is presumed, in direct contradiction with the historical record of the fate of philosophy, despite the most strenuous efforts toward domestication.

With finance in view, it can be seen that division and separation have key antecedents arising from the realities of finance and financial calculation. It should be recalled that the division of labour was always a question of finance. In 1832 Charles Babbage clarified and elaborated the financial reasoning as to why it is that manufacturers seek in practice to divide labour. In an astute reading of Babbage's account of the differential pricing of labour, Harry Braverman (1974) emphasizes how the division of labour is motivated by differentiation of the functions of labour in order that the purchaser of labour (i.e., the capitalist) pays for no more than the minimum level of skill required for the completion of one fragment of the total work to be performed. What thus appears with remarkable clarity in Babbage is an emphasis on how the division of labour was ultimately a financial question relating to the differential cost of different forms of labour (see Babbage, 1832, chap. 19). The point is that finance is always a matter of the pure differential between the capacities of bodies (this point is elaborated in Jones, 2015).

If economic thought is a historical condition of thought and its institutions, then today we see finance increasingly ordering the institutions of public education. The logic of division and separation is central to finance, resting at the heart of the price mechanism but moreover at the base of the possibility of arbitrage opportunities. In finance this goes well beyond the basic capitalist dynamics of product differentiation and the articulation of the 'unique selling proposition' of anything actually or potentially for sale. Recall, following Martin, how finance moves between difference and association, even if difference can be celebrated while association is simultaneously the necessary but unacknowledged condition of finance.

Finance is both the condition of separation and the prospect for its overcoming. Finance is not restricted to one domain, and its spread takes at least the appearance of universal scale. Thus in the institutions of public learning and above all in the university, one can see how finance has displayed a displacement of boundaries that potentially exceeds the spread of any other object of analysis. Even where not explicitly represented, finance establishes itself as the condition of representation in the university, whether in the practicalities of the funding of science and engineering or in the spread of techniques and notions of risk and leverage that are today taken up as grounding presuppositions of science and knowledge as such.

As Martin emphasizes, though, division is only one side of the story. The disciplines, even when they represent finance, do so in astonishing separation from one another, remaining separate and distinct even when seeking to arbitrage advantages across their differences. Finance here figures as a mode of intellectual sectarianism even while at the very same moment it constitutes new modes of association by infiltration. Hence the importance of reclaiming notions such as circulation and association from finance, even as the current disciplinary institution of the university is so often designed to sever circulation and association. Finance as ground offers exactly this prospect, which follows from the fact that, as Martin puts it, the dynamics of finance "roam through rooms that once held different knowledge forms apart from one another" (2009a, p. 111).

As the terminal decline of capital continues its long march and everything that is imaginable is done to make it seem to have a semblance of sense, our challenges are clearly political, but they are also problems of knowledge and are figured in the divisions that cut through the university as institution and prospect. These divisions are structural between and within the parties to discipline. Finance stands at the end of the disciplines and has concrete potential for those with the courage to simultaneously respect what is distinct in disciplinary areas but also to register the costs of separation. This rests in the recognition that, as Martin writes, "The means to craft education otherwise through critical interdisciplinary initiatives are already at hand" (2011a, p. 162). This is so because financialisation "joins and travels through interdisciplinary worlds. Its intellectual force permits a fuller circulation of critical thought and engagement" (Martin, 2009a, p. 108). Beyond an interdisciplinarity that might figure as a derivative of disciplines already established, finance also promises, even as it cannot abide it, forms of association outside anything recognisable as discipline as such.

PUBLICS

What presents itself as the future does not come from a distant future but from the immediate present and our action upon its inconsistencies. There should be no sense of anything utopian in the effort to seize from our situation a quite different future than what is widely presented. The future of public education and the public can be found neither by stabilising what apparently is nor in abstractly dreaming of a new golden age. New relations between bodies are at hand in the university and outside it and the question is how these new relations will become manifest.

It should be stressed that new forms of association and reconfiguration of public education are not matters of education alone. Although one of the nodes in this picture relates to education, to focus on education alone or education within institutions such as the university is again to focus only on one moment. To think that education alone will resolve everything is to fall prey to idealism, the idealism of imagining that the whole world in the end boils down to ideas. At first it might seem obvious that the great temptation of those sequestered within institutions of higher learning would be toward idealism. This is however only a contingent articulation, based on the distinction and separation of intellectual labour from other forms of labour.

The real world of finance renders untenable any notion of an intellectuality emanating from the university that might one day run into a blunt unthinking world of practice. Quite the contrary, finance is already run through with theoretical premises, as the detailed accounts of, for example, Hirokazu Miyazaki make clear. In his ethnographic work Miyazaki seeks to expose "the complexities, intricacies and subtleties of thinking afforded by the sensibilities of arbitrage" (2013, p. 8), emphasising the fact that "many traders (and other financial market professionals) are not simply decision makers but also thinking subjects engaged in dialogue with a variety of broader intellectual debates and projects" (p. 6).

Not only is the idea that education or any educational institution is ostensibly separated from the real world invalidated by finance, so too are so many facile carvings up in which the university somehow stands on the side of theory while the world of practical reality awaits it on the outside. As Martin puts it, "Contemporary finance would seem to be the influence-minded academic's dream, a world where theory is practice, where abstract mathematical modeling that garners professional respect gains widespread application" (2010b, p. 420). The lesson to be taken from this is that finance is so profoundly theoretical that the forms of knowledge circulating in the university are often today less theoretically astute than the abstractions of finance and thus with respect to theory the university has been caught napping by the tortoise that is finance. When the university is run through with finance, a call is issued for the university to turn not to the immediacy of the world but to the way that one particular set of theoretical commitments are in the course of remaking the world—and potentially ending it.

It should also be known that the prospect of the end of the disciplines does not result in vagueness, indeterminacy or indistinction between knowledge forms and claims. If there is a great virtue of training in a discipline then it is the mastery of the skills and embrace of the presuppositions of one particular domain. While mastery can be a defence again dilettantism it equally produces the amateurism that comes with ignorance of what is going on elsewhere. What is at stake here is the current situation of intellectual sectarianism. What is called to account by new forms of association and circulation are "those who wish to bury their heads in stale sand, thereby complacently and comfortably ignoring momentous intellectual upheavals going on all around them outside of their scholarly zones of specialisation" (Johnston, 2013, p. 7).

At stake is a form of specialisation that has established itself both within and outside the university, which takes reality to be partitioned in such a way that it offers itself differentially to the gaze of observers who can pick up those chunks of it that are most immediately amenable to them. Thus, as Susan Buck-Morss notes,

> When the separate aspects of history are treated in disciplinary isolation, counterevidence is pushed to the margins as irrelevant. The greater the specialization of knowledge, the more advanced the level of research, the longer and more venerable the scholarly tradition, the easier it is to ignore discordant facts. It should be noted that specialization and isolation are also a danger for those new disciplines such as African American studies, or new fields such as diaspora studies, that were established precisely to remedy the situation. Disciplinary boundaries allow counterevidence to belong to someone else's story. (2009, p. 22)

A good part of the social sciences and the humanities have sought to defend themselves by building a thick layer of insulation between themselves and a hostile outside in which unknown practices and forms of knowledge circulate in lands of mystery. In the name of the disciplines questions such as 'is it sociology?' or 'is it philosophy?' are taken to trump questions of the reality that the discourse evokes or its veridical and moral grounds. Internally within each particular discipline, enclaves have formed that each justifies its increasingly narrow focus by the unexplained and unexamined claim that 'this paper will take such and such a perspective,' that a research project will draw on a particular tradition, or that a contribution to knowledge will be found at the narrowest meeting point between the smallest of debates.

Likewise on the other side of the 'two cultures' that still divide the university (see Snow, 2012 or Husserl, 1970), a focus on scientific or instrumental technique so often relegates social, moral, and political questions to an equally lonely outside. Having apparently divorced oneself from such concerns they return with a vengeance in the most unconsidered and violent form. Thus the sciences and the technosciences today partake in a massive outsourcing of responsibility in which concern over social or environmental issues is taken to be something that takes place outside of them, or alternatively, are placed into the hands of an agent of blame or salvation such as the mechanisms of the human brain or 'the market' (see Foley, 2006; Jones, 2013).

With finance the separation of the seemingly technical from the social, cultural, political and ideological is in the strict sense invalidated. It is precisely in the technical apparatus of finance that its social and political effects are embedded.

The ideological import of finance is written into how particular forms of technical inscription operate. Faced with finance there is often no immediately apparent ideological opponent, and in this way finance is perfectly 'post-political' and 'post-ideological' in the precise sense that, presenting itself as pure technique, finance oversteps the bounds of any previously held ideological or political positions. The ideology of finance, if it any longer makes sense to speak of such a thing, is not clearly distinguishable from the design of an algorithm for investment or an equation for pricing derivatives. As social studies of finance have made clear, if there is something ideological at stake, then it is in this now foreclosed distinction between the technical matters of finance and its ideology (see MacKenzie, 2006; 2009).

The question of whether finance is technical or social is a badly posed question, one that obfuscates the intermeshing of finance and actual social reality. Equally, given the place of finance in framing the experience of what is taken as reality and its effects in reordering real things in the world, it becomes implausible to think that finance does not have a phenomenology and ontology of its own. At the same time, any philosophical reflection on the nature of experience or being that is ignorant of the dynamics of finance dooms itself to outright abstraction. In short: no finance without ontology, no ontology without finance.

Finance enjoins us to new levels of complexity and this should never be confused with muddy indifference. The objects that we seek to know and the forms of knowledge required to comprehend them may well be distinct, but that does not mean that they are or need be separate. Clarity and discernment comes not, as was argued by Locke, in the distinct and separate, but rather in the capacity for distinction and association. Thus if the disciplines might live on after finance then it would be in the distinct moments that are elucidated by their claims and not in their separation. The promise is of new forms of association, and as always association comes out of respect for the distinct singularities of the bodies that are conjoined. This, again, is one element of the promise offered by finance.

> Given its reach and implications, the study of financialization promises to draw committed minds out of their separate rooms and into an intellectual commons where together they might craft a fuller grasp of the politics that accompany each of capital's myriad reincarnations. Financialization, therefore, is not simply a stable object of inquiry that awaits bright lights, but an occasion at self-reformation around an expanded political arena. (Martin, 2009a, p. 116)

If the division and separation of the university internally and from its outside are being called into question by the practical reality of finance and its new modes of circulation and association, then an even deeper prospect results from the dynamics of the contestation of particularity and the new universalities that arise from infinite extension. Finance presents itself as practice and knowledge that is all embracing, that literally knows no limit and sees no end (Amato & Fantacci,

2012). For many finance is not so much too big to fail as it is too overwhelmingly massive to think it might be anything other than universal. Finance presents itself and is widely taken as being both universal reality and universal knowledge.

There are however at least two risks to any pretending universalism. Most obviously, any claim to universality that does nothing more than the universalisation of a particular is far from universal. This was quite clearly demonstrated as the historical premise and consequence of many of the apparent claims to universality that accompanied the global spread of European universalism, in which the sectional interests of dominant elites claimed to act in the long-term interests of all in order to justify immediate suffering (among many other sources see, for instance, Wallerstein, 2006).

Universalisation of a particular is extended particularism, which is at best a false universal. Working through the consequences of this kind of particularism has been the experience of the twentieth century, in the practical politics of contestation of particular claims to universality that are found in various racisms and fascisms. If the lesson learned from the refusal of racism and fascism is a reassertion of particularism then this is a bitter victory. The false universal that is particularism is a form of opportunism that involves little more than immediate registering of what is and seeking one's particular advantage in that.

This is the meaning of Hegel's critique of what he calls the 'merely abstract universal.' For anything to be meaningfully universal it needs to include particularity within it. This is the case whether thinking about the inclusion of bodies in a social situation or the need for knowledge to account for the richness of the particularities found across the various sciences. Thus in the context of his insistence on familiarity with other sciences Hegel stresses that "Only after a profound acquaintance with the other sciences does logic rise for subjective spirit from a merely abstract universal to a universal that encompasses within itself the riches of the particular" (2010, p. 37).

Finance teaches cool lessons in particularism by arbitraging advantage at the point of endlessly extending pricing differentials. Even in the practical politics of constraining finance the lesson of the limits of any strategy short of universal is again taught. Financial transaction taxes or any other impositions made against finance that are applied only regionally have been repeatedly shown to fail as financial elites evade and openly mock any state agency lacking universal jurisdiction. The prospect of a differentially regulated outside offers the path of least resistance, and here the global mobility of capital and its transnational bodies of association show themselves to outwit any nation-state seeking anything other than local advantage.

The other manner in which universality can be effaced is through the levelling of all particular content by an abstract universal. This is one of the very real reasons for the fear of universalism, in a context in which universal prospects can present a totalitarian eradication of all differences. Any meaningful idea of universality must be grounded in the presupposition of multiplicity. Hence the need "to create an expansive universal discourse, constructed out of, not against, the proliferation of particularisms of the last few decades" (Laclau, 2000, p. 306). Multiplicity as ontological starting point stands out as one of the many important achievements of the work of Alain Badiou. If the project of progressive politics is to create association and unities in a way that does not destroy singularities but instead maintains or better elevates them, then there is a pressing need today to think difference and association again.

UNDISCOURAGEMENT

I have argued that although finance reframes the operation of institutions such as the university and the categories through which they are understood, at the same time the world of finance is far from total. It is both contested by resistance and protest, and numerous important mobilisations in recent years have displayed remarkable courage in the face of barbarous particularism. I have sought to show in this chapter that finance also contains within it elements that run against its drive to divide, separate, and particularise. Here as elsewhere it is in the inconsistencies of finance that a vast range of possibilities reside.

Very real possibilities for thinking and performing the university differently arise at the heart of finance. If my conclusion is that the divisions between the university and its outside, and divisions of the disciplines and the particularisms on which they rest could by and large be set aside, I do not seek to offer this as a negative or critical conclusion. On the contrary, just as Marx found the prospect of a free association of producers in the cooperative forms of fully socialised capital, the prospect for the construction of an association of the producers of knowledge starts out from the already existing relations of association and interdependence that already exist in the production of knowledge.

If those who have been entrusted with the leadership of higher institutions of public education have been largely ineffective in resisting the destruction of the institution that was earlier in their lives the condition of their possibility, then this has been at least in part a result of a "crisis of the imagination" (Haiven, 2014) and of being on the losing side of the "war for the imagination" that has been waged and in large part won by regressive forces (Graeber, 2012). But imagination is one thing, and what is being proposed here is a concrete programme of alternatives that arises from the state of the situation of today, a situation that is marked by marauding financial violence and at the same time radical possibilities for association and interdependence. If finance has been 'realistic' in recent years then it has been so in utter disregard for what was otherwise imagined to be possible. In doing so, as Randy Martin puts it, "The capitalist juggernaut careened past its checkpoints and goalposts, beyond its own wildest expectations" (2002a, p. 11).

The youth of today on arriving in university lecture halls have been told that nothing is impossible and have learned from the practice of our masters the old Hegelian lesson that the identification of limits involves their supersession. What lesson can they learn from those entrusted with the social, human, and cultural sciences when told that there is nothing better than to respect limits and boundaries? As the apparently critical becomes damage control, the sciences of the manipulation of nature and other people promise the infinite. These sciences of manipulation naturally meet their limits in practical terms when they run up against the recalcitrance of nature and of human will. But when the will can be sequestered into differential conditions and differential willingness to be brutalised, vast spaces for manipulation remain and finance exhorts the dominant to be always on the move in order to seek them out and exploit them.

It is for the fact of these continued divisions that Badiou has argued that courage is the cardinal virtue of our age. Courage is not stubborn persistence or dogmatic ignorance but involves converting the sense of impotence into an enduring encounter with what is presented as impossible (see Badiou, 2008, chap. 5). This is crucial because we are in a situation today in which anyone who claims a position that might be defensible beyond a particular locale leads quickly, as Alberto Toscano (2010) has so astutely observed, to the charge of 'fanaticism.'

From a position of fear one can imagine that the safest strategy is flight into a hole and defence of that small safe space. As the university is now finally subjected to the same rampage that was unleashed with fury in wave after wave from the 1970s on, finance calls each and every one out of their hiding place. The alternative is to come out all together, and to come out announcing not that all is well, but that if the university is to be radically reconfigured then the terms on which this reconfiguration will be effected are in fact up for grabs. Coming out together, which has been increasingly taking place throughout the world in recent years, means saying that the criteria of finance that threaten to do the evaluation can themselves be drawn out of their hiding place and exposed for the particularity they represent.

Thus the embers of truth in the ashes of finance were already there all along. They exist in what Stefano Harney and Fred Moten (2013) have so importantly dubbed the 'undercommons' of the university. They advance this concept against the tut-tutting of those who consider that nothing is possible or are so inclined to believe that students are duped and that if they see critical thought in their students then even this can be dismissed as naive utopianism or fully incorporated obedience to old dogma. This opens the very real prospect of opening critical spaces with students on the basis of the equality of intelligence and for entering into alliance with others in distinct disciplines who already and maybe unsurprisingly do not hold positions that even approximate the caricatures that circulate about them. It invites the prospect of forming solidarities with others in the institution that do anything so mundane as discuss with students their financial hardship and psychological distress and prepare their food. It involves forming bonds with others outside the university, which does not mean those with particular financial or political interests who seek something in return.

The important thing about the undercommons is that it is not something that needs to be created, fostered, or encouraged. If anything, what needs undoing is the discouragement that comes from isolation, separation, and fear. Students and others do not need encouragement or to be called out from above. What is required instead is a repeated 'undiscouragement.' Such undiscouragement seeks to put to rest the voices that tell them that they and their experiences are nothing and that they should be afraid to speak because they have nothing to say. Yes, we live in discouraging times and to have the courage to be a scholar today means to become a militant at the very least. At the same time the responsibility of those who seek to construct responsible institutions is to find that there, right there, staring them in the face for so many years, is the very spark of truth that one had been waiting for all along.

REFERENCES

Amato, M., & Fantacci, L. (2012). *The end of finance.* Oxford: Polity.

Babbage, C. (1832/2008). *On the economy of machinery and manufactures.* Teddington, UK: Echo.

Badiou, A. (2005). *Being and event* (O. Feltham, Trans.). London: Continuum.

Badiou, A. (2008). *The Meaning of Sarkozy* (D. Fernbach, Trans.). London: Verso.

Badiou, A. (2009). Logics of worlds: Being and event, 2 (O. Feltham, Trans.). London: Continuum.

Balibar, E. (2013). *Identity and difference: John Locke and the invention of consciousness* (W. Montag, Trans.). London: Verso.

Baucom, I. (2005). *Specters of the Atlantic: Finance capital, slavery and the philosophy of history.* Durham, NC: Duke University Press.

Blyth, M. (2013). *Austerity: The history of a dangerous idea.* Oxford: Oxford University Press.

Braverman, H. (1974). *Labor and monopoly capital: The degradation of work in the twentieth century.* New York: Monthly Review.

Buck-Morss, S. (2009). *Hegel, Haiti and universal history.* Pittsburgh, PA: University of Pittsburgh Press.

Daellenbach, S. (2015). Who's afraid of public financial literacy? In M. A. Peters, J. Paraskeva, & T. Besley (Eds.), *Global financial crisis and educational restructuring.* New York: Peter Lang.

de Goede, M. (2005). *Virtue, fortune and faith: A genealogy of finance.* Minneapolis: University of Minnesota Press.

Duménil, G., & Lévy, D. (2011). *The crisis of neoliberalism.* Cambridge, MA: Harvard University Press.

Engelen, E., Ertürk, I., Froud, J., Johal, S., Leaver, A., Moran, M., Nilsson, A., & Williams, K. (2011). *After the great compliance: Financial crisis and the politics of reform.* Oxford: Oxford University Press.

Foley, D. (2006). *Adam's fallacy: A guide to economic theology*. Cambridge, MA: Harvard University Press.

Giroux, H. (2011). Beyond the swindle of the corporate university. In M. Bailey & D. Freedman (Eds.), *The assault on universities: A manifesto for resistance*. London: Pluto Press.

Graeber, D. (2012). Revolution at the level of common sense. In F. Campagna & E. Campiglio (Eds.), *What we are fighting for: A radical collective manifesto*. London: Pluto Press.

Haiven, M. (2011). Finance as capital's imagination? Reimagining value and culture in an age of fictitious capital and crisis. *Social Text, 29*(3), 93–124.

Haiven, M. (2014). *Crises of imagination, crises of power: Capitalism, creativity and the commons*. London: Zed Books.

Harney, S., & Moten, F. (2013). *The undercommons: Fugitive planning and black study*. Wivenhoe, UK: Minor Compositions.

Hegel, G. W. F. (2010). *The science of logic*. (G. di Giovanni, Trans.). Cambridge: Cambridge University Press.

Husserl, E. (1970). *The crisis of the European sciences and transcendental phenomenology: An introduction to phenomenology* (D. Carr, Trans.). Evanston, IL: Northwestern University Press.

Johnston, A. (2013). *Prolegomena to any future materialism, Vol. 1: The outcome of contemporary French philosophy*. Evanston, IL: Northwestern University Press.

Jones, C. (2013). *Can the market speak?* Winchester, UK: Zero Books.

Jones, C. (2014). Finance, university, revolt. *Argos Aotearoa, 1*, 44–50.

Jones, C. (2015). *The world of finance*. Manuscript, under review.

Kant, I. (1798/1979). *The conflict of the faculties* (M. Gregor, Trans.). Lincoln: University of Nebraska Press.

Kant, I. (1785/1996). Groundwork of the metaphysics of morals. In *Practical philosophy*. Cambridge: Cambridge University Press.

Laclau, E. (2000). Constructing universality. In J. Butler, E. Laclau, & S. Žižek (Eds.), *Contingency, hegemony, universality: Contemporary dialogues on the left*. London: Verso.

Lapavitsas, C. (Ed.). (2012). *Financialization in crisis*. Chicago: Haymarket Books.

Lapavitsas, C. (2013). *Profiting without producing: How finance exploits us all*. London: Verso.

Locke, J. (1690a/2004). *An essay concerning human understanding*. (R. Woolhouse, Ed.). London: Penguin.

Locke, J. (1690b/1988). *Two treatises of government* (P. Laslett, Ed.). Cambridge: Cambridge University Press.

Locke, J. (1697/1993). Draft of a representation containing a scheme of methods for the employment of the poor. In D. Wootton (Ed.), *Political writings*. Indianapolis, IN: Hackett Publishing.

Losurdo, D. (2011). *Liberalism: A counter-history* (G. Elliot, Trans). London: Verso.

MacKenzie, D. (2006). *An engine, not a camera: How financial models shape markets*. Cambridge, MA: MIT Press.

MacKenzie, D. (2009). *Material markets: How economic agents are constructed*. Oxford: Oxford University Press.

Martin, R. (Ed.). (1999). *Chalk lines: The politics of work in the managed university*. Durham, NC: Duke University Press.

Martin, R. (2002a). *Financialization of daily life*. Philadelphia, PA: Temple University Press.

Martin, R. (2002b). *On your Marx: Relinking socialism and the New Left*. Minneapolis: University of Minnesota Press.

Martin, R. (2007). *An empire of indifference: American war and the financial logic of risk management*. Durham, NC: Duke University Press.

Martin, R. (2009a). The twin towers of financialization: Entanglement of political and cultural economies. *The Global South, 3*(1), 108–125.

Martin, R. (2009b). Whose crisis is that? Thinking finance otherwise. *Ephemera: Theory and Politics in Organization, 9*(4), 344–349.

Martin, R. (2010a). Specters of finance: Limits of knowledge and the politics of crisis. *Journal of Communication Inquiry, 34*(4), 355–365.

Martin, R. (2010b). The good, the bad, and the ugly: Economies of parable. *Cultural Studies, 24*(3). 418–430.

Martin, R. (2010c). What's in it for us? Rethinking the financial crisis. *Rethinking Marxism, 22*(2). 187–194.

Martin, R. (2011a). Taking an administrative turn: Derivative logic for a recharged humanities. *Representations, 116*(Fall), 156–176.

Martin, R. (2011b). *Under new management: Universities, administrative labor and the professional turn.* Philadelphia, PA: Temple University Press.

Martin, R. (2012). A precarious dance, a derivative sociality. *TDR: The Drama Review, 56*(4), 62–77.

Martin, R. (2013). After economy? Social logics of the derivative. *Social Text, 31*(1), 83–106.

Martin, R. (2014). What difference do derivatives make? From the technical to the political conjuncture. *Culture Unbound, 6*, 189–210.

Martin, R. (forthcoming). *Knowledge ltd: Toward a social logic of the derivative.* Philadelphia, PA: Temple University Press.

Marx, K. (1867/1976). *Capital: A critique of political economy,* Vol. 1 (B. Fowkes, Trans.). London: Penguin.

McGettigan, A. (2013). *The great university gamble: Money, markets and the future of higher education.* London: Pluto Press.

Miyazaki, H. (2013). *Arbitraging Japan: Dreams of capitalism at the end of finance.* Berkeley, CA: University of California Press.

Poovey, M. (2008). *Genres of the credit economy: Mediating value in eighteenth- and nineteenth-century Britain.* Chicago: University of Chicago Press.

Ruskin, J. (1853/2004). The stones of Venice, II: The nature of gothic. In D. Birch (Ed.), *Selected writings.* Oxford: Oxford University Press.

Smith, A. (1759/2000). *The theory of moral sentiments.* Amherst, NY: Prometheus Books.

Smith, A. (1776a/1986). *The wealth of nations, Books I–III* (A. Skinner, Ed.). London: Penguin.

Smith, A. (1776b/1999). *The wealth of nations, Books IV–V* (A. Skinner, Ed.). London: Penguin.

Snow, C. P. (2012). *The two cultures.* Cambridge: Cambridge University Press.

Toscano, A. (2010). *Fanaticism: On the uses of an idea.* London: Verso.

Wallerstein, I. (2006). *European universalism: The rhetoric of power.* New York: New Press.

NOTE

1. Earlier versions of this chapter were presented at the Sociological Association of Aotearoa (New Zealand) and at the Centre for Global Studies of Education at the University of Waikato. I would like to thank all participants for their feedback and specifically to thank Shanti Daellenbach, Stefano Harney, Anna-Maria Murtola, Sean Sturm, Warwick Tie, and Stephen Turner for critical feedback on an earlier draft and Michael Peters for encouragement throughout.

CHAPTER SEVEN

Instrumental Reasoning qua Capitalist Rationality

The Embedding of Capitalism within Educational Discourse

HOWARD GIBSON

INTRODUCTION

There are three parts to this chapter.[1] The first seeks to explain the philosophical origins and assumptions of instrumental rationality. This is the "useful but blind" (McGuigan, 2006, p. 171) variant of reason that is concerned for procedures and leaves unquestioned the purposes of reasoning. The second attempts to show how instrumental rationality has inveigled its way into educational discourses of late and becomes normalised. The third links instrumental rationality with capitalism by showing that many of the secreted purposes contained in these educational discourses are primarily destined to secure a trained and disciplined labour force.

Horkheimer is a key figure in the emergence of the term 'instrumental reason.' In *Eclipse of Reason* he describes it in terms of "the adequacy of procedures for purposes more or less taken for granted and supposedly self-explanatory. It attaches little importance to the question whether the purposes as such are reasonable" (2004/1947, p. 3). Here he implies a distinction between reason as a content-free, value-neutral instrument, a tool that Schopenhauer cast as having "no material but only a formal content" (1974, p. 171), and reason as having purposes and consequences within the world where actions and behaviours convey a normative component inextricably bound to its instrumental function. This is clearly Horkheimer's position, for whom the purposes and ends of reasoning were an intimate guiding component of reasoning itself. O'Neill makes the point that "instrumental reasoners may show that it is necessary to break eggs if one wants to make an omelette, but they have nothing but 'subjective' or 'arbitrary' preferences to cite as reasons for making or not making omelettes" (1998). In other words, instrumental reasoners retreat to the personal or subjective domain when verifying moral or political decisions and deny the significance of wider issues in deciding between issues of choice and value. To extend her analogy, while instrumental reasoning may be essential for the *skilful* or *efficient* preparation of omelettes, that the *purpose* is to embarrass a vegan or kill a cholesterol-laden diner, or is linked with any explicit purpose apart from the 'subjective,' is deemed unrelated and extraneous. Procedures are fundamental. Purposes are disconnected from or considered irrelevant to this form of reasoning.

The chapter starts with an examination of some of the philosophical antecedents of instrumental rationality in the work of David Hume and sociology of Max Weber. The tensions and limitations that emerge are then used to reflect upon three current educational discourses in England that employ reason instrumentally. Managerial discourses use phrases like 'the pursuit of excellence' while failing to suggest what content or purpose such terms might serve as a standard to judge the quality of a new headteacher (DfES, 2004a); the development of 'communication skills' illustrates the problem of perceiving such an activity in an instrumental way in so far as it contains, in both senses, a preference for an undisclosed normative agenda; and 'personal financial capability' that becomes part of the National Curriculum in 2014 and aims to teach pupils how "to manage their money on a day-to-day basis, and plan for future financial needs" (DfE, 2013), side-lines reflection with pupils about the purpose of the state and possible economic alternatives. The final section speculates about the link of instrumental with what Marcuse called "capitalist rationality." In the 1960s he argued that, despite its claim to formality or inertness, instrumentalism was coupled with a specific economic agenda. In the 1980s Lyotard's account of modernity was explained through the eclipse of deliberation upon these underlying purposes, the rise of discourses concerned with performativity and the efficient and effective expansion of "the system" (Lyotard, 1984, p. xxiv). The chapter asks, then, if instrumental reasoning and performativity are now historically aligned with a set of entrenched normative assumptions about the world that education now services and maintains.

HUME'S INSTRUMENTALISM

Hume is renowned for his sceptical doubt about the limits of human reason and for his epistemological modesty: "Reason is, and ought only to be the slave of the passions, and can never pretend to any other office than to serve and obey them" (1973, p. 458). If the function of reason is to serve an individual's passions, and "since a passion can never, in any sense, be call'd unreasonable," Hume surmised that "tis impossible that reason and passion can ever oppose each other" (1973, p. 416). If these non-cognitive desires cannot be contrary to reason then, he concluded, "Tis not contrary to reason to prefer the destruction of the whole world to the scratching of my finger" (1973, p. 416). Because of this portrayal of reason as a tool that discovers the best action to achieve a subject's purposes, underpinned by a profound scepticism regarding the possibility of the rational deliberation of those purposes, some have concluded that "'Humean" now serves as a virtual synonym for "instrumentalist'" (Setiya, 2004, p. 365; see also Audi, 2002, p. 236).

Some loyal Humeans have acknowledged pitfalls and lacunae within the master's original account of reason but have sought to explain how it might be profitably reshaped (e.g., Baier, 1991, p. 161; Setiya, 2004, p. 370; Garrett, 1997, p. 95. See also Hubin, 2001; Audi, 2002; Lillehammer, 2007). While they have proffered arguments favouring modifications of the original depiction of reason, others have warned against tenuous reinterpretations. Hampton (1996, 1998) and Korsgaard (1997), for example, have argued that such notions may sequester more fundamental problems at the heart of instrumentalism. Their proposals are detailed, convoluted, and distinct but both try to show how Humean reason is untenable precisely *because* it omits an explicit conception of what is right or just. They have argued that normativity is inescapable in a conception of instrumental reasoning and that this omission is sufficient to unravel the fallacy that reason can serve as an inert tool. Thus, they argue, in identifying passions considered important to a subject, instrumental reasoners still need to address the problem of *coherence* and the likelihood that subjective preferences may compete with each other; or that judgements will still need to made about whether, in the *longer term*, passions could be best maximised by temporary postponement now; or whether planning for the *future* could involve reason speculating about currently unfelt, but rationally perceivable, preferences. Thus, says Korsgaard, "in order to distinguish rational desire from actual desire, it looks as if we need to have some rational principles determining which ends are worthy of preference or pursuit" (Korsgaard, 1997, p. 230). Such rational principles, says Hampton, entail values that are in Hume assumed: "Any theory of instrumental reason is just as hip-deep in normativity as any moral theory, and therefore just as metaphysically problematic as any moral theory" (1998, p. 206). In short, if reason cannot deliver straightforward attachments to subjective preferences without making judgments between purposes and possible ends, Hume's notion "that reason is perfectly inert" (1973, p. 458) is untenable. Any moral theory based upon it faces an insuperable dilemma: "The authority of this instrumental form has to be understood non-instrumentally ... understood as an imperative, it is categorical and not hypothetical" (Hampton, 1998, p. 140, n. 22).

Thus, despite the tendency for an instrumentalist like Hume to "dislike the inclusion of norms in their theory" (Hampton, 1998, p. 198), there are good arguments to show that reason cannot be limited to an instrumental function, that the purpose of reasoning is *inescapably* tied to a normative agenda. In Hume's epistemology this would appear as egoism and prudence and emerges in the problem he faced when shifting his construal of reasoning from philosophy to social and political judgement. This transferral was not achieved by Hume nor was it his intention. However, some have speculated that his "pensive melancholy" at the start of the *Enquiry* was a consequence of a philosophical position that, by his own admission, bore no "direct reference to action and society" (Hume, 1996, p. 9). While latter parts of the *Treatise* contain discussion of what philosophy can do for society, Hume's persistent scepticism regarding the remit of reason prevented him from making connections between his philosophical thought and the values that emerged in his writings on social, political, and economic matters. Like his conservative companions, Edmund Burke and Michael Oakeshott, custom and tradition would provide the guide to practical action. Some have compared him with Bertrand Russell in this regard, whose writing on mathematics and epistemology displayed no obvious relationship to his musings on social themes like marriage and morals (see Moore, 1976; Russell, 1961). Indeed, when a critic remarked on this comparison Russell expressed his delight, denying that there needed to be any logical connection between the two domains and suggested he was merely following Hume's example, with whom he agreed on philosophical assumptions but with whom he wholly disagreed on social and political ones (see Schilpp, 1971, p. 727).

Because of Hume's empiricism and the way he dislocated philosophical from practical reason, Horkheimer described him as "the father of modern positivism": "The acceptability of ideas, the criteria for our actions and beliefs, the leading principles of ethics and politics, all our ultimate decisions are made to depend upon factors other than reason" 1974/1967, p. 6). While reason in Hume is not able to arbitrate between the relative merits of scratching one's finger or destroying the world, contemporary Humeans, too, bypass substantive moral, social, or political claims by focussing upon what Hampton dubs "trivial and whimsical" preferences for inconsequential subject matter (Hampton, 1998, p. 193). Wanting to see a film (Raz, 2005, p. 7), deciding whether to go to a spa (Hubin, 2001, p. 450) or put parsley on the moon (Nagel, 1970, p. 45), are the sorts of examples chosen to illustrate a socially minimised and inconsequential discussion of practical reason. In short, Hampton's accusation of triviality is an outcome of the prohibition of a form of reasoning withdrawn from the adjudication of more significant issues than these, a form of disinfected reasoning permitted to deal with nothing more complex than the efficacy of solutions to everyday personal choices. Some have argued, however, that when reasoning in its instrumental form serves as a barrier to interpretations of complex socio-economic practices then the consequences of a philosophy that feigns "arbitrary preference" (O'Neill, 1998) is ideologically suspect, and here Weber has been a target.

WEBER'S INSTRUMENTALISM

Weber's reflections on the meaning of reason and rationality are scattered and unmethodical and have been variously described as "confusing" (Levine, 1981, p. 13), "fragmentary" (Habermas, 1984, pp. 143, 170) or "ambiguous" (Swidler, 1973, p. 35). In *The Protestant Ethic* Weber acknowledged he had difficulty with the term (1930, p. 194, n. 9) and in *The Economic Ethics of the World Religions* considered the "very different things that 'rationalism' can mean" (Weber, 1948, pp. 293–294; see Levine, 1981, p. 23). However, only in *Economy and Society* did he write more clearly of four types: "traditional," "affectual," "instrumental/formal" (*Zweckrationalität*) and "value/substantive" (*Wertrationalität*) rationality (Weber, 1968, pp. 24–25):

> The term "formal rationality of economic action" will be used to designate the extent of quantitative calculation ... The concept of "*substantive rationality*", on the other hand, is full of ambiguities. It conveys ... certain criteria of ultimate ends, whether they be ethical, political, utilitarian, hedonistic, feudal, egalitarian or whatever. (Weber, 1968, pp. 85–66)

It is Weber's construal of formal and substantive rationality that is of interest here.

In *The Protestant Ethic* he reflected upon the portentous expansion of market forces under capitalism but concluded that they would do so anyway for humanity was entrapped by the laws of modernity. In the context of inexorable economic forces and the growing disenchantment with religion, human reason was denuded of any vestige of its former qualities in pre-capitalist times:

> Man is dominated by the making of money, by acquisition as the ultimate purpose of his life. Economic acquisition is no longer subordinated to man as the means for the satisfaction of his material needs. This reversal of what we should call the natural relationship, so irrational from a naïve point of view, is evidently as definitely a leading principle of capitalism as it is foreign to all people not under capitalistic influence. (Weber, 1930, p. 53)

With the constant expansion of science and technology that fed the rise of capitalism, along with adjudicating and administrative procedures at hand to establish the dependable regulation of business, Weber prophesised that "progress" toward the bureaucratic state was imminent. The rationalisation of society was leading to an ever-increasing growth of a social and economic system whose values, ends and goals were irrational but unchangeable: "The capitalist economy of the present day is an immense cosmos into which the individual is born, and which presents itself to him ... as an unalterable order of things in which he must live" (1930, p. 54). Instrumental rationality had taken hold of the world and presented itself to humans as a necessary system where functional imperatives dominated. Weber described entrapment within this "iron cage" (1930, pp. 181–182) as "relentless" (Weber, 1968, pp. 1156, 731), "irresistible" (1968, p. 1403), "unalterable" (1930, p. 54), "escape proof" (1930, pp. 1401–1402) and "unavoidable" (1958, p. 60).

It was the structural condition of humanity in industrial nations that rationalisation would forever emend its efficiency and scope until "the last ton of fossilized coal is burnt" (1930, p. 181).

It was the universality of Weber's depiction of the effects of instrumental reason upon the social fabric that raised the ire of the Frankfurt School in the 1970s. While they concurred with his analysis, that Protestantism had been an important precursor for the development of capitalism and that capitalism had provided a matrix in which instrumental reason could flourish, Marcuse condemned him for presenting it in terms of historical fate:

> Who decrees the fate? … Weber's concept of fate is construed "after the fact" of such coercion: he generalizes the blindness of a society which reproduces itself behind the back of individuals, of a society in which the law of domination appears as objective technological law. However, in fact, this law is neither "fatal" nor "formal". The context of Weber's analysis is the historical context in which economic reason became the reason of domination. (1972, pp. 213–214)

For Marcuse the rise of instrumental reason was not to blame per se for the "chaotic, frightening and evil aspects of technological civilisation"; rather, it was the way in which rationalization was organised under capitalism that accounted for the "irrationality of this rationalization." Horkheimer similarly fought against the reduction of reason to a tool that fore-grounded means rather than ends and, in a *Critique of Instrumental Reason*, sought "to rescue thought from this fate":

> "Reason" for a long period meant the activity of understanding and assimilating the eternal ideas which were to function as goals for men. Today, on the contrary, it is not only the business but the essential work of reason to find means for the goals one adopts at any given time … Reason is considered to come into its own when it rejects any status as an absolute … and accepts itself simply as a tool. (1974/1967, pp. vii–viii)

In short, Weber stood accused of fusing the apparent inexorable growth of instrumental reasoning with the progress of capitalism and by so doing arriving at an ideologically unacceptable position of foreclosure upon the possible emergence of historical and political alternatives.

For Habermas, the error of the Frankfurt theorists was to present their "unrelenting critique from the ironically distanced perspective of an objective reason that had fallen irreparably into ruin" (1984, p. 377). While their critique of Weber was valid, their explanatory model of rationality was flawed (1984, p. 350). A more convincing way, he argued, was to redefine Weber's *Wertrationalität* while retaining *Zweckrationalität* as a distinct but essential and compatible component of human reasoning (1971). Instrumental rationality was more clearly defined therefore as that which considered means and consequences in a quantifiable and calculable way, a form of rationality where actions were judged by the ultimate goal of maximum efficiency. In contrast, substantive (or "communicative") rationality was based upon principles of justice, fairness, and truthfulness. This form of rationality entered people's lives through their culture and community and was thus subject to the vagaries of particular customs and traditions of power. Whereas instrumental rationality had technical rules, substantive rationality rested upon morality and social norms. Whereas instrumental rationality used context-free language—the language of mathematics, measurement, and replication—substantive rationality rested upon inter-subjectively shared everyday language. Whereas systems of instrumental rationality involved learning skills and manifesting formal qualifications to demonstrate scientific and technical prowess, substantive action drew upon internalised roles gained from convention and tradition: "skills put us in a position to solve problems" while traditions motivate us "to follow norms." Transgressing the rules of instrumental rationality led to inefficiency while the failure of substantive action involved the reprisal of authority. And whereas the rationalisation of systems of instrumental action involved the growth of productive or capitalist forces through the incessant, quasi-autonomous expansion of scientific and technical control, in communicative interactions there was the possibility of what Habermas called, albeit vaguely, emancipation.

To sum up so far: First, the roots of instrumental reasoning are found in elements of empiricist philosophy and social theory. Second, critics of instrumentalism in Hume (Korsgaard and Hampton) and in Weber (Marcuse and Horkheimer) argue strongly against the pretence that reason can be conceived solely as a means-seeking activity that presupposes human purposes that are "taken for granted and supposedly self-explanatory." They are reproached for secreting normative assumptions (in Hume) or ideological dispositions (in Weber) that go unacknowledged. Third, Habermas's development of two forms of rationality provides a useful model that extends Weber's *Wertrationalität* while retaining *Zweckrationalität* as distinct and complex components of human reasoning. The next three sections explain the way in which instrumental reasoning has come to permeate educational discourse and colonise its substantive partner.

MANAGEMENT AND INSTRUMENTALISM

Ball has argued that 'new public management' (NPM) has become "the key mechanism in the political reform and cultural re-engineering of public sectors for the last 20 years" (Ball, 2008, p. 47). One of the key terms in NPM has been 'effective,' as in "effective school leadership" (see Teddlie & Reynolds, 2000). For some, however, the term is controversial. Bottery has suggested that 'effective' is a word normally taken to be a neutral term, something that simply describes a relationship between means and ends, and so has argued that the School Effectiveness

Movement has facilitated the spurious belief that there was nothing problematic in their declarations. This, he says, has enticed researchers to think of the study of the 'effective school' as a matter of mere empirical investigation: "If there are no values involved, or if it is so evidently good, then all we need to do is get on and investigate it" (Bottery, 2000, p. 115). Similarly, Blake, Smeyers, Smith, and Standish have argued: "It is the notion of effectiveness, and its close relation efficiency, that have above all replaced proper consideration of ends" (1998, p. 132). Pring has likewise proposed that the effectiveness debate has severed educational from moral discourses resulting in "a theory of effectiveness which ignores the question 'effective for what?'" (2005, p. 13). Again Wrigley has argued that research surrounding school effectiveness "avoids a debate about the *purposes* of education" (2006, p. 35, my emphasis), that he also attributes to its successor, the School Improvement Movement, which is "virtually silent about the purpose of schooling" and "gives rise to some very strange writing. Dozens of books are published every year about styles of leadership but few even consider where they are leading to" (2006, p. 38). Managerialism is part of a culture where the devising of means has become a dominant activity and where "consideration of values, of the ends to which means lead, no longer takes place to any significant extent' (Blake et al., 1998, p. 133). For MacIntyre:

> Managers themselves and most writers about management conceive of themselves as morally neutral characters whose skills enable them to devise the most efficient means of achieving whatever end is proposed. Whether a given manager is effective or not is on the dominant view a quite different question from that of the morality of the ends which his effectiveness serves or fails to serve. Nonetheless there are strong grounds for rejecting the claim that effectiveness is a morally neutral value. (2007, p. 74)

In short, many observers are united in their judgement that the term 'effective' has been used instrumentally as a means for excluding issues that might call into doubt the neutrality or self-evident goodness of desired changes in public policy, in this case management structures.

Since 2004 those wishing to become senior managers in state schools in England must hold, or be working toward, National Professional Qualifications for Headship (NPQH), for which they will be assessed against government determined Standards: "The Standards recognise the key role that headteachers play in engaging in the development and delivery of government policy and in raising and maintaining levels of attainment in schools in order to meet the needs of every child" (DfES, 2004a). The *National Standards for Headteachers* lists the qualities, activities, and attributes necessary for the job:

- maintaining effective partnerships
- shaping the future
- create a productive learning community

- ensuring that the school moves forward
- carry the vision forward
- the pursuit of excellence
- develops and maintains effective strategies

What is missing here is acknowledgement of the normative or substantive domain that would give meaning to implied purposes. For example, there are thirty-eight references to the word 'effective' but no explicit discussion of what the *content* of an 'effective partnership' might be. Similarly, there is no discussion about the values underlying disparate 'visions' headteachers might have. Some may argue that a school 'moving forward' should 'shape the future' in one direction rather than another, driven, on the one hand, by a radical concern for the ecological catastrophe a headteacher may think now faces the planet, or, on the other, by the need to create more students primed with qualities and skills to duplicate the existing trajectory. How these disparate 'visions' are to be evaluated goes unmentioned. In avoiding underlying purposes the *National Standards for Headteachers* employ a technical language that contains values that are indefinite or sustain an instrumental discourse that dodges issues of a substantive nature. These remain implicit and unstated. Together with NPM it gives the appearance of providing technical solutions to educational problems and for some is clearly ideological: "New managerialism … is very clearly an ideological rather than simply a technical reform of higher education and one that is firmly based on interests concerning relations of power and dominance" (Deem & Brehony, 2005, pp. 231–232). For others it is a procedure for "keeping silent about human values" and for strengthening an ideological position while reinforcing "the sense of inevitability and fatalism that neo-liberal politicians use to quell dissent" (Wrigley, 2006, p. 38).

SKILLS AND INSTRUMENTALISM

Under Fagin's tutelage Oliver Twist was taught five skills for efficient pickpocketing. These were "nimbleness," retreating from sight when closing upon a victim, the need for "extraordinary rapidity of movement," the knack of accurate timing, and developing appropriate reactions for "accidental stumbling" (Dickens, 1966, pp. 54–55). But the skills revolve in a paradigm that is unquestioned. The substantive issue of thieving per se is placed outside the frame and Fagin's reasoning appears instrumental because his education of Oliver involved merely the teaching of efficient methods of thieving bound to unquestioned purposes.

In educational policy unstated assumptions about purposes are less convincing. Skills have always been an outcome of education but were conventionally viewed as its by-product. Today not only does the National Curriculum enshrine them in law (DfEE, 2000a) but until recently the Department for Education *and Skills* championed the very term in its title. This has coincided with an anxiety about whether education "prepares young people adequately for the challenges of the new global economy" (DfES, 2005a) and the push to create a flexible, team-thinking workforce suitably equipped to sustain the nation's economic future within an unpredictable global context:

> Skills are fundamental to achieving our ambitions, as individuals, for our families and for our communities. They help businesses create wealth, and they help people realise their potential. So they serve the twin goals of social justice and economic success. (DfES, 2005a, para. 1. See also DfES, 2005b)

Whether skills divorced from specific bodies of knowledge or physical challenges *are* transferable is a debate that has gone on elsewhere. The concern here is to establish how skills are linked with instrumental reasoning.

Take 'communication skills,' the first of the Key Skills in the National Curriculum (DfEE, 2000a, pp. 20–21). Communication skills are commonly presented as a conduit devoid of content, that is to say, not communication about an issue or the *substance* of something but, rather, about the transferable, *content-less* skill of communication. The substantive issues contained in communication are often assumed to reside elsewhere. British Telecom, for example, in its education initiative *Communication Skills for Life* (BT, 2006), claims that its aims are: "To help everyone in the UK understand and enjoy the benefits of improved communication skills." What it omits to explain is how such understanding, benefit, and improvements might be measured in terms of political or moral criteria. It aims "to make a difference," but *to whom* and *why* are issues not raised. BT aspires to get communicators "constantly engaged" but refuses to explain for *what reason*, nor that the contested nature of engagement is often highly problematic. It values communicators who are "open to ideas, opinions and questions," but whether this openness extends to *argument* about poor ideas or merely to the *reception* of any ideas no matter what their content, remains highly ambiguous. In short, BT's portrayal of communication skills proffers no epistemological concern for the content of ideas and, in the absence of a position about how contested values might be communicated, mechanisms to ensure politeness and tolerance substitute for a complex explanation of how substantive disputes might be resolved. It is, in short, an instrumental view of communication that again contains, in both senses, a normative agenda.

In reality the proximity of "communication" with "skill" overflows with values embedded in political and cultural practices:

> The phrase 'communication skill' names a cultural construct, not a natural phenomenon with an objective existence in the world. Whether some person, or group of people, has good, bad or indifferent communication skills is entirely dependent on what 'communication' is taken to be, and what is thought to constitute 'skill' in it. (Cameron, 2000, p. 128)

In other words, the *same* discursive features of communication could be seen as a skill in one historical period or culture but as pathological in another. Argument, for example, in a primary classroom in Russia is currently deemed to be a valuable skill (Alexander, 2000) but less so in English primary schools today where non-judgementalism has emerged as culturally more worthy in practices like "circle time" (Middlesbrough EiC Partnership, 2006) and "peer mediation": "One of the most crucial components of the mediation process is that it remains non-judgemental" (Holmes, 2006; see also Teachernet, 2006). In essence, the content of communication skills varies from age to age and from culture to culture, and the façade of neutrality is revealed by historical evidence of shifts in content and by a comparison of assumptions from different contemporary practices.

Moreover, the contemporary preference for non-judgementalism as a communicative skill in education in England is itself both revealing and problematic. On the one hand, such a skill in, say, peer mentoring could be seen as replicating therapy-like discourses that resolve everyday conflicts in school without the construction of winners or losers, where questions of right and wrong are deemed unimportant in the quest to move forward in pragmatic and effective response. On the other hand, such practices could be seen as an example of discourses structured to undermine or bypass the search for the truth about particular instances of bullying and, in refusing to isolate culprits, gloss over issues of social justice in the haste for closure. The prohibition on judging others, be it their feelings, values or power, taken to its logical conclusion would undermine the liberal justification for reasoning and presuppose that the world is already just (see Cameron, 2000). When the substantive dimension is missing in this portrayal of communication skills the liberal tradition of contestation, refutation, and contradiction is not simply removed from the agenda but represented as distressing and inappropriate (see Ecclestone & Hayes, 2009). Although pupils may disagree with one another, their skill is measured by their ability *not* to judge and the competence to avoid argument. They may have personal desires and opinions, in a Humean sense, but the skill of communicating, instrumentally contrived, demands tolerance of the other, where tolerance is cast as an interpersonal or psychological construct disassociated from its epistemic root. Moral relativism is one possible consequence of this form of instrumentalism (see Lukes, 2008), a situation where the platform upon which differences can be explored has been dismantled and where substantive issues of value are considered subjective and abstracted from communication.

FINANCIAL CAPABILITY AND INSTRUMENTALISM

These problems explaining 'good communication' are mirrored in advice given to teachers when managing classroom discussion of financial skills. Guidance suggests that teachers should "listen carefully to what everyone has to say, valuing all contributions non-judgementally so that young people from different financial backgrounds are able to contribute to discussions on an equal footing and with equal confidence" (DfEE, 2000b, p. 12). Such pedagogical advice might be seen as appropriate and sensitive and avoiding the embarrassment a pupil may feel when encountering others from "different financial circumstances" (DfEE, 2000b, pp. 9, 11). Equally, it could be interpreted as prohibiting discussion of structural inequalities where substantive values associated with comparative wealth are placed beyond judgement and run counter to the liberal justification for communicative engagement by presenting the world as if it were already fair and wise.

Moreover, it would place beyond question the broader policy agenda that has driven the introduction of financial capability into English schools in recent years. Although government policy for teaching financial capability has been fragmentary and non-statutory, there has been considerable resolve to find it a place within the National Curriculum over the last decade. In 2000 the Department for Education and Employment (DfEE) noted "the Government's wish to include financial capability as a topic at all key stages" (2000b, p. 3):

> Financial capability is an important life skill for everyone: the ability to make financial decisions is the key to identifying and making best use of the opportunities in today's changing world ... Developing financial understanding is the first step in ensuring that young people leaving school have the skills required to deal with everyday financial issues. (DfEE, 2000b, pp. 4, 6)

In 2004, as part of the *Every Child Matters* programme, New Labour made it statutory for all pupils to "achieve economic wellbeing" (DfES, 2004b, p. E4), although what this meant remained diffuse and contested (see Gibson, 2012). In 2005 the Qualification and Curriculum Authority suggested that "financial capability" was "an important life skill" that would help young people "look after money" and "move into adulthood with confidence in their ability to deal effectively and efficiently with the range of financial decisions they will have to make" (QCA, 2005). In 2006 the Financial Services Authority "reviewed in depth what works in improving financial capability", arguing that there should be "a new road map for delivering a step change in the financial capability of the UK population" (FSA, 2006a, p. 1), and recommended that pupils should learn about "bank accounts, spending, looking at mobile phone tariffs and how to access needs" (FSA, 2006b). A year later the government drew up limited statutory provision for 11–14-year-olds who would learn about the "essential financial life skills through functional maths and in Personal Social and Health Education," that is, "learn about risk and reward; investment and trade; personal budgeting; mortgages; interest rates; and balancing credit cards" (DCSF, 2007). In 2009 the Macdonald Review again urged the government to improve the status of financial capability and made a "firm recommendation" that Personal, Social, Health, and Economics (PSHE) education should become "part of the statutory National Curriculum in both primary and secondary phases" (Macdonald, 2009, p. 5). In essence there has been mounting pressure to make "financial skills" part of the compulsory curriculum for state schools in England and, at the time of writing, the Conservative Secretary of State for Education, Michael Gove, has approved a new National Curriculum for 2014 in which secondary-age pupils will soon be taught how "to manage their money," "make sound financial decisions" and "plan for future financial needs" (DfE, 2013).

The process, however, has been one in which financial skills have been systematically uncoupled from the broader economic backdrop and reduced to a set of competences of a personal ("manage *their* money") and prudential nature. In such a way it gives the appearance of responding pragmatically to inevitable historical necessities while diminishing reflection upon, and critical engagement with, the particular historical period that cradled it. The principal mechanism for naturalising this process has been a language game where verb-less inventories of things that pupils "will need to learn" have been expressed in noun lists or nominal form—"income and expenditure, credit and debt, insurance, savings and pensions, financial products and services, how public money is raised and spent." Nominalisation is an option in English grammar that is used to avoid explicit contact with preferences implicit within policy recommendations (see Fairclough, 1989). For example, OFSTED and the Financial Services Authority (FSA) use nominalisation to secrete assumptions in their description of financial capability, as in "the development of ideas" (OFSTED, 2004, p. 6) or "the drive to make ideas happen" (FSA, 2006a), as well as in the use of agent-less passives, as in "tackling a problem," "identifying a need," "breaking down tasks" and "planning an activity" (OFSTED, 2004, p. 6). This not only distorts the representation of choice by leaving attributions of causality and responsibility unclear (Fairclough, 1989, p. 124) but omits consideration of value. This realm lies beneath the *choice* of "a problem" (such as who is empowered to choose and define "the" problem), resides in broader *assumptions* regarding what is or is not "a need" (such as equal- or over-consumption), and is concerned with the *consequences* of "an activity" (as upon the environment). In other words, the language surrounding the emergence of financial capability rallies collusion by presuming concurrence with unspoken values. In Horkheimer's terms these are "self-explanatory" (because "the economy is rapidly changing" and "flexible labour market," "short term contracts," and "greater longevity" will "all have serious implications for how we undertake financial planning") and the curriculum that emerges is presented as self-evidently un-contentious.

An alternative explanation is that the context underpinning the introduction of financial capability in schools has been part of a broader macroeconomic programme for socio-economic change in England since Prime Minister Thatcher in the late 1970s. On the one hand was an intentional economic shift toward neoliberalism enacted through a programme of market de-regulation, privatising state-owned enterprises, constructing public-sector market proxies in the residual state sector, reducing direct taxation, abolishing tariffs and subsidies, lifting control on foreign investments to encourage the mobility of capital, labour, and so on. On the other was a parallel agenda for social regulation that came to dominate New Labour discourses on 'individual responsibility,' opportunity, and a renewal of citizenship. This involved the preparation of citizens for a move away from a culture of dependency upon the welfare state, portrayed as costly, overburdened, inefficient, incapable of eliminating poverty, and orientated to cash entitlements, and its replacement with a 'welfare to workfare' programme. Here incentives and skills were to be provided for people to find employment and enable 'personal empowerment'—'a hand up rather than a hand out.' In essence, the Keynesian welfare state was to be dismantled and replaced by a Schumpeterian workfare one where the state's role was to create the structures for the successful operation of the market in which private individuals would increasingly need to take risk and compete and plan for themselves.

Education became one of the central carriers of this socio-economic project, acting as a conduit for ensuring that the new vision for social regulation was congruent with the economics of neoliberalism. Financial capability formed part of the attempt to naturalise and endorse it, or, in Jessop's phrase, "to make the continuing neoliberal transformation acceptable and sustainable rather than to question or challenge it" (Jessop, 2003). It is challengeable insofar as it takes technological change and globalisation as given, depersonalises and fetishises markets, and makes scant reference to the economic, political, and social forces that drive these preferences forward. The economic system is presented as natural and inevitable and imbued with a Weberian spirit where human actors are concealed in the construction of socio-economic activity, a process in which 'they' (economic forces) are presented as objective and inevitable, and 'we' (actors, subjects, 'people') are required to adapt to them. The absence of any obvious agency helps bind 'us' to the necessity of such economic propositions because "financial decisions impact," "choices and decisions" are made, and "changes happen" (see DfEE, 2000b), as with the introduction of student fees in higher education in England. 'People' are things to which events occur: "People need to … be skilled in managing their financial affairs" (DfEE, 2000b, p. 5); "problems can arrive when people fail to manage their money" (DfEE, 2000bibid, p. 5); "people are, more than ever before, being asked to take responsibility for managing their finances" (FSA, 2006b). Not agencies and actors like multinational companies, transnational banks, strategic alliances among giant companies, the military-industrial complex, the World Economic Forum, the International Monetary Fund, the World Bank, the Organisation for Economic Co-operation and Development, the World Trade Organisation, or trans-national elite (Robinson, 2004). Certainly not actors like trade unions.

Thus, the way the social-economic system is presented is not as a preference but a necessity, not a project but a Weberianesque inevitability, where 'personal financial capability' demands that pupils learn competencies and skills for use in a context cast as unalterable and where human agency enters through the need for personal survival. The current Minister of Education's depoliticising of the curriculum for economic education—"I'm not going to be coming up with any prescriptive lists, I just think there should be facts" (Gove, 2011)—emerges as policy in which pupils are to learn the facts of personal finance but are not enabled to question or critique the assumptions and values upon which they are based. One of the consequences, says Davies, is that in England, as in the US and Australia, young people will continue "to leave school with an inadequate understanding of their current economic system, and ... know even less about the economic alternatives among which they, as citizens, could choose" (Davies, 2006, p. 22).

CAPITALISM AND INSTRUMENTALISM

These educational discourses on managerialism, skills, and finance education exemplify instrumental reasoning in practice. The chapter has suggested that the way they are currently presented side lines reflection upon substantive assumptions by their disengagement from epistemic and normative realms that underpin and sustain them. Issues of purpose and value are presented as unproblematic, "taken for granted and supposedly self-explanatory" (Horkheimer, 1947/2004, p. 3), and consensus and agreement too often feigned or contrived. The paper has argued, however, that beyond their instrumental function they are *necessarily* tied to a normative agenda, are "hip-deep in normativity" to use Hampton's phrase, but are reticent to acknowledge their moral or political a priori. In 1972 Marcuse argued that the normative a priori underpinning Weber's instrumental rationality coincided with "capitalist rationality" in so far as its purpose was calculable efficiency and increased profit:

> Its rationality organizes and controls things and men, factory and bureaucracy, work and leisure. But *to what purpose* does it control them? Up to this point, Weber's concept of reason has been 'formal' ... But now the limits of formal reason emerge: neither the specific purpose of the scientific-technical construction nor its materials (its subjects and objects) can be deduced from the concept of reason; they explode from the start this formal, 'value-free' concept. (pp. 205–206. See also McGuigan, 2006, p. 14; Habermas, 1971, p. 82; Lyotard, 1984, p. 12)

Instrumental reasoning qua capitalist rationality helps explain the emergence of managerialism in education, the prominence of skill development today, and the ascendancy of finance capability in English schools. I take them in turn. Above it was argued that in discourses on managerialism "talk of effectiveness is not so agnostic about ends as it pretends" (Blake et. al., 1998, p. 132) inasmuch as substantive values are imported under the guise of ethical neutrality. One way of explaining this is to view these sequestered purposes as associated with compliance and efficiency and linked with a central requirement of capitalism to minimise costs by securing efficiency gains through the surveillance, control, and management of the labour market. For some this would help explain the de-politicisation of the public sphere as a site of potential instability, coupled with the associated fragmentation of communities and crises of political legitimation (Habermas, 1988). For others managerialism is comprehensible as a facet of capitalism insofar as it is "inseparable from a mode of human existence in which the contrivance of means is in central part the manipulation of human beings into compliant patterns of behaviour" (MacIntyre, 2007, p. 74). Manipulation, in short, is the moral and political a priori that underpins managerialism, its unclaimed purpose.

Skill development is also underpinned by capitalist rationality and accounted for when explaining historical shifts in content. Above it was argued that 'good' communication skills in school today preference certain linguistic behaviours commonly associated with girls, whereas boys in the past were thought "more likely to argue openly and to voice strong opinions" (OFSTED, 1993. See also QCA, 1998). But the transformation over the past two decades, from enabling female students to become more assertive to today's dominant paradigm were boys are required to become "better communicators" by becoming less judgemental, can be linked with labour and employability. Some have argued that the current content of communication skills in education might not simply be associated with "feminised language" but reflect a more general cultural shift toward manufacturing "the flexible worker" and "the responsible citizen" (see Cameron, 2000; 2008). In other words, the instrumental take on communication skills may actually be part of a broader response to an employability agenda where members of either sex are required not only to be economically creative and technically skilled but compliant "team players," malleable and collegiate in their outlook, and disposed to communicative compromise rather than argue a case or contest assumed values. Capitalist rationality demands it:

> Employers are usually best placed to judge how to develop their business, and what skills their current and future employees will need. Training is more likely to have an impact if the employer is engaged in its design and delivery, and is motivated to deploy the new skills effectively. (DfES, 2005a, para. 52–53. See also CBI/Universities UK, 2009)

From what already has been said, the link between capitalist rationality and the National Curriculum for personal financial capability is unambiguous. However, what is also clear is the new explicit curriculum for 2014 will run merely in tandem to an ongoing and *implicit* one that has gone on for years to ensure, in Whitty's phrase, "pupils are taught the right lesson": "We have not yet seen the life and teachings of Adam Smith written in the school timetable, but we should not assume that the lessons of neoliberalism are not being learnt" (Whitty, 2002, p. 94). Here he implies that while pupils may not have been explicitly taught the necessity for market deregulation they have for decades absorbed unreflectively a set of neoliberal assumptions. These lessons go undetected, derive from everyday common sense activities, and are tacitly endorsed when schools engage uncritically with such things as the collection of supermarket savings vouchers, the raising of money for charities, or engage in entrepreneurial challenges. Supermarket giants like Tesco and Sainsbury's issue vouchers for parents to collect in exchange for goods like computers for their child's school. By so doing they presumably seek community validation to counter those who would vilify them for colonising the high street (see Tescopoly, 2011). Schools also commonly teach children the virtues of charitable donation and so, from hunger lunches to cake fairs, sponsored runs to school discos, money is often raised and donated to good causes. It is an implicit curriculum for economics that fits seamlessly with Prime Minister Cameron's plan for a "Big Society" where state provision is to be replaced by "a new social norm around volunteering or charitable giving" (Cameron, 2009). What is not so evident is schools' willingness to teach pupils about the political and economic *assumptions* underpinning philanthropic donation and the degree to which state institutions, like the National Health Service, should come to rely upon charity (see Gibson, 2012, p. 646; 2008, pp. 62–64). Similarly, entrepreneurial challenges like Tenner Tycoon (2013) or the mimicking Dragon's Den in schools are part of an implicit curriculum for economics. The latter is a popular TV programme in England that sets entrepreneurs before investors, requiring them to argue a case to win sponsorship. It is an implicit lesson in neoliberalism endorsed by the school inspectorate:

> Through this work last year and the evolving work on trade and economy pupils gained valuable skills that were developed in their own version of Dragon's Den, where pupils' ideas for developing trade were tested out by other pupils. Through such activities pupils develop key skills that prepare them well for their future lives. (OFSTED, 2009, p. 6)

CONCLUSION

The chapter has tried to show how instrumental reasoning has colonised substantive or communicative reasoning. One consequence has been that beneath the veneer of procedural certainty where purposes are assumed and "taken for granted and supposedly self-explanatory," educational discourses reveal them to be often "hip-deep in normativity" and *necessarily* bound to an unacknowledged set of values. This deception operates not only in policy discourses on management, skills and financial capability, but extends to areas like "creativity" in education where it too can be shown to be linked with capitalist rationality. Apparently, the need to identify "value" and "purpose" is crucial when defining creativity: "imaginative activity fashioned so as to produce outcomes that are both original and of value" (DfEE, 1999; OFSTED, 2003). Seltzer and Bentley also see the importance of linking creativity with value: "Creativity is the application of knowledge and skills in new ways to achieve a valued goal" (1999, p. viii). However, because discussion of what *is* of value is omitted, the *purpose* is left free-floating. In the absence of any sustained epistemological or ethical discussion of what *are* valued goals, creativity appears supine to the needs of the economy with education policy following closely at heel: "To boost competitiveness in the knowledge economy, we must make radical changes to the educational system" (Seltzer & Bentley, 1999, p. viii). In other words, beneath these Weberianesque uses of creativity for instrumental ends lies a set of values directly attributable to the requirements of capitalism (see Gibson, 2005).

Habermas has argued that "in modern societies, economic and bureaucratic spheres emerge in which social relations are regulated only via money and power" (1987, p. 154). This he explains in terms of the economic and bureaucratic "system" penetrating the "lifeworld," the realm of substantive rationality (*Wertrationalität*), and corrupting its ability to mediate among norms, identities, and social traditions. Although he presents the lifeworld in terms of idealised communicative practices, rather than as a realm of contrasting social identities and competing values where forms of domination and power operate (see Fraser, 1985, p. 106; Jessop, 2003, p. 7), it is a model that can help explain the withering of the sphere in which liberal notions of reasoning were meant to operate, the domain where contestation, refutation, and argument were designed to judge between competing purposes.

Habermas has not written in detail about the way education is involved in ratifying or opposing this trend. Others, however, have suggested that his idea of the colonisation of the lifeworld can help explain how education has increasingly become "a vehicle for maintaining or enhancing the nation's economy" and how "teaching, learning and the curriculum are … themselves increasingly shaped by the model of economic exchange" (Deakin Crick & Joldersma, 2007, p. 82). Others have focussed more on the normative core within substantive rationality and the need for education to shift from its current preoccupation with the development of appropriate skills and attitudes in preparation for employment, to the development of students' readiness to engage in making value-judgements about the world (see Habermas, 1979, pp. 84–85. See also Carleheden, 2006; Englund, 2010). In these sorts of ways, education would engender what Habermas has called the epistemic need for a "persistent critique" of latent purposes and expose the substance and assumptions implicit in human reasoning (Habermas, 1984, p. 345). This would curtail the intensification of instrumental rationality (*Zweckrationalität*) as capitalism evolves, a process that "has reduced reason to a potential for knowledge that has lost, together with its critical sting, its commitment, its moral decisiveness and has been separated from such a decision as from an alien element" (Habermas, 1974, p. 258).

REFERENCES

Alexander, R. (2000). *Culture and pedagogy: International comparisons in primary education.* Oxford: Blackwell.

Audi, R. (2002). Prospects for a naturalization of practical reason: Humean instrumentalism and the normative authority of desire. *International Journal of Philosophical Studies, 10*(3), 235–263.

Baier, A. C. (1991). *A progress of sentiments: Reflections on Hume's treatise.* Cambridge, MA: Harvard University Press.

Ball, S. (2008). *The education debate.* Bristol: Policy.

Blake, N., Smeyers, P., Smith, R., & Standish, P. (1998). *Thinking again: Education after postmodernism.* London: Bergin & Garvey.

Bottery, M. (2000). *Education, policy and ethics.* London: Continuum.

BT (British Telecom). (2006). *BT education programme: Communication skills for life.* Retrieved 28 June 2006, from http://www.bteducation.org/communication

Cameron, D. (2000). *Good to talk? Living and working in a communication culture.* London: Sage.

Cameron, D. (2008). *The myth of Mars and Venus.* Oxford: Oxford University.

Cameron, D. (2009). *The big society.* Prime Minister Speech, 10 November. Retrieved 24 November 2013, from http://www.conservatives.com

Carleheden, M. (2006). Towards democratic foundations: A Habermasian perspective on the politics of education. *Journal of Curriculum Studies, 38*(5), 521–543.

CBI/Universities UK. (2009). *Future fit: Preparing graduates for the world of work.* UK.

Davies, P. (2006). Educating citizens for changing economies. *Journal of Curriculum Studies, 38*(1), 15–30.

DCSF (Department for Children, Schools and Families). (2007). *Key stage 3 curriculum review.* London: Crown.

Deakin Crick, R., & Joldersma, C. W. (2007). Habermas, life-long learning and citizenship. *Studies in Philosophy and Education, 26*(2), 77–95.

Deem, R., & Brehony, K. (2005). Management as ideology: The case of 'new managerialism' in higher education. *Oxford Review of Education, 31*(2), 217–235.

DfE (Department of Education). (2013). *The national curriculum in England.* London: Crown.

DfEE (Department for Education and Employment). (1999). *All our futures: Creativity, culture & education. (National Advisory Committee on Creativity and Cultural Education).* London: DfEE.

DfEE. (2000a). *The national curriculum: Handbook for primary teachers in England.* London: DfEE/QCA.

DfEE. (2000b). *Financial capability through personal financial education: Guidance for schools at key stages 1 & 2* and *3 & 4.* London: DfEE/QCA.

DfES (Department for Education and Skills). (2004a). *National standards for headteachers.* London: DfES.

DfES. (2004b). *Every child matters.* London: DfES.

DfES. (2005a). *Skills: Getting on in business, getting on at work.* London: HMSO.

DfES. (2005b). *Skills for productivity*. London: DfES.

Dickens, C. (1966). *Oliver Twist*. Oxford: Clarenden.

Ecclestone, K., & Hayes, D. (2009). *The dangerous rise of therapeutic education*. Abingdon: Routledge.

Englund, T. (2010). Educational implications of the idea of deliberative democracy. In M. Murphy & T. Fleming (Eds.), *Habermas, critical theory and education* (pp. 19–32). Abingdon: Routledge.

Fairclough, N. (1989). *Language and power*. London: Pearson.

Fraser, N. (1985). What's critical about critical theory? The case of Habermas and gender. *New German Critique, 35*, 97–131.

FSA (Financial Services Authority). (2006a). *Financial capability in the UK: Delivering change*. Retrieved 22 November 2013, from http://www.fsa.gov.uk/

FSA. (2006b). *Financial capability in the UK: Creating a step change in schools*. Retrieved 22 November 2013, from http://www.fsa.gov.uk

Garrett, D. (1997). *Cognition and commitment in Hume's philosophy*. Oxford: Oxford University.

Gibson, H. (2005). What creativity isn't: The presumptions of instrumental and individual justifications for creativity in education. *British Journal of Educational Studies, 53*(2), 148–167.

Gibson, H. (2008). Ideology, instrumentality and economics education: On the secretion of values within philanthropy, financial capability and enterprise education in English schools. *International Review of Economics Education, 7*(2), 57–78.

Gibson, H. (2011). Management, skills and creativity: The purpose and value of instrumental reasoning in education discourse. *Oxford Review of Education, 37*(6), 699–716.

Gibson, H. (2012). Economic wellbeing: Critical reflections upon policy and practice in English primary schools. *Journal of Curriculum Studies, 44*(5), 631–658.

Gove, M. (2011). *We need to have facts in the curriculum*. Interview with Justin Webb, Radio 4, Today programme, Thursday 20 January 2011. Retrieved 24 November 2013, from http://news.bbc.co.uk/today/hi/today/newsid_9367000/9367626.stm

Habermas, J. (1971). *Toward a rational society: Student protest, science, and politics*. London: Heinemann.

Habermas, J. (1974). *Theory and practice*. London: Heinemann.

Habermas, J. (1979). *Communication and the evolution of society*. London: Heinemann.

Habermas, J. (1984). *The theory of communicative action, Vol. 1: Reason and the rationalization of society*. (T. McCarthy, Trans.). London: Heinemann.

Habermas. J. (1987). *The theory of communicative action, Vol. 2: The critique of functionalist reason* (T. McCarthy, Trans.). London: Heinemann.

Habermas, J. (1988). *Legitimation crisis*. Cambridge: Polity.

Hampton, J. (1996). On instrumental rationality. In J. B. Schneewind (Ed.), *Reason, ethics, and society* (pp. 84–116) Chicago: Open Court.

Hampton, J. (1998). *The authority of reason*. Cambridge: Cambridge University Press.

Holmes, E. (2006). *Peer mediation*. Retrieved 2 June, 2006, from http://66.249.93.104/search?q=cache:gCPlqX8S5-YJ

Horkheimer, M. (1974/1967). *Critique of instrumental reason*. New York: Seabury.

Horkheimer, M. (2004/1947). *Eclipse of reason*. New York: Continuum.

Hubin, D. (2001). The groundless normativity of instrumental rationality. *The Journal of Philosophy, 98*(9), 445–468.

Hume, D. (1973). *A treatise of human nature*. Oxford: Oxford University.

Hume, D. (1996). *Enquiries concerning human understanding and concerning the principles of morals* (3rd ed.). Oxford: Clarendon.

Jessop, B. (2003). *Good governance and the urban question: On managing the contradictions of neo-liberalism.* Lancaster: Department of Sociology, Lancaster University. Retrieved from http://www.lancs.ac.uk/fass/sociology/research/publications/papers/jessop-gender-selectivities.pdf

Korsgaard, C. M. (1997). The normativity of instrumental reason. In G. Cullity & B. Gaut (Eds.), *Ethics and practical reason* (pp. 215–254). Oxford: Clarendon.

Levine, D. N. (1981). Rationality and freedom: Weber and beyond. *Sociological Inquiry, 51*(1), 5–25.

Lillehammer, H. (2007). *Companions in guilt: Arguments for ethical objectivity.* Basingstoke: Palgrave Macmillan.

Lukes, S. (2008). *Moral relativism.* New York: Picador.

Lyotard, J.-F. (1984). *The postmodern condition: A report on knowledge.* Manchester: Manchester University Press.

Macdonald, A. (2009). *Independent review of the proposal to make personal, social, health and economic (PSHE) education statutory.* London: DCSF.

MacIntyre, A. (2007). *After virtue: A study in moral theory* (3rd ed.). London: Duckworth.

Marcuse, H. (1972). *Negations: Essays in critical theory.* Middlesex: Penguin.

McGuigan, J. (2006). *Modernity and postmodern culture* (2nd ed.). Buckingham: Open University Press.

Middlesbrough EiC Partnership. (2006). *Circle time.* Retrieved 20 June 2007, from www.eic-middlesbrough.gov.uk

Moore, J. (1976). Hume's theory of justice and property. *Political Studies, 24*(2), 103–119.

Nagel, T. (1970). *The possibility of altruism.* Princeton, NJ: Princeton University Press.

O'Neill, O. (1998). Practical reason and ethics. In *Routledge encyclopaedia of philosophy* (pp. 613–619). London: Routledge.

OFSTED. (1993). *Boys and English.* London: SCAA.

OFSTED. (2003). *Expecting the unexpected: Developing creativity in primary and secondary schools.* London: HMI.

OFSTED. (2004). *Learning to be enterprising: An evaluation of enterprise learning at Key Stage 4.* HMI 2148. London: HMI.

OFSTED. (2009). *Freshford C of E Primary—School Inspection Report.* Retrieved 31 March 2011, from www.ofsted.gov.uk

Pring, R. (2005). *Philosophy of education: Aims, theory, common sense and research.* London: Continuum.

QCA (Qualification and Curriculum Authority). (1998). *Can do better: Raising boys' achievement in English.* Hayes: QCA.

QCA. (2005). *Sex and relationship education, healthy lifestyles and financial capability: Teacher's handbook and units of work.* London: QCA/05/1695.

Raz, J. (2005). The myth of instrumental rationality. *Journal of Ethics and Social Philosophy, 1*(1), 2–28.

Robinson, K. (2004, 12 March). At long last a break in the clouds. (Supplement). *The Times Educational.*

Russell, B. (1961). *Marriage and morals.* London: Unwin.

Schilpp, P. A. (1971). *The philosophy of Bertrand Russell.* (4th ed.). Chicago: Open Court.

Schopenhauer, A. (1974). *On the fourfold root of the principle of sufficient reason.* Chicago: Open Court.

Seltzer, K., & Bentley, T. (1999). *The creative age: Knowledge and skills for the new economy.* London: Demos.

Setiya, K. (2004). Hume on practical reason. *Philosophical Perspectives, 18*, 365–389.

Swidler, A. (1973). The concept of rationality in the work of Max Weber. *Sociological Inquiry, 43*(1), 35–42.

Teachernet. (2006). *Circle Time*. Retrieved 2 June 2005, from http://www.teachernet.gov.uk/teachingandlearning/library/circletime/

Teddlie, C., & Reynolds, D. (2000). *The international handbook of school effectiveness research*. London: Falmer.

Tenner Tycoon. (2013). *It's in your hands*. Retrieved from 23 October 2013, from http://www.tenner.org.uk

Tescopoly. (2011). Retrieved 9 November 2011, from www.tescopoly.org

Weber, M. (1930). *The Protestant ethic and the spirit of capitalism*. London: Unwin.

Weber, M. (1948). *From Max Weber: Essays in sociology*. New York: Oxford University.

Weber, M. (1958). Zur Lage der bürgerliche Demokratie in Russland. In J. Winckelmann (Ed.), *Gesammelte Politische Schriften*. Tübingen: Mohr.

Weber, M. (1968). *Economy and society*. 2 Vols. (G. Roth & C. Wittich, Eds.). New York: Bedminister.

Whitty, G. (2002). *Making sense of education policy*. London: Sage.

Wrigley, T. (2006). *Another school is possible*. London: Bookmarks & Trentham.

NOTE

1. This chapter is based upon a paper first published in the *Oxford Review of Education*, 2011.

CHAPTER EIGHT

Financial Fantasy Documents and Public Learning

The Case of the U.S. Financial Crisis Inquiry Report

JAMES REVELEY AND JOHN SINGLETON

> It is not by means of a metaphor that a banking or stock-market transaction, a claim, a coupon, a credit, is able to arouse people who are not necessarily bankers ... Desire is present wherever something flows and runs, carrying along with it interested subjects—but also drunken or slumbering subjects—toward lethal destinations.
>
> —Deleuze & Guattari, 2009, 104–105

INTRODUCTION

This chapter looks at the interplay between fantasy and the United States variant of financialised capitalism. The quotation immediately above serves as the springboard to our discussion. Consistent with their materialism, Deleuze and Guattari (2009) argue in their masterwork *Anti-Oedipus* that "it is not possible to attribute a special form of existence to desire, a mental or psychic reality that is presumably different from the material reality of social production" (p. 30). Desire permeates the social field; it is just as "present" in flows of money capital as it is in seminal flows. The corollary is that "fantasy is never individual: it is group fantasy"; simply put, fantasies are "secondary expressions" of how desire manifests in social production and its specifically capitalist forms (Deleuze & Guattari, p. 30, emphasis omitted).

How desire enters into finance capital circuits is a topical issue. Crosthwaite (2010) describes stock market traders as self-destructive actors, impelled by a death desire, in a libidinal economy that culminated in the global financial crisis.

Other researchers make the connection between financialised capitalism and culturally derived collective fantasies that circulate within society at large. In the British context, Glynos, Klimecki, and Willmott (2012) attribute the lack of large-scale public resistance to post-crisis austerity measures to the operation of a "fantasmatic logic" that functions like a social pressure release valve to restore faith in financialisation as the key to future prosperity. Indeed, Foster and McChesney (2012) argue that economic policies in the U.S. are currently directed at "the reinstitution of financialization" (p. 46)—the sheer irrationality of which can be taken as a sign that finance has economic policymakers entranced.

Official reports by government inquiries provide yet another window to understanding how the fantasy world of finance obtrudes upon the social field. We seek to illustrate this point by looking at the 2011 report issued by the U.S. Financial Crisis Inquiry Commission (FCIC), also known as the Angelides Commission after its Chairman Phil Angelides. Though we find Deleuze and Guattari's materialist theory of group fantasy helpful, ours is not primarily a psychoanalytic study nor is it an exercise in fine-grained textual or discourse analysis. Rather, we draw on work by sociologists and organisational theorists who conceptualise official reports as fantasy documents that fulfil a social function. We therefore look at the FCIC report as a social fact in its own right, rather than merely as a source of information about the crisis. We also track the report's engagement with a wider social fantasy about the existence of a new period—immediately prior to the 2008 financial crisis—of finance-driven growth. For that task we supplement the fantasy documents literature with work by economists whose crisis theories have an affinity with an emergent psychoanalytic literature on this topic.

Our chapter has the following structure. After providing a brief overview of the FCIC, we introduce the theory of fantasy documents. Then we identify how the FCIC report channels two types of fantasy, thus supporting our contention that it is a financial fantasy document. A brief conclusion rounds out the discussion.

ORIGINS AND STRUCTURE OF THE FCIC REPORT

Created in 2009 by means of the Fraud Enforcement and Recovery Act (FERA), the FCIC's ten members comprised six Democrat nominees and four Republican nominees. A Californian politician, gubernatorial candidate, and former state treasurer, Chairman Phil Angelides came from the Democratic side of U.S. politics.[1] As the rubric in FERA states, the Commission's purpose was "to examine the causes, domestic and global, of the current financial and economic crisis in the United States."[2] FCIC hearings took place during 2010, and the voluminous report, which ran to more than 600 pages, was published in January 2011.

The Commission's bipartisan nature meant that the die was cast from the beginning: the commissioners could not agree on the findings. The latter part of the report contains two dissenting statements—one jointly written by three Republican commissioners (Keith Hennessey, Douglas Holtz-Eakin, and Bill Thomas), and the second—more substantive—statement written by the remaining Republican appointee Peter J. Wallison.

Despite the discordant element that the dissenting statements introduce into the latter part of the report, it is structured in a way that carries the reader along. Each chapter subsection is headed with a bracing quote from a key actor that frames the points made. The report has five sections comprising 22 chapters in total and is written in an accessible style. This is no accident. Like the 1932 Pecora Commission of inquiry into the causes of the Wall Street Crash, the FCIC commissioners were clearly playing to the public gallery. Indeed, it would be worthwhile to analyse the tropes the report's authors use to tell a particular story about the crisis and to apportion blame for the event. Whittle and Mueller (2012) have done just such an analysis of the 2009 British Treasury Select Committee hearings into the collapse of the banking industry. However, to recapitulate, our interest is not in the report's internal narratological properties but rather in the external social function which it fulfils. To that end we turn now to explain how the theory of fantasy documents can be applied to the text.

FINANCIAL FANTASY DOCUMENTS

The term "fantasy document" was coined by the sociologist Lee Clarke (1999) in a study of the symbolic functions of disaster planning. National level disaster plans, he says, are fantasy documents when they are created for the rhetorical purpose of reassuring the general public that the potential for disaster can be controlled—in circumstances where "high uncertainty" makes such control nigh on impossible (Clarke, 1999, p. 4). Channelling the political theorist Murray Edelman, Clarke argues that in the national arena fantasy documents function as a "political palliative" to the extent that they "offer the public soothing solutions to difficult problems" (p. 145).

To transfer this theory to the financial realm we draw on Birkland (2009) who adapts the idea of pre-disaster planning documents as convenient fictions and applies it to official inquiries into the causes of disasters. Though he does not examine financial disaster inquiries, what he says is relevant to them. The reports of disaster investigations he terms "fantasy learning documents" on the basis of their overriding rhetorical function (p. 146). Birkland makes the connection with public learning in the sense that the rhetoric of "lessons learned" masks the fact that "these documents and the processes that create them are mere reflections of a group's or interest's preferred social construction of a problem and its 'target populations'" (p. 154). Our analysis is informed by this approach but takes one step beyond it. We look at how the FCIC report reproduces a fantasy akin to the type Birkland identifies. Yet, at the same time, we maintain that the FCIC report exposes a wider social fantasy about reaching a new era of endless economic prosperity.

The two fantasies can be labelled as follows. First, the FCIC report responds to a recurrent collective fantasy of living in a new era of unlimited growth and stability. Using a phrase from Reinhart and Rogoff (2009), we call it the "This Time is Different" fantasy. We argue that the FCIC was not able fully to break free of that fantasy's spell. Second, in an attempt to offer public reassurance that policymakers have learnt lessons from the financial crisis, the report perpetuates the fantasy of objective explanation and the achievement of consensus within a highly politicised—and formally bipartisan—official inquiry. We call this the "We Can Explain What Went Wrong" fantasy.

THE FIRST FANTASY: "THIS TIME IS DIFFERENT"

This fantasy stems from a defect in the economic imagination that gives rise to what we will call "new era thinking." This fault has deep cultural taproots as people refract economic conditions through culturally supplied sensemaking devices. Prime among these is the narratological framework of storytelling (Frank, 2010). Economists have begun to realise that stories are not merely irrational glitches in the otherwise rational deliberations of the neoclassical figure of *homo economicus*, but rather are central to people's thinking and decision making and thus play a decisive role in economic life. In a break with the neoclassical tradition, Akerlof and Shiller (2009, p. 167) show how "stories that interpret the economy" are responsible for mood swings of economic confidence or pessimism. Confidence-boosting "new era stories" are "those that purport to describe historic changes that will propel the economy into a brand new era" (Akerlof & Shiller, p. 55).

Prior to the financial crisis, two intersecting storylines accompanied the housing boom and mortgage securitization bonanza in the U.S. The first was a tale that people told themselves and others about housing prices. As Akerlof and Shiller insightfully observe:

> The story in this case was that the price of housing had never declined (that is only a story, and it is actually untrue) and therefore that it would just continue to go up and up. There was nothing to lose. (2009, p. 170)

The second story was about Wall Street's expertise and foresight in bundling (securitization) and slicing-and-dicing of home loans into a variety of derivatives.

In financial circles, the "story of the go-go years was that all of these securitizations and derivatives were about 'risk management'" (Akerlof & Shiller, 2009, p. 87).

In short, new era-type storytelling expresses the recurring social fantasy that a period of permanent stability, unlike anything experienced in the past, has been reached. Stated in terms that Reinhart and Rogoff (2009) employ in their magistral history of financial crises, this fantasy manifests as the "This-Time-is-Different Syndrome" (p. 15). They identify a consistent pattern to this zeitgeist's emergence in boom periods that precede crises:

> Each time, society convinces itself that the current boom, unlike the many booms that preceded catastrophic collapses in the past, is built on sound fundamentals, structural reforms, technological innovation, and good policy. (p. xxxiv)

In the U.S., prior to the financial crisis, the euphoria of apparently limitless growth and opportunity was sustained by new era thinking that saw crises as a historical—and indeed a foreign—curiosity. Reinhart and Rogoff put it this way:

> The thinking at the time: Everything is fine because of globalization, the technology boom, our superior financial system, our better understanding of monetary policy, and the phenomenon of securitized debt ... Housing prices doubled and equity prices soared, all fuelled by record borrowing from abroad. But most people thought the United States could never have a financial crisis resembling that of an emerging market. (2009, p. 20, emphasis omitted)

By an emerging market they mean a developing country. So this instance of new era thinking is yet another twist on the theme of American exceptionalism.

In its depiction of the pre-crisis euphoria, the FCIC report, in effect, is an attempt to puncture the This Time Is Different fantasy. To the extent that the report documents how the actions of the Federal Reserve and pronouncements by its governor Alan Greenspan sustained that fantasy, it succeeds in doing so. Read this way, the first part of the report (consisting of chapters 1–10) is a study in how collective economic fantasies are reinforced by central bankers. We will now provide some excerpts to support this reading.

The FCIC report argues that in the run-up to the near collapse of the financial system in 2008 there was a widespread belief in the U.S. that the economy was insulated from calamity by official agencies including the Federal Reserve. Faith in "the Fed" had built over the preceding twenty or so years. After orchestrating the bailout of the hedge fund of Long-Term Capital Management in 1998 in the wake of shockwaves from Russia defaulting on its national debt payments "Federal Reserve Chairman [Alan] Greenspan became a cult hero—the 'Maestro'—who had handled every emergency since the 1987 stock market crash" (FCIC, 2011, p. 59). The Fed's actions in cutting interest rates after the bursting of the tech (or "dotcom") bubble in 2000 and the events of 9/11 only served to reinforce "investor's faith that the Fed would keep the capital markets functioning no matter what" (FCIC, 2011, p. 61). The FCIC quotes from testimony by Lawrence Lindsay, a former governor of the Fed, that "we had convinced ourselves that we were in a less risky world" (FCIC, p. 61).

The report paints a picture of regulators, central bankers, investors, and others being entranced by the seemingly limitless money-making opportunities in finance. The trance was not easily broken. For one, "Greenspan argued the financial system had achieved unprecedented resilience" (FCIC, p. 83). Such pronouncements did nothing to stop new era thinking cascading down from the financial elite to working and middle-class homeowners. Driven by cheap mortgage credit, many expanded their disposable income by leveraging their houses in the belief that house prices would continue their upward trend.

> As home prices rose, homeowners with greater equity felt more financially secure and, partly as a result, saved less and less. Many others went one step further, borrowing against the equity. The effect was unprecedented debt: between 2001 and 2007, mortgage debt nationally nearly doubled. (FCIC, p. 83)

Congress and by implication the general public continued to be reassured by the Fed that the risk of an economic calamity was low. In mid-2005 Greenspan's advice to Congress's Joint Economic Committee was as follows:

> That growth in nonprime mortgages was helping to push home prices in some markets to unsustainable levels, 'although a "bubble" in home prices for the national as a whole does not appear likely.' (FCIC, p. 158)

This was not the view of Greenspan alone, but rather accords with the assessment by Federal Reserve economists at the time. Drawing on internal Fed documents the report offers the following summary:

> Even in the face of a large price decline, they [the economists] argued, defaults would not be widespread, given the large equity that many borrowers still had in their homes. Structural changes in the mortgage market made a crisis less likely, and the financial system seemed well capitalized. (FCIC, p. 159)

The report succinctly summarises the view of financial sector regulators with the mantra "Markets Will Always Self-Correct"; within regulatory agencies there was "a widely held view that market participants had the situation well in hand" (FCIC, pp. 170–171).

The situation was a long way from being in hand. Tellingly, chapter 10 of the report is titled "The Madness." It refers to developments in 2006–2007, when house prices began to fall, yet still "everyone wanted a piece of the action" (FCIC, p. 189). The mania was fuelled by Collateralized Debt Obligations (CDOs), particularly those of the "synthetic" variety, which were just financial instruments built upon other financial instruments. Synthetic CDOs were "composed not of real mortgage securities but just of bets on other mortgage products" (FCIC, p. 8). Credit default swaps were integral to synthetic CDOs. Here is how they worked:

> Investors in these CDOs included 'funded' long investors, who paid cash to purchase actual securities issued by the CDO; 'unfunded' long investors, who entered into swaps with the CDO, making money if the reference securities performed; and 'short' investors, who bought credit default swaps on the reference securities, making money if the securities failed. (FCIC, p. 142)

The riskiest versions of these CDOs "were bought by hedge funds that were often engaged in complex trading strategies: they made money when the CDOs performed, but could also make money if the market crashed" (FCIC, p. 188). Hence the continuing demand for mortgages to securitize even after house prices began to decline.

The FCIC argues that as the housing bubble began to burst, early in 2007, government officials—including the then Fed Chairman Ben Bernanke and Treasury Secretary Henry Paulson—underestimated risks to the wider economy. Paulson is quoted as saying at the time that "from the standpoint of the overall economy, my bottom line is that we're watching it closely but it appears to be contained" (FCIC, p. 234). When banks and other financial institutions began to fail, the report maintains, a crisis of confidence in the financial system resulted. The initial government response did not help matters:

> The inconsistency of federal government decisions in not rescuing Lehman after having rescued Bear Stearns and the GSEs, and immediately before rescuing AIG, added to uncertainty and panic in the financial markets. (FCIC, p. 343)

Panic, indeed—if we were asked to choose a single sentence that summarises the tonality of the FCIC report, it would be this: "countless Americans joined in the financial euphoria that seized the nation" (FCIC, p. 4). The report's use of the language of emotion—panic, optimism, and so forth—is not insignificant. By connecting the report's emotional leitmotif with its economic lineage, we think it is possible to make a link back to the fantasy realm.

In its attempt to lift the veil of the "This Time Is Different" fantasy, the FCIC report falls into line with an established body of economic thought about the origins of economic and financial crises. It is traceable back to John Maynard Keynes (1936) and continued in a slightly different way by Hyman Minsky (1982), as well as by Charles Kindleberger and Robert Aliber (2011) in their popular book about financial manias. Each deals at least implicitly with fantasy worlds because the key message in their work is that individuals are less to blame for crises than are swings in optimism. In the euphoric phase there is a systematic underestimation of risk and an ignoring of uncertainty. The FCIC report can be read to suggest that the Fed did nothing to dampen the euphoria and may well have fuelled it.

When economists such as Kindleberger use a term such as 'euphoria' to describe aspects of a financial bubble, they come close to the language of neo-Freudian psychoanalysis regarding unconscious fantasy. Reflecting on the dotcom bubble of the late 1990s, Tuckett and Taffler (2008) argue that financial assets become "phantastic objects" representing the deepest desires of investors. In their paranoid-schizoid state investors suppress all doubts and make light of the risks they are bearing, but when the markets turn against them they resort "to denial, to anger, and then to paranoid efforts to find scapegoats" (Tuckett & Taffler, p. 404). In the same vein, Stein (2011) discusses the "manic culture" that gripped financial markets in the years leading up to the 2008 crash.

Yet, despite the report displaying the FCIC's intuitive grasp of how quirks of collective psychology and unconscious investment in fantasy worlds were implicated in the financial crisis, it too was mesmerised by at least one element of the "This Time Is Different" fantasy. Based on an economist's close reading of the FCIC report, Barba (2011) argues that the FCIC was captivated by the realm of circulation—high finance and money—to the exclusion of non-financial factors in the crisis. He identifies, in particular, the role of rising household debt due to credit-based consumption that, since the 1980s, underpropped U.S. consumption demand. His critique of the FCIC ("the Commission") is worth quoting at length:

> Precisely because of the incapability to assess the role of the financial system and its lending practices in connection with economic conditions generally (i.e. to the non-monetary causes of the crisis), the Commission has been unable to focus its reconstruction of events on the constraints the government was trying to overcome by monetary means. This was, in some way, an inevitable mistake. The economic debate before the outbreak of the crisis was so taken by the idea that capitalism had finally entered a phase of stable growth that a systemic crisis like that which occurred in 2007–08 was unthinkable. This attitude was so strong that it survived the crisis. Many still see it as a highly unlikely catastrophic event (the black swan), an occurrence that can certainly happen without challenging the conventional vision that must hold most of the time. (p. 96)

In other words, the FCIC's explanation of the crisis in purely financial terms is explicable in terms of the pervasiveness of the "This Time Is Different" fantasy. Despite the FCIC's attempts to puncture this fantasy, it seeped into the text of the report.

THE SECOND FANTASY: "WE CAN EXPLAIN WHAT WENT WRONG"

In general, this fantasy is expressed through public learning rhetoric in which 'lessons learned' is a narrative resource politicians and those charged with investigating a crisis use in an attempt to craft a neat-and-tidy 'official' account of why it occurred and, by implication, how such a thing can be prevented from happening again. To the extent that the FCIC tries to distil lessons so as to reassure the public, the report perpetuates this fantasy and hence it can be described not just as a financial fantasy document—on the grounds that it reproduces the "This Time Is Different" fantasy—but as a fantasy public learning document. It is a document from which an 'educated' public can see lessons that supposedly will be or have been learnt by policymakers.

Some say objective explanation is itself a culturally derived—Western world—fantasy (Latour, 2010). We do not go that far. Instead, what we are saying is that the explanatory fantasy in the FCIC case is based on the belief that consensus is achievable within a bipartisan inquiry into a complex economic event. The notion that a commission of inquiry can sit for several months and derive an explanation of what happened is fanciful. Yet this is just what the FCIC tried to do. The reason the report succumbed to the explanatory fantasy is due to the latent social function that it—and indeed all reports of this nature—fulfil. Writing about official inquiries into the global financial crisis, Glynos et al. (2012) call it the public "soothing" or "cooling out" function. Though their explanation focuses on Britain, it is eminently applicable to the FCIC report.

A brief explanation of the theoretical base from which Glynos and his co-authors derive this function is in order. They draw on the argument about the importance in everyday interactions of "cooling out" made by the sociologist Erving Goffman in his classic interactionist paper, "On Cooling the Mark Out" (1952). For Goffman, "the mark" is someone who suffers a loss in self-esteem due to experiences that challenge their self-definition. For those who do not see themselves as being easy to dupe, getting ripped off is a prime example of what Goffman is talking about. David Denby's (2004) *American Sucker*, his autobiographical account of foolishly blowing all his money in Internet stocks in 2000, superbly illustrates how failed investors can be construed as marks. In Goffmanesque terms the "cooling out" process entails adjusting to the loss, often assisted by "coolers" such as counsellors and others who offer sympathetic advice (pp. 456–458).

Glynos et al. (2012) take the cooling methods that Goffman documents at the micro-social level and transpose them up to the level of society as a whole. In the financial crisis, the "marks" were the public at large and the "cooler" function is fulfilled by official inquiries and reports. Looking at how two reports on finance and banking in the British context were received, they conclude that "key reports … are important (restorative) cooling devices that reaffirm the value of neoliberal finance capital" (p. 308). Cooling or 'soothing' reports seek to allay public concern about financialisation and to restore faith in finance-based capital accumulation as providing a path back to prosperity.

Considered this way, the FCIC report was an exercise in cooling out the American public. In Clarke's (1999) terms, the report provides a socio-political palliative dressed up in the rhetoric of lessons learned. Yet due to the dissent the report contains, this function was only partially fulfilled. No amount of gloss can hide the fact that more than 100 pages of the report are devoted to the dissenting views.

Barba (2011) shows that the cleft in the FCIC was evident by mid-2010, as political developments overtook the commissioners' deliberations. As he explains, this is when

> President Obama signed a lightweight financial reform [the Dodds-Frank Act or DFA], which was declared by both Republicans and Democrats as final ... After the enactment of the DFA, commissioners found themselves in the unpleasant position of having to conclude a 'preliminary work' for a financial reform bill that the Congress had already passed. (p. 78)

The level of dissent demonstrates that the notion that official inquiries can explain what went wrong, especially so soon after the event and in a politically charged environment, is little more than a fantasy. As a cooling device, the FCIC report is the quintessential fantasy public learning document.

CONCLUSION

Hopefully, by showing how crisis-prone financialised capitalism is buttressed by official reports that perpetuate enduring social fantasies, we have succeeded at inserting some new ideas into the financialisation debate. With regard to the "We Can Explain What Went Wrong" fantasy, we have argued that the FCIC report pressed into service a "lessons learned" trope in which public and policymaker "learning" is merely a form of rhetoric by which its authors—whether consciously or unconsciously—sought to fulfil a latent cooling out function. A financially literate public is a desirable thing; yet far from promoting this goal the FCIC report's cooling out role is at odds with it. Cooling out is not about *educating* but rather *soothing* the general public concerns about finance capital's role in the crisis. This makes perfect sense if one accepts Foster and McChesney's (2012) thesis that policymakers in the U.S. are currently looking to financialisation to reinvigorate a largely stagnant economy.

We want to finish with a brief reflection on one philosophico-theoretical implication of the FCIC report's bolstering of the "This Time Is Different" fantasy. This point takes us full circle, back to our opening quotation. The FCIC's focus on financial factors alone, which Barba (2011) documents, and especially the commissioners' preoccupation with optimism, confidence, euphoria, and so forth, risks a purely subjective crisis explanation that lacks a materialist anchor in capitalist economic conditions. To be sure, such an explanation is congruent with neo-Freudian accounts of how fantasy plays out in financial circles. Yet, an unreconstituted psychoanalytic theory without a materialist foundation is, as Deleuze and Guattari (2009) argue, at best incomplete and at worst socio-politically regressive. The challenge is to ground the analysis of the fantasies of financialised capitalism in as materialist a foundation as possible, without losing sight of subjectivity. By focusing on one particular kind of textual-material artefact that circulates in Western societies at times of financial crisis—the official inquiry report—our chapter just scratches the surface. More work is needed to mine a Deleuze–Guattarian vein for insights into financial fantasy worlds.

REFERENCES

Akerlof, G. A., & Shiller, R. J. (2009). *Animal spirits: How human psychology drives the economy, and why it matters for global capitalism*. Princeton, NJ: Princeton University Press.

Barba, A. (2011). The US Congress inquiry on the financial and economic crisis. *Contributions to Political Economy, 30*(1), 77–98.

Birkland, T. A. (2009). Disasters, lessons learned, and fantasy documents. *Journal of Contingencies and Crisis Management, 17*(3), 146–156.

Clarke, L. (1999). *Mission improbable: Using fantasy documents to tame disaster*. Chicago: University of Chicago Press.

Crosthwaite, P. (2010). Blood on the trading floor. *Angelaki: Journal of the Theoretical Humanities, 15*(2), 3–18.

Deleuze, G., & Guattari, F. (2009). *Anti-Oedipus: Capitalism and schizophrenia*. New York: Penguin.

Denby, D. (2004). *American sucker*. Melbourne: Text.

FCIC. (2011). *The financial crisis inquiry report*. Washington, DC: U.S. Government Printing Office.

Foster, J. B., & McChesney, R. W. (2012). *The endless crisis: How monopoly-finance capital produces stagnation and upheaval from the USA to China*. New York: Monthly Review.

Frank, A. W. (2010). *Letting stories breathe: A socio-narratology*. Chicago: University of Chicago Press.

Glynos, J., Klimecki, R., & Willmott, H. (2012). Cooling out the marks: The ideology and politics of the financial crisis. *Journal of Cultural Economy, 5*(3), 297–320.

Goffman, E. (1952). On cooling the mark out. *Psychiatry: Journal of the Biology and the Pathology of Interpersonal Relations, 15*(4), 451–463.

Keynes, J. M. (1936). *The general theory of employment, interest, and money*. London: Macmillan.

Kindleberger, C. P., & Aliber, R. Z. (2011). *Manias, panics, and crashes: A history of financial crises*. Basingstoke: Palgrave Macmillan.

Latour, B. (2010). *On the modern cult of the factish gods*. Durham, NC: Duke University Press.

Minsky, H. P. (1982). The financial-instability hypothesis: Capitalist processes and the behaviour of the economy. In C. P. Kindleberger & J. P. Laffargue (Eds.), *Financial crises: Theory, history & policy* (pp. 13–39). Cambridge: Cambridge University Press.

Reinhart, C. M., & Rogoff, K. S. (2009). *This time is different: Eight centuries of financial folly*. Princeton, NJ: Princeton University Press.

Stein, M. (2011). A culture of mania: A psychoanalytic view of the incubation of the 2008 credit crisis. *Organization, 18*(2), 173–186.

Tuckett, D., & Taffler, D. (2008). Phantastic objects and the financial market's sense of reality: A psychoanalytic contribution to the understanding of stock market instability. *International Journal of Psychoanalysis, 89*, 389–412.

Whittle, A., & Mueller, F. (2012). Bankers in the dock: Moral storytelling in action. *Human Relations, 65*(1), 111–139.

NOTES

1. The other commissioners and their political affiliations are as follows: Bill Thomas (Republican), Brooksley Born (Democrat), Byron Georgiou (Democrat), Bob Graham (Democrat), Keith Hennessey (Republican), Douglas Holtz-Eakin (Republican), Heather H. Murren (Democrat), John W. Thompson (Democrat), and Peter J. Wallison (Republican).
2. http://en.wikipedia.org/wiki/Financial_Crisis_Inquiry_Commission

CHAPTER NINE

The Rationality Crisis IN U.S. Higher Education[1]

CLYDE W. BARROW

> By the second section of the intelligible world you may understand me to mean all that unaided reasoning apprehends by the power of dialectic ... like a flight of steps up which it may mount all the way to something that is not hypothetical, the first principle of all ... never making use of any sensible object, but only of Forms, moving through Forms from one to another, and ending with Forms. I understand, he said, though not perfectly; for the procedure you describe sounds like an enormous undertaking.
>
> —PLATO, *THE REPUBLIC*

CAPITALISM, CRISIS THEORY, AND THE UNIVERSITY[2]

The capitalist system is frequently conceptualized as a matrix of three interdependent, but relatively autonomous subsystems: the economic system, the political system, and the ideological system.[3] The most important institutions associated with the economic subsystem are the relations of production between classes in the workplace and relations of exchange between buyers and sellers in the marketplace. The ideological subsystem, from which individuals derive normative values, includes the family, educational institutions, religion, and cultural outlets. Finally, in late capitalism, the political subsystem consists primarily of those institutions organized as the state and the policies implemented through the state apparatuses.

Although each subsystem encompasses concretely identifiable institutions, the capitalist system as a whole is often posited as the *network of relationships* among these institutions, which produces consequences *through* institutions, but is therefore never reducible *to* institutions.[4] Claus Offe maintains, for example, that the capitalist system is a "superordinate level of mechanisms that generate 'events'."[5] However, the superordinate reality of the system is only observable empirically when the institutional mechanisms that fulfill systemic maintenance functions fail to suppress or displace the underlying contradictions of the capitalist mode of production. A contradiction, according to Offe, "is the tendency inherent within a specific mode of production to destroy those very pre-conditions on which its survival depends."[6] Consequently, the historical development of a contradiction must inevitably culminate in some crisis event that makes the contradiction empirically perceptible as a crisis.[7]

Jürgen Habermas provides the most comprehensive and analytically coherent typology of potential crisis conditions within late capitalism.[8] Habermas argues that "crises arise when the structure of a social system allows fewer possibilities for problem solving than are necessary to the continued existence of the system. In this sense, crises are seen as persistent disturbances of system integration."[9] Important, the difference between a crisis and a mere problem is that crises ultimately cannot be resolved within the system's boundaries, because they are generated by system imperatives that are mutually incompatible; that is, contradictory.

Habermas suggests that crises of capitalism may be generated from within any of its three subsystems. However, it is generally agreed—at least among radical political economists influenced by Marx—that the underlying economic contradictions of capitalism are often displaced onto the political and ideological subsystems that become responsible for managing, deflecting, or absorbing the economic crisis in various ways.[10]

THE FISCAL CRISIS OF THE STATE

In *The Fiscal Crisis of the State* (1973), James O'Connor argues that beginning in the early twentieth century, contemporary capitalist states have managed the economic contradictions of capitalism by socializing many of the costs of production in capital intensive sectors of the economy.[11] O'Connor observes that the steady increase in state spending throughout the last century provided the basis for continuing economic growth in these sectors, because their profitability is heavily dependent on state outlays for physical, human, and more recently, intellectual capital. At the same time, and to insure its popular legitimacy, the state must respond to escalating material demands from classes seeking access to the public goods and services required to participate in economic growth or to ameliorate the costs of capitalist economic growth, such as unemployment, injury and disability, environmental damage, and urban deterioration. Thus, there is constant political pressure on state elites to increase state expenditures on education, social insurance, social welfare, housing, health care, and environmental remediation. A structural gap develops between the expenditures necessary to maintain both capital accumulation and popular legitimacy and this structural contradiction becomes a fiscal crisis of the state that is empirically observable as a chronic structural deficit.

THE RATIONALITY CRISIS OF THE STATE

Claus Offe and Jürgen Habermas have each suggested that efforts by state elites and state managers to surmount the political contradiction between accumulation and legitimation are hindered by systemic limitations on state rationality.[12] Offe calls attention to a potential contradiction between the democratic legitimacy and capitalist functions of the state apparatus. In modern states, the legitimacy of state policy inheres in formal rules and procedures whose observation by political authorities obligates citizens to comply with the state's laws and decisions. However, Offe makes the important observation that the legitimating status of formal rules and procedures is linked to an assumption that their application and observation by state officials will systematically result in functional consequences that contribute to the common and individual welfare. Thus, while the formal legitimacy of bureaucratic procedures is based on strict adherence to bureaucratic rules and consistent enforcement of those rules, over the long-term their substantive legitimacy resides in our common expectation that these rules are functionally effective in achieving an identified outcome, whether that outcome is new job creation, environmental protection, a fair trial, or student learning.

However, as Habermas notes:

> During the course of capitalist development, the political system shifts its boundaries not only into the economic system, but also into the socio-cultural system. While organizational rationality spreads, cultural traditions are undermined and weakened. The residue of tradition must, however, escape the administrative grasp, for traditions important for legitimation cannot be regenerated administratively.[13]

Thus, according to Habermas, systemic output crises of the state apparatus take:

> the form of a *rationality* crisis in which the administrative system does not succeed in reconciling and fulfilling the imperatives received from the economic system … The rationality crisis is a displaced systemic crisis which, like economic crisis, expresses the contradiction between socialized production for non-generalizable interests and steering

> imperatives. This crisis tendency is converted into the withdrawal of legitimation by way of a disorganization of the state apparatus.[14]

The dilemma faced by state managers is that they must simultaneously balance two competing forms of rationality: (1) a formal rationality that inheres in the strict observation of formal-bureaucratic procedure and (2) substantive rationality that inheres in functional effectiveness.[15] The ability to balance these two forms of rationality requires that means and ends be aligned with each other, but to the extent that the two forms of rationality diverge, state managers must choose between short-term formal legitimacy based on appeals to position and authority or substantive legitimacy based in the long-term functional effectiveness of their decisions and administrative practices. However, Offe and Habermas suggest that the two forms of rationality are diverging as a systemic effect of capitalist development and this divergence leads to a dichotomy in state administrative practices and decision-making processes. The result is a type of state administration that constantly oscillates between the two horns of this dilemma, but which does not resolve the contradiction itself. Moreover, state managers cannot resolve the contradiction within current systemic constraints, because the wholesale pursuit of either strategy risks a legitimation deficit or substantive failure.[16] Both outcomes have the potential to implode the administrative system and generate popular upheavals demanding a new system of relationships that restore democratic accountability and functional effectiveness to the failed state administrative system. The other alternative is for state elites to relieve pressure on the state administrative system by shrinking its boundaries and withdrawing from public functions through privatization, marketization, and commodification policies, which ostensibly "de-politicize" these social relations by transferring them back to the private sector.[17]

These contradictory pressures in the administration of higher education are now generating a form of decision-making that I call *fictitious rationality*. Fictitious rationality is a derivative of formal rationality, which as Herbert Marcuse observed almost a half-century ago, focuses exclusively on administrative *means*, such as rules, procedures, and efficiency calculations.[18] Substantive rationality focuses on *ends* and it is therefore evaluative, normative, and even political. It asks whether an administrative process achieves its purpose, however narrowly or broadly conceived, and even questions whether that purpose is worthwhile or in the best interests of those who are the objects of formal rationality. Consequently, an administrative process based exclusively in formal rationality does not incorporate the *substantive reasons* for its existence or understand the normative purposes it serves as an instrumentality. Thus, when the failure of formal rationality is challenged by substantive rationality, its adherents solipsistically justify the need for *more* formal rationality with redundant appeals to the need for more rules, more process, greater efficiency, and more productivity without questioning why there is a crisis in the first place. Marcuse observes that the climax of formal rationality in late capitalism occurs when this rationality appears "in a new light—in the light of its [substantive] irrationality."[19] Formal rationality becomes fictitious rationality when it is divorced from social or organizational ends and no longer subjects itself to the evaluative requirement that it be functionally effective.

In higher education, fictitious rationality is the structural ideological effect of occupying a position within the administrative system where managers exclusively monitor and regulate the academic labor process, rather than produce educational values, such as teaching (learning) or research (information and knowledge).[20] Fictitious rationality is the ideological illusion of individuals who observe the academic labor process, but are *not* directly part of that process. Consequently, as I will subsequently illustrate, higher education administrators who occupy this position in the social relations of production increasingly seek to regulate that labor to achieve greater efficiency, because they view it as a net cost to the organization, rather than the producer of its value. Thus, the illusory solution to the fiscal crisis in higher education is to monitor, regulate, and reduce the costs of intellectual production, but to do so requires an ever larger, and more coercive, administrative apparatus. This rationality crisis leads to an intensification of the fiscal crisis in higher education, which leads to a deepening of the rationality crisis, as higher education administrators seek to suppress this contradiction coercively with authoritative appeals to formal legitimacy, which potentially transforms the rationality crisis in higher education into a political crisis of the university.

THE UNIVERSITY AND THE CRISES OF THE STATE

Over the course of the last century, many of the stresses and contradictions of advanced capitalism have been displaced onto colleges and universities, which are now directly attached to the state—whether legally, politically, or financially—as an important component of the ideological and economic state apparatuses.[21] Consequently, the problems associated with fiscal crises have often been a catalyst to institutional reform in American higher education and a persistent theme of those reforms has been to promote increased "academic efficiency."[22] Orthodox economists define academic efficiency as a policy that uses "the minimum necessary resources for *intended* (as opposed to actual) results."[23]

It is now clear that the recession of 1990–1991 marked the beginning of a prolonged fiscal crisis in American higher education. In fact, during the last fifteen years, state appropriations to U.S. colleges and universities per Full-Time Equivalent (FTE) student have declined substantially after adjusting for inflation, while dependence on tuition and fees as a primary source of revenue has grown during the same time.[24] Moreover, the fiscal crisis in higher education emerged just as corporate and state elites began to pressure colleges and universities to assume a more prominent role in the general maintenance function by increasing their direct support for business through expanded workforce development and technology transfer.[25] Corporate and state elites began demanding that faculties reorient their teaching and research toward the immediate problems of global economic competitiveness, while also becoming more efficient and productive in their use of financial and physical resources.[26] The contradictory imperative that universities respond to the challenges of building a globally competitive post-industrial economy and the demand for increased access to higher education, while simultaneously coping with a fiscal crisis has generated a rationality crisis in college and university administrative systems that is leading to their disorganization and functional collapse.

THE FETISHISM OF PLANNING[27]

By the spring of 1991, 71% of college and university administrators in the United States had come to view adequate finances as the main challenge facing higher education institutions.[28] Similarly, two-thirds of state higher education executive officers, such as governing and coordinating board officials, identified declining state support as the dominant issue in higher education policy.[29] Consequently, administrators responded to the burgeoning fiscal deficits in higher education budgets by rapidly shifting from short-term problem solving to crisis management and then strategic planning for a prolonged fiscal crisis. Strategic planning is a direct descendant of Frederick Taylor's principles of scientific management.[30] Strategic planning quickly became the fetish *de jour* among the state elites and state managers who oversee the higher education apparatus,[31] but unfortunately the proponents of strategic planning rarely stopped to consider that its pitfalls, fallacies, and exaggerated claims had already rendered it a dubious venture by the time it was implemented in colleges and universities.[32] Strategic planning originated in the 1950s primarily as a budget-planning exercise among corporate financial officers. It spread quickly through the corporate sector, particularly in the United States, and by the mid-1960s, it was "a virtual obsession among American corporations."[33] Yet, even at the pinnacle of its popularity with U.S. corporate elites, management consultants from within the private sector were already observing that "the word 'planning' is currently used in so many and various senses that it is in some danger of degenerating into an emotive noise."[34] The identified limitations of strategic planning included (1) the inability of strategic planners to agree on how best to implement a strategic planning process, (2) a lack of real commitment to strategic plans by high level managers, who were disempowered by strategic plans, (3) a tendency toward risk aversion and a reluctance to embrace change among middle managers who therefore obstruct implementation of the strategic plan once it is adopted, and (4) a strategic plan's tendency to generate an obsession with micro-management and financial controls that not only stifles real creativity, independence, and entrepreneurialism in large organizations, but overloads the management system with decision-making bottlenecks and an endless quest for more information through centralized data systems, official forms, and multiple signature authorities.[35]

Indeed, the strategic planning movement failed to prevent the collapse of moribund U.S. corporations in the 1970s, but the recognized limitations and failures of strategic planning did not forestall its export to government by political conservatives, who saw it as a key to running government like a business.[36] The fundamental problem, of course, is not only that government is not a business; that is, it produces public goods and services and not private goods and services, but it was now going to be managed using a business planning and decision-making system that by the 1980s was already being abandoned by U.S. corporations for leaner, flatter, and more flexible forms of organization and decision-making.[37] Indeed, as early as 1973, the conservative political scientist Aaron Wildavsky was reiterating warnings from the private sector that "planning protrudes in so many directions the planner can no longer discern its shape."[38]

Nevertheless, as I have documented elsewhere, by the early 1990s state elites and state managers in higher education ostensibly began linking system- and campus-level resource allocations to a strategy of selective excellence that depended on strategic planning.[39] The strategy of selective excellence is a form of strategic planning designed to rationalize the American higher education system by clearly differentiating the missions of individual institutions, eliminating programs that do not support that mission, and by shifting research activities into applied research that directly supports government and business. The central objective of this strategy was to manage the burgeoning fiscal crisis in higher education by downsizing individual institutions, while enabling the system as a whole to adjust to the needs of the new economy. Thus, higher education elites began adopting a business strategy that had been abandoned by corporate elites at least a decade earlier and it was already failing in the wider state sector for reasons that were well understood by corporate elites, business consultants, scholars, and government officials.

UNIVERSITY OF MASSACHUSETTS: A CASE STUDY OF THE RATIONALITY CRISIS

The on-going attempt to systematically restructure public higher education in the Commonwealth of Massachusetts exemplifies the strategy of selective excellence as a response to the fiscal crisis, and I use it to illustrate the limitations and failures of strategic planning as a form of crisis management.[40] The combination of a fiscal crisis and the collapse of the state's economic base in the late 1980s and early 1990s resulted in the exertion of two simultaneous pressures on the public higher education system. First, the size and persistence of reduced state appropriations created chronic financial pressures that were only partially offset by student fees increases. Second, corporate and state elites officials increasingly turned to the state's public colleges and universities as an untapped source of human and intellectual capital that could support the implementation of state and regional economic development strategies.[41] In the context of these dual pressures, governors, state legislators, and boards of trustees initiated a long-term effort to systematically restructure the state's entire public higher education system.

The blueprint for restructuring the university system was prepared in 1989 by the Commission on the Future of the University of Massachusetts. The Commission, chaired by David Saxon, former president of the University of California, was created by the University of Massachusetts Board of Trustees to build support for increased funding for the University. The Commission recommended that Massachusetts "build a world-class public university" beginning with the consolidation of the state's five university-level campuses into a single University of Massachusetts System with campuses at Amherst, Boston, Dartmouth, Lowell, and Worcester.[42] The Commission's political objective in proposing a five-campus system was to stabilize funding for the University of Massachusetts by creating a state-wide base of support, because the proposed system would now have a campus in each of the state's five major regions. However, the report failed to capture the state legislature's attention until the depth of the 1990–1991 recession, at which point, university officials adopted the opposite rationale and suggested that consolidation would yield cost efficiencies at the system level. Thus, amid promises of renewed fiscal efficiency, rather than increased funding, a five-campus University of Massachusetts System was created in September 1991.[43]

The new Board of Trustees (consisting mainly of Massachusetts business executives) spent its first year consolidating the new system's central administration, instituting a series of tuition and fee increases, and preparing a "Vision Statement" for the new five-campus system. The Vision Statement identified "centers of excellence" on each campus that were supposed to build on existing campus strengths and deliver greater efficiency within the system by differentiating each campus through its leading programs. The Amherst campus was designated as the system's traditional research university that would continue to offer a broad range of PhDs where quality and student demand continued to justify such effort. The Boston campus was designated as the state's "urban university" with the goal of serving non-traditional students and providing applied research on urban problems. The Dartmouth campus was identified as a small undergraduate teaching university with selected emphasis on graduate education and applied research in marine- and technology-related fields and in applied professional areas, such as technical writing, public policy, and education. The Lowell campus was to build on long-standing strengths in high-technology and engineering, while Worcester is the system's medical school focused on training general practitioners.[44]

At the same time, the Trustees created a Public Policy Working Group (1992), which initiated an extensive planning process that resulted in a document entitled, *Planning to Plan*.[45] This process resulted in a new vision statement and a comprehensive framework to guide further strategic planning by the individual campuses. The central thesis of the Trustee's vision statement was that the University of Massachusetts should define a distinctive niche by reclaiming its original land-grant mission, which they defined as student access, program excellence, economic development, and public service. The long-range objective was to strive for world-class status by renewing the university-state partnership and by creating university-business partnerships, and this vision was reaffirmed in a "Statement of System Priorities" (1993) the following year.[46]

In February 1995, former President Michael Hooker released an "Action Plan for the Year 2000" that was supposed to implement the strategic plans adopted by the system and by each of the individual campuses.[47] The Action Plan 2000 was based on the assumption that the University of Massachusetts is in a "permanent state of fiscal stress," but notwithstanding the fiscal crisis it must provide qualified citizens with access to a first-rate education (while raising tuition and fees) "in order to ensure their own success in the workplace and to ensure the State's competitiveness in the global economy." The Action Plan also emphasized the University's special obligation to provide quality research and technology transfer in areas important to the state's economy. As the final step in a four-year strategic planning process, the Action Plan required each campus to evaluate all existing programs on the basis of centrality to campus mission, quality, cost, and student demand. By December 1995, every program, center, and department was to be rated on the basis of these evaluative categories and designated for expansion, stasis, or reduction/elimination. In accordance with these decisions, each campus was required to document that it was reallocating 3% of its base budget each year over the next five years toward designated areas of selective excellence.

Each UMass campus administration responded to the system-level imperative by initiating a campus-based (top down) strategic planning process that was supposed to operate within the limitations laid down in the system level vision statement and the planning framework articulated in *Planning to Plan* (1992). For example, in 1992, the University of Massachusetts Dartmouth released its first campus strategic plan entitled, *Building on Our Strengths*, which reaffirmed the commitment to "access and excellence" for students, while stimulating regional economic development through technology transfer and innovation in selected areas, such as advanced technology, marine science and technology, textiles, education, business management, and public policy.

The main outcome of *Building on Our Strengths* was the creation of a new Academic Planning Task Force that, in response to faculty resistance to the established plan, was supposed to incorporate more faculty input into the strategic planning process. The campus had just completed its first strategic plan, but the Academic Planning Task Force was charged by the Chancellor with "developing a planning process" for the campus. Although the five-campus consolidation had promised "economies of scale" and "systemic efficiencies," while identifying UMass Dartmouth as an undergraduate institution, the campus-based planning process immediately veered off unrestrained in the opposite direction. The new Task Force was charged by the campus administration with exploring a variety of new initiatives that would increase costs to the campus and fundamentally diverge from the campus mission established at the system level by the president and board of trustees. These initiatives included increasing student enrollment by 50% over ten years, doubling dormitory capacity, increasing the number of graduate programs, including at the doctoral level, and increasing non-academic support staff, while contracting out academic decisions to paid management consultants in areas such as new program development and academic space utilization. These expanded campus goals were reaffirmed three years later, when a reconstituted Academic Planning Task Force issued *Building on Our Strengths Revisited* (1995), which was followed two years later by the Task Force's *Shared Academic Agenda* (1997).

Each iteration of the campus-based strategic planning process was launched by a new chancellor, an interim chancellor, a new provost, or an interim provost, who wanted to expand the campus mission with new initiatives attributable to them.[48] Thus, following the appointment of yet another new Chancellor at UMass Dartmouth, the campus launched another round of strategic planning in 1999. This round of planning, which was the most extensive to date, involved 150 faculty, staff, and administrators in focus groups, sub-committees, and research groups over a one-year period only to conclude that henceforth: "Planning is an on-going activity at the University." Strategic planning has become a fetish that consumes more and more faculty, staff, administrative, and clerical time in deliberating what faculty should do, and how to evaluate it, rather than doing it. The new report entitled, *Engaged, Embedded, and Evolving* (2000) layered new priorities on top of the old ones, including greater community involvement and public service by faculty, and new programs, staff, and buildings to support those goals. A significant outcome of this strategic planning process was the addition of a $12 million Advanced Technology Manufacturing Center in Fall River, Massachusetts, a downtown arts school in New Bedford, Massachusetts, and a $10 million School of Marine Sciences and Technology. Each of the new facilities was supposed to be a "self-supporting revenue generator," a "profit center," or it was funded by direct state appropriations outside the university budget, which were terminated due to the state's current budget deficit.[49]

After seven years, the campus convened another group that produced Engaged, Embedded, and Evolving, 2000–2007: The University of Massachusetts Strategic Plan; A Report on Progress,[50] and the campus just completed its third iteration of Engaged, Embedded, and Evolving, 2008–2012.[51] During this time, each college and school at UMass Dartmouth was also required to develop a strategic plan. These plans built around the core mandates established at the system and campus level, but just as the campus had done, each of them went beyond the boundaries of higher level plans, by capitalizing on vaguely stated or overly broad objectives to justify new departments, programs, research centers, and other initiatives. Consequently, each new iteration of "the" strategic plan became more expansive, more costly, and more self-contradictory so that it came to replicate, institutionalize, and intensify all the original problems of the multiversity model. Thus, as the strategic planning process evolved it became clear that neither the UMass System, nor its individual institutions, were really prepared to break radically with the post–World War II model of the multiversity.[52] Indeed, the chasm between the bold rhetoric of state elites and the self-serving incrementalism of university managers has produced more institutional chaos than institutional change.

First, faculty resistance to strategic planning has moved administrators toward a form of politicized irrationality, where despite elaborate planning models and formal criteria for program development and evaluation, the administrative implementation of strategic planning objectives becomes a highly charged political process. Administrators attempt to soften political resistance to planning objectives with concessions to internal and external constituencies that often have competing visions of higher education, which results in strategic plans that not only accrete over time, but incorporate contradictory or self-defeating objectives. For example, prior to the first strategic plan at UMass Dartmouth, an interim chancellor had identified the departments of textiles chemistry and textiles technology for elimination, because they were legacy programs introduced early in the twentieth century, when the region was a center of global textiles production. However, in response to intense political pressure from local textiles company executives, a new chancellor successfully inserted the textiles industry in the first strategic plans as a key area for academic program development and technology transfer. Ironically, textiles was already a declining regional industry, but the campus invested in faculty, students, and capital equipment to support an industry that has virtually disappeared from New England.[53] Similarly, in response to the state's 1990–1991 budget crisis, the same interim chancellor had slated the education department for a phased elimination. This process was well underway when the new chancellor immediately reversed course and began expanding the undergraduate department just as the Massachusetts Education Reform Act of 1993 abolished the undergraduate education degree and rendered the program obsolete. Meanwhile, later strategic plans called for the establishment of a new department of public policy, but other social science departments concerned about a reallocation of resources successfully blocked its creation for seven years even though it was mandated by a faculty-approved campus strategic plan.

In this respect, strategic planning becomes a forum for intensified and concentrated political conflicts that inject an additional centrifugal force into an already diffuse multiversity. Departments and colleges compete against each other for funding and personnel. Faculty salaries are juxtaposed against the provision of additional student services. Facilities and capital improvements compete with personnel needs. In the end, the strategic-planning process generates more competition within the campus, rather than any agreement on strategic goals with the result that fragmentation and chaos ensue as smaller and smaller units of organization seek to institutionalize some minor advantage in a strategic plan that will not guide administrative decision making anyway.

Second, most university administrators have proven to be poor strategic planners. They embrace the rhetoric of twenty-first-century business enterprise, while clinging to an outdated model of corporate bureaucracy. Administrators promote the concept of faculty entrepreneurialism, but they attempt to manage and control it with an industrial era corporate bureaucracy. In fact, administrators' commitment to the corporate ideal that I examined in *Universities and the Capitalist State* (1990) has actually intensified in response to the contemporary fiscal crisis as exemplified by the fact that universities no longer have chancellors, provosts, and vice-chancellors, but chief executive officers, chief academic officers, chief financial officers, and chief information officers. University administrators refer to deans, directors, and chairs as middle managers. This change in nomenclature also signals a shift in the composition of administrative personnel from career academic administrators, who at least started out as faculty and often had a distinguished record of teaching and scholarship, to a new stratum of career education managers, who often come from business or politics with no previous experience in higher education. It is becoming more and more difficult to find a PhD in university management, which is now populated by assistant chancellors, special assistants, assistant vice-chancellors, executive directors, and assistant or associate deans without PhDs or other academic experience, but who enter the university with a bachelor's degree in accounting, management information science, an M.B.A., a law degree, or the now ubiquitous doctorate in educational administration.[54] Given this stratum's lack of substantive academic knowledge, and their reluctance to incorporate faculty expertise in a system of co-determination, the new managerial stratum has come to rely more and more on outside consultants, auditors, and lawyers when making academic policy decisions.

Third, despite all the rhetoric, the fact is that most administrators will not survive the implementation of a strategic plan and, consequently, decisions are actually made around short-term considerations of individual advancement intended to launch them into their next position at a new institution, where the entire process begins anew. Administrators are short-term, but strategic plans are long-term, usually with a five- to ten-year horizon. Successful plans require long-term consistency, but turnover among administrators is frequent. Each new administration starts its own planning process and rarely builds on prior efforts. Strategic plans accrete over time or veer off in competing directions that whipsaw the entire institution. The result is a strategic planning and restructuring movement that creates chaos rather than change, while plunging higher education institutions into deeper fiscal and rationality crises.

Moreover, as short-timers, top university administrators typically lack the political will to actually implement strategic plans even when directed to do so by state elites. The result is that bureaucratic decision making devolves to lower and lower levels of the administration, who move to fill this vacuum, where non-academic middle managers compete with each other like warlords in a failed state, while admonishing the faculty that they "do not understand" the magnitude of the institution's fiscal crisis. As non-academic middle managers grasp for more and more control of the minutiae of university operations, the institution spirals further out of control as a confused network of administrative diffusion makes it more and more difficult for faculty to fulfill their role in implementing institution's basic educational mission.[55]

The Center for Policy Analysis (CFPA) at UMass Dartmouth illustrates this pattern of administrative diffusion and organizational disintegration. A decade ago, the Director of the Center for Policy Analysis reported directly to the Provost for administrative purposes, although its day-to-day operations were supervised by the Director, while its mission, budget, and project development was governed by a faculty executive board. The Director had full scope of authority over day-to-day operations, including hiring, project development, purchasing, accounts payable, and billing, subject to oversight by the faculty Executive Board.[56] As an organized research unit, most of its financial operations, purchasing, personnel, and research contracts were organized through the UMass Dartmouth Foundation (a 501(c)3 non-profit corporation) under the double signature authority of the CFPA Director and the Foundation's Executive Director. Financial operations and expenditures were post-audited annually by an accounting firm retained by the Foundation.

However, in 2008, the CFPA was transferred to a new School for Education, Public Policy, and Civic Engagement (SEPPCE), which entailed dispersing most of its administrative and financial operations from the CFPA and Foundation Director to the university's Division of Administrative and Fiscal Services. This division is an umbrella that houses independent departments of Administrative Services, Human Resources, Purchasing, Accounts Payable, and Auditing. The CFPA's facilities management was transferred to the Division of Facilities and Planning, while its research operations were placed under the Office of Grants and Research Contracts, although some semblance of academic authority was retained by the Dean of SEPPCE and the Provost. In this manner, a fundamentally academic enterprise was turned into an administrative and facilities function. Moreover, the effort to establish centralized controls and accountability over an independent research unit actually dispersed its operations among so many competing non-academic middle managers that it became impossible to execute contracts, hire personnel, or complete research projects in a timely manner.

As figure 9.1 documents, an organization that previously operated under the supervision of an academic director and faculty governing board had its operations dispersed among fifteen different non-academic administrative supervisors, each of which has the authority to veto the decision of the academic director, faculty executive board, and academic dean without any requirement that they consult with each other or with academic personnel on such decisions. If one extrapolates this "disorganization chart" across 65 academic departments and programs, 46 research centers, projects, and partnerships, 100 student clubs and other student services, then one begins to glean the daily chaos generated by this administrative system; not to mention the plethora of decision-making bottlenecks created by non-academic middle managers, who have neither the time nor the expertise to make decisions in a timely or informed manner.[57]

The daily stresses of organizational disintegration and its decision-making bottlenecks are politically charged in a university, because non-academic middle managers lack any of the formal symbols that convey substantive legitimacy within the university, such as an earned doctorate in a substantive field, teaching experience, scholarly publications, or even significant administrative experience within the university's academic division. Consequently, their decision-making authority must rely entirely on strict adherence to the external rules of formal-legal legitimacy, appeals to their "superior" place in the organizational hierarchy, their command of arcane administrative and accounting rules, and their acumen with official forms. However, the middle managers have no real independent authority, but must invoke the formal authority of their own superiors or the external authority of laws and regulations. Consequently, middle-management decisions are inherently risk aversive and it is this pattern of decision-making characteristic that was one of the primary failures of corporate strategic planning.

Middle managers constantly work in fear of their organizational superiors, internal and outside auditors, lawyers, press investigations, faculty criticism, and mutual sabotage for purposes of self-advancement. This form of administration not only loses any semblance of substantive legitimacy within the university

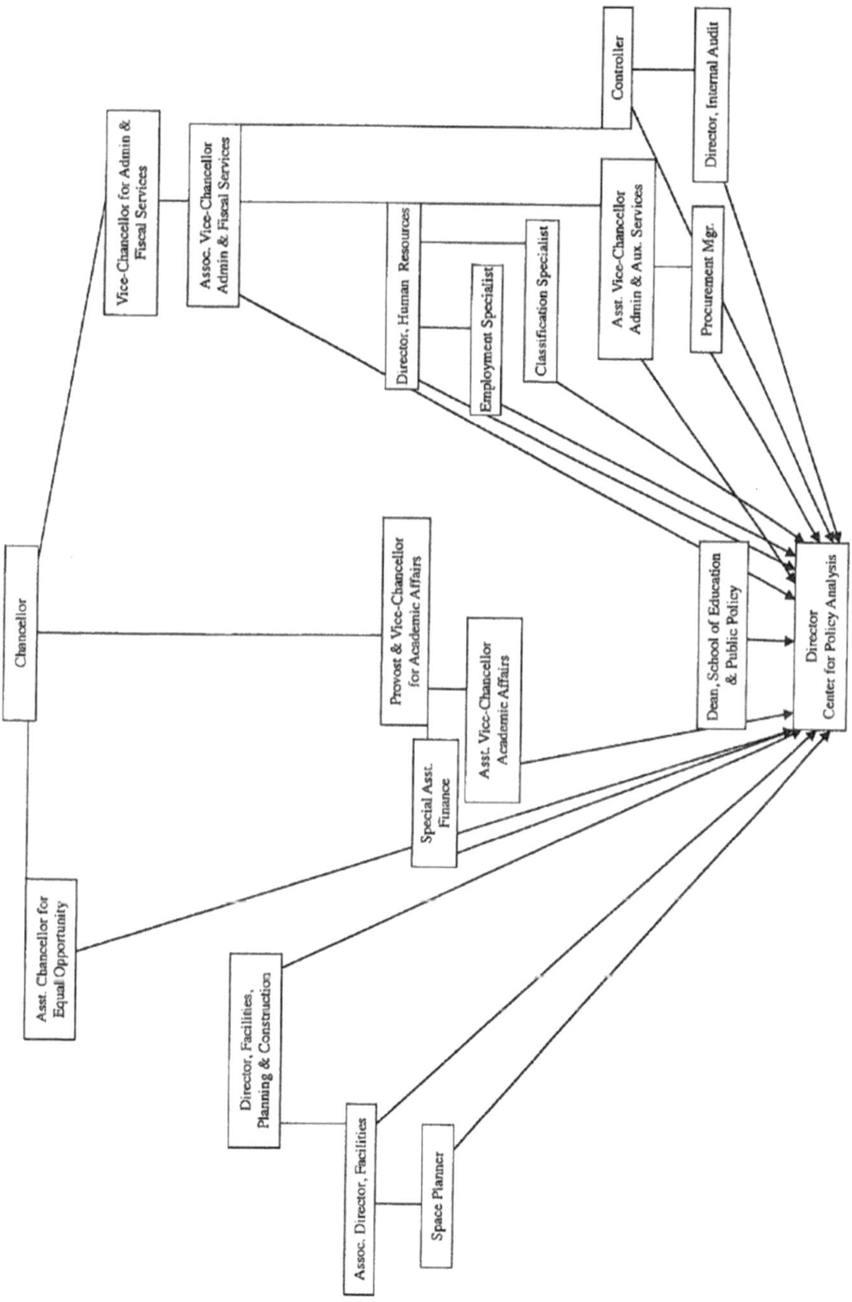
Chancellor
Vice-Chancellor for Admin & Fiscal Services
Assoc. Vice-Chancellor Admin & Fiscal Services
Controller
Director, Internal Audit
Director, Human Resources
Classification Specialist
Employment Specialist
Asst. Vice-Chancellor Admin & Aux. Services
Procurement Mgr.
Provost & Vice-Chancellor for Academic Affairs
Asst. Vice-Chancellor Academic Affairs
Special Asst. Finance
Dean, School of Education & Public Policy
Director Center for Policy Analysis
Asst. Chancellor for Equal Opportunity
Director, Facilities, Planning & Construction
Assoc. Director, Facilities
Space Planner

Figure 9.1

faculty, administrators' attempts to legitimate their authority in the name of "efficiency" are directly undermined by the daily routines of faculty, who must spend more and more of their time doing clerical and administrative work created by the middle managers. Meanwhile, decisions about teaching, curriculum, and research are made by accountants, auditors, clerks, grants officers, compliance officers, controllers, and other career education managers. The university gradually devolves into a chaos of dispersed administration, where non-academic middle managers make the important academic and personnel decisions, while the bureaucratic processes that implement these decisions are shifted onto faculty, who become an extension of the administrative system. As faculty time is diverted into non-academic activities, the university is less and less able to produce the substantive outputs and values—teaching and research—that generate revenue for the institution. Thus, strategic planning intensifies the fiscal crisis in higher education by institutionalizing a fictitious rationality that generates political dissensus on campus and further deepens the fiscal crisis by implementing structural inefficiencies justified by this fictitious rationality.

Despite the strategic planning rhetoric about system integration and administrative streamlining, the University of Massachusetts Dartmouth is actually a welter of overlapping, inconsistent, and self-contradictory administrative practices that generate operational chaos as the primary system output. The strategic-planning process, and the numerous policies and administrative practices it generates, now consume so much administration, staff, clerical, and faculty time that the university's former Vice-Chancellor for Administrative and Fiscal Services eventually issued a "Policies on Policies" in an effort to slow down the proliferation of new policy and planning initiatives across the campus.[58] However, the *Policy on Policies* has been completely ignored as the university's equivalent of a central bank has been unable to steer the institution out of its fiscal crisis, or to reestablish control over its own administrative procedures.[59] This theoretical conclusion is again illustrated with two case studies that should be read as a phenomenology of the fiscal crisis, because the cases reveal how faculty experience the fiscal crisis as a rationality crisis in their everyday routines on campus.

FORMS AS THE METAPHYSICS OF STRATEGIC PLANNING

One outcome of the strategic planning process at the University of Massachusetts Dartmouth has been an "administrative streamlining" initiative designed to reduce costs and increase employee productivity. A phenomenological reconstruction of that process from below demonstrates how this initiative systematically generates policy failure within the institution that intensifies administrative chaos throughout the administrative system. When the five-campus University of Massachusetts

System was created in 1991, it was soon discovered that the various campuses utilized three different financial software systems that prevented system integration and centralized system management, monitoring, and control from the President's Office in Boston. After a great deal of debate, and in the midst of a financial crisis, the University agreed to purchase PeopleSoft software for $150 million, notwithstanding that it is a system plagued with numerous difficulties, including a level of user unfriendliness that requires extensive training and re-training at considerable additional expense.[60]

PeopleSoft was corporate America's dominant supplier of software for human resource operations when it decided to first enter the higher education market in 1994. Thus, it had an immediate appeal to state elites and state managers intent on running the university like a business. PeopleSoft first entered the higher education market with its financial-management systems, and then introduced "integrated" applications for managing human resources, student information, fund raising, and grants. One could write an entire paper on the continuing problems with PeopleSoft, particularly how it takes control of routine decision-making processes, rather than implementing or facilitating them. However, this paper will focus on UMass Dartmouth's travel reimbursement process, because it is an administrative practice familiar to all faculty. The travel reimbursement system at UMass Dartmouth was comparatively simple ten years ago before the adoption of PeopleSoft. Faculty submitted a travel reimbursement form with copies of receipts for airfares, meals, lodging, conference fees, and so forth. The form was filled out by a department secretary, signed by the department chair and dean, submitted to a payroll clerk, and then a reimbursement check was mailed within one or two weeks. This system was deemed "inefficient," because it lacked the multiple managerial controls that administrators and trustees considered necessary to reign in non-essential or excessive spending by the academic division.

In contrast, PeopleSoft mandates management "controls" that require multiple additional signature authorities and approvals, including the budget control officer, the human resources director, purchasing director, an associate vice-chancellor for administration and finance, and finally a payroll clerk. Thus, once again, what was previously an administrative practice performed within the academic division for academic purposes was transformed into an administrative and fiscal services function controlled entirely by non-academic middle managers. The new controls were ostensible to insure that sufficient funds existed in the travel account being billed, and to insure compliance with university travel policies, but the additional controls assume therefore that department chairs and deans are either not capable of understanding their own budgets and travel policies, or they are inherently prone to overspend their travel budgets and to authorize reimbursements in violation of university policies. Not only does PeopleSoft infantilize faculty and academic administrators, the new reimbursement procedures turned a two week process into a six week process, primarily because middle managers were frequently off-campus attending system level "software integration" meetings, off-site PeopleSoft training sessions, or they simply did not consider faculty reimbursements a daily priority. The significant element of this change, however, is the subtle transformation of an academic function previously controlled by academic personnel with PhDs (chairs and deans) and *implemented* by administrative and fiscal clerks, into a middle management function supervised by accountants, payroll clerks, and human resource managers with the authority to veto the decisions of academic chairs, deans, and directors.[61] It also institutionalizes the anti-intellectual culture that academic personnel are not capable of managing budgets or complying with reasonable procedures without the constant supervision and monitoring by non-academic personnel. The assumption underlying this managerial anti-intellectualism is that faculty are responsible for the fiscal crisis in higher education, because of their uncontrolled spending or low productivity, although faculty generally have less control over university budgets than administrators and it is actually the growth of middle management and professional staff that accounts for the largest increases in higher education spending over the last two decades.[62]

This logic of academic disempowerment was carried further when it was decided by middle managers that the reporting details on business expense reimbursements were not sufficient to allow for "proper controls" over how faculty spent funds for academic and business purposes, such as faculty recruitment dinners. UMass Dartmouth previously required faculty to submit a "Direct Reimbursement Form" with a credit card receipt, which identified the purpose of the business expense, such as a faculty recruitment dinner. This form too was signed by the department chair and the dean, who then submitted it directly to an accounts payable clerk for payment from a department or college account.

In its effort to clamp down on "unnecessary expenses" by implementing "appropriate financial controls," the UMass Board of Trustees issued a new policy discouraging, but not prohibiting, the expenditure of university funds on alcohol at official dinners or functions. Consequently, to encourage compliance with the policy, middle management decreed that faculty would now have to attach the original itemized restaurant receipt—not the summary credit card receipt—in order to be reimbursed for a faculty recruitment dinner or other academic function, such as a guest lecturer's dinner. When the itemized restaurant receipts failed to have the anticipated stigma necessary to discourage the purchase of alcohol, a new Direct Reimbursement Form was issued that requires one to attach the original itemized receipt, state the purpose of the dinner, and the location, date, names, titles, and affiliations of all persons who attended the dinner. What was previously a two minute process became a twenty minute process with the obvious result that more time was being spent filling out and processing forms across the campus than money was being "saved" as a result of the new process.

However, it was eventually determined by the middle managers in administrative and fiscal services that the Direct Reimbursement Form could properly be used only for the reimbursement of out-of-pocket expenses, such as emergency office supplies.[63] Instead, faculty recruitment and guest lecturer expenses had to now be submitted on a new "Business Expense Reimbursement Form," which is submitted by the department chair directly to the Division of Administration and Finance (bypassing the dean), where it must be approved by the human resources director, purchasing manager, an associate vice-chancellor for administrative and fiscal services and, finally, an accounts payable clerk. When this procedure met resistance from deans, who no longer had signature authority over expenditures from their own accounts, middle managers decided that *in addition to* the new Business Expense Reimbursement Form, faculty would now *also* submit the old Direct Reimbursement Form with all required documentation. The problem with this integrated procedure was that Direct Reimbursement Forms went from the dean to payroll, while the Business Expense Reimbursement Forms went from the associate-vice chancellor to an accounts payable clerk and the two forms sat on two desks unpaid until an irate faculty would call to find out why two months had passed without a reimbursement.

Thus, the author and his dean met with the Vice-Chancellor of Administrative and Fiscal Services, who ostensibly supervises these myriad functions, and explained the "irrationality" of the campus reimbursement system and they were informed that a "streamlined electronic solution" would be implemented as soon as possible. The PeopleSoft solution was supposed to streamline the reimbursement process, but it actually added new layers of forms and costs to an already cumbersome system. The PeopleSoft reimbursement process starts with a "self-service" function that now requires each faculty member, rather than a department secretary, to electronically enter their Business Expense Reimbursement Form. What was previously performed by employees earning $15 to $20 per hour is now performed by employees earning $50 to $75 per hour, and faculty who attempt to circumvent these new responsibilities are continually reminded by the IT middle managers that it is a punishable violation of the university's information technology policy to give another person, such as a departmental secretary, access to their PeopleSoft password or account.

Once the new streamlined electronic reimbursement system was implemented in the Fall of 2009, faculty were also informed that after entering the reimbursement information into the electronic Business Expense Reimbursement Form, one then has *to print out a hardcopy*, sign it, secure the department chair's signature, and then have it signed by the Purchasing Manager. Furthermore, after submitting the new "electronic" hardcopy to purchasing, one must *also* submit the old paper Business Expense Reimbursement Form *and* the old paper Direct Reimbursement Form. Consequently, the electronic system not only duplicates the old paper system at a much greater expenditure of labor and capital, it actually adds a third layer of paperwork—three forms instead of two forms—becomes administrative streamlining in the world of doublethink, because it now incorporates the use of a user unfriendly $150 million software system. The true impact of this streamlining has probably been to triple or quadruple the total cost of implementing reimbursement processes, which has essentially done nothing more than shift a clerical and non-academic administrative function onto the faculty workload. However, layered on top of what even Frederick Taylor would recognize as a basic inefficiency has been the expenditure of millions of dollars on multiple rounds of training and retraining for clerks, faculty, and staff, which has also diverted administrative and fiscal staff time into training as opposed to administration, but it also requires the continuing support of PeopleSoft consultants and trainers (at considerable additional expense).

By "streamlining" the reimbursement system with PeopleSoft, UMass Dartmouth added a third form, another layer of signature authority, and added further delays to the process, because it is still the case that none of these forms ever intersect in a single place, so a department clerk still has to track them down, reassemble them, and finally insure that they all end up on one desk, which is difficult because no one person is actually responsible for concluding the process. The standard time for a reimbursement is now three months and it requires more time and more people than previously and it requires the use of more expensive labor, not less expensive labor.[64]

THE LAGRASSA PARADOX

The LaGrassa Paradox was first identified at the University of Massachusetts Dartmouth in 2009 following a decision by Michael LaGrassa, the Assistant Vice-Chancellor for Administrative Services, to terminate all purchases of Poland Springs water on the campus.[65] The rationale for the decision was that it would save the university approximately $30,000 to $50,000 annually and, thereby, reduce the institution's $9.8 million structural deficit.[66] The small benefit of this "strategic decision" was quickly offset by the costs of its implementation in faculty time, clerical time, and lost productivity, as well as the administrative payroll expended on more "strategy meetings," audits, notices, and other enforcement actions by the middle management authority. These costs, while difficult to quantify, no doubt far exceed the savings attributable to this strategic decision. For example, when the institution's Center for Policy Analysis refused to comply with the unilateral decree on grounds that it purchased Poland Springs water with privately generated funds, the response on November 30, 2009, was a one inch thick audit report from the University Controller. This extensive audit package documented that the UMass

Dartmouth Center for Policy Analysis had spent $163.27 on Poland Springs water from July 1, 2009, through October 30, 2009. It is estimated that several thousand dollars were expended in audit, clerical, and other middle management payroll to document this small figure and to demand that the Center's employees "pitch in" to personally reimburse the University for their drinking water. When this example is extrapolated to the entire campus, it becomes readily evident that the cost of implementation was exceeding any savings to the campus.

The audit confrontation reached its crisis when the UMass Dartmouth Director of Physical Plant forwarded an email from the Town of Dartmouth to all university employees, (informing them four days late and after most units had discontinued the purchase of Poland Springs water), that the town water available on campus was contaminated with *E. coli* bacteria. According to the official communication:

> These microbes can make you sick, and are a particular concern for people with weakened immune systems. Dartmouth Water Division routinely provides disinfection adequate to remove fecal bacteria, but it does not reach the current standard to confidently remove viruses from drinking water.[67]

Thus, not only did the Poland Springs ban *not* save university funds, it incurred additional financial and health care costs that were shifted onto employees at precisely the same time that contributions to health insurance premiums (+67%), physician co-pays (+33%), prescription co-pays (+25%), and annual deductibles (+$250–$750) were being increased for all UMass employees, although under the new campus policy, no other source of public drinking water was available to faculty. The health costs and lost workdays was not factored into the original decision. The alternative option proposed by faculty was to eliminate the position of the Assistant Vice-Chancellor for Administrative Services for a real savings of $98,000 annually, which would have yielded cost savings two to three times greater than the decision to terminate the purchase of Poland Springs water, even before accounting for the payroll, auditing, and health care costs of a fundamentally irrational decision which generated the opposite output of its stated objective.[68]

The LaGrassa Paradox is not an isolated occurrence in American higher education, but an example of the fact that higher education managers rarely incorporate the costs of implementation, the cost of their own time, or the cost of lost faculty productivity into their calculations about cost reductions and efficiency. The irony of these preposterous policies is that UMass Dartmouth has grown from 4,800 students in 1998 to more than 9,500 (+98%) students in 2009, while the number of full-time tenure line faculty employed by the campus increased by only 7.3% in the same time (from 303 to 313).[69] Concurrently, UMass Dartmouth has greatly expanded their research and public service efforts with a numerically static faculty, with sponsored research growing from $5 million to $17 million annually. These figures lead to the obvious conclusion that teaching and research "productivity" by the tenure line faculty has increased dramatically, even as the fiscal crisis has deepened, but for that reason a systematically rational administration would calculate that the diversion of this high value labor power into lower cost clerical or low level administrative tasks is a net loss in real dollars to the university's revenue streams in the form of lost student tuition and research grants. In fact, as middle managers have continued diverting faculty time away from their primary missions of teaching and research, the dollar value of sponsored research has begun to decline in the last two years, and UMass Dartmouth was the only UMass campus to experience a decline in undergraduate applications for academic year 2010–2011.

The institution's managers concluded that these declines were due to a lack of strategic planning support personnel, professional grants administrators, grants compliance officers, and enrollment management personnel![70] Consequently, as documented by the UMass Faculty Federation, the campus has been on a middle management hiring spree even as it lays off clerical personnel, part-time faculty, and implements faculty pay "raises" of 0%-0%-0% from AY 2010–2012. However, as faculty productivity increases, publicly available data provided by the UMass Dartmouth administration indicates that the Chancellor's Office was the fastest growing division of the university over the last 3 years (2006–2009), which expanded from 11 to 24 FTE. This 112% growth in personnel compares to average campus FTE growth of only 12.4% over the same time. Similarly, FTE employees in the Provost's Office grew by 33%, which is nearly three times the campus average during the same three years. These figures do not include the addition of purchasing, auditing, and financial controllers, whose jobs have been shifted from the campus payroll to the system payroll, or administrative positions that have been converted into "consultants" in order to hide the real administrative payroll from legislative auditors and faculty. Thus, as faculty productivity increases, these gains are expropriated through an uninterrupted expansion of managerial personnel, whose ongoing proliferation is beginning to counteract the institutional foundation of those productivity gains.

On its surface, the LaGrassa Paradox appears to be a radical exception to the rational actor market logic of neo-classical economics. Indeed, how does one explain decisions taken in the midst of a fiscal crisis to adopt and implement policies with costs that far exceed the benefits, when an alternative rational decision was readily available; for example, to eliminate an assistant vice-chancellor whose irrational decisions were systematically imposing new costs on the institution? The solution to this paradox in higher education administration exemplifies the continuing relevance of Marxian value theory; namely, the mere fact that a fictitious commodity commands an exchange-value does not mean that it has a use-value.[71]

Marx's distinction between the value of a commodity and the price of a commodity is useful in understanding and solving the LaGrassa Paradox.

Marx observes that:

> As the *exchangeable values* of commodities are only *social functions* of those things, and have nothing at all to do with the *natural* qualities, we must first ask: What is the common *social substance* of all commodities? It is *labour* ... And I say not only *labour*, but *social labour*. A man who produces an article for his own immediate use, to consume it himself, creates a *product*, but not a *commodity*.[72]

While Marxian value theory takes us part of the way toward solving the LaGrassa Paradox, a complete solution of the problem must draw on the related concept of unproductive labor, which creates *neither a product, nor a commodity*, but is incorporated into systems of higher education accounting as having use value, but no price.[73] The fictitious rationality that underlies the LaGrassa Paradox is that university administrators place a high use value on their labor, but incorrectly price their own labor at $0 in exchange value, despite being paid a considerable salary (price) for in fact contributing no use value to the institution. In contrast, university administrators incorrectly assign a use value of zero to the work of academic employees, because they do not conceptualize that it is *value producing labor*. Thus, if we assume that all unproductive administrative labor has zero cost and a high use value then the expenditure of administrative labor will be factored into a cost-benefits equation as zero cost, while faculty labor is factored into the equation as having zero use value, but a high exchange value (price). In fact, the *price* we pay for administration now far exceeds the financial and other benefits of their decisions, while the *price* we pay for faculty labor generates the only real outputs of a university in the form of teaching and research. The idea that the university should be run "like" a business collapses in contradiction, because if it was run like a business, it would be out of business.[74]

CONCLUSION

The rationality crisis in American higher education manifests itself politically in the struggle between faculty and students, on the one hand, and a strata of state elites and state managers in the higher education system. As the fiscal crisis in higher education continues to intensify, these elites and managers will increasingly choose strict adherence to ever more complex, arcane, and authoritarian administrative rules over fulfilling the substantive functions of the college and university. One choice adheres to the external rules of formal-legal legitimacy and fictitious rationality, backed by the coercive legal authority of the state, while the other relies on the internal substantive legitimacy of faculty expertise within the college and university and a commitment to access and affordability for students. The traditional cultural norms of faculty and students are focused on teaching and research, and the ability to perform these functions effectively is the cornerstone of substantive legitimacy, which is being withdrawn from the university by faculty at every type of institution.

However, within the current boundaries of the corporate university, higher education administrators cannot respond to demands for substantive legitimacy, because it would mean shifting the focus of administration away from the fictitious rationality of formal rules and financial controls onto those areas where faculty rightly claim substantive expertise; that is, educational goals, curriculum, and research techniques.[75] It would also require a greater focus on affordability and access for students as opposed to viewing them as a source of revenue and profit.[76] This shift in focus would undermine the very foundations of the new managerial apparatus in higher education and deprive it of its claim to formal legitimacy, which is based in the authoritative enforcement of rules and procedures and its alleged (though failed) efforts to bring greater efficiency and profitability to the higher education institutions.[77]

The rationality crisis in the administrative apparatus has been explored through an analysis of the strategic-planning process at the University of Massachusetts, but it is the author's contention that this case is not *sui generis*, but one that illustrates a systemic rationality crisis in U.S. higher education and the state apparatuses. In fact, Marcuse suggests that the extension of formal rationality from the economic system to the political and ideological subsystems of capitalism is a structural characteristic of late capitalism that unfolds as it subsumes and commodifies ever wider swaths of the social order. However, he observes:

> "... when the bureaucratic administration of the capitalist apparatus in all its rationality remains a means, and thereby dependent, it reaches its own limits as rationality. Bureaucracy subordinates itself to a power above and beyond bureaucracy—a power "alien to administration". And when rationality is incorporated into administration and *only* incorporated there, then this law-enforcing power must be *irrational*.[78]

The rationality crisis has also been illustrated through an examination of two case studies at the University of Massachusetts Dartmouth. If these examples are extrapolated across the entire campus, and then multiplied by layering these policies on top of still more policies, then one can start to conceptualize the degree to which fictitious rationality has become so embedded in the organizational structure of the institution that it is incapable of extracting itself from the rationality crisis while working within its existing structures of fictitious rationality.[79] Furthermore, the irrationality of this administrative system layers cost upon cost and, thus, the administrative apparatus that is charged with resolving the fiscal crisis in higher education is incapable of doing so, because its decision-making process *is* the problem. However, the perceived administrative solution to this problem is to do more of the same—the very essence of a fetish—a bureaucratic system which culminates with an administration administering an administration.[80]

The logical outcome of the fiscal and rationality crises would seem to be an implosion of the university. Structural implosions of the state apparatus open political space for the organization of new state forms.[81] In contrast, the general tendency of economic globalization has been to ease the rationality crisis by ceding state sovereignty to global markets and transnational corporations and this process is evident too in higher education.[82] At the present time, the fastest growing sector in American higher education is the for-profit private sector, while the transnationalization of this sector is being actively facilitated through the General Agreement on Trade in Services and various regional free trade agreements.[83] These trends, and numerous other forms of privatization, may potentially resolve the rationality crisis and its underlying fiscal crisis by marketizing higher education and shifting system boundaries in a way that remove the state from this region of the economic and ideological subsystems. A more progressive resolution of the crisis would be a new social compact between higher education, the state, and the public, which must include a restoration of faculty and students to a central place in higher education decision-making processes. The progressive alternative will not be realized until faculty and students retake physical control of their campuses and join with other social movements to reconstruct power relations within those institutions and redefine their relationship to the state.

NOTES

1. This chapter appeared as C. W. Barrow (2010) "The Rationality Crisis in US Higher Education," *New Political Science, 32*(3), 317–344. It is published here with permission from Taylor & Francis.
2. This section is an abridged and revised version of the argument in Clyde W. Barrow, *Critical Theories of the State: Marxist, Neo-Marxist, Post Marxist* (Madison: University of Wisconsin, 1993), chap. 4.
3. Ralph Miliband, *The State in Capitalist Society* (New York: Basic Books, 1969); Nicos Poulantzas, *Political Power and Social Classes* (London: Verso, 1978), pp. 1–33.
4. Poulantzas, *Political Power and Social Classes,* p. 115, fn. 24, defines an institution as "a system of norms or rules which is socially sanctioned … On the other hand, the concept of structure covers the *organizing matrix* of institutions." Similarly, David Gold, Clarence Lo, and Erik Olin Wright, "Recent Developments in Marxist Theories of the Capitalist State, Part I," *Monthly Review*, 27:5 (1975), p. 36, fn., observe that the concept of a structure "does *not* refer to the concrete social institutions that make up a society, but rather to the systematic functional interrelationships among these institutions."
5. Claus Offe, *Contradictions of the Welfare State* (Cambridge, MA: MIT Press, 1984), p. 37.
6. Ibid., p. 132.

7. Ibid., p. 116, fn. 15.
8. Jürgen Habermas, *Legitimation Crisis* (Boston: Beacon Press, 1975), part 2, chaps. 1–8. See also, James O'Connor, *The Meaning of Crisis: A Theoretical Introduction* (New York: Basil Blackwell, 1987); Patrick Dunleavy and Brendan O'Leary, *Theories of the State* (New York: Macmillan, 1987), pp. 259–270.
9. Habermas, *Legitimation Crisis*, p. 2.
10. James O'Connor, *The Fiscal Crisis of the State* (New York: St. Martin's Press, 1973).
11. On the continuing relevance of this analysis, see the new edition of this book, James O'Connor, *The Fiscal Crisis of the State*, with a new introduction by the author (New Brunswick, NJ: Transaction, 2002).
12. For purposes of this analysis, federal officials, governors, state legislators, boards of trustees, system offices, and other high-ranking higher education boards are considered state elites, while campus-based administrators are considered state managers. On the distinction, see Barrow, *Critical Theories of the State*, pp. 28–29.
13. Habermas, *Legitimation Crisis*, p. 47.
14. Ibid., p. 46.
15. Herbert Marcuse, "Industrialization and Capitalism," *New Left Review* 30 (March–April 1965), pp. 3–17.
16. Claus Offe, *Disorganized Capitalism* (Cambridge, MA: MIT Press, 1985), pp. 303–307; Habermas, *Legitimation Crisis*, p. 47. Offe and Habermas's hypothesis on the possibility of rationality crisis is non-empirical in the sense that it does not examine the actual rules that govern action in specific state bureaucracies. Thus, they only postulate a hypothetical divergence between the two criteria of administrative rationality.
17. Claus Offe, *Modernity and the State* (Cambridge, MA: MIT Press, 1996).
18. Herbert Marcuse, *Negations: Essays in Critical Theory* (Boston: Beacon, 1968), pp. 201–226.
19. Marcuse, "Industrialization and Capitalism," p. 6.
20. For background, see John Smyth, (ed.), *Academic Work: The Changing Labour Process in Higher Education* (Buckingham, UK: Open University Press, 1995).
21. Louis Althusser, "Ideology and Ideological State Apparatuses: Notes Towards an Investigation," in *Lenin and Philosophy and Other Essays* (New York: Monthly Review Press, 1978), pp. 127–186. On the concept of the state economic apparatus and its increasingly important role, see Nicos Poulantzas, *State, Power, Socialism* (London: Verso, 1978), p. 170. For this reason, college and university faculty occupy a social location at the nexus of the economic, political, and ideological sub-systems. They not only fulfill multiple functions within the capitalist system, but are peculiarly subject to its many contradictions and, therefore, they are in a position to experience and observe those contradictions in the *quotidian*; see Henri Lefebvre, *Critique of Everyday Life* (London & New York: Verso, 2008).
22. For historical studies, see Clyde W. Barrow, *Universities and the Capitalist State* (Madison: University of Wisconsin Press, 1990); Barbara Ann Scott, *Crisis Management in American Higher Education* (Westport, CT: Praeger, 1983); David N. Smith, *Who Rules the Universities?* (New York: Monthly Review, 1974). On the class war character of institutional responses to the current fiscal crisis in higher education, see the excellent argument by Peter Phillips, "The Fiscal Crisis in Higher Education Protects the Wealthy," *The Daily Censored*, November 22, 2009, see http://dailycensored.com/2009/11/22/the-higher-education-fiscal-crisis-protects-the-wealthy/
23. Kent Halstead, *State Profiles: Financing Public Higher Education, 1978 to 1989* (Washington, DC: Research Associates, 1989), p. 41. This concept was first introduced by Morris L. Cooke,

Academic and Industrial Efficiency (New York: Carnegie Foundation for the Advancement of Teaching, 1910).

24. For an empirical documentation, see, The Delta Cost Project, *Trends in College Spending* (Washington, DC, 2009), pp. 14–15.
25. Commission on the Skills of the American Workforce, *America's Choice: High Skills or Low Wages!* (Rochester, NY: National Center on Education and the Economy, 1990). Esther Rodriguez, *Building a Quality Workforce: An Agenda for Postsecondary Education* (Denver: State Higher Education Executive Officers, 1992).
26. Sheila Slaughter, *The Higher Learning and High Technology: Dynamics of Higher Education Policy Formation* (Albany: State University of New York Press, 1990), identifies numerous organizations created during this period specifically to promote a new strategic alliance between business, government, and higher education. Slaughter documents how such organizations have argued convincingly that higher education policy should be linked explicitly to the goal of regaining a competitive advantage for American business mainly by promoting "advanced applied technology, technology transfer, and the training of a competitive scientific and professional labor force," p. 2. See also, Clyde W. Barrow, "Will the Fiscal Crisis Force Higher Education to Restructure?" *Thought and Action: The NEA Higher Education Journal* 9 (Fall 1993), pp. 25–39; Clyde W. Barrow, "The New Economy and the Restructuring of Higher Education," *Thought and Action: The NEA Higher Education Journal* 12 (Spring 1996), pp. 37–54. More recently, see Sheila Slaughter and Gary Rhoades, *Academic Capitalism and the New Economy: Markets, State, and Higher Education* (Baltimore: Johns Hopkins University Press, 2004).
27. I have applied the anthropological concept of a fetish to strategic planning in higher education, because a fetish is an object or ritual that is believed to have magical properties. Thus, a shaman believes that if a rain dance is performed properly, it will rain. However, if it does not rain, this does not lead the shaman to conclude that the ritual is a superstition. It leads the shaman to demand more dancing, or to accusations that the dancers lack the appropriate faith, or that the dance was performed incorrectly in some minor detail. If the shaman is lucky, and the dance continues long enough, eventually it will rain, although not because of the dance; or the entire village may die of thirst and starvation because they keep dancing, but it never rains.
28. "Administrators' Views of Challenges Facing Institutions in the Next Five Years," *The Almanac of Higher Education, 1992* (Chicago: University Chicago Press, 1992), p. 72.
29. Alene Bycer Russell, *Faculty Workload: State and System Perspectives* (Denver: State Higher Education Executive Officers, 1992), pp. 13–19.
30. Henry Mintzberg, *The Rise and Fall of Strategic Planning* (New York: Free Press, 1994), pp. 21–22, 225–226.
31. For a sampling of the early planning movement, see, Western Interstate Commission for Higher Education, *Meeting Economic and Social Challenges: A Strategic Agenda for Higher Education* (Boulder, CO: WICHE, 1992); Western Interstate Commission for Higher Education, *Joined or Unconnected?: A Look at State Economic Development and Higher Education Plans* (Boulder, CO: WICHE, 1992); Richard B. Heydinger and Hasan Simsek, *An Agenda for Reshaping Faculty Productivity: State Policy and College Learning* (Denver, CO: SHEEO, 1992); D. B. Johnstone, "The Costs of Higher Education: Worldwide Trends for the 1990s," in P. G. Altbach and D. B. Johnstone (eds.), *The Funding of Higher Education: International Perspectives* (New York: Garland Publishing, Inc., 1993), pp. 3–24; W. F. Massy and J. W. Meyerson, *Strategy and Finance in Higher Education* (Princeton, NJ: Peterson's Guide, 1992); D. F. Finifter, R. G. Baldwin, and J. R. Thelin, *The Uneasy Public Policy Triangle in Higher*

Education: Quality, Diversity, and Budgetary Efficiency (New York: American Council on Education & Macmillan Publishing Co., 1991).

32. Mintzberg, *Rise and Fall of Strategic Planning*, chaps. 3–4.
33. Ibid., p. 6.
34. B. J. Loasby, "Long-Range Formal Planning in Perspective," *The Journal of Management Studies* 4:3 (1967), pp. 300–308.
35. Mintzberg, *Rise and Fall of Strategic Planning*, pp. 159–160.
36. Barry Bluestone and Bennett Harrison, *The Deindustrialization of America* (New York: Basic Books, 1982).
37. For example, William H. Davidow and Michael S. Malone, *The Virtual Corporation: Structuring and Revitalizing the Corporation for the 21st Century* (New York: Harper Collins, 1992); Michael Hammer and James Champy, *Reengineering the Corporation: A Manifesto for Business Revolution* (New York: Harper Business, 1993).
38. Aaron Wildavsky, "If Planning Is Everything Maybe It's Nothing," *Policy Sciences* 4:2 (1973), pp. 127–153.
39. Clyde W. Barrow, "The Strategy of Selective Excellence: Redesigning Higher Education for Global Competition in a Postindustrial Society," *Higher Education* 31:4 (1996), pp. 447–469. See also Clyde W. Barrow, "Social Investment in Massachusetts Public Higher Education: A Comparative Analysis," *New England Journal of Public Policy* 7:1 (Spring/Summer 1991), pp. 85–110.
40. In June 1992 the Massachusetts Higher Education Coordinating Council (HECC) adopted "The Mission of the Public Higher Education System of the Commonwealth," which states: "The public college and university system of Massachusetts exists to make accessible to the people of the Commonwealth programs of excellence in higher education."
41. Massachusetts Executive Office of Economic Affairs and the University of Massachusetts, *Choosing to Compete: Statewide Strategy for Job Creation and Economic Growth* (Boston: Commonwealth of Massachusetts, 1993); Massachusetts Department of Economic Development and the University of Massachusetts, *Toward a New Prosperity: Building Regional Competitiveness Across the Commonwealth* (Boston: Commonwealth of Massachusetts, 2002); Massachusetts Department of Housing and Economic Development, *Regional Economic Development Framework* (Boston: Commonwealth of Massachusetts, 2009), see http://www.mass.gov/?pageID=ehedmodulechunk&L=1&L0=Home&sid=Ehed&b=terminalcontent&f=Framework_For_Action&csid=Ehed
42. Commission on the Future of the University of Massachusetts, *Learning to Lead: Building a World-Class Public University in Massachusetts* (Boston: University of Massachusetts, 1989); Commission on the Future of the State and Community College System, *Responding to Change: New Directions for Public Colleges in Massachusetts* (Boston: Massachusetts Higher Education Coordinating Council, 1992).
43. In line with this commitment, state funding for the UMass System is currently below its 1988 funding level in real dollars. The state appropriation for UMass Dartmouth has fallen from 72% of university revenues in 1989 to 25% of revenues in 2009; see Grant Welker, "A 'Tale of Two Stories'," *Fall River Herald News*, August 14, 2009, which also reports that "the state's share of the UMass budget has fallen—from $441 million in fiscal 2001 to $310 million in fiscal 2009, when adjusted for inflation." Chancellor Jean F. MacCormack, Campus-wide Town Meeting Presentation (North Dartmouth, Massachusetts, May 14, 2009), see http://www.umassd.edu/chancellor/updates/campus_town_meeting051409.pdf. Also, Grant Welker, "Another Round of Cuts Coming to UMD," *Fall River Herald News*, May 15, 2009.

44. "University of Massachusetts Vision Statement" (Boston: University of Massachusetts Board of Trustees, Revised Doc. T91–107, 1991).
45. Public Policy Working Group, *Planning to Plan: A Proposal for Trustee Action* (University of Massachusetts Board of Trustees, 1992).
46. "The University of Massachusetts Statement of System Priorities" (Boston: University of Massachusetts Board of Trustees, June 2, 1993).
47. Michael K. Hooker, *The President's Action Plan for the Year 2000: Improving Quality and Responsiveness at UMASS Through Restructuring, Reallocation, and Reinvestment* (Boston: University of Massachusetts Board of Trustees, 1995).
48. It is a well-accepted principle of state theory that state elites and state managers are self-interested maximizers whose main interest is to enhance their own institutional power, prestige, and financial resources, see Barrow, *Critical Theories of the State*, p. 125.
49. In fact, the New Bedford arts building and the ATMC combined now account for $4.3 million (44%) of a $9.7 million structural deficit in the UMass Dartmouth budget, see Grant Welker, "UMD Still Scrambling Due to Cuts in Funding," *Fall River Herald News*, May 21, 2009. In the last twenty years, there has not been a single new program, building, or laboratory at UMass Dartmouth that has achieved self-sufficiency or evolved into a profit center for the university. Despite this incontrovertible fact, the campus will launch a law school in the Fall of 2010 with the promise that it will be self-sufficient and eventually generate millions of dollars in new revenue for the campus even though no public law school in the United States operates without a state subsidy. Outside reviews of the plan estimate that the law school will increase the campus's structural deficit by $2 million to $10 million annually, depending on enrollments, even as faculty were told to adopt a new collective bargaining agreement with no raises, because "there is no money" to fund them; see Jeff Jacoby, "The Price of UMass Law School," *Boston Globe*, February 7, 2010.
50. See http://www.umassd.edu/chancellor/strategicplanupdate.pdf
51. See http://www.umassd.edu/chancellor/Introduction.pdf
52. Clyde W. Barrow, "Beyond the Multiversity: Fiscal Crisis and the Changing Structure of Academic Labour," in John Smyth (ed.), *Academic Work: The Changing Labour Process in Higher Education* (Buckingham, UK: Open University Press, 1995), pp. 159–178.
53. Clyde W. Barrow, *Economic Impacts of the Textile and Apparel Industries in Massachusetts* (Boston: Donahue Institute of Governmental Affairs, 2000).
54. Gary Rhoades, *Managed Professionals: Unionized Faculty and Restructuring Academic Labor* (Albany: State University of New York Press, 1998).
55. Clyde W. Barrow, "Author's Post-Script," *Thought and Action: The NEA Higher Education Journal* 16 (Fall 2000), pp. 77–88, available at http://www.nea.org/he/heta00/f00toc.pdf
56. It is not surprising that strategic planning experiments throughout the world have consistently found that people are more productive and more satisfied with their jobs when they operate under their own unit plans instead of externally imposed plans, see B. M. Bass, "When Planning for Others," *Journal of Applied Behavioral Science* 6:2 (1972), pp. 151–171.
57. One such example is the UMass Dartmouth "Classification and Compensation Specialist," who blocked the hiring of a research associate due to the claim that such an employee belonged in the clerical union. It was pointed out that the Director of the Center for Policy Analysis had authored the language on research associates in the faculty union contract while serving as the union's treasurer, and only then did the Classification "Specialist" reluctantly concede the point, and only after two sponsored research projects had been lost due to the hiring delay.

58. The purpose of the Policy on Policies "is to establish a formal mechanism to create, approve, rescind, and periodically revise campus policies and procedures, including a standardized format and reference numbering system," see, http://www.umassd.edu/policies/policy.cfm
59. This process exactly parallels the restructuring of central state apparatuses worldwide, where an internal realignment of power within the state apparatus privileges the institutions, offices, and agencies in closest contact with the centers of the global economy, while subordinating or disempowering those offices and agencies that draw support from domestic constituencies. The offices of presidents and prime ministers, treasuries, and central banks now assume the leading role in state policy, while ministries of commerce, labor, health, welfare, and education, among others, are being subordinated ideologically to the tenets of international competitiveness and further disempowered through budget and staffing reductions. See Leo Panitch, "Globalisation and the State," in Ralph Miliband and Leo Panitch, (Eds.), *Socialist Register, 1994* (London: Merlin Press, 1994), p. 72. In universities, it is the academic and student divisions that are being subordinated to divisions of administration and finance.
60. Florence Olsen, "Delays, Bugs, and Cost Overruns Plague PeopleSoft's Services," *Chronicle of Higher Education*, September 22, 1990; Wendy Leibowitz, "Officials of 7 Large Universities Complain to PeopleSoft About Its Programs," *Chronicle of Higher Education*, December 14, 1999, reports that "the provosts and vice-presidents of seven of the eight 'Big Ten' universities that use PeopleSoft software on their campuses wrote a joint letter to the company last month, complaining that the 'performance of the systems, in terms of responsiveness, is simply unacceptable'." See, also, John Huston, "Village Dumps PeopleSoft," *Oak Leaves* (Oak Park, IL), January 14, 2009.
61. Ironically, after the author had completed this paper for presentation at the annual meeting of the American Anthropological Association, he received an email from the Accounts Payable Department informing him that "the system will not allow it [his travel] to be approved." Evidently, "the system" at UMass Dartmouth has now commandeered the authority to veto academic travel arrangements even after they have been approved by the department chair and college dean.
62. See Delta Cost Project, *Trends in College Spending*, pp. 17–20, which documents that most increases in higher education spending are due to increased expenditures on operations, student services, and academic support personnel and activities, while direct research and instructional budgets have languished at the same time.
63. It should be noted that any cost-benefits analysis of these policy changes should incorporate the fact that middle managers actually held numerous "strategy meetings" at the expenditure of significant administrative payroll to arrive at these monumental decisions. Those decisions then had to be communicated to faculty, while clerks and faculty had to be re-trained on the new forms and procedures.
64. In an electronic mail received December 14, 2009, from Administrative Services, the university explicitly refers to the travel reimbursement system just described as "administrative streamlining," when in fact the new procedure actually costs more money to capitalize, requires more signatures, and takes more time to implement than the previous system, while relying on faculty labor, rather than clerical labor.
65. On December 1, 2009, the Center for Policy Analysis received an official "Bottled Water Reminder" from Michael LaGrassa, Assistant Vice-Chancellor for Administrative Services at UMass Dartmouth, restating "that effective as of July 1, 2009 the University will no longer support with University funds, the purchase of bottled water, associated dispensers or rental of such. This includes small personal sized bottled water as well as jugs of water used in conjunction with dispensers."

66. This alleged savings constitutes approximately 0.51% of the institution's structural deficit.
67. Electronic mail from David Ferguson, Director of Physical Plant to the Campus Community, "Town of Dartmouth Drinking Water Notice," December 5, 2009.
68. The author eventually filed a grievance against the Assistant Vice-Chancellor of Administrative Services on grounds that the Poland Springs decree violated the university's own Policy on Policies, because it had not gone through the review and approval process required by this policy. The grievance was withdrawn after it was agreed that the Center for Policy Analysis would be allowed to provide its employee with Poland Springs water so long as the water was purchased with non-state revenues.
69. University of Massachusetts Dartmouth, *NEASC Draft Report: Standard Five Faculty* (North Dartmouth, MA: Office of the Provost, 2009), see http://www.umassd.edu/provost/neasc/standard5_11-16-09.doc
70. Only a non-academic middle manager would conclude that students chose to attend a college or university because of its enrollment managers or that faculty chose not to write grants because the institution lacks a sufficient number of grants compliance officers.
71. On the concept of a fictitious commodity, see Karl Polanyi, *The Great Transformation* (Boston: Beacon Press, 1949).
72. Karl Marx, *Value, Price, and Profit* (New York: International Publishers, Inc., 1974), p. 30.
73. The basis of this distinction is Karl Marx, *Capital: A Critique of Political Economy* (London: Penguin Books, 1978), Vol. 2, p. 208, who observes, that "The dimensions assumed by the conversion of commodities in the hands of capitalists can naturally not transform this labour, which does not create value, but only mediates a change in the form of value, into value-creating labour ... These third parties will certainly not put their labour-power at the disposal of the capitalists for the sake of their blue eyes. It is similarly immaterial for the rent collector of a landlord or the porter at a bank that their labour does not add one iota to the magnitude of the value of the rent, nor to the gold pieces carried to another bank by the sackful."
74. Habermas, *Legitimation Crisis*, pp. 47–48, identifies motivation crisis as a third crisis possibility within the cultural subsystem, but it is beyond the scope of this paper to address that possibility. The intensification of the labor process in higher education, as in other sectors of the economy, is stressing the balance between work and family (and leisure). Faculty can devote less time to family and personal matters, which contributes to a motivational crisis, or faculty can reconcile the contradiction by attending to family and personal matters, which feeds back into the economic system as sub-optimal performance.
75. Henry Steck, "Corporatization of the University: Seeking Conceptual Clarity," *Annals of the American Academy of Political and Social Science* 585:1 (2003), pp. 66–83.
76. The author recently attended a meeting called by a UMass Dartmouth administrator to discuss the importance of websites as a source of student recruitment, where said administrator referred to students as "human ATMs."
77. Stanley Aronowitz, *The Knowledge Factory: Dismantling the Corporate University and Creating True Higher Education* (Boston: Beacon Press, 2000); Henry A. Giroux and Kostas Myrsiades, *Beyond the Corporate University: Culture and Pedagogy in the New Millennium* (Lanham, MD: Rowman & Littlefield, 2001).
78. Marcuse, "Industrialization and Capitalism," p. 13.
79. It is assumed that readers will empathetically recognize equivalent, or even identical processes, at their own colleges and universities. It is hoped that similar case studies will be produced by other scholars as a measure of the rationality crisis throughout the U.S. higher education system.

80. Max Weber, "Politics as a Vocation," in Hans H. Gerth and C. Wright Mills (Eds.), *From Max Weber: Essays in Sociology* (New York: Oxford University Press, 1958), p. 128.
81. See Karl Marx, *The Civil War in France* (New York: International Publishers, 1940). Specifically, on higher education, see Clyde W. Barrow, "What Is to Be Undone?: Academic Efficiency and the Corporate Ideal in American Higher Education," *Found Object* 10 (Spring 2001): 149–180; Barrow, *Universities and the Capitalist State*, pp. 175–177; Henry A. Giroux and Kostas Myrsiades (Eds.), *Beyond the Corporate University: Culture and Pedagogy in the New Millennium* (Lanham, MD: Rowman & Littlefield, 2001).
82. Clyde W. Barrow, "Trade Liberalization and the Emergence of Multinational For-Profit Colleges and Universities," *Global Education* 8 (2004): 88–109.
83. Roberta M. Bassett, *The WTO and the University: Globalization, GATS, and American Higher Education* (New York: Routledge, 2006); Clyde W. Barrow, Sylvie Didou-Aupetit, and John Mallea, *Globalisation, Trade Liberalisation, and Higher Education in North America: The Emergence of a New Market Under NAFTA?* (Dordrecht, The Netherlands: Kluwer Academic Publishers, 2003); Clyde W. Barrow, "Globalization, Trade Liberalization, and the Higher Education Industry," in Stanley Aronowitz and Heather Gautney (Eds.), *Implicating Empire: Globalization and Resistance in the 21st Century* (New York: Basic, 2003), pp. 229–254.

CHAPTER TEN

Neoliberal Pedagogy of Debt vs. Debtor Pedagogy

The New Neoliberal Commodities

JOÃO M. PARASKEVA AND SHEILA L. MACRINE

> Underlying the market orientation of education is the ascendance, almost worldwide, of market capitalism and the principles of neoliberal economics.
>
> —*World Bank Report* (Johnstone et al., 1998)

INTRODUCTION

If we concede that pedagogy concerns the teaching/learning political relationships that exist in formal and informal educational settings, and that pedagogies themselves are shaped by the socio-political worlds in which they exist, what, for example, might a neoliberal pedagogy look like? What are the ideological effects? Paulo Freire wrote extensively about the 'pedagogy of the oppressed': a classed, raced, and gendered pedagogy within a eugenic capitalist system at the onset of neoliberalism's heyday. Freire was also one of the pioneers in alerting us to the looming social tsunami swept in by neoliberalism's policies and politics. Subsequently, other public intellectuals have challenged the oppressive dynamic of dominant pedagogical forms. Giroux (1981) ferociously unmasks the lethal consequences of segregational pedagogical perspectives framed within the reductive and dangerous cult of positivism. Apple (2000) questions the very selective nature of curriculum knowledge that permeates the daily lives of students in schools. Both Giroux and

Apple are sentient about the impact of hidden curriculum in the production and reproduction of oppressed communities. The late educational philosopher Maxine Greene (1995, p. 5) insightfully and sharply argued for an education that fosters the utopian thinking, one that "refuses mere compliance, that looks down roads not yet taken to the shapes of a more fulfilling social order, to more vibrant ways of being in the world [one] that re-shapes imagination [based] on permanent dialogue."

McLaren (1989) denounces the oppressive nature of dominant technocratic pedagogies witnessed in his ethnographic study by bringing to light the intense clash between upper-class cultural rules and the nefarious cultural forms of the hope-deprived underclass students. Further, Macedo (1994) condemns the dominant pedagogical matrices that foster potentially dangerous educational practices that privilege specialization while ignoring the need to make linkages using critical literacy. Macedo refers to this pedagogy of big lies as stupidification that fosters potentially dangerous educational practices that rely on eugenic institutional mechanisms to undermine independent thought. Antonia Darder (2012) also raises her voice against the cleansing forms of cultural oppression imposed on minorities on a daily basis in the classrooms via curriculum content. In her book, Darder stressed how minority students "do not learn about their environment from the perspective of their own reality, but from the white wealthy man" (p. 5). She further claims that the US educational system plays a key role in the class power structures serving as "an effective vehicle for the dominant culture to *civilize* bicultural populations to ensure that society remains orderly and safe" (p. 6).

Angela Valenzuela addresses the cultural politics of the daily school life of Chicano and Latino oppressed communities. She elegantly framed and coined this metamorphous of such pedagogies as 'subtractive schooling,' which is a framework for understanding the patterns of immigrant students' underachievement and how schools subtract resources from youth. Valenzuela (1998) writes that this happens in two major ways: first by dismissing their definition of education and second, through assimilationist policies and practices that minimize their culture and language. A key consequence, for Valenzuela, is the erosion of students' social capital evident in the absence of academically oriented networks found among acculturated U.S.-born youth. These pedagogical insights expose both the Orwellian manipulations of society and the political economy propaganda model advanced by Edward S. Herman and Noam Chomsky's "manufacturing of consent" or "engineering of consent" involved in the ideological production determined by the late capitalist society, in general, and the educational system, in particular (Apple & Weis, 1983).

In this chapter we expand on Williams's notion of debt education (2006) to help explicate Macrine's (2012) concept of a neoliberal pedagogy of debt, which she describes as a materialist interpretation of the development of neoliberal capitalism's chief predatory weapon that of debt subjugation; we argue that in order to reveal the true ideological productive/reproductive practices of a neoliberal pedagogy of debt, it becomes necessary to make the other side of this predatory tool that being a 'debtor pedagogy' explicit, which helps to articulate the citizen/worker responses to such oppression and subjugation. In order to accomplish this (1) we define the 'neoliberal pedagogy of debt' and introduce the concept of 'debtor pedagogy,' which is the flip side of the same predatory coin; (2) we unmask how such pedagogies have been crucial in feeding the school-to-prison pipeline, and force-outs, and; (3) we examine how certain pedagogies have been determined by the needs of the current market-based culture of society asphyxiated by austerity policies and practices. We end by suggesting alternative avenues to challenge these dominant neoliberal pedagogical matrices. Our goal in this article is not to rehash neoliberal theories and practices and their apocalyptic impacts on the realization of democratic and liberatory ideals—these issues have been taken up elsewhere (Eagleton, 2011; Harvey, 2005; Giroux, 2013; Lipman, 2011; Saltman, 2012), rather, our goal is to add to the literature and to provide a language that public intellectuals, scholars, educators, and cultural workers might employ to challenge and utilize in posing alternative and transformative possibilities.

MAKING THE ECONOMY SCREAM: NEOLIBERALISM AND THE CULTURAL POLITICS OF AUSTERITY

The current global recession leaves little doubt about the excesses of late capitalism. In fact, Fraser, Murphy, and Kelly (2013) argue that the current economic crises "raise numerous questions about neoliberal ideas and practices, not the least of which is whether neoliberalism can survive it" (p. 38). If there is something that the current global recession has demonstrated is that "it is impossible to define neoliberalism purely theoretically" (Saad-Filho & Johnston, 2005, p. 1). According to David Harvey (2005),

> Neoliberalism is in the first instance a theory of political economic practices that proposes that human well-being can best be advanced by liberating individual entrepreneurial freedoms and skills within an institutional framework characterized by strong private property rights, free markets, and free trade ... Furthermore, if markets do not exist (in areas such as land, water, education, health care, social security, or environmental pollution) then they must be created, by state action if necessary. But beyond these tasks the state should not venture. State interventions in markets (once created) must be kept to a bare minimum because, according to the theory, the state cannot possibly possess enough information to second-guess market signals (prices) and because powerful interest groups will inevitably distort and bias state interventions (particularly in democracies) for their own benefit. (p. 2)

As a philosophy of a specific political economic praxis, neoliberal market totalitarianism paves the way for the crises unleashed by the very austerity measures set in place to address such crises. Not unlike neoliberalism, austerity measures emerge as the only alternative to rescue—so neoliberals argue—nations and the state. One cannot understand a neoliberal philosophy of praxis without viewing it as an attack on the state, and its resultant deregulation policies. Austerity policies and practices play within the very core of the wrangle Fordism-post-Fordism-neoliberalism; they are cause and consequence. Paul Passavant unveils the argument insightfully, when he contextualizes such wrangle within the epicenter of urban governance. Conversely to Fordism (defined by mass production, mass consumption, welfare state) post-Fordism (loss of manufacturing in the U.S., economies demanding flexibility in labor) is intricately associated "with neoliberalism that [promotes] privatization, market-based logics" (2011, p. 89) and asphyxiates the state or any state form of intervention that puts in danger the dynamics connected with the market.

Rationales about neoliberalism's crisis-driven modus operandi by Slavoj Žižek (2010) and John Bellamy Foster and Robert McChesney (2012) deserve to be highlighted. While the former places the emphasis on state of permanent crisis, the latter focuses on the need to understand the crisis between the pendulum of financialization and stagnation as the tout court framework of the current economic havoc.

In the introduction of *The Endless Crisis: How Monopoly-Finance Capital Produces Stagnation and Upheaval from United States to China*, also published subsequently as an article in *Monthly Review*, Foster and McChesney (2012) subscribe that "the United States, Europe, and Japan, remain caught in a condition of slow growth, high unemployment, and financial instability, with new economic tremors appearing all the time and the effects spreading globally"; they also assert that "for a general consensus among informed economic observers that the world capitalist economy is facing the threat of long-run economic stagnation, sometimes referred to as the problem of 'lost decades'" (p. 1). That is, the emphasis should be put on the swamp propelled by the stagnation of the capitalist economy, and not just on the financial crisis or recession. The big question worldwide, they argue, is the impact of stagnation and its multifarious consequences.

Foster and McChesney (2012) draw on works by Paul Krugman, Tyler Cowen, and Thomas Palley to highlight the differing metamorphic changes that each of the major crises faced by the capitalist system. They contend that the current crisis has a dangerous commonality with the anemic impulses of recovery that introduces each new phase of the crises, which is, simply put, the issue of stagnation. Foster and McChesney claim that "the defining characteristic of such depressions was not negative economic growth, in the trough of the business cycle, but rather protracted slow growth once economic recovery had commenced" (p. 2).

One of the reasons for such a puzzled state is what Foster and McChesney (2012) refer to as the explicit "denial of history" (p. 2). Such cultural politics of denial, as we would frame, chirurgically crosses many turfs. Beyond the arrogance of a new political lexicon that intentionally burned key concepts into the minds of the public to address current reality (this is so overtly visible in education, with concepts such as oppressed, urban, among others), the majority of economic experts refuse to pay attention to an economy that long ago started screaming for help. Acknowledged by leading political economists such as John Galbraith and Joseph Schumpeter, as well as Foster and McChesney (p. 4), crucial economic mistakes of the last four decades were driven by a systematic neglect of history. As Foster and McChesney argue,

> Indeed, it is the slow growth or stagnation that has been festering for decades which explains not only financialization, manifested in a string of financial bubbles, but also the deep economic malaise that has set in during the period of financial deleveraging. A realistic analysis today thus requires close examination of the dangerous feedback loops between stagnation and financialization. (p. 5)

That is, the fact that these hegemonic economic models were designed to pro-act immediately before a crisis certainly speaks volumes over who needs to be blamed. Worse, such models positively excluded the very possibility of a crisis (Foster & McChesney, 2012, p. 4). Notwithstanding with such a crumbly economic framework, a red flag was raised in a number of different venues, not just by dissenting voices but also by mainstream economists and above all by the daily state of the real(ity). Foster and McChesney state:

> In fact warnings of a housing bubble and the threat of a severe financial collapse in the four years leading up to the crisis were so numerous as to make it difficult, if not impossible, to catalogue them all. The problem, then, was not that no one saw the Great Financial Crisis coming. Rather the difficulty was that the financial world, driven by their endless desire for more, and orthodox economists, prey to the worship of their increasingly irrelevant models, were simply oblivious to the warnings of heterodox economic observers all around them. Mainstream economists had increasingly retreated back into a Say's Law view (the notion that supply creates its own demand), which argued that severe economic crises were virtually impossible. The failure of orthodox economics to perceive the financial bubble prior to the Great Financial Crisis is now well established in the literature. What we are suggesting here, however, is something different: that the same economics of innocent fraud has hindered orthodox economists from perceiving until now an even bigger fault line of the mature capitalist economy, the tendency to long-term economic stagnation. (2012, p. 5)

Thus, stagnation has become the new normal of the current economic mayhem, a condition that is actually propelled by the contradictions of monopoly capitalism. That is "the very conditions of exploitation (or high price markups on unit labor costs) meant both that inequality in society increased and that more and more surplus capital tended to accumulate actually and potentially within the giant firms and in the hands of wealthy investors, who were unable to find profitable investment outlets sufficient to absorb all of the investment-seeking surplus" (Foster & McChesney, 2012, p. 7). Echoing Paul Sweeny's insightful rationale, Foster and McChesney argue that new conundrums such as globalization(s), stagnation—which does not mean necessarily negative growth—and financialization inaugurates a totally different historical phase that they refer to as "monopoly-finance capital," a moment paced by ambiguity in global competition forced by "a slowing down of growth due to overaccumulation" (Foster & McChesney, p. 7) pushed dangerous envelopes to address a complex wrangle between the demands of an ever-demanding market and the crude reality of a pallid economy. In fact, and in frontal opposition to what seems to be perceivable at an open eye, Foster and McChesney contextualize China's growth and other so labeled emergent economies (Brazil and Angola, we would say) within such yarn of perpetual disaster. Clearly, the solution, which comes out of the Foster and McChesney's *The Endless Crisis: How Monopoly-Finance Capital Produces Stagnation and Upheaval from United States to China* and addresses the current crisis, relies outside of the current financial/economic capitalist system. It is impossible as the *The Endless Crisis* overtly shows to even interrupt the current state of affairs without destroying the current socio-economic framework of the capitalist system pumped by specific and unacceptable conditions and relations of production. It is actually such a take that we see in Samir Amin's *The Implosion of Contemporary Capitalism* (2013). According to Amin the current monopoly-financial capitalism is imposing ever-demanding yet unsustainable changes within the civil archeology that puts the system in a kind of self-destruction mode since it is incapable of finding the right formula to address its own unsuitable demands. The system is exhausted because it exhausted its very social matrix. Needless to say, the impact of such a conflictive state has serious implications on education. Education and educators are under the gun to come up with answers for a problem that is beyond their jurisdiction. Education and educators are in a permanent tourniquet to maintain and revitalize an economy that shows daily signs of unsustainability. More than ever before, education is playing a crucial part in the new equation of the current political economy (Lipman, 2011). The best way to address such a crisis is to unravel the rampage of austerity politics. Disconcertedly, the idea is to rescue the system, not the people. Education and other social public spheres, such as health care, have been subjugated to severe cuts to feed the so-called structural adjustment plans imposed on governments (Roy, 2014).

Leading world philosopher Slavoj Žižek (2010) presents a similar position when he describes the current crisis as "a permanent economic emergency" (Žižek, 2010). According to Žižek there are good and bad elements on both sides of the aisle. Relying on the Eurozone as *plus qui parfait* scenario to examine austerity politics, Žižek argues that the draconian measures imposed on nations, such as Greece, Italy, Ireland, and Spain (and we would add Portugal), deepened the unfathomable abyss between two complex perspectives. The first is the self-proclaimed neutral mainstream that "proposes a de-politicized naturalization of the crisis, [that is,] the regulatory measures are presented not as decisions grounded in political choices, but as the imperatives of a neutral financial logic—if we want our economies to stabilize, [then] we simply have to swallow the bitter pill" (p. 85); and second is the position led by social groups, such as "protesting workers, students and pensioners, [that] see the austerity measures as yet another attempt by international financial capital to dismantle the last remainders of the welfare state" (p. 85). According to Žižek, both perspectives are mired with elements of both truths and fallacies, which frame a shocking paradox. Before we unveil the paradox, we concur with Žižek, that institutions like the IMF did not even blink at unleashing this inhumane recovery plan—a plan that is just concerned with the economy forcing nations into a permanent state of debt in order to address debt. Concomitantly, suffering nations are forced to play in this game, even though they know full well that the equation of 'debt to pay debt' is an unresolvable equation of restructuring. Nevertheless, the IMF is very comfortable with all of this since they benefit directly from the interests already banked and indirectly from the outcomes of rushed austerity-driven privatizations of state assets. Mark Blyth and Tom Willis's (2013) description is telling:

> Now public debt is a wonderful thing because if you think about it it's a great scam. You are the state and I am the capitalist. And I want my property protected. But I also want to be able to control you in some way. So I've got this thing called a debt instrument. I will give you money and you will use it to protect me. But the privilege of doing so means that I've got you on a leash and you also have to make interest payments to me. And at the end of the term you give me all the money back! I mean could there be a better deal than this in the world? But Hume figures out that there's a problem here. In order to make that work you're going to have to pay a rate of interest on the bill, which is as good, if not higher, than you would get in the private market.

Odd as it might be, debt has become a crippling global crisis. That is, the fiscal chaos perpetrated by uncontrolled markets has paved the way for stricter and stricter austerity measures that impose fiscal consolidations, as well as *spartan* economic policies that have broader effects at all levels including the state level. According to the Center for American Progress, austerity measures such as deficit cutting, reduced spending, and slashed public services are not going anywhere—they will be with us for years to come and it is not just in the U.S. With debt levels unacceptably high, many countries are being forced to make dramatic cuts to avoid default. Privatization policies are currently in progress in more than 80 countries throughout the world. These austerity measures come with serious economic, political, and social implications.

The push for the adoption of financial and political tools to rapidly cut social and economic programs like austerity measures allow the market to expand its tentacles through privatization mechanisms and other fiscal solutions. Take Portugal, for example. The government issues golden resident visas, which give foreign investors who spend at least 500,000 euros on a property the right to live in Portugal and the promise of citizenship. Growth schemes like this one are cropping up all across Europe. The Portuguese Golden Residence Visa or the Investor Residence Permit are a vivid examples of how even during the current economic tsunami, the world's 1% are still capable of multiplying their assets. Instead of bailing out the poverty stricken, the neoliberal model of getting out of the crisis is to bail out the rich. As for the paradox, as we promised to highlight, the truth of the matter is that all of this is happening within the so-called laudable democratic societies under the auspices of an overtly non-democratic structure that is the IMF, democracies that the West is imposing all over the world even at the cost of human lives.

It is actually here that one of the cruxes of the current crises resides. As the stagnation (Foster & McChesney, 2012), or permanent economic emergency (Žižek, 2010), keeps growing, or as we would say, instability stabilizes, democracy keeps shrinking to a point that, for instance, in the case of Europe, "the true message of the Eurozone crisis is that not only the Euro, but the project of the united Europe itself is dead" (Žižek, 2010, p. 86). While identity is at stake here, such challenges need to be seen as an opportunity for new utopias, or as Boaventura de Sousa Santos (2006) would argue, alternative ways in order to build more coherent alternatives. That is, in the face of all the de-politicizing attempts, the current social terrain frames the strategies to address the crisis as 'neutral' or as Žižek (2010) argues "a re-politicized Europe, founded on a shared emancipatory project" (p. 86). Such a trend needs to "avoid the temptation to react to the ongoing financial crisis with a retreat to fully sovereign nation-states, easy prey for free-floating international capital, which can play one state against the other. More than ever, the reply to every crisis should be *more* internationalist and universalist than the universality of global capital" (Žižek, 2010, p. 86). This is the best way to address the new period facing dominant and counter-dominant tranches.

After decades of the welfare state, where cutbacks were relatively limited and came with the promise that things would soon return to normal, we are now entering a state of economic emergency that is becoming a permanent way of life. It brings with it the threat of far more savage austerity measures, cuts in benefits, diminishing health and education services, and more precarious unemployment. As Žižek points out the Left faces the difficult task of emphasizing the fact that we are dealing with a *political* economy—that there is nothing 'natural' or 'neutral' in such a crisis,

> The existing global economic system relies on a series of political decisions—while simultaneously being fully aware that, insofar as we remain within the capitalist system, the violation of its rules effectively causes economic breakdown, since the system obeys a pseudo-natural logic of its own. So, although we are clearly entering a new phase of enhanced exploitation, rendered easier by the conditions of the global market (outsourcing, etc.), we should also bear in mind that this is imposed by the functioning of the system itself, always on the brink of financial collapse. (2010, p. 86)

According to Žižek (2010), the goal, explicit or implied, is to regulate capitalism—through the pressure of the media, parliamentary inquiries, harsher laws, honest police investigations—but never to question the liberal-democratic institutional mechanisms of the bourgeois state of law; this remains the "sacred cow" (p. 87). Foster and McChesney (2012) also unveil such a framework as the "tough bone to chew." That is while challenging the excesses of a threadbare market and the need to mercilessly regulate the markets, too many counter-dominant intellectuals and movements refuse to put their finger in the pie and destroy the very social mechanisms that maintain such a state of affairs. There is obviously a reason for such refusal according to Žižek (2010). To challenge the very mechanisms that maintains—a kind of market socialism, or capitalism with a human face—implies the disruption of the relations and conditions of production, thus promoting what Žižek calls "transformative social relations of production" (p. 88).

Žižek's (2010) analysis allows one to perceive the real underbelly of the economy as an ideological form, and how a simple set of tourniquets in the financial veins of a particular nation will make that economy scream, thus asphyxiating the government, as was the case in Allende's Chile. In a way Žižek is also simultaneously challenging and complexifying the commonsensical cliché of the invisible hand of the market arguing that "in the current economic emergency, we are clearly not dealing with blind market processes but with highly organized, strategic interventions by states and financial institutions, intent on resolving the crisis on their own terms" (p. 89). The idea that the economy is the zone of non-ideology is one of the most ferocious ideological claims. With that said, the economy needs to be seen as ideology (Žižek, p. 90).

Education is the terrain that proves the irrefutability of such a statement. Education and educators have no other option, either they assume to be the accelerator of this new economic momentum or they have will be left with no voice or social place. Hence, education and educators have been victims of a system that was designed to fail the challenges for more social and cognitive justice (see Sousa Santos, 2014), which is now mercilessly cornered and charged with the responsibility of eliminating the social malaises. That education was always a crucial device within the political economic matrix was always defended, not just by Karl Marx and Friedrich Engels but also by heavy-weight Marxist and neo-Marxist intellectuals, such as Antonio Gramsci, Louis Althusser, Samuel Bowles, and

Herbert Gintis and others not without intense criticism—sometimes unfairly yet expectedly sarcastic—even within the very Left platform. Unsurprisingly the very same claim—that is, education as a crucial piece within the puzzle of political economy—has been now harangued by center, center-right, right, and far right intellectuals. As one of us argued elsewhere (Paraskeva, 2008) it looks like currently some of the best Marxists are on the right and center right.

Stephen Ball's (2008) masterpiece *The Education Debate* insightfully addresses such issues from its very roots by highlighting Tony Blair's (2005, as cited in Ball, 2008) assertion that the role of education in neoliberal times "is our best economic policy. [The UK] will succeed or fail on the basis of how it changes itself and gears up to this new economy, based on knowledge. Education is now at the center of economic policy making for the future" (p. 14). The attacks "on teachers unions, closing of schools in minority and poor communities, students being erratically pushed to a kind of permanent transferred position, meaningless public participation, gentrification of African American and Latino/a working class neighborhoods, and families pushed farther out of the city" (Lipman, 2011, p. 2) leaves little doubt about the nefarious consequences of how education has been positioned to catalyze the new political economy. This manifestation of destructively creative neoliberalization according to Pauline Lipman (2011) is the local consequence of "the global project to gear education to [the so called] economic competitiveness [thus] imposing a market discipline in all aspects of schooling" (p. 3). Odd as it might be, one of the avenues seized by neoliberals to achieve such competitiveness are tough austerity policies that legitimize a full-on neoliberal pedagogy of debt.

THE SUBJECTIFICATION OF DEBT

The literature is now vast drawing attention to the lethal impact of neoliberal polices in higher education. From Stanley Aronowitz's *Knowledge Factory*, through the seminal works of Clyde Barrow's *Universities and Capitalist State*, Gary Roades and Sheila Slaughter's *Academic Capitalism*, Benjamin Ginsberg's *The Fall of Faculty*, Henry Giroux's *University in Chains*, Piya Chatterjee and Sunaina Maira's *The Imperial University*, as well as Jeffrey Williams's *Debt Education*, to our notions in the *Neoliberal Pedagogy of Debt and Debtor Pedagogy*, the common theme is how neoliberalism legitimizes a new paradigm for higher education. At the very root of these new articulations of pedagogical paradigms is the shift in higher education as a service to society to a business model driven by the bottom line and intrinsically connected to various funding policies, including the rationale of extreme austerity and the virtual inevitability of higher educational revenue diversification, such as some forms of cost-sharing, in most countries (Johnstone, 2004). That is the neoliberal pedagogy of debt imposed and legitimized by neoliberal policies is more complex and has repercussions in pedagogical daily matters. The neoliberal pedagogy of debt is more than a mode of finance. It is also a pedagogical device that opens the door for the analysis of a myriad of connected complex issues including student loan debt. Here, Williams (2006) examines the upward cost of higher education during the last three decades, which is not only alarming but also highlights the tremendous costs being absorbed by students:

> The average undergraduate student loan debt in 2002 was $18,900. It more than doubled from 1992, when it was $9,200. Added to this is charge card debt, which averaged $3,000 in 2002, boosting the average total debt to about $22,000. One can reasonably expect, given still accelerating costs, that it is over $30,000 now. Bear in mind that this does not include other private loans or the debt that parents take on to send their children to college. (Neither does it account for "post-baccalaureate loans," which more than doubled in seven years, from $18,572 in 1992–1993 to $38,428 in 1999–2000, and have likely doubled again)

Williams (2006) argues, "The reason that debt has increased so much and so quickly is that tuition and fees have increased, at roughly three times the rate of inflation. Tuition and fees have gone up from an average of $924 in 1976, when I first went to college, to $6,067 in 2002." Naturally this upward financial curve puts "disproportionate burden on students and their families—hence loans [to a point that] although it is difficult to measure these costs separately, paying for college no doubt forms part of the accelerating indebtedness of average [U.S.] families." The chirurgical defunding of public higher education establishes a "principle that citizens should pay more directly for public services, and public services should be administered less through the state and more through private enterprise" (Williams, 2006); that is "the state's role is not to provide an alternative realm apart from the market but to grease the wheels of the market, subsidizing citizens to participate in it and businesses to provide social services" (Williams, 2006). While this is a disquieting reality, it is just one side of the coin. The other side of the coin is that it opens the door for the private model of management and philanthropic impulses. Arundhati Roy (2014) states that "as the IMF enforced structural adjustments and arm-twisted governments into cutting back on public spending on health, education, child care, development, the NGO's moved in. [That is] the privatization of everything has also meant the NGO-ization of everything" (p. 32). The truth of the matter is that the very reality "everything" is very selective. The market is only targeting educational apparatuses capable of producing profits. Student loan debts have eclipsed both auto loans and credit cards, making student loan debt the largest form of consumer debt outside of mortgages. Student loan debt is the only form of consumer debt that has grown since the peak of consumer debt in 2008.

The issue of philanthropism is also exposed by Henry Giroux (2011) and Stephen Ball (2012). Henry Giroux in his *Education and the Crisis of Public Values* frames such austerity policies as a form of violence, a violence that is perpetrated by a policy of cruelty. As he states,

> When I refer to a culture of cruelty and a politics of humiliation, I am talking about the institutionalization and widespread adoption of a set of values, policies, and symbolic practices that legitimate forms of organized violence against human beings and lead inexorably to hardship, suffering, and despair. Forms of humiliation in which the character, dignity, and bodies of targeted individuals and groups are under attack more and more accompany such practices. An extreme form is evident in state-sanctioned torture practices, such as those promoted by the Bush administration in Iraq and on full display in the images of humiliation that emerged from the torture chambers of Abu Ghraib prison. The politics of humiliation also works through symbolic systems, diverse modes of address, and varied framing mechanisms in which the targeted subjects are represented in terms that demonize them, strip them of their humanity, and position them in ways that invite ridicule and sometimes violence. (2011, p. 14)

In education, Giroux (2011) adds, that such culture of cruelty and humiliation needs to be contextualized within "a formative politics of dislocation and misrepresentation." He (2011) challenges us to frame the philanthropic approach to education within "the hidden fallacies of an insulting generosity" (Paraskeva, 2013, p. 706). Henry Giroux (2011) states,

> Bill Gates (Microsoft), Philip Anschultz (Denver Oil), Jeff Skoll (eBay), and other members of the corporate elite use their power and money-soaked foundations to pour millions into a massive public pedagogy campaign that paints the American system of public education, teacher unions, and public school teachers in terms that are polarizing and demonizing. Humiliation, in this case masquerades as generosity, coupled with an attempt to divert attention from the real problems and solutions needed to improve American public education. Real problems affecting schools such as rising poverty, homelessness, vanishing public services for the disadvantaged, widespread unemployment, re-segregation of public schools, massive inequality in wealth and income, overcrowded classrooms, and a bankrupt and iniquitous system of school financing disappear in the educational discourse of the super rich. Moreover, the policies promoted by such anti-public reformers are endlessly legitimated through a massive public relations campaign that is one sided, politically reactionary, and sectarian in its attempts to disparage and drown out more critical and progressive voices. (p. 16)

Stephen Ball's (2012) workbook *Global Education, INC*, which is "a sequel to *Education PLC* (2007)," not only corroborates Giroux's (2011) approach but also offers "an account of contemporary trends in education in particular on the increasing role of business, social enterprise and philanthropy in education service delivery and education policy" (p. 1). Ball (2012) alerts us to how these new forms of educational management that he refers to as hierarchies represent "dynamic and very immediate changes that have a national and global significance in relation to educational policy, education reforms, democracy, social opportunity and equity and the meaning and practice of education" (p. 1). This research drew upon "a series of research studies of philanthropy, privatization and policy reform in education and cognate fields between 2004 and 2011 [covering] extensive and exhaustive internet searches around particular edu-business, corporate and family philanthropies, philanthropists and philanthropically funded programs" (p. 4) and unveils accurately the promiscuous interplay between such turfs and education.

As one of us (Paraskeva, 2013) had the opportunity to analyze elsewhere the "policies of disinvestment in public education are in fact a strategy for the global salvation of a group of corporations and billionaires that are suffering in the current economic crisis, a strategy that helps capitalism back on its track and ensures that no philanthropic superman is left behind, it is also a severe attack on intellectual freedom and democracy" (p. 706). Philanthropism, Giroux (2011) argues, is the institutionalization of "a collective suicide whose victims will include not only education, but democracy itself" (p. 26).

The impact of such a new paradigm has huge implications for pedagogical practices in general. Our claim is that the neoliberal pedagogy of debt is not just a financial framework that pushes people to a quasi-irremediable oppressed position, it is also the pedagogical fiber that permeates the daily lives of the oppressed. It is not a discursive matter; quite the opposite, it institutionalizes a concrete space and time that imposes on the oppressed a subjectivity that is systematically defined by its deficits.

Within this critical analysis, the *neoliberal pedagogy of debt* is a political tool that articulates a neoliberal pedagogy that permeates the cultural politics of everyday life. It is a financial virus hegemonically embedded within our commonsense. Clearly, oppressed communities already in debt know full well that the only way to survive is to be a zombie engaged in a path of debt. Such framework reframes completely the ethical and moral terrain as it fabricates a new ethics and morals of consent by legitimizing subjugation through predatory debt that has lethal impacts within not just students' performance but also in access policies and praxis.

Needless to say, we are not here subscribing any kind of social and cultural reproductionist's platform. However, to challenge and interrupt such complex issues, it is important to understand the totalitarian impulses of such pedagogy. The oppressed working classes and the poor are the ones that shoulder the brunt of the costs of debt whether it be individual debt, as in student loans, subprime mortgages, nation-state debt, or Third World debt, it is impossible to exist without debt unless you are a member of the 1%. The truth of the matter is that such neoliberal pedagogies need to be seen as a hegemonic tools mediating between the global corporate centers of power and the mundane disposable citizen who cannot exist outside of being in debt. Late capitalism has created a system where one cannot exist outside of a debtor society, one needs a credit card to buy groceries, a loan to buy a car, and so forth. We live in a system that needs to fabricate more debt to sustain its financial system that pushes society into more and more oppressed status, a democracy that supports a middle class condemned to disappear. The neoliberal pedagogy of debt teaches individuals their places, their roles, and their responsibilities as economic pawns in this global financial chess game.

Mauricio Lazzarato's (2011) approach helps us understand neoliberal economy as a process of subjectification. Neoliberal economy, Lazzarato argues, is a "subjective economy" (p. 37) framed within the wrangle 'creditor-debitor,' a wrangle that relies at the very core of social relations. Objectively, such relation(ships) subjectifies "everyone as a debtor" (Lazzarato, p. 7) within a finance matrix increasingly dominated by the totalitarianism of the concubinage creditor-debitor. Lazzarato) states:

> Viewing debt as the archetype of social relations means two things. On one hand it means conceiving economy and society on the basis of an asymmetry of power and not on that of a commercial exchange that implies and presupposes equality. On the other hand, debt means immediately making the economy subjective, since debt is an economic relation, which in order to exist, implies the molding and control of subjectivity such that labor becomes indistinguishable from work in the self. (p. 33)

Needless to say that such wrangle creditor-debitor is a power relation—or fuels and it is fueled by power relations—"since it is itself a power relation, one of the most important and universal of modern-day capitalism" (Lazzarato, p. 30), thus "intensifying the mechanisms of exploitation and domination at every level of society" (p. 7).

The neoliberal economy is not a finance economy but a debt economy. To be more precise, within the complex neoliberal global mantra, "what we call finance is indicative of the increasing force of the creditor-debitor relation" (Lazzarato, 2011, p. 22). The subjectification of debt, Lazzarato (p. 31) claims, is cultivated daily and it is ultimately and ideological position.

DEBTOR PEDAGOGY

Neoliberal financialization has dramatically expanded the scope and reach of neoliberal approaches to credit/debt and its predatory devices, such as subprime mortgage-driven homeownership. Neoliberalism opened up new frontiers for punitive operations of debt advocating: self-discipline by indebted masses who are engulfed by the financialized economy and refashioned governmentalities. These include economic policies and the attending discourse of personal that furnished the grounds for the symbiosis of debt and discipline (Mahmud, 2013). The prescription of subjectivity to obtain interiorization of the market's goal in the context of precariatization of labor is accomplished through generalization of debt

(Mahmud, 2013). Rose (1999) adds that the result is an assemblage of citizens that "accepts" itself as a homo economicus, "a dependent subjectivity, an 'individual' subjectivity conforming to capital," and in which "a dependent subjectivity, a subjectivity conforming to capital, and in which the rationality of homo economicus, of human capital, replaces the idea of social rights and common goods" (p. 178). This ensures self-discipline whereby time and life both within and outside the bounds of any specific site of production remain subjected to value production. The use of this methodology has provocative implications concerning what might be learned about forging a link between the individual struggle for change against neoliberal pedagogy of debt's policies/practices and a collective consciousness to develop and to reposition individuals in order that they may explore a range of methodological and interpretive strategies for challenging power relations and the ways in which this innovative pedagogy can be empowering beyond the research situation.

As we state in the beginning, we believe the evolution of more and more neoliberal pedagogies, such as a neoliberal pedagogy of debt, needs a responsive pedagogical paradigm to empower citizens with the language and strategies to fight back. Under debtor pedagogy, citizens are expected to take responsibility to adapt by upgrading their skills through life-long learning, changing their attitudes to become less "risk-adverse" and more "entrepreneurial." The overall goal of neoliberal communitarian citizenship is to ensure that citizens, for the cause of global competitiveness, become less reliant on the state for welfare protection and more "employable" in order to adapt to "more flexible labor markets" and "flexible working conditions" (Bieling, 2003, pp. 65, 67).

For three decades, neoliberal financialization combined with globalization contained the crisis of profitability and produced debt-encumbered, self-disciplined working classes (Mahmud, 2013). In response to this neoliberal reorganization of capitalism, we find that hegemony of finance capital displaced the Keynesian compromise. This transformation, according to Mahmud, entails the rollback of the welfare state, breaking the power of organized labor, precarization of labor markets, financialization of the economy, and exponential expansion of debt. In this ensemble, debt maintains collective demand, fuels liquidity to lubricate financialization, and facilitates assemblage of entrepreneurial subjects responsible for their own economic security and insecurity (Mahmud, 2013).

It is this point precisely that brings us to a citizen response to the neoliberal pedagogy of debt—we refer to the citizen response to this predatory subjugation as debtor pedagogy. Here the citizen is expected to develop strategies alone in response to overwhelming odds. In others words, *how* do citizens respond, react, and retaliate against neoliberal financialized machines? Foucault (1983) argues, "He who is subjected to a field of visibility, and who knows it, assumes responsibility for the constraints of power; he makes them play spontaneously upon himself;

he inscribes in himself the power relation in which he simultaneously plays both roles; he becomes the principle of his own subjection." Further, according to Foucault (1983), these are "modes of subjectivation … in which people are invited or incited to recognize their moral obligations" (p. 264).

While critical political economy helps uncover macro-level neoliberal economic transformations, Foucault's constructs focus on the attendant micro-level processes of market-mediated subject formation. Of particular utility are Foucault's constitution of the constructs of governmentality, bio-power, and assemblage of self-caring. We are all aware of the differences between corporate privilege and individual privilege—just look at how the banks were bailed out during the recent crisis and their credit ratings readjusted. There is no safety net in place for the individual citizen and in particular students. In fact, Congress voted to prevent students from declaring bankruptcy on student loans, so students carry loans from school to the grave in some case. Right now students are in over $13 billion in credit ratings and adjustments. The federal government is making a profit from student loans. Massachusetts Senator Elizabeth Warren (2013) said, "While students are paying more, the federal government is boosting its own profits—$51 billion from our student loan programs in 2013 alone."

An urgent challenge is to explore agendas, coalitions, and organizational forms of resistive social movements suitable to pursue popular democratization of finance. Also needed are designs of political and economic governance conducive to organizing banking and finance as public utilities. The current crisis has opened up the possibility of alternative social orders and modes of life. What shape the future will take depends in no small measure on how contending social forces will confront the perennial question of finance and the relationship between debt and the citizen (Mahmud, 2013).

One such collective response is in the case of the state of Mississippi, where the whole state is suing one of the three largest credit-reporting agencies, Experian. The lawsuit accuses Experian of knowingly including error-riddled data in the credit files of millions of Americans, jeopardizing their ability to obtain loans and sensitive government security clearances, and fouling employment-related background checks. Experian has even wrongly reported that consumers are on a federal terrorism watch list, the lawsuit says. The newspaper, *The Dispatch*, investigated and found that consumers virtually are powerless to correct credit-report error with the three big national credit-reporting agencies, documenting the plight of thousands who could not correct even the most obvious error: "I am not dead." However this is only one state against one credit-reporting bureau, and it is not enough. Citizen consumers are perilously at risk and powerless to do anything about it as individuals.

Not without resistance—among the most notable one needs to flag the case of the Chicago teachers' unions—the *neoliberal pedagogy of debt* is paving the way for debtor *pedagogy*. That is, the neoliberal pedagogy of debt is an instrument that is destructive, a de-humanizing pedagogy that capitalism institutionalizes as a way (the only way) of existence by keeping people in debt, and supporting a system that does this both overtly and implicitly. On the other hand, debtor pedagogy expresses how people become critically aware of the late capitalism's pervasive system à la Freire's (1978) *Pedagogy of the Oppressed* and neoliberal pedagogy of debt (that's us) versus debtor pedagogy (the banks, capitalist, etc.). The concept of a neoliberal pedagogy of debt and a debtor pedagogy acts dialectically to entrap and then coerce people into their own economic destruction. So, it is through the deconstruction of this pedagogy that allows people to become aware of this system in order to transform it. Based on Freire's conviction that every human being is capable of looking critically at his/her world in a dialogical encounter with others, and that provided with the proper tools for such encounters he/she could gradually perceive personal and social reality and deal critically with it and transform it. "I work, and working I transform the world." As the person learns and is able to make such statements, his/her world becomes radically transformed and he is no longer willing to be a mere object responding to changes occurring around him/her (Freire, 1970, p. 57).

Neoliberalism cannibalizes the poor and working classes. As a result, there are fewer opportunities in the new economy world order that no longer assumes responsibility for the social needs of its people. These neoliberal economic forces are effectively breathing new life into sanctioned slave labor and creating disposable people across the globe. Here, in the U.S., the prevailing logic of neoliberalism and its pursuit of greater profits are attained through outsourcing and flexible production that has given rise to wage slavery and disposable populations at home (Giroux, 2004). Since they are the two faces of the same coin, both the neoliberal pedagogy of debt and the debtor pedagogy are the new *Panopticon* of late global neoliberalism that only allows one to exist in perpetual debt.

The neoliberal pedagogy of debt frames teaching and learning relationships that take place outside of formal schooling, fulfilling the goals of neoliberalism in global, nation-state, and individual contexts and making visible their predatory practices, and at the same time colonializing new generations in such a way that asphyxiates identity and agency, jeopardizing democracy, critical thinking, and fostering inequality.

The *debtor pedagogy* is a consequence of the *neoliberal pedagogy of debt* that pervades the classrooms of too many nations around the world. That is a financial and cultural framework that hurts almost irremediably minorities, people of color, and women, not just through curriculum content, with the high-stakes testing, tracking and common assessments, and the latest Common Core, but also through policies such as No Child Left Behind and Race to the Top (basically No Child Left Behind on steroids), forcing neoliberal solutions such as charter schools and innovation schools, as is the current case in the state of Massachusetts that are really masked exclusionary policies of "choiceless choices" (Macedo, 2013). The *debtor pedagogy* shows precisely how a huge generation of minority kids is actually facing epistemological debt (Paraskeva, 2011) through a curriculum that is based on a selective tradition and that attempts to fabricate not democratic citizens with a social conscious but consumers in which their existence and identity relies on their capacity to survive in permanent debt, as well as the non-homogeneous actions against the impact of such pedagogies portrayed by educators, community leaders, activists, and public intellectuals.

FINAL CONSIDERATIONS: A COUNTER-HEGEMONIC CRITICAL DEBTOR PEDAGOGY

We live in perilous times. Citizens are in debt over their heads, and this is no accident according to Geisst (2013), who writes that Wall Street orchestrated the current predatory debt-crisis. The idea is that people do not choose to be poor or oppressed or perpetually in debt, although the bourgeois would like us to believe otherwise. Today, under the mantle of neoliberalism, it is easy to see that those in power keep the poor and powerless in subservient positions, through different mechanisms, but in this case predatory debt subjugation. Everyone has their own story of oppression, of people they know or family members who are struggling to end that poverty cycle, to the best of their individual and collective ability.

Unfortunately, oppressive dynamics fueled by the neoliberal pedagogy of debt are not simply the result of ignorance of the other; rather they were developed to justify economic and political exploitation by claiming that the working class, the poor, and other visible minorities are physically and morally inferior. Moreover, it also needs to be contextualized within the secularized cultural policies of eugenics, an ideological strategy that permeates all the dominant pedagogical forms. Therefore, only by examining the historical construction of oppression can we begin to eliminate the destructive ideologies that promote and justify political and economic inequality. The seduction of the market economy with public passivity and a general lack of outrage within the industrialized nations form what the advent of corporate rule has come to mean for most of the world's people (Bauman, 2007). Needless to say, such dominant pedagogical forms have been on the frontline to produce, reproduce, and legitimate the particular forms of common sense that frame society hegemonically. Hegemony is 'the master concept' of neoliberalism as the current dominant philosophy of praxis.

Marx (1992) addresses oppression by emphasizing class dynamics quite related with the complex dynamics propelled by political economy. In so doing, he and Engels (1848) define "the modern working class—as a class of laborers who live only so long as they find work, and who find work only so long as their labor increases capital" (p. 479). The working class for Marx is everybody who has to work for a wage and sell his or her labor in order to survive.

Antonio Gramsci (1971) developed the idea of "hegemony," which he referred to as the dominance of one group of people, or one ideology, based on consent and persuasion, rather than by brute force. In other words, hegemony means the oppressed accept their oppression, internalizing and perhaps even outwardly arguing for the mythology of their rulers and thoroughly being indoctrinated with the mythology of capitalism—seeing the system as positive and liberating, rather than violent and destructive as it actually is (Knight, 2010). So, it is much easier to rule over people if they believe it is for their own good. The acceptance of oppressive dynamics is quite connected to what Freire (1997) calls the banking form of education. Such a dehumanizing pedagogical praxis has been dissected by Giroux (1981) as praxis based on a dangerous cult of positivism, a zombie politics with a meta-narrative that arrogantly determines the scientificity of science.

Constant struggles by the poor and the oppressed to escape their bondage *become ideologically relevant today.* The neoliberal pedagogy of debt (Williams, 2006; Macrine, 2012) is the explication of neoliberalism's predatory tool that mediates between the global corporate centers of power and the common citizen, fabricating neoliberal policies as a total. This illustrates the conditions in which it operates, and how individuals learn their place, their roles, and their responsibilities as economic pawns in this global financial chess match. Our claim is that a 'critical debtor pedagogy,' is a meme or the fundamental unit of information in an emerging revolutionary theory of culture; it is the response to this oppression and contributes to the debate on and against the logic of the neoliberal regimes. It helps to expose how their predatory practices form a hegemonic pedagogy that teaches us to accept our oppression (see Freire, 1980) and to accept the decoupling collective interests from individuals/workers who are left without any recourse or protection of the rights of citizenship, who are ultimately left without a safety net. In fact, commonsensically under the neoliberal regime rights have been converted to privileges. This incendiary hegemonic pedagogy constitutes the coercion of the public's own "construction of consent" or "consensual control," whereby individuals "'voluntarily' assimilate the world-view or hegemony of the dominant group" (Ransome, 1992, p. 150). This hegemony contributes to the strength of neoliberal ideology and legitimizes widespread dismantling of welfare state policies and validates the neoliberal rhetoric of individual freedoms and personal responsibility through meritocracy. Antonio Gramsci's assertion that "every relationship of 'hegemony' is necessarily an educational relationship" (1971, p. 350) supports the processes of popular consent to the hegemony of the dominant cultural industry, then the matter becomes pedagogical (Dutton & Mann, 2003). Individuals are told to either work hard or suffer the consequences of failure with no one to blame but themselves. According to Rose (1990), neoliberal governments psychologically police citizens to become enterprising selves irrespective of class barriers. To challenge this hegemonic pedagogy, we argue for the development of counter-hegemonic critical debtor pedagogy in order to explore and create alternative pedagogical sites to supplant neoliberalism's savage capitalism.

> "Hegemony" goes beyond "culture", as previously defined in its insistence on relating the "whole" social process to specific distributions of power and influence ... In a class society these are primarily inequalities between classes. Gramsci therefore introduced the necessary recognition of dominance and subordination in what has still, however, to be recognized as a whole process. (Williams, 1977, p. 108)

In short, a critical debtor pedagogy is a useful response to the neoliberal pedagogy of debt in two ways: first, it serves as a model for uncovering the hidden curriculum of neoliberal policies and practices as it engages nation-states and citizens in a collective and critical response through which their sense of self in relation to others becomes the groundwork for themes to repudiate and reject such predatory practices. As a model for the citizen-community relationship, it teaches citizens how to critically think about the different values and beliefs held by transnational corporations and banks that have become neoliberal purveyors and how to begin to recognize themselves as victims in relation to their place in society. A citizen's responsibility for change is then translated into communal action, whereby one contributes to the greater good while finding her or his place among others (Prilleltensky, 1997). In this process, citizens may realize their individual and collective power to refute oppression and gain strength from their community.

To address these concerns, we advocate a critical debtor pedagogy, one that challenges the use of debt subjugation to secure particular forms of authority; by questioning how power operates in a commodified knowledge arena, while redefining what is taking place all around us. Today, we are experiencing the full impact of neoliberal capitalism's need to become, more than ever before, a fully internationalized and integrated system of socio-economic control and domination—the global system that many commentators have suddenly remembered Marx and Engels (1848) presciently forecast in the *Communist Manifesto* (Mayo, 2007).

The development of a critical debtor pedagogy helps us recognize the need for personal liberty and collective consciousness that can help us to solve these challenges to the public interest and academic freedom in this diminishing democracy and culture of freedom (Giroux, 2004). Finally, we seek to disrupt neoliberalism's hegemonic pedagogical practices and policies by naming and theorizing its most effective weapons, a 'critical debtor pedagogy,' a pedagogy that increases poverty as it eliminates individual and nation-state sovereignty, while it increases political and economic subordination and dissolves democracy. This 'critical debtor pedagogy' describes a praxis of the politics of disposability (Giroux, 2006), in which deeply indebted countries, nation-states, and workers find themselves without a voice with which to challenge and battle their oppressors against subjugation and enslavement. The "neoliberal pedagogy of debt" and 'critical debtor pedagogy' are two halves of the same coin of oppression, politics, and economics. Both stand as an insidious political teaching and learning tool used to convince us that the interest of capital should come at the expense of human life, democracy, dignity, and responsibility toward the future. We advocate for a discursive and collective action against the predatory nature of neoliberalism's most successful pedagogies. We believe that through the articulation of these pedagogies that we can give citizens the tools necessary to live, in the Freirean sense, with the hope and possibility of an open terrain.

REFERENCES

Adeleke, T. (2002). Globalization and the challenges of race-based pedagogy. *Globalization*. Retrieved from http://globalization.icaap.org/content/v2.2/adeleke.html

Amin, S. (2013). *The implosion of contemporary capitalism*. New York: Monthly Review.

Apple, M. (1982). *Education and power*. New York: Routledge.

Apple, M. (1993). *Ideology and curriculum* (2nd ed.). New York: Routledge.

Apple, M. (2000). *Official Knowledge*. New York: Routledge.

Apple, M., & Weis, L. (1983). Ideology and practice in education: A political and conceptual introduction. In M. Apple & L. Weis. *Ideology and practice in schooling* (pp. 3–33). Philadelphia: Temple University Press.

Ball, S. (2005). *Education policy and social class: The selected works of Stephen J. Ball*. New York: Routledge.

Ball, S. (2008). *The education debate*. Bristol: Policy.

Ball, S. (2012). *Global education: New policy networks and the neoliberal imaginary*. New York: Routledge.

Bauman, Z. (2007). *Consuming Life*: London: Polity.

Bieling, H. J. (2003). European employment policy between neo-liberal rationalism and communitarianism. In H. Overbeek (Ed.), *The political economy of European employment: European integration and the transnationalization of the (un)employment question*. London: Routledge.

Blyth, M., & Willis, T. (2013). Power & prejudice: The politics of austerity (Part 1). *The New Left Project*. Retrieved from http://www.newleftproject.org/index.php/site/article_comments/power_prejudice_the_politics_of_austerity_part_1

Bourdieu, P. (1998). *Acts of Resistance: Against the Tyranny of the Market*. New York: Free Press.

Brubaker, M., Tlanusta, M., Garrett, M., Rivera, & Tatec, K. (2010). Justice making in groups for homeless adults: The emancipatory communitarian way. *The Journal for Specialists in Group Work, 35*(2), 124–133.

Cheung, S. L. (2000, September 8). Economic orthodoxy in theory and practice. *An Australian Review of Public Affairs*. http://www.australianreview.net/

Country for sale: How Cambodia's elite have captured the country's extractive industries. (2009, 5 February). Global Witness, London. Retrieved from http://www.globalwitness.org/media library detail.php/713/en/country for sale

Darder, A. (2012). *Culture and power in the classroom: A critical foundation for the education of bicultural students*. Boulder, CO: Paradigm.
Debord, G. (1990). *Comments on the society of the spectacle*. New York: Verso.
Debord, G. (1995). *The society of the spectacle*. (D. Nicholson-Smith, Trans.). Cambridge, MA: MIT.
Dutton, T., & Mann, L. H. (2003, July–September). Affiliated Practices and Aesthetic Interventions: Remaking Public Spaces in Cincinnati and Los Angeles. *The Review of Education, Pedagogy, and Cultural Studies, 25*(3), pp. 75–93.
Eagleton, T. (2011). *Was Marx right?* New Haven, CT: Yale University Press.
Engels, F. (1964). *The condition of the working class in England*. Chicago: Academy of Chicago.
Farmer, P. (1999). *Infections and inequalities: The modern plagues*. Berkeley: University of California Press.
Farmer, P. (2005). *Pathologies of power: Health, human rights, and the new war on the poor*. Berkeley: University of California Press.
Fitzsimons, P. (2002). Neoliberalism and education: The autonomous chooser. *Radical Pedagogy*. http://radicalpedagogy.icaap.org/content/issue4_2/04_fitzsimons.html
Foster, J. B., Magdoff, H., & McChesney, R. (2004, April). The stagnation of employment. *Monthly Review, 55*(11), 3–17.
Foster, J., & McChesney, R. (2012, April). Global stagnation and China. *Monthly Review, 55*(11), 3–17.
Foucault, M. (1983). *Discourse and truth*. UC Berkeley Campus in October and November 1983.
Foucault, M. (1990). *The history of sexuality, Vol. 1* (R. Hurley, Trans.). New York: Vintage.
Foucault, M. (1995). *Discipline and punish: The birth of the prison* (A. Sheridan, Trans.). New York: Vintage.
Foucault, M. (2003). *Society must be defended*. Lectures at the College de France, 1975–1976. (D. Macey, Trans.). New York: Picador.
Fraser, A., Murphy, E., & Kelly, S. (2013). Deepening neoliberalism via austerity and reform: The case of Ireland. *NUIM, 6*(2), 38–53.
Freire, P. (1970). *Pedagogy of the oppressed*. New York: Herder and Herder.
Freire, P. (1973). *Education for critical consciousness*. New York: Continuum.
Freire, P. (1978). *Pedagogy in process*. New York: Seabury.
Freire, P. (1980). *Pedagogy of the oppressed*. New York: Continuum.
Freire, P. (1997). *Mentoring the mentor: A critical dialogue with Paulo Freire*. New York: Peter Lang.
Freire, P. (1998). *Pedagogy of freedom: Ethics, democracy, and civic courage* (P. Clarke, Trans.). Lanham, MD: Rowman & Littlefield.
Freire, P. (2000). *Pedagogy of the oppressed*. New York: Continuum.
Geisst, C. R. (2013). *Beggar thy neighbor: A history of usury and debt*. Philadelphia: University of Pennsylvania Press.
Giroux, H. (1981). *Ideology, culture and the process of schooling*. Philadelphia: Temple University Press, London: Falmer.
Giroux, H. (1983). *Critical theory & educational practice*. Victoria, Australia: Deakin University Press.
Giroux, H. (1988). *Teachers as intellectuals: Toward a critical pedagogy of learning*. Westport, CT: Bergin & Garvey.
Giroux, H. (2004). *The terror of neoliberalism: Authoritarianism and the eclipse of democracy*. Boulder, CO: Paradigm.
Giroux, H. A. (2004). Public pedagogy and the politics of neo-liberalism: Making the political more pedagogical. *Policy Futures in Education, 2*(3), 494–504.
Giroux, H. (2006). *Stormy Weather: Katrina and the Politics of Disposability*. Boulder, CO: Paradigm Publishers.

Giroux, H. (2010, October). Lessons from Paulo Freire. *Chronicle of Higher Education, Chronicle Review.* Retrieved 15 March 2013, Retrieved from http://chronicle.com/article/Lessons-From-Paulo-Freire/124910/

Giroux, H. (2011). *Zombie politics in the age of casino capitalism.* New York: Peter Lang.

Giroux, H. (2013). America's education deficit and the war on youth: Reform beyond electoral politics. New York: *Monthly Review Press.*

Goldstein, R., Macrine, S., & Chesky, N. (2012). Welcome to the "New Normal": The news media and neoliberal reforming education. *Journal of Inquiry and Action in Education, 4*(1), Article 6. Retrieved from http://digitalcommons.buffalostate.edu/jiae/vol4/iss1/6

Gramsci, A. (1971). *Selections from the prison notebooks of Antonio Gramsci.* New York: International.

Greene, M. (1995). *Releasing the imagination. Essays on education, the arts and social change.* San Francisco: Jossey-Bass.

Hardt, M., & Negri, A. (2000). *Empire.* Cambridge, MA: Harvard University Press.

Harvey, D. (2005). *A brief history of neoliberalism.* Oxford: Oxford University Press.

Herman, E., & Chomsky, N. (2002). *Manufacturing consent: The political economy of the mass media.* New York: Pantheon.

Heywood, A. (1994). *Political Ideas and Concepts: An Introduction.* London: Macmillan.

Hinkelammert, F. (1953). Changes in the relationships between third world countries and first world countries. *Mission Studies, 12*(2), 133ff.

Hodgson, D. (2002). "Know your customer": Marketing, governmentality and the "new consumer" of financial services. *Management Decision, 40*(4), 318.

hooks, b. (2003). *Teaching community. A pedagogy of hope.* New York: Routledge.

Jameson, F. (2005). *Archaeologies of the future: The desire called utopia and other science fictions.* New York: Verso.

Johnstone, D. B. (2004). The economics and politics of cost sharing in higher education: Comparative perspectives. [Special Issue] *Economics of Education Review, 23*(200), 403–410.

Kincheloe, J. (2008). *Critical pedagogy primer.* New York: Peter Lang.

Knight, A. (2010). Zombie-Marxism Part II: What Marx got right. Retrieved from http://www.countercurrents.org/knight051110.htm

Lazzarato, M. (2011). *The making of the indebt man.* Amsterdam: Semiotext.

Lipman, P. (2002). Making the global city, making inequality: The political economy and cultural politics of Chicago school policy. *American Educational Research Journal, 39*(2), 379–419. Retrieved from http://www.jstor.org/stable/3202527

Lipman, P. (2011). *The new political economy of urban education: Neoliberalism, race, and the right to the city.* New York: Routledge.

Macedo, D. (1994). *Literacies of power: What Americans are not allowed to know.* Boulder, CO: Westview.

Macedo, D. (2013). *Voices and Silences of Social and Cognitive Justice.* Keynote address at the University of Massachusetts Dartmouth – Doctoral Program in Educational Leadership and Policy Studies, November 16.

Macrine, S. L. (2009). *Critical pedagogy in uncertain times: Hope and possibilities.* Education, Politics, and Public Life Series. New York: Palgrave Macmillan.

Macrine, S. L. (2011). Capitalist education: Neoliberal pedagogy of debt. Paper presented at AERA, New Orleans, LA.

Macrine, S. L. (2012). Neoliberalism's neoliberal pedagogy of debt. Paper presented at AERA, Vancouver, British Columbia, Canada.

Macrine, S. L. (2013). *Critical pedagogy in uncertain times: Hope and possibilities.* Education, Politics, and Public Life Series. New York: Palgrave Macmillan.

Mahmud, T. (2013). Debt and discipline: Neoliberal political economy and the working class. *Kentucky Law Journal, 101*(1). Retrieved from http://digitalcommons.law.seattleu.edu/faculty/125

Marx, K. (1992). *Das kapital: A critique of the political economy, Vol. 1*. New York: Penguin.

Marx, K., & Engels, F. (1848). *The communist manifesto*. London: Verso.

Mayo, P. (2007). *Public intellectuals, radical democracy and social movements. A book of interviews*. New York: Peter Lang.

McLaren, P. (1989). *Life in schools: An introduction to critical pedagogy in the foundations of education*. New York: Longman.

McLaren, P. (2000). Paulo Freire's Pedagogy of Possibility. In S. Steiner, H. Krank, P. McLaren, & R. Bahruth (Eds.), *Freirean pedagogy, praxis and possibilities: Projects for the new millennium* (pp. 1–22). New York & London: Falmer.

Miller, F., & Wertheimer, A. (2009). *The ethics of consent: Theory and practice*. New York: Oxford University Press.

Paraskeva, J. M. (2006). Portugal will always be an African nation. A Calibanian prosperity or a prospering Caliban? In D. Macedo & P. Gounari (Eds.), *The globalization of racism* (pp. 241–268). Boulder, CO: Paradigm.

Paraskeva, J. M. (2008). Neo-Marxismo com Garantias. In J. M. Paraskeva, D. Hursh, & W. Ross (Eds.), *Marxismo e educacao* (pp. 4–28). Porto, Portugal: Profedicoes.

Paraskeva, J. M. (2011). *Conflicts in curriculum theory. Challenging hegemonic epistemologies*. New York: Palgrave.

Paraskeva, J. M. (2012). Challenging the neoliberal global Minotaur. Henry A. Giroux: Education and the crisis of public values: Challenging the assault on teachers, students and public education. *Policy Futures in Education, 10*(6), 700–716.

Paraskeva, J. M. (2013). *Rituals and student identity in education: Ritual critique for a new pedagogy*. Education, Politics, and Public Life Series. New York: Palgrave.

Paraskeva, J. M., & Torres Santome, J. (2012). *Globalisms and power*. New York: Peter Lang.

Passavant, P. (2011). Mega-events, the Superdome and the return of the repressed in New Orleans. In C. Johnson (Ed.), *The neoliberal deluge: Hurricane Katrina, late capitalism, and the remaking of New Orleans* (pp. 87–129). Minneapolis: University of Minnesota.

Polyani, M. (1962). *Personal knowledge. Toward a post-critical philosophy*. Chicago: University of Chicago.

Prilleltensky, I. (1997). Values, assumptions, and practices: Assessing the moral implications of psychological discourse and action. *American Psychologist, 52*, 517–535.

Ransome, P. (1992). *Antonio Gramsci: A New Introduction*. New York: Harvester/Wheatsheaf.

Rose, N. (1990). *Governing the Soul: The Shaping of the Private Self*. London: Routledge.

Rose, N. (1999). *Powers of freedom: Reframing political thought*. Cambridge: Cambridge University.

Roy, A. (2014). *Capitalism. A ghost story*. Chicago: Haymarket.

Saad-Filho, A., & Johnston, D. (2005). Introduction. In A. Saad-Filho & D. Johnston (Eds.). *Neoliberalism: A critical reader* (pp. 1–6). London: Pluto.

Said, E. (2002). The public role of writers and intellectuals. In H. Smalls (Ed.), *The public intellectual* (pp. 19–39). New York: Blackwell.

Saltman, K. (2007). *Capitalizing on disaster: Taking and breaking public schools*. Denver, CO: Paradigm.

Saltman, K. (2012). *The failure of corporate school reform*. Boulder, CO: Paradigm.

Sousa Santos, B. (2006). *The rise of the global left. The world social forum and beyond*. London: Zed.

Sousa Santos, B. (2014). *Epistemologies of the south. Justice against epistemicide*. Boulder, CO/London: Paradigm.

Springer, S. (2011). Articulated neoliberalism: The specificity of patronage, kleptocracy, and violence in Cambodia's neoliberalization. *Environment and Planning, 43*, 2554–2570.

Stewart-Harawira, M. (2005). Cultural studies, indigenous knowledge and pedagogies of hope. *Policy Futures in Education, 3*(2), 153.

Stiglitz, J. (2013). *The price of American inequality*. New York: W. W. Norton.

Valenzuela, A. (1998). *Subtractive schooling: U.S.-Mexican youth and the politics of caring*. New York: State University of New York.

Walzer, M. (1983). *Spheres of justice*. Oxford: Robertson.

Warren, E. (2013). Federal Student Loan Program will earn $51 billion in 2013. *Washington Post*, July 11, 2013. Retrieved from http://www.washingtonpost.com/blogs/fact-checker/post/elizabeth-warrens-claim-that-the-us-earns-51-billion-in-profits-on-student-loans/2013/07/10/7769a3c2-e9b8-11e2-aa9f-c03a72e2d342_blog.html

Weidner, J. R. (2007, February). People, Places, Things: Towards a Critical Theory of Globalization. Paper presented at the annual meeting of the International Studies Association 48th Annual Convention, Chicago, IL. Retrieved June 26, 2013, from http://www.allacademic.com/meta/p180961_index.html

Williams, J. (2006). Debt education: Bad for the young, bad for America. *Dissent. A Quarterly of Politics and Culture*. Retrieved from http://www.dissentmagazine.org/article/debt-education-bad-for-the-young-bad-for-america

Williams, R. (1977). *Marxism and literature*. Oxford: Oxford University Press.

Žižek, S. (2010, July–August). A permanent economic emergency. *New Left Review, 64*. Retrieved from https://newleftreview.org/article/download_pdf

Žižek, S. (2010, September 25). Žižek in the New Left Review; Elections as Experiences. In *Blographia Literaria*. Retrieved from http://www.blographia-literaria.com/2010/09/zizek-in-new-left-review-elections-as.html

CHAPTER ELEVEN

Crowding Out Knowledge

Efficiency, Innovation, and Higher Education

SHARON RIDER AND ALEXANDRA WALUSZEWSKI

PRELIMINARY REMARKS

One of the most salient features of contemporary culture is the ongoing dissolution of once clearly delimited modern institutions (universities, hospitals, schools, but also banks, factories, and laboratories) into seemingly amorphous and transient networks of mutual relations, interests, and dependencies. Local and national companies and other actors are subsumed under multinational conglomerates as suppliers or partners, basic publicly funded city and state services are outsourced and put on the international auction block, pupils are customers, patients are clients, citizens are consumers: all solid boundaries evaporate, as Marx and Engels might say. At the same time, this blurring of the borders or boundaries of publicly funded social, scientific, and cultural institutions is occurring at the same time as new and harder ones are being fabricated in order to identify discrete unitary and accountable bases of production that can be assessed according to predetermined performance indicators.

Michael Sandel[1] makes three plain points about the monetization and marketization of the social and cultural sphere—to which science and education must be included, for reasons that we shall elaborate shortly—(1) it is not morally neutral; (2) it can be objected to on the basis of issues of fairness; (3) it can be objected to on the basis of the notion of value(s). In what follows, we shall not address issues of fairness or morality, but will concentrate on the third with regard to the transformation of the publicly funded organization of higher education, research and scholarship (for which we will use the shorthand term "the university"). But we will not be making the sort of normative claims with which Sandel is concerned; rather, following Max Weber, we will make certain observations about the relationship between means and ends, as well as the role of certain concepts that are part and parcel of the idea of "research and innovation," a forced marriage arising out of expectations regarding the role of the university system in advanced liberal democracies. We leave it to the reader to evaluate the ethical import of these observations.

Taking our cue from Waluszewski & Håkansson's (2014) critique of market-theoretical notions of efficiency and innovation, we will consider the meaning and implications of the increasingly porous boundaries between companies and public agencies, between customers and suppliers, between clients and citizens.[2] To begin with, certain basic notions of classical liberal, democratic society become diffuse: we mean modernist notions of "autonomy," "agency," "responsibility," and so forth. This is a natural consequence of the blurring of boundaries, or diffusion of agency, described in our introductory remarks. Seemingly innocuous policies aimed at encouraging interaction between university research and industry, for instance, have deeper implications. As a case in point, take the following description of the activities of the Swedish Governmental Agency for Innovation Systems, a description typical for similar agencies in other advanced liberal democracies:

> We promote collaborations between companies, universities, research institutes and the public sector. We do this by stimulating a greater use of research, by making long-term investment in strong research and innovation milieus and by developing catalytic meeting places.

The explicit government policy governing the directives of the agency is (1) to promote efficient use of publicy funding in university research, and (2) to stimulate innovation and growth through these efficiently used investments. But one consequence of blurring the boundaries of the university is that it becomes difficult to ascertain who is doing what for whom and in which capacity she is doing it. When publicly funded research activities are directed at and linked to specified external counterparts, it becomes unclear what is to count as "the university" within the system. A second, perhaps more ominous consequence of encouraging direct interaction between university research and companies, organizations, and/or non-governmental organizations is that the university's research activities necessarily have to be adapted to the requirements of the latter. If the research is to offer direct benefits to some specified company or organization, it has to accommodate their specific interests and needs. In short, research has to be adapted to the established structures and strategies of the organization or corporation in question. Similarly, if educational programs are to meet the direct labor needs of stakeholders, it is the interests and strategies of the stakeholders that must direct the form and content of the education to be provided. When it is noticed that the basic organization of higher education and scientific inquiry must be altered in order to achieve efficiency, two questions arise: what exactly is being made more efficient, and in what does the efficiency consist?

EFFICIENCY

Efficiency means, in economic terms, that a certain good (product or service) is supplied at a lower cost with no loss in quality.[3] This latter characteristic is essential to the notion of efficiency: without equal or superior quality, the lower cost of production is not to be regarded as demonstrating efficiency, but merely a reduction in price at the expense of quality. There is a tacit assumption in many attempts to make the production and maintenance of public goods and services (the case in point here being higher education and research) more efficient that (1) efficiency is a value in and of itself; and (2) that there is such a thing as "absolute" efficiency, that is, a scale of efficiency according to which any particular service or function can be measured. But efficiency is, of course, a relative term; efficiency can only be measured in relation to something. Thus, in order to assess the efficiency of a given function (let us say teaching at the tertiary level), we would first have to know what the *function* is, what the activity *aims* at, in order to see if the means utilized are those best suited for achieving the *ends*.[4] We would also have to take into account unintended or unforeseen consequences, that is, how any given planned or expedited change might affect the achievement of the overall aim. Only then would we be in a position to assess if the implementation of the reform or the introduction of the new element actually increases efficiency.

Our point above is simply that assessing efficiency is no simple task, but one requiring a thorough transillumination of precisely which activities are performed by which organizational units (departments, faculties, management, research groups, etc.), as well as of how these directly or indirectly contribute to the function (once defined) that one wishes to run efficiently (that is, to produce a service or product of as high or higher quality as previously at less expense).

"New Public Management" (NPM) is an umbrella term which we will use as shorthand for policy aiming at improving efficiency in publicly funded organizations through simplifying and quantifying efficiency by means of the construction of artificial markets consisting of neoteric organizational units, that is, through the *creation of new divisions*. These boundaries are not based on the aim or content of the activities involved, but rather on economic models. Indeed, one of the main criticisms that has been leveled at the application NPM on the organization of the universities has been that in modeling the organization of higher education on the market principles of economic theory, it has effectively altered the fundamental aims of the university and thus cannot be said to achieve greater efficiency with regard to the original ones. Rather, it has replaced the values, norms, and principles incarnated in the university with other ones, namely market principles, and achieves greater or less efficiency with regard to achieving goals based on *those new and different principles and values.* The idea that the university's organizational form (its division into "faculties," for example) is neither necessary nor "natural" is not new. As Derrida has noted, already Kant introduces his defense of the autonomy of the "philosophical faculty" with a reflection that "it wasn't a bad idea" of "whoever it was who first hit on the notion of a university" to "handle the entire content of learning (really, the thinkers devoted to it) by *mass production* so to speak—by a division of labor."[5] What is particular to NPM with regard to the organization of the university is the assumption that there *is* a universally applicable form of rationality that legitimately accounts for and justifies divisions in the university (or any other organization), although not as a reflection of the Idea of Reason in the Kantian mode,[6] but rather the Idea of Efficiency.

One of the most important aspects of NPM is the relationship between organization and efficiency, the idea being that functions can be separated from each other and treated independently when assessing efficiency. The rationality of this modus operandi is sound insofar as the empirical landscape on which the precepts of NPM are applied have the same characteristics as assumed in the market principles, that is, to the extent that the value of what is to be exchanged is independent of its context. A crucial feature of market logic is that given full and free access to relevant information and individual freedom of choice, price competition will force economic actors to maximize efficiency in the supply of products. Ideally, price competition is a kind of efficiency engine, guaranteeing that inefficient suppliers are sorted out from the market.

Applied to universities and other publicly funded organizations, the aim of NPM is to utilize the engine of price competition for the better use of public funds, in a vision of perpetually improved efficiency. In this ideal of a planned market, every university, department, research group, and so forth will strive to achieve maximum efficiency. But how the divisions are established (what constitutes a research group, department, or faculty, for instance) is determined not by some intrinsic scientific, scholarly, or educational goal but by external measurements, that is, within artificially created organizational borders. Since neither resources nor actors are assumed to be affected by how they are combined or are related to one another, the efficiency is thought to be reached without any loss of quality. It will be recalled that the overall goal of NPM is to create an organizational landscape that will resemble as closely as possible the market model as it is conceived in economic theory, which is in terms of homogeneous resources and independent actors.

According to the model, students and taxpayers alike will benefit. And that would be the case, if all the elements necessary to reach an overall function were not only in theory but also in fact independent of each other. As soon as there is a variation between resources, and as soon this variation affects the overall function, market logic tends rather to hinder efficiency. NPM compels its adherents to neglect qualitative aspects of interdependencies across organizational borders and economic divisions. More important, it compels them to neglect the effects of the introduction of market mechanisms on overall function in terms of the aims of the activity to be made "more efficient."

The general goal of NPM, as we said, is the creation of a market that will resemble as closely as possible the market model as it is conceived in economic theory. A crucial feature of this model is that organizational units carry their own costs in competition with each other. This is thought to create incentives for efficient use of public funds, in a vision of perpetually improved efficiency. Ideally, every university, department, research group, and so on will strive to achieve maximum efficiency in this artificial market without any loss of quality. According to the model, students and taxpayers alike will benefit. But that is, of course, if the insertion of the market mechanism has no necessary effects on the overall function on the basis of which we can ascertain if the function or service is of higher or lower quality. Sandel argues that even if we were to disregard all other practical effects, the very intrusion of market incentives into spheres of human action previously considered as primarily "moral" carries with it an implicit imperative of another sort, namely, to consider all human affairs as fundamentally and irreducibly subject to the calculus of cost and benefits and hence in the last analysis a question of private gain. The prevalence of utilitarian explanation and prediction leads to a "crowding out" of the language of values in favor of the terms of a rational calculus of costs and effects in which the individual seeks to maximize her benefits. Everything else is romance, nostalgia, or poetry. As we shall see in the final section, this "crowding out" effect described by Sandel with regard to morality is also discernible in questions formerly considered "aesthetic" or "epistemological."

As we remarked earlier, there are two related principles at the core of the market model. These are the notions of competition and independence: autonomous actors compete to supply a good or service at the lowest cost, leading to the optimization of the process and benefits to society in general, and the consumers of the good in particular. The slew of reforms we have seen in the last twenty years with the introduction of the market mechanism, de-regulation and the re-organization that follows from it, budget responsibility in lieu of direct regulation, recurrent audits and evaluation exercises, and so on, are all direct consequences of the implementation of this model on the assumption that its two basic notions (autonomy and competition) are intrinsic to efficiency. But in order for the free-market model to work, certain conditions must be met.

To begin with, the assumption is that less efficient actors will automatically be out-competed by better ones. A well-functioning market is an assurance that society's resources are being distributed in the most rational way, that is, in accordance with the free choices and preferences of clients and customers, who are assumed to seek greatest benefit at minimum cost. A functioning market is one in which potential customers can at any given point select the best available option, that is, the good or service that best fulfills her aims or needs at the lowest price. This entails that cartels are excluded from the ideal market. Further, to the extent that the customer is bound to long-term engagements, she is not free at any juncture to select the service or good she prefers in accordance with the benefit-lowest cost criterion. Such diachronic interdependencies are therefore also excluded from the model.

Thus, we have accounted for two prerequisites for the attainment of the efficiency sought, both of which can be described in terms of autonomy or independence (the client cannot be bound to a given supplier, the suppliers may not be bound to each other). There is a third. The model assumes that the singularly decisive feature, the piece of information to the consumer or client that is the economic sine qua non for a functioning market, is *price*. Each product, service, or good must be conceived as an isolated phenomenon, its value distinct, separate, and unaffected by the other products, services, or goods in which that value is embedded. These three conditions taken together make it clear that the model assumes an atomistic picture of market relations, in which there are already in advance of any interaction, connection, or relation, real and distinct actors and units of value. Another way of putting the point is to say that in the ideal-typical free market, the resources of an organization are taken as clearly delimited, that is, as independent of each other as well as of other organizations. This means that the value of the goods and services are understood as existing independently of their relation to other goods and services: they are conceived as economically homogenous. Again, notice the paradoxical nature of the requirement. On the one hand, market actors are conceived as unambiguous, isolated, and distinct. At the same time, the value of their respective activities is treated as indistinguishable (or "equivalent") except with regard to price. Efficiency becomes an Absolute in the Idealist sense, a featureless identity, or, to borrow a phrase from Hegel, "the night in which all cows are black."

We have called this market model "ideal-typical" because it is a starting point for empirical analysis rather than the product of one. In the real world, of course, price is rarely if ever the only relevant feature in deciding the value of a service or good. Rather, the value is determined with regard to two fundamental considerations:

1. Qualitative differences, or "comparative qualitative value."
2. The role of the good or service, or rather its contribution, in relation to other factors, for the achievement of a certain end. One might call this "relational value."

Something that is a given for any consumer is ignored by the ideal-type of the free market, namely, that the defining characteristic of "efficiency," that the same or equivalent good or service is to be had at a lower cost, is an abstraction. An infinite complexity is concealed behind the seemingly innocuous term "equivalent." The "equivalence" of the good or service offered, especially when applied to things like academic training or basic research, is a purely theoretical equivalence. In fact, something has to change if the financial cost is to be lessened. But the consequences of those changes, for example in the role the good or service plays in relation to other relevant considerations and other functions, have no place in the model, and are therefore not considered as part of the "value." Rather, such effects are always at the outset assumed to be marginal by definition.

The deregulation of the university in Europe is guided by the market model described above not only as model for the purchase and sale of goods and service in the public sector but also as a principle of organization. Insofar as the public sector is expected to behave as actors on the market, it has to be organized so that its agencies behave as autonomous buyers, reacting to the price signals. The consequence is that those responsible for the activities of schools, hospitals, police stations, daycare centers and universities focus on the budget and production figures of "this school," "this hospital unit," "this college faculty," rather than on "education," "curing and healing," "crime prevention," or "the advancement of science" as such; further, the parameters in which they organize and assess their "own activities" make it impossible to take into account the complex qualitative relations between and dependencies among agents and elements involved in schooling, criminal justice, healthcare, and other parts of the public sector. And this is not by accident, but by design. A fundamental precept of New Public Management is that publicly financed organizations are to behave as market actors so that citizens (taxpayers) can benefit from the efficiency achieved by economic competition between actors. Arguments on the basis of quality are difficult to justify on this model.

Let us say that a university wants to argue that the very existence of a professorship in Latin is of value to the community at large, including the business community, as well as to all students at the university, even those who are studying more "practical" subjects with a view toward direct employment. The value, the vice-chancellor might argue, is a complicated affair: it is good for the engineering student to come in contact with students studying ancient languages, since it broadens both students' horizons. It is good that we maintain the capacity to teach Latin, given how much of our culture and science has its roots in the language and culture of Rome (the organizational form of the first universities, for example). It is good for students and scholars in astronomy, history, medicine, and languages to have access to such expertise. It is good for a society to know its past, so forth and so on. Thus a university that offers teaching and contributes to scholarship in Classics has qualities that a university without such institutions and activities does not, and this quality is relevant for the society of which it is a part. These consequences and effects are not so easily translated into the sort of argument that can be summed up in a specification of requirements, however detailed, that will allow for a direct comparison with regard to the costs between the two. To the contrary, the requirement that there be a single value in splendid isolation from others is exactly what is not met. So let us say that the university cuts Latin from its curriculum, since it is just an added cost. How are we to ascertain and assess the difference in the quality of the education offered and the contribution to society made? Note that in this scenario, it is not being argued that the university management has after serious consideration of aims and means concluded that neither the university nor the society of which it is a part "needs" Latin, or that it "can't afford it." (Such an argument can surely be made.) Rather, what has happened is that its potential or real benefits are not at issue at all, since they are not of the kind that fits into the buyer-seller model of isolated, homogenous goods.

INNOVATION

What kind of goods and services are expected from the university today? Few words have created such a flurry of enthusiasm in research and higher education policy as has "innovation" in recent years.[7] It is also a word the meaning of which has undergone some transformation. In the high modernist epoch of the middle of the last century, the term connoted heavy investments and risky business, since it entailed large-scale production and distribution. As interpreted by OECD and EU policy today, it designates the result of ideas that can meet some pre-defined need to a better relative performance than existing solutions. The main obstacle to overcome is the challenge of making these ideas available in the form of commercial products on the market—which is assumed to have the characteristics described above. For knowledge to be "packaged" into commercial products, capital is required to put it on the market where, assuming that this knowledge corresponds to existing needs, it will be transformed into successful innovations. Thus the post-modern idea of innovation is to create favorable conditions for innovation, for instance, by directing university research toward the perceived needs of the market, enhancing entrepreneurial agency in research design and setting the process in motion with seeding and venture capital. Innovations are treated as self-subsistent phenomena that, once created, have only foreseeable effects and consequences.

Let us now consider what an innovation is, in economic terms. To begin with, an innovation is the broad diffusion and utilization of something new. The invention or discovery of something is not enough to make it an innovation. It has to be used, and used on a large scale. Thus it can be said to have three components: (1) a new idea, technique, process, and suchlike; (2) which is integrated into a production and dissemination process so that it can be made readily available;

(3) which is then integrated into a broad range of user structures and organizations. It seems fairly obvious that the latter two entail substantial costs and require a fair bit of investment in advance of any foreseeable revenue.

If the novelty or invention proves useful or beneficial at all three stages, there is potential for revenue at the end of the process. (There is, however, no guarantee that those who invested the most, for example, in the development of a prospective innovation, will be those who reap the greatest economic rewards.) Whether the yield will be greater than the investment, and who will profit from the changes and effects produced by the successful launching of an innovation, can only be determined with certainty in hindsight. But the innovation strategy one finds described by the OECD, for example, attributes a kind of clairvoyance to the market model. The picture that seems to guide the strategy is that there is some "thing" that is entirely "new," a seed requiring nourishment in the form of capital to grow and flourish (into a patent, a prototype, a process, a product, a service, or an organizational solution), which can then be tested and modified to meet determinate market needs. And, on this basis, it makes sense to create an environment in which a plurality of "new ideas" are developed and nourished, from conception to marketing, without interfering with each other or with established technological, social, and economic structures. The most radical new ideas, the ones that promise the most sweeping effects but that have been hitherto underutilized, are thought to be found in university-based research and science.

A different picture of the nature of innovation emerges when we approach it not from the viewpoint of a market model but from the viewpoint of history and society.[8] If we see the model described earlier not as the only possible or relevant method for understanding scientific development and educational success, but as one approach with a particular problem in its focus (efficiency understood as equivalent goods and services provided at a lower cost and innovation understood as knowledge transfer), then we are inclined to attend to other features as well, from a different starting point. From this point of view, one must begin by considering the already existing context in which an innovation is to be introduced and established. The future role of an innovation is not decided exclusively by the planning and execution of the service or product developed, but primarily by what its introduction would mean in relation to the technical, social, cultural, and economic state of affairs in which its novelty is to be integrated. If one takes this view, it is difficult if not impossible to identify any given innovation in isolation from a long and continuous process of changes in society as well as in science, which can only be evaluated honestly and with any rigor retrospectively. A central issue for any innovation is what changes would be required and what consequences might be expected from the widespread use of the new technology on the problem that the innovation was designed to solve. Potential innovations, be they products, services, technologies, processes, logistical solutions, or something else, arise in a context of already existing and related technical, economic, organizational, cultural, and social factors. The novelty of the new and the value of the novelty are dependent on the previous and the present.

The complex relation between the new and the already existing cannot be accounted for in the model of innovation appealed to by the OECD and EU as the policy panacea that will ensure universal economic growth while at the same time addressing "social and global challenges." Universities are a major expenditure for many OECD countries and are thus subject to ever-increasing demands from governing agencies to account for their direct contribution to social and economic development and growth, that is, for their role in the innovation system. But innovation processes are unsure and erratic: the costs are relatively certain and immediate, while revenues are dicey and deferred. Just as venture capitalists aren't primarily interested in the processes involved in realizing innovation, today's research, higher education and innovation policy formulated by the OECD and the EU is not concerned with content (knowledge) or process (learning, discovery) as such. Rather, on the assumption that the market will automatically convert commercialized knowledge that fulfils a need into innovations, the innovation strategies are intended to construct models and incentives that enable the innovation process to get started. The concept of knowledge, especially in the form of sophisticated technologies and the research that gives rise to them, is construed in terms of its role as an integral element or factor in the development process, leading to the construal of universities as central suppliers of the research and trained labor that would satisfy stipulated market demands. In the university construed as the motor of an innovation system, there is constant pressure to yield research results and educational programs that can be "packaged" as components of the system of commercialization. Whatever doesn't fit into such a package cannot be regarded as "knowledge" in the sense in which the term is operative in innovation policy and strategy. The crucial feature of "knowledge" in current parlance is not the long-term investment in the future of science or society, but "exit," the potential for economic return on investment.

Given a specialized and interdependent economic landscape, if universities are to become key actors in innovation processes as envisioned by OECD policy, they will have to adapt their research to established technological and social investments of companies and organizations. In order to be of direct economic benefit, universities will have to accommodate their research to the ongoing activities and strategies of industry. At the same time, as companies seek to cut costs in research and development, they will naturally look to "outsource" these activities to publicly funded research, the direction of which they will then want to influence so as to suit their needs.[9]

As universities take on an ever increasing share of the research and development activities formerly conducted "in-house" by companies and organizations, the relationship between the academy and the society it serves will no longer be that of an autonomous authority (science as a common good) and the legitimate interests of a state or community, but that of a market actor and its 'clients.' And if the university, as an actor on the market, intends the innovations that it delivers to be actualized on a large scale (industrialized and widely disseminated), its organization and aims will develop so as to meet the existing needs of its clients and customers. What that actually means is that science will no longer seek to extend our knowledge and understanding beyond what already is known and understood, but will settle on minor modifications of the old and established, that is, current technological, social, and economic structures. But the autonomy of the academy that can ensure renewal is not that of economic agency, but of what Derrida calls "the advent of something entirely other." And it is this possibility, let us label it "the openness of the future", that is lost along with the free agency of a scientific pursuit and educational mission that is not beholden to any determinate set of present interests.[10] Such a loss ultimately undermines any possibility of radical innovation, almost by definition.

"CROWDING OUT" SCIENCE AND SCHOLARSHIP: REIFIED EXPECTATION AND EPISTEMOLOGICAL PREJUDICE

Nothing that we have said up to this point is intended as a normative argument against the use of market models on the basis of their inherent unfairness. Those arguments have been made well elsewhere by others, and there is surely something to be said for the objections raised regarding the ostensible free agency of the buyer on the market. Our effort here, however, has been merely to describe, in the most general terms, the way the market model gives a certain inflection to our ideas and conduct with regard to knowledge, education and science, in much the same way as it gives a certain inflection to our ideas and conduct with regard to health/healthcare, justice/the criminal justice system, and so on. We do this because we think that Sandel is correct in pointing out that the insertion of the market mechanism is not merely a further extension of our freedoms but also has the effect of colonizing our reason. And it does so because the idealized market model dissolves certain fundamental functions of human society (the preparation of the youth for civil and professional life, the care of the sick and elderly, the safeguarding of personal safety, and others) into isolated constituents of an economy rather than acknowledging that these functions can be rationally described and evaluated in other ways (as integrated features of a human form of life, for example).

The cultural and social roots of economism grow deep. At bottom we find what the authors are inclined to call an "epistemological prejudice," namely, the prejudice that reason and realism (1) are synonyms, and (2) require that we view all human affairs in terms of a cost-benefit analysis, that everything else is nostalgia, utopianism, or sentimentality. Thus the deeper philosophical issue is not economism as such, which is rather a symptom or practical manifestation of something else, namely, a kind of dogmatic irrationalism that takes at its starting point that it has no need to account for itself, its most fundamental assumptions, or the grounds out of which they have arisen. Monetization is not the cause of what ails us, it is rather a symptom of a deeper malaise: we don't really know what it would mean to *think* in any other terms. One might say that Lyotard's approving reference to Luhman's hypothesis that "in postindustrial societies, the normativity of laws is replaced by the performativity of procedures" constitutes a correct description of our collective and individual social, economic, political, and cultural life.[11] And, oddly enough, this postmodern condition, as we shall see, has its origins in an attitude of procedural rationality at the heart of liberal political theory. Or, in George Lakoff's somewhat drastic formulation: "Oxford philosophy reigns supreme, right? Oxford philosophy is killing the world."[12] In what follows, we will conclude with a number of observations concerning the relationship between the economization of knowledge, on the one hand, and a certain conception of rationality and realism, on the other.

An early critic of the conception of rationality that finds expression in the kinds of epistemological assumptions described above was R. G. Collingwood. One of the main thrusts of his critique was that the utilitarian prejudice prevents us from distinguishing the moral, political, and economic aspects of our (individual and collective) actions and decisions. Utilitarianism, he concluded, "offers an account of economicity when professing to offer one of morality."[13] By the same token, one can argue that our contemporary models, by collapsing questions concerning science and teaching into the notion of innovation "offer an account of market economics when professing to offer one of science and education." We will not recapitulate Collingwood's philosophy here, but it is useful to consider his main criticisms of the thought forms of his own period, as they are pertinent to our current situation and the present discussion:

1. Any philosophy will be not only unconvincing but also actually nonsensical to a person who does not understand the kind of problem it is intended to solve. Thus, for instance, questions regarding the nature of knowledge or science not directly related to commercial activity and revenue become nonsensical in a model in which innovation is the core concept. (We use the term "nonsensical" here in the "austere" manner, that is, as synonymous with unintelligible, to describe a sign that has no use.)
2. The politics of a democratic, enlightened society are self-correcting because policies are matured in the open air of free and informed consideration

and discussion in the polity. The government is not "a post office for distributing ready-made policies to a passively receptive country."[14] This formulation echoes classical Enlightenment ideas about the relationship between rationality and autonomy, the idea being that it is only through unconstrained intellectual interchange that both theoretical and practical reason can be exercised and effective.

3. The whole system breaks down if the electorate and its representatives cease to be able to distinguish between special and general interests, or between questions of expediency and questions of principle. If the notion of a common good is considered isomorphic with the aggregate of private goods (the greatest good for the greatest number), and further, these goods are understood in terms of profit and gain, then even here the notion of intrinsic value loses meaning.

In the spirit of Collingwood, we wish to point out that ideas about general education and basic research that do not fit into the innovation model are not obsolete, naïve, or irrational in themselves, but are deemed so on the basis of certain determinate values in which they have no natural place within the defining model. To put the matter another way, we have the system of higher education and research that we *choose* on the basis of the values that we as a society de facto embrace in creating the systems we have. Second, if the fundamental values upon which our models of assessment are grounded (with efficiency as the highest value) are assumed as absolute and non-negotiable (except as an exercise in free but uninformed and ineffective speech), then the entire idea of the modern research university is in effect obsolete, since science requires open and informed discussion concerning its presuppositions, aims, and methods in order to be "self-correcting," or to progress. Finally, if there is no specific value or "good" associated with academic pursuits and their norms and institutions other than measurable expediency, there is no reason to suppose that the university can "supply" anything that cannot be produced elsewhere—presumably at a lower cost.

NOTES

1. Michael Sandel, *What Money Can't Buy: The Moral Limits of Markets* (New York: Farrar, Straus & Giroux, 2012).
2. See Alexandra Waluszewski & Håkan Håkansson, *Bakom marknadsfasaden* (Hedemora, Sweden: Gidlunds, 2014). For more on heterogeneous economic resources rather than standard market models as a starting point of analysis, see *Business in Networks,* H. Håkansson, D. Ford, L.-G. Gadde, I. Snehota, & A. Waluszewski, Eds. (Chichester, UK: Wiley, 2009).
3. See R. Bocconcelli & H. Håkansson, "When a market solution is not enough. Ducati making a turnaround," *IMP Journal, 2*(2), 2008; and Waluszewski & Håkansson 2014, pp. 28–39.

4. See S. Rider, "Higher Heteronomy: Thinking through Modern University Education," in *Transformations in Research, Higher Education and the Academic Market: The Breakdown of Scientific Thought*, Eds. S. Rider, Y. Hasselberg, & A. Waluszewski (Dordrecht, The Netherlands: Springer, 2013).
5. Immanuel Kant, *The Conflict of the Faculties*, trans. M. Gregor. (Lincoln: University of Nebraska Press, 1979); Jacques Derrida, "Mochlos; or, the Conflict of the Faculties," trans. R. Rand & A. Wygant, in *Logomachia: The Conflict of the Faculties* (Lincoln: University of Nebraska Press, 1992).
6. For an extended treatment of the tension between contemporary and classical notions of autonomy with regard to higher education, see Sharon Rider, "The Very Idea of Higher Education: Vocation of Man or Vocational Training?" in *The Humboldtian Tradition: Origins and Legacies*, P. Josephson, T. Karlsohn, & J. Östling, Eds. (Leiden, The Netherlands: Brill, 2014).
7. See Magnus Eklund, "Science Policy in a Socially Embedded Economy" (Rider et al., 2013, pp. 111–124). See also H. Håkansson & A. Waluszewski, Eds., *Knowledge and Innovation in Business and Industry. The importance of Using Others* (London & New York: Routledge, 2007).
8. See Alexandra Waluszewski, "Contemporary Research and Innovation Policy—A Double Disservice?" (Rider et al., 2013).
9. See, e.g., Philip Mirowski, *Science-Mart: Privatizing American Science* (Cambridge, MA: Harvard University Press, 2011).
10. This argument is worked out in more detail in Sharon Rider, "The Future of the European University: Liberal Democracy or Authoritarian Capitalism?" in *Culture Unbound, 1*, 2009, pp. 83–104.
11. J.-F. Lyotard, *The Postmodern Condition: A Report on Knowledge* (Minneapolis: University of Minnesota Press, 1984, p. 45).
12. http://www.theguardian.com/books/2014/feb/01/george-lakoff-interview
13. R. G. Collingwood, *An Autobiography* (Oxford: Clarendon, 1939, p. 149).
14. Ibid., p. 154.

CHAPTER TWELVE

Who's Afraid of Public Financial Literacy?[1]

SHANTI DAELLENBACH

The idea of financial education for the public is not a new one. However, the widespread enthusiasm with which financial literacy programmes are being embraced by governments and financial institutions in the context of the latest financial crisis suggests the public have not yet learnt their lessons. Or perhaps the problem is that they have. Since what Randy Martin has called the "global bailout of finance" (2014, p. 203) in 2008, publics around the world have become increasingly involved in discussions around the failings of the financial system and how it should operate in the future. Public dissent over government austerity policies and financial sector bailouts are now a common feature of the global political scene. Issues around financialisation and its social consequences have featured centrally in many of the protest movements that have enveloped the world in recent years; from the Icelandic Revolution, anti-austerity movements in Spain and Greece, and student-led movements in Chile and Canada around debt and the financialisation of education to protests in Brazil and Turkey over government acts of financial expropriation that benefit the few. While it would seem that people are becoming critically literate in the mechanisms of finance on their own, the growing emphasis on financial literacy education around the world operates on the assumption that the public receiving it remains illiterate.

At stake within this dynamic is not only what can be said about finance and by whom but the parameters around what constitutes literacy and illiteracy as such, and what positions in the world of finance these categories allow a person to inhabit. The content of financial literacy curriculum and policy have been well analysed by the likes of Chris Arthur (2012a; 2012b; 2014), Laura Pinto (2012) and Elizabeth Coulson (Pinto and Coulson, 2011), and Toni Williams (2007). This chapter contributes to discussions on the appearance of a particular idea of financial literacy education in the wake of the 2008 financial bailout, sensitive to the fact that ideas can have profound material consequences, and that different ideas and material relations exist and, therefore, different outcomes are possible.

I will begin by accounting for the process of financialisation, and how its key tendencies of risk-shifting and the socialisation of risk emerge as a response to the threat of literate and collectively organised publics that gain political momentum in periods of crisis. I argue that this is the context out of which the current and increasingly popular iteration of the idea of financial literacy education emerges. I then map the construction of this logic of financial literacy education and the presuppositions about the givenness of the world of finance and the relations of inequality and expropriation on which it is premised. The 'worlding' of the world of finance necessitates the socialisation of subjects whose status as literate and capable citizens is assessed not via their knowledge but the nature of their financial participation. The conclusion of this section is that the criteria that distinguish the literate from the illiterate subject operate to de-politicise finance and de-centre financial responsibility through the internalisation of risk and the framing of unequal redistributions of wealth as individual pathology.

I will draw on the work of Jacques Rancière and his idea of the explicative order in order to think financial logic in pedagogical terms. Financial literacy education teaches a distribution of the sensible in which everyone is accorded a relative position of mastery or ignorance that determines their measure of legitimate participation in a given society. Contrary to the usual assumption of the ignorant pupils' dependence on the enlightened master, I argue that it is the explicator, the financier, and the state who rather rely on an illiterate public to maintain this structuring logic of inequality. I do not set out to prove one narrative of class struggle over another of capitalist domination, but instead to see what becomes thinkable and possible, what can be done and *is* done when people proceed from the assertion of the equal capacity and intelligence of anybody. The Icelandic Revolution and the Occupy Wall Street movement serve to illustrate the materiality of critical and publicly produced financial literacies and the different forms of financial participation and social organisation these make possible.

People's daily experiences in navigating their exposure to risk and debt in a financialised world are not markers of financial ignorance but testify to their being well versed in its exploitative operations and exclusionary effects. This lies at the heart of why explication of financial logic in the classroom has become so necessary for finance in recent years. What finance has to fear today is nothing less than a public literate in the logic and language of finance, and their constitutive place within it.

RESISTANCE FROM ABOVE

An analysis of financial literacy education must first be located within the context of financialisation. Costas Lapavitsas identifies financialisation as a global process spurred by "the asymmetric growth of financial compared to real accumulation during the last four decades" (2013, p. 201). As real accumulation begins to reap more precarious returns, the capitalist class, requiring new sources of profit, turn their attention toward workers as a source of "financial expropriation" (Lapavitsas, 2009, p. 126). This has, according to Greta Krippner, operated to massively expand financial sector profits while also "reorientating nonfinancial firms toward financial sources of income" (2011, p. 57). As Lapavitsas explains, financialised capitalism is characterised by "the spreading of new and exploitative relations across society as financial markets grow and as individuals are increasingly drawn into the formal financial system" (2013, p. 146–147).

Capital's response to the threat of systemic crises plays a significant role in the development of financialisation. For Max Haiven, financialisation also constitutes a direct response to a threat of a different sort, a politically influential labour movement claiming significant gains for workers over the middle of the twentieth century. "The financial sphere emerges," he argues, "as capitalists seek to share risk collectively and to collaborate as a class, and they do so because they feel under threat" (2012, p. 89). As such, financialisation is a reactive strategy by which capital seeks to harness and control the creative power of reproductive labour upon which it relies (Haiven, 2014a, p. 117). We can think of financialisation then as a means of expropriation that fits with Mario Tronti's analysis of capitalist exploitation in general.

> Exploitation is born, historically, from the necessity for capital to escape its *de facto* subordination to the class of worker-producers. It is in this very specific sense that capitalist exploitation, in turn, provokes workers' insubordination. The increasing organisation of exploitation, its continual reorganisation at the very highest levels of industry and society are then, again, responses by capital to workers' refusal to submit to this process. (2007, p. 31)

Financialisation as a symptom of the continual reorganisation of exploitation occurs precisely because labour's subordination to capital is neither total nor certain. This is also why ideological instruments such as education were considered paramount for the likes of Louis Althusser (1971), Pierre Bourdieu, and Jean-Claude Passeron (1977) to the question of the reproduction and perpetuation of capitalist ideology and class relations. It should come then as little surprise that today the households of the working classes are the central target of financial literacy education strategies.

Central to the tendencies of credit expansion and volatility is the characteristic of risk and risk exposure. Dick Bryan and Mike Rafferty (2011) describe the process of financialisation as one of "risk-shifting." As the retrenchment of the welfare state has required increasing engagement with financial instruments such as mortgages, credit cards, and individualised superannuation schemes, the risk and instability of finance has been increasingly displaced onto labour and households (Bryan & Rafferty, 2011). This dual process further enabled changes over this period to dis-empower organised labour and obscure class relations, producing what Bryan and Rafferty call an "asset class." In a financialised world, Bryan and Rafferty explain, "Labour is not only a supplier of waged work, and a consumer of commodities, it is also a manager of assets (including human capital) and liabilities" (p. 50). If financialisation is centred upon the further imbrication of risk into previously non-financial aspects of people's lives, of concern in this chapter is what role financial literacy education plays in how this comes to be accepted by those who must bear this risk as not only a given but also as a constituent measure of a good life.

While Stefano Harney and Fred Moten note that "work against risk can be harvested without end" (2013, p. 77), the relationship between financialisation and risk goes beyond one of mitigating risk. As Edward LiPuma and Benjamin Lee argue, risk has become the "objective means of organising social relations within the sociostructures of circulation" (2004, p. 153). As such, risk as something to be hedged against in financial transactions is supplemented by a generalised notion of risk that becomes the constitutive basis of financial relations marked by mutual interdependence and connectivity. Risk is presupposed in finance to the extent that to decide not to engage with it at some level is to be excluded from virtually any financial practice and from sociality more generally. As such, social inclusion becomes predicated on financial participation, in which risk appears as part of the natural foundation of all social relations. This is why Claire Le Berge states that, contrary to common assumptions, "finance concretises what was heretofore abstract" (2014, p. 101). The issue is not whether financial literacy education is teaching people to take risks or to protect themselves against them, but rather how either way it functions to incorporate its recipients within a logic in which risk is presupposed in every social interaction.

Randy Martin (2014) observes that as financialisation produces greater interdependence and mutual indebtedness, financial crisis increases these in turn through the redistribution of risk and wealth in the form of publicly funded bailouts. It is because of capital's need to disavow this debt that labour and households must be implicated by governments and financial institutions as having played a central role in the crisis and by logical extension playing their part in its remedy.

Locating labour and household's financial decisions at the root of the current crisis has, however, not seen calls to increase state regulation around their participation in financial markets. On the contrary as Bryan and Rafferty note, following the 2008 crisis "the key message now is that household risk management capacity must be improved as part of financial stability" (2011, p. 50).

Financial literacy education emerges during the post-crisis period as a key instrument toward this end. Laura Pinto (2012) notes that while already peripherally on the policy agenda in some countries and organisations such as the OECD since the early 2000s, financial literacy education took on a whole new level of importance and urgency for governments worldwide post-2008. As of 2013, 45 countries have implemented or are close to establishing a national strategy on financial education (OECD/G20, 2013). The connection between crisis and the idea of financial literacy is also clearly observable in the myriad of policy recommendations being produced by proponents of financial literacy education across the developed world. For example, in 2012 the OECD's International Network on Financial Education (2012) stated,

> In the aftermath of the financial crisis, financial literacy has been increasingly recognised as an important individual life skill in a majority of economies … In addition, the consequences of the financial crisis have demonstrated the potential implied costs and negative spill-over effects of low levels of financial literacy for society at large, financial markets and households. (pp. 2–3)

Financial literacy education is regarded as an effective process through which individual and household relations to financial risk and debt will take a particular form in the context of economic austerity. This is a context in which they are required to engage with financial products and their concomitant risks on an increasing scale. Financial literacy education is aimed at both eliciting everyone's acceptance of risk and normalising the use of an expanding range of financial products, and in the process incorporating labour, alongside the capitalist class, as once again full and willing participants in a world of finance premised on relations of ever growing inequality and exclusion.

THE LOGIC OF FINANCIAL LITERACY EDUCATION

In order to think the logic of finance, Campbell Jones (2012) suggests that we draw on Gayatri Spivak's notion of 'worlding.' Financial literacy education is part of a process of writing or inscribing the world within a logic of finance, and this worlding occurs precisely through the most mundane, insidious, and everyday activities. For example, he explains, "The worlding of the world in the image of finance takes place in financial literacy programs in schools and in the invitation to all citizens to think of themselves today as 'human capital' into which they must invest" (p. 5). Key, here, is how this process presupposes the world before it is understood in financial terms as un-inscribed and ignorant. Within this context the idea of financial literacy emerges as a vehicle to enlightenment, a path out of ignorance and naiveté, and in this way it appears entirely natural and good to incorporate education into the practices and mechanisms of finance. The endgame of this process of worlding is what Haiven calls the "financialised imagination," the characteristic of a society in which "our visions of the future are increasingly individualised and foreclosed" (Haiven 2014b, p. 106).

Financial literacy education is one method by which individuals are adjusted to this reality of the world of finance in crisis, in which risk, debt, and general immiseration are routine, and which grounded only in the present also appears as the natural state of things. Indeed, the financial productivity that risk engagement generates may be secondary to financial literacy education's role in worlding the world of finance. Not all students of financial literacy education will engage in the same levels of risk or consume financial products as productively as others. However, all recipients of financial literacy education, regardless of their success or failure are subjected to its ordering principles and measured by its values to the exclusion of every other reality, actual or possible. As Arthur puts it, financial literacy education "reduces the risk of systemic change so that our future possibilities are limited to the present's power relations and imagination" (2014, p. 157). This requires the production of a particular type of subject.

According to its proponents, financial literacy education promises financial productivity by producing citizens who are empowered to participate fully in financial life, who can carry the risk this transfers to themselves and the responsibility for individual and systemic failure that may come with it. According to the OECD (2013):

> Financially literate consumers can make more informed decisions and demand higher quality services, which will encourage competition and innovation in the market. They are also less likely to react to market conditions in unpredictable ways, less likely to make unfounded complaints and more likely to take appropriate steps to manage the risks transferred to them … All of these factors will lead to a more efficient financial services sector and potentially less costly financial regulatory and supervisory requirements. They can also ultimately help in reducing government aid (and taxation) aimed at assisting those who have taken unwise financial decisions—or no decision at all. (p. 141)

One can detect here, as Chris Arthur has, a commitment to Adam Smith's notion of the regulatory virtues of individual self-interest (Arthur, 2012b). The financially literate subject will not only successfully serve his or her own interests but through competition and consumer demand will create a more efficient and beneficent financial system. In addition, this very material burden of responsibility for financial risk placed on the subject also serves a political end, as what Toni Williams calls the "empowerment rationale" and the "responsibilisation thesis" of financial literacy education "provide justifications for de-centered regulation" (2007, p. 231). In this way, the state, while in reality central to maintaining finance (exemplified by the post-crisis bailouts) becomes invisible in the operation of financial markets and both in turn invisible in the misfortunes of those who fail to take responsibility for their own prosperity. By the same token, as responsibility is de-centred away from governments and financial institutions, crisis also becomes conceptualised as an individualised experience that requires an individual response. This works to obscure the systemic nature of crisis while capital's indebtedness to labour as the source of surplus value and social reproduction can similarly be denied. When political issues are presented as individual ones, the systemic nature of inequality and the possibility of social change become very difficult to see.

Financial literacy education seeks to enlighten its recipients to the apparent realities of the present, taking finance and the risks financial participation involve as somehow natural or given rather than shaped through conscious political decisions by those who may benefit. While finance in crisis, as it is framed in financial literacy discourse, may not appear the most redeeming of ordering principles, financial literacy education operates fundamentally on the idea that through pupils' increased participation it may be made virtuous and more productive. It was this fiction of a unity of interests between labour and capital that the global financial bailout saw publics across the world beginning to call into question. Such is what Harney and Moten have identified as the danger for capital emergent in this imperative of financial participation, that is a crisis of participation "provoked by the wrong participation of the wrong(ed)" (2013, p. 81). This wrong(ed) part is exemplified in the financially illiterate pupil who, having not yet learned his or her place, presumes to speak from the position of expert or make unpredictable or financially unproductive decisions. Through the ideas of responsibilisation and empowerment, financial literacy education presents to us a potentially seamless world of finance limited and marred only by an ignorant public in need of correction.

THE PEDAGOGICAL ORDER OF FINANCE

Financial literacy education in the classroom is significant because the school is a site for the creation of citizens, who, under the tutelage of financial discourses will take a particular form. This section considers how financial literacy education is dependent on a particular pedagogical logic that extends out beyond educational institutions into the world of finance as a whole. Jacques Rancière proposes that contemporary capitalist society "presents itself as a vast school, with its savages to civilize, and its problem students to put right" (2010a, p. 13). It is therefore important to consider the role financial education plays in the worlding of finance, as well as the possibilities embodied in different forms of public financial education outside the master's classroom.

According to Rancière (2010a), education is usually based on a pedagogical structure of explication from the literate master to the never-as-literate pupil. Contemporary conceptions of the function of education and the role of the school in society find their origin in enlightenment thinking in which education was considered an avenue to emancipation. Similarly, Rancière observes how pedagogical theories concerned with reducing social inequalities through education tend to be premised on a notion of emancipation through demystification that encounters similar inegalitarian contradictions (2010a). The problem is that while the emancipator exists above the realm of ignorance, those yet to be educated remain reliant on them for their emancipation. This establishes an inequality between the literate explicator and those who, as pupils, will never know as much as their teacher, a relation that appears as one of incapacity or dependence.

In the idea of financial literacy education, the pedagogical structure of explication creates a division between the experts who can legitimately know finance and therefore speak about it and the public who learns before all else their own ignorance in such matters. These respective places of relative enlightenment and ignorance are ascribed different functions within the world of finance. While individuals may indeed ascend this hierarchy through successful financial participation, a distribution of differentiated positions remains in place, as there will always be many more ignorant and also more intelligent than oneself. Charles Bingham and Gert Biesta (2010) explain that this inegalitarian relation is reproduced through educational institutions in the way that these essentially operate to "set a limit on interpretation" (p. 149). Rancière's scrutiny of the inegalitarian nature of explication is also socially important for Bingham and Biesta as it illustrates "the extent to which explanation also operates in society—as a social logic—thus modeling social and policing relations according to an explicative notion of schooling" (Bingham & Biesta 2010, p. 149). This ordering of relations according to a particular social logic of explication involves what Rancière calls a "distribution of the sensible."

The distribution of the sensible refers to the "system of self-evident facts of sense perception that simultaneously discloses the existence of something in common and the delimitations that define the respective parts and positions within it" (Rancière, 2004, p. 12). This distribution can be thought as the ordering of a particular common world, such as the world of finance. The differentiation of places and the social roles that are ascribed to them come to determine the boundaries of what appears as sensible, knowable, and natural in a given world, which in turn defines who can legitimately speak, act, and participate within it. For Rancière this is not a question of who is legally allowed to speak or not, but rather how one's speech is interpreted within this distribution of the sensible; for example, as logical argument or inarticulate noise. Similarly, Jones (2013) describes the way that capitalism "codes speech in the language of the market, and that language denigrates all other languages as degenerate and inferior if not outright incomprehensible" (p. 67). The language of finance is only comprehensible by and to those who are accorded a literate part within the distribution of the sensible, whose role it is to, like the financial trader or economist, deal in the complexities of finance too difficult for ordinary people to grasp. This is a distribution that for Rancière (1991) is fundamentally predicated on the presupposition of the inequality of intelligences.

Arthur suggests that the social logic of finance can be understood in terms of what Rancière calls the "police order" (Arthur, 2012b). The police order denotes the mechanisms by which a particular distribution of the sensible is upheld and as such its function is one of ensuring consensus, which beyond verbal agreement signals an alignment "between a mode of sensory presentation and a regime of meaning" (Rancière, 2010b, p. 144). This description of the consensual tendency of police indeed fits well with the reality-oriented and de-politicising logic observable in financial literacy education discourse. Rancière explains that the police "consists, before all else, in recalling the obviousness of what there is, or rather of what there is not, and its slogan is: 'Move along! There's nothing to see here!'" (2010b, p. 37). Such a command implies the absence of any exceptional occurrence, the absence of any subject or idea to contradict the facts of the world as it appears in the innocuous and everyday world of finance. Furthermore, because its grounds for legitimation are based so much on its unquestioned givenness in the present, the logic of finance requires constant reiteration so that one does not peer at its claims of obviousness too closely. Marieke de Goede (2005) highlights the disciplinary tendency in this reiteration of financial lessons, which she notes are required not only of the young or financially unsuccessful but increasingly of financial agents and experts as well. Financial literacy education is an expression then of the pedagogical logic of finance, a form of explication and reiteration that apportions some the part of literate and most the part of relative ignorance.

However, Rancière's argument is not that the police order of finance dictates that the poor must always remain poor and excluded. An individual worker can certainly become literate in the speculative art of finance in ways that elevate him or her to the position of successful entrepreneur, skilled trader, or savvy investor. The point is rather that one cannot, within the logic of finance, occupy more than one position simultaneously. The worker, *as a worker*, can never also be an economist, or as a worker speak coherently about finance except to express the desire to become less ignorant about it, that is, to escape the ascribed part of the worker altogether. This is the same myth that dismisses as naive and irrational the idea of a society of producers immanent to capital (Martin, 2014), a society in which workers would occupy no less than the position of producer and manager of the collective surplus at the same time. Financial literacy education purports emancipatory intentions, while it presupposes the continuation of both intellectual and material inequality by arbitrarily setting the limits on what counts as literate and illiterate, sensible and incomprehensible participation in the world of financialised capitalism.

FINANCIAL LITERACY FROM BELOW

According to Martin the ideas of risk-shifting, responsibilisation, and individualised choice that financialisation requires in its subjects simultaneously gives rise to "a nascent literacy in the face of a manufactured illiteracy around what finance is and does" (2014, p. 207). This emergent literacy is what I propose to call public financial literacy or financial literacy from below. In Rancière's schema another mode of social participation emerges in contradiction to the manufactured consensus of police, which he calls "dissensus." When sensory perception no longer matches up with the logic of the police there is dissensus, and this break or disjuncture is for Rancière "the essence of politics" (2010b, p. 38). Dissensus can be thought as a form of social participation that disrupts the alignment between what is perceived as given reality, such as the incapacity or capacity of people to be already literate in finance, and the regime of meaning on which this world is premised, that is, the presupposition of pedagogical inequality. Dissensus is concerned with changing what can be seen and heard within the sensible limits of the logic of finance by the placing of one world in another. As Rancière explains,

> Political demonstration makes visible that which has no reason to be seen; it places one world in another—for instance, the world where the factory is a public space in that where it is considered private, the world where workers speak, and speak about the community, in that where their voices are mere cries expressing pain. (2010b, p. 38)

Such activity requires that this other, previously excluded, world in which anybody can be literate in finance and articulate financial alternatives already exists within the given world of finance, present but not interpreted as such or interpreted as something else, for example unproductive or illiterate financial participation. In order to show how this is not fantasy but is a concrete reality today let us look at how this political demonstration of literacy plays out in, for example, social movements and revolutions such as the Icelandic Saucepan Revolution and the Occupy Wall Street movement.

In 2008 Iceland's banking sector collapsed, seeing banks default on approximately $85 billion (Valdimarsson, 2012). The Icelandic public responded with waves of escalating protests that led to the dissolution of the government and managers of the collapsed banks and the head of the financial authority being forced to step down to meet public demands (Júlíusson & Helgason, 2013). These protests were much more than the loud noise of discontent that gave the Saucepan

Revolution its name. Árni Júlíusson and Magnús Helgason note how following the collapse, weekly "citizens meetings" were held to discuss the problems at hand and their possible solution, at which bankers and politicians identified as responsible for the crisis were invited along to explain themselves and be questioned by the public, sometimes even to a national television audience. Citizen-initiated organisations, such as the Association for Sustainability and Democracy (ALDA), began to form around proposals for constitutional change, and developing programs for social banking (to eliminate derivative trading practices, for example), shortening the working week and regulating wage differences to not exceed 9:1 (ALDA, 2011). Public pressure also saw changes to the legal and financial systems, with 200 people facing criminal changes for their role in the banking crisis, and banks forgiving $1.6 billion worth of household debt under court and government orders (Valdimarsson, 2012).

These proposals and demands demonstrate both an assertion of public capacity to understand how finance operates and to engage in serious discussions about concrete ways its structure and effects could be changed. The public response to the crisis went well beyond expressions of unarticulated discontent or demands for an abstract equality. It demonstrated acute public awareness of the way in which seemingly abstract speculative financial practices are grounded in material relations that produce unequal distributions of wealth. This awareness brings with it an understanding of where this financial wealth in fact originates, in which direction the debt actually flows, and whose it is to forgive, claim, and redistribute (Joseph, 2014). It was in this way a demonstration of equality through the realization and assertion of public determination over the government and the financial sector, carried out under the claim of the equal capacity of anybody to be literate in and make decisions about finance on a national scale, that is, to occupy the position of worker and economist simultaneously.

The Declaration of Occupy Wall Street, ratified by the New York City General Assembly in September 2011, performed a similar dissensual function in that it articulated the myriad ways in which the American public, despite not being residents of the trading floor, were already intimately knowledgeable in the workings of finance. This financial literacy was one developed out of the firsthand experiences of exploitation listed in the Declaration: the loss of homes through illegal foreclosures; the use of taxpayer money to bail out financial institutions; the ways in which financial interests shaped the experience of discrimination in the workplace, or benefited from weak labour regulations, outsourcing, and student indebtedness; how a lack of market regulation had produced monopolies and market bubbles, rendering the necessities of life unaffordable for many; and so on (New York City General Assembly, 2011). The occupation in New York, and those that followed around the globe, made visible within the world of finance a public with a concrete understanding of the productive mechanisms of risk-shifting, debt, financial expropriation, and the constitutive place of themselves within these. This was also a public that could speak articulately not only about finance but the possibility of changing it, a public that was also becoming critically literate in alternatives to finance capitalism.

Public demonstrations of financial literacy like the Icelandic Revolution and Occupy Wall Street help to make visible some of the internal contradictions in the idea of financial literacy education as well as some of the possibilities immanent to it. Literacy as framed by financial literacy education is fundamentally reliant upon the consensual participation of its recipients in the world of finance. This means that if such participation is not given, but rather participation that contradicts the explicative order of the world of finance, such as the worker who engages in writing economic policy or forgiving debt, then this order loses its logical foundation. Furthermore, financial education premised on the presupposition of the equality of intelligences is not only possible but is already actualised in every performance of a public's equal capacity to read about, understand, write, and speak about finance.

Such is what Rancière (1991), following nineteenth-century French educator Joseph Jacotot, calls universal teaching. Jacotot, who undertook his teaching from the premise of the equality of intelligences, found that he was able to teach his students that which he himself did not know, as under such an approach, anyone had the capacity to learn anything for themselves. The point for Rancière in thinking equality in this way, is not to empirically prove its existence over inequality but rather in "seeing what can done under that supposition" (1991, p. 46). As Biesta argues, "To act on the basis of this assumption requires a constant verification of it—not in order to check whether the assumption *is* true in the abstract, but in order to *practice* the truth of the assumption, that is, to *make* it true in concrete situations" (2010, p. 57). What an intelligence is capable of under the supposition of equality is in fact the verifying or making real of the equality of anybody.

Public performances of financial literacy like Occupy Wall Street or the Icelandic Revolution are expressions of what I am calling financial literacy from below. That these moments are occurring in greater numbers following the financial bailout is not just a problem for financial institutions or for states' capacity to extend financial expropriation and mete out risk, they undermine the very pedagogical foundations on which the logic of finance operates. This is the sum of the political and emancipatory potential in financial education approached from another starting point to that of explication, which radically changes the limits of interpretation on the subject, specifically in ways that do not take finance as a given. It also explains the renewed presence of financial literacy education on the agenda of almost every financial institution and government body in the developed world today.

When financial literacy is considered from the starting point of equality, the contradictory characteristics of the explicative order of finance itself become apparent. If explication is not necessary for the so-called ignorant to learn, this changes where the relation of dependency lies. As Rancière explains, "Explication is not necessary to remedy an incapacity to understand. On the contrary, that very incapacity provides the structuring fiction of the explicative conception of the world. It is the explicator who needs the incapable and not the other way around; it is he who constitutes the incapable as such" (1991, p. 6). One can find a nice parallel of this contradiction in the workerist assertion that this chapter's analysis of financialisation began from. Tronti's hypothesis back in 1964 that "at both national and international level, it is the specific, present, political situation of the working class that both necessitates and directs the given forms of capital's development" (1979: 1) may indeed be closer to the truth of our situation than any story of domination and incapacity. If finance is already being thought and performed from below, the task today is to make this world appear.

CONCLUSION

The idea of financial literacy education that has gained popular sway with governments and financial institutions since the 2008 financial bailout is an instance of what Harney and Moten call "resistance from above" (2013, p. 76). It follows that within labour's participation in finance, in the way workers share in the debts and risks that finance both shies from and relies upon, there is something for finance to fear.

Part of the broader trend of financialisation that has been shaping social and economic life over the last four decades, financial literacy education is an instrument that operates to implicate its recipients within financial mechanisms, increasing labour's risk-bearing capacities and individualising responsibility for personal and systemic failures. On the one hand, financial literacy education is also concerned with worlding the world of finance, premised on its givenness in the present and a distribution of social positions and financial behaviours to which its pupils are adjusted. The construction of a distinction between the literate and illiterate subjects of financial literacy education serves as a measure for social inclusion or disqualification premised not on an individual's knowledge of finance but on the consensual nature of their participation in the market.

Looking beyond this story of domination, an analysis of financial literacy education in the context of financial crisis can provide insights into how financial literacy also comes from below. In the aftermath of the global financial bailout, explication of financial logic in the classroom is called upon to reinforce the givenness of finance's inegalitarian logic in an attempt to occlude the ways in which publics may be already literate in finance in a very material sense. The idea of the public's emergent literacy is grounded on a sensibility of the collective generative capacity of labour as the basis of surplus value and social reproduction. To proceed from this supposition radically changes what is sensible, knowable, and sayable in and about the world of finance. Martin (2014) invites us to do just this when he suggests we consider the financial bailout not in terms of what was robbed from the public to do so but rather in terms of "what it means to be able to suddenly muster trillions of dollars and to undertake a public deliberation over what might be done with a social surplus that was never acknowledged as such to be one" (p. 207). Before the master economist or trader, and before the responsibilised risk-laden citizen, finance is indebted to the phenomenal social surplus generated by labour's collective productive forces. If, as Martin contends, "the money is there, the mutuality exists, the means to make what is desired are at hand" (2013, p. 102) then financial participation premised on the maxim of equality is indeed something for finance to fear. A public literate in their constitutive part in the world of finance should not be the goal of financial education today, rather it should be, in the tradition of Jacotot and Rancière, its starting point.

REFERENCES

Althusser, L. (1971/2001). *Lenin and philosophy and other essays* (B. Brewster, Trans.). New York: Monthly Review.

Arthur, C. (2012a). *Financial literacy education: Neoliberalism, the consumer and the citizen*. Rotterdam: Sense.

Arthur, C. (2012b). Financial literacy education for citizens: What kind of responsibility, equality and engagement? *Citizenship, Social and Economic Education, 11*(3), 163–176.

Arthur, C. (2014). Financial literacy education as public pedagogy for the capitalist debt economy. *TOPIA, 30–31*, 147–163.

Association for Sustainability and Democracy (ALDA). (2011). *Our vision*. Retrieved from http://en.alda.is/?page_id=22

Biesta, G. (2010). A new logic of emancipation: The methodology of Jacques Rancière. *Educational Theory, 60*(1), 39–59.

Bingham, C., & Biesta, G. (2010). *Jacques Rancière: Education, truth, emancipation*. London: Continuum.

Bourdieu, P., & Passeron, J.-C. (1977). *Reproduction in education, society and culture*, trans. R. Nice. London: Sage.

Bryan, D., & Rafferty, M. (2011). The new class politics of financial risk. *D!SSENT, 37*(Summer), 47–51.

Commission for Financial Literacy and Retirement Income (CFLRI). (2012). *National strategy for financial literacy*. Retrieved from www.cflri.org.nz/financial-literacy/national-strategy/documents

de Goede, M. (2005). *Virtue, fortune and faith: A genealogy of finance*. Minneapolis: University of Minnesota.

Haiven, M. (2012). Finance depends on resistance, finance is resistance, and anyway, resistance is futile. *Mediations, 26*(1–2), 85–106.

Haiven, M. (2014a). The creative and the derivative: Historicizing creativity under post-Bretton Woods financialization. *Radical History Review, 118* (Winter), 113–138.

Haiven, M. (2014b). *Crises of imagination, crises of power: Capitalism, culture and resistance in a post-crash world.* London: Zed.

Harney, S., & Moten, F. (2013). *The undercommons: Fugitive planning and black study.* New York: Minor.

Jones, C. (2012). *The World of Finance.* Paper presented at the Australasian Society for Continental Philosophy Annual Conference, Auckland, 10–12 December.

Jones, C. (2013). *Can the market speak?* Winchester, UK: Zero.

Joseph, M. (2014). *Debt to society: Accounting for life under capitalism.* Minneapolis: University of Minnesota Press.

Júlíusson, Á., & Helgason, M. (2013). The roots of the saucepan revolution in Iceland. In C. Flesher Fominaya & L. Cox (Eds.), *European movements: New social movements, global justice struggles, anti-austerity protest* (pp. 189–202). London: Routledge.

Krippner, G. (2011). *Capitalizing on crisis: The political origins of the rise of finance.* Cambridge, MA: Harvard University Press.

La Berge, L. C. (2014). The rules of abstraction: Methods and discourses of finance. *Radical History Review, 118*(Winter), 93–112.

Lapavitsas, C. (2009). Financialised capitalism: Crisis and financial expropriation. *Historical Materialism, 17*(2), 114–148.

Lapavitsas, C. (2013). *Profiting without producing: How finance exploits us all.* London: Verso.

LiPuma, E., & Lee, B. (2004). *Financial derivatives and the globalisation of risk.* London: Duke University.

Martin, R. (2013). After economy? Social logic of the derivative. *Social Text, 114*(31), 83–106.

Martin, R. (2014). What difference do derivatives make? From the technical to the political conjecture. *Culture Unbound, 6*, 189–210.

New York City General Assembly. (2011, September 29). *Declaration of the occupation of New York City.* Retrieved from http://www.nycga.net/resources/documents/declaration

Organisation for Economic Co-operation and Development (OECD). (2013). *PISA 2012 Assessment and analytic framework: Mathematics, reading, science, problem solving and financial literacy.* OECD Publishing. http//dx.doi.org/10.1787/9789264190511-en

Organisation for Economic Co-operation and Development and G20 OECD/G20, (2013), *Advancing national strategies for financial education: A joint publication by Russia's G20 presidency and the OECD.* OECD Publishing.

Organisation for Economic Co-Operation and Development International Network on Financial Education OECD/INFE. (2012). *High-level principles on national strategies for financial education.* OECD Publishing.

Pinto, L. (2012). When politics trumps evidence: Financial literacy education narratives following the global financial crisis. *Journal of Education Policy, 28*(1), 95–120.

Pinto, L., & Coulson, E. (2011). Social justice and the gender politics of financial literacy education. *Journal of the Canadian Association for Curriculum Studies, 9*(2), 54–85.

Rancière, J. (1991). *The ignorant schoolmaster: Five lessons in intellectual emancipation* (K. Ross, Trans.). Stanford, CA: Stanford University Press.

Rancière, J. (2004). *The politics of aesthetics* (G. Rockhill, Trans.). London: Continuum.

Rancière, J. (2010a). On ignorant schoolmasters. In C. Bingham & G. Biesta (Eds.), *Rancière: Education, truth, emancipation* (pp. 1–24). London: Continuum.

Rancière, J. (2010b). *Dissensus: On politics and aesthetics* (S. Corcoran, Trans.). London: Continuum.

Tronti, M. (1964/1979). Lenin in England. In, *Working class autonomy and the crisis: Italian marxist texts of the theory and practice of a class movement: 1964–79* (pp. 1–6). London: Red Notes.

Tronti, M. (2007). The strategy of refusal. In S. Lotringer & C. Marazzi (Eds.), *Autonomia: Post-political politics* (pp. 28–35). Los Angeles: Semiotext(e).

Valdimarsson, O. (2012, February 19). Icelandic anger bring debt forgiveness in best recovery story. *Bloomberg online.* Retrieved from http://www.bloomberg.com/news/2012-02-20/icelandic-anger-brings-record-debt-relief-in-best-crisis-recovery-story.html

Williams, T. (2007). Empowerment of whom and for what? Financial literacy education and the new regulation of consumer financial services. *Law and Policy, 29*(2), 226–256.

NOTE

1. I would like to thank Jai Bentley-Payne, Rea Daellenbach, Campbell Jones and Helen Tregidga for their valuable feedback and insights on earlier versions of this chapter.

CHAPTER THIRTEEN

Financialization AND THE Production OF New Financial Elites through Business Education

SARAH HALL

INTRODUCTION

This chapter examines the changing relationship between elite financial labour markets in the City of London and education. Historically at least, membership of the 'old boys networks' from a small number of public (fee-paying) schools and elite universities, particularly Oxford and Cambridge, was an important way of displaying the required forms of cultural capital needed to secure entry into financial services labour markets in the City of London (Augar, 2001). In particular, this educational background was seen to inculcate the "narrative of the gentleman" into new recruits, "based on values of honour, integrity, courtesy and so on, and manifest in ideas of how to act, ways of talk [and] suitable clothing" (Thrift, 1994, p. 342). These discourses played an important role in shaping the nature of work within the City as well as the 'soft touch' regulatory environment favoured by the Bank of England that was built around an understanding that a "gentleman's word was his bond" (Pryke, 1991). However, the relationship between education and elite financial labour markets changed markedly following the deregulatory changes of 1986 collectively known as Big Bang. Among other developments, this regulatory change facilitated the entry of overseas banks, particularly US investment banks that relied less on educational background and in so doing stimulated greater demand for skilled labour—demand that could not be met through the public school system and Oxbridge alone (Leyshon & Thrift, 1997).

As a result, whilst educational background still features in recruitment decisions into elite labour markets (Faulconbridge & Hall, 2014), education after completion of a first bachelor's degree has played an increasingly important role in securing entry into and upward mobility within elite financial labour markets in London, in common with other international financial centres (see Ho, 2009, in the case of Wall Street). Interdisciplinary research into the role of education in elite formation and reproduction provides a valuable starting point for examining this growing role of postgraduate education including graduate training courses, MBA degrees and specialist courses offered by for-profit business education service firms, emphasising how individuals use education to secure themselves a positional advantage within increasingly competitive financial elite labour markets (Brown & Hesketh, 2004). However, understandings of how individuals use credentials acquired in what remain largely national higher education systems to secure access into elite labour markets that have been increasingly labelled as global or transnational in nature remain limited (although see Waters, 2012).

In this chapter, I respond to this lacuna by reporting on original empirical research conducted with early career elites working in financial services in the City of London. This research reveals the importance of ongoing education within financial services labour markets, particularly that provided by for-profit education companies, as a bridge between under- and postgraduate degrees embedded within national education systems and the more networked and trans-local nature of elite financial services work in which individuals frequently move between different international financial centres over the course of their career (Beaverstock & Hall, 2012). This analysis is both theoretically and empirically important because it reveals the situated nature of positional advantage acquired through higher education credentials within elite labour markets, highlighting how highly valued higher education credentials in domestic labour markets can be comparatively less valued in international settings. In so doing, and reflecting wider calls to incorporate a greater sensitivity to space and place in understandings of work and employment (Ward, 2007; Herod, Rainnie, & McGrath-Champ, 2007), this argument qualifies claims of the emergence of a relatively homogeneous group of transnational elites (Sklair, 2001; Sassen, 2012) by revealing the persistence of geographical differences between international financial centre labour markets and the ways in which these impact the relative value of different higher education credentials held by early career financial elites. Empirically, my research reveals the important but understudied role of forms of education and training beyond higher education, particularly that provided by rapidly growing for-profit education companies, in shaping the working practices and (im)mobility of contemporary early career financial elites. My analysis therefore intervenes in wider debates concerning the formation, reproduction, and changing nature of elites at the start of their careers as well as demonstrating the importance of a range of forms of financial education in shaping the working practices of financial elites who were at the heart of reproducing financialisation during the rapid expansion of finance-led capital in the 2000s and the continued (re)production of the international financial system in the wake of the financial crisis of 2007–2008.

I develop this argument over five sections. Next, I combine work on contemporary elite labour markets with work on graduate employability in order to advance understandings of the situated nature of positional advantage within financial labour markets. I then introduce the nature of postgraduate education offered to early career financial elites in the City of London. In the next two sections of the chapter, I examine why individuals undertake such additional education in financial labour markets, demonstrating how it acts as a bridge between national higher education systems and the trans-local nature of contemporary financial services labour markets. I conclude by outlining the significance of these findings for research on intersecting education, work, and employability within elite labour markets generally and financial services in particular.

EDUCATION AND EARLY CAREER FINANCIAL ELITE LABOUR MARKETS FORMATION

Two significant periods of change have been experienced by the City of London's elite financial labour market that have implications for the role of education within it in the last 30 years. First and most recently, finance and related professional services such as law were at the heart of a period of rapid finance-led economic growth and innovation throughout the 2000s (Engelen et al., 2010; Froud et al., 2006). The resulting growth of financial services in financial centres, including London, led to a diversification in the relationship between education and financial elites. In particular, as noted above, 'old school tie' recruitment networks of the 1980s were unable to provide the volume of new recruits demanded (Leyshon & Thrift, 1997) and greater emphasis was placed on the technical competencies of individuals. This growth and change in financial services built on the second key set of changes that altered the relationship between financial labour markets and education in London—the set of deregulatory policies introduced by the Thatcher Government in 1986, collectively known as Big Bang, which facilitated the internationalisation of the City in terms of headquarter location of the financial firms that were eligible to operate within it (Augar, 2001). In terms of education, this shift was significant because it meant that whilst the education systems in which financial elites are trained remained predominately nationally organised, financial labour markets became increasingly global in scope (Beaverstock &

Hall, 2012). In these labour markets, it is typical, over the course of a career, to work in several different financial centres whilst being employed by an international firm that operates globally, either through short-term expatriation or longer-term secondments or periods of highly skilled migration (Beaverstock, 2005). Indeed, international investment banks, in common with related producer service firms such as law firms, are eager to emphasise their 'global' office networks and standards of customer service (Faulconbridge, 2008; Jones, 2005) whilst executive search firms that play an important role in encouraging elite mobility between different jobs emphasise their ability to conduct global searches (Faulconbridge, Beaverstock, et al., 2008). Meanwhile, national governments have used the discourse of a global "war for talent" (Michaels et al., 1997) as part of wider justifications for attempting to upskill their domestic workforce in the face of greater international competition. This spatial imagination of a global competition for skilled workers extends to studies of the elites who work in such labour markets through work on, for example, the "creative class" (Florida, 2002), the "transnational capitalist class" (Sklair, 2001) and "new international professionals" (Sassen, 2012).

Whilst this literature clearly demonstrates the impact of globalisation on elite labour markets, research has developed a subtle but significant spatial understanding of these processes by exploring the trans-local nature of elites and their working practices in which national and regional differences exist alongside processes of globalisation such as labour market migration and global and supra-national regulatory regimes. For example, in the case of financial services, this intersection between place-based norms and international influences has given rise to a globally networked international financial system co-ordinated through a small number of financial centres that have retained distinct working practices, norms, and cultures (Clark & Wójcik, 2007; Beaverstock, Smith, & Taylor, 2000; Hall & Appleyard, 2011). It is particularly important to consider this intersection between the global and the local when considering the intersection between education and financial elite labour markets because there is considerable debate concerning the extent to which education continues to be predominately embedded within national education policymaking arenas. For example, whilst King, Marginson, and Naidoo (2011) question the future role of the nation-state in higher education provision and emphasise the more homogeneous nature of postgraduate training, others have pointed to the persistence of national and regional differences in education provision, labour market expectations and working practices (Brockmann, Clark, & Winch, 2011). In this chapter, I contribute to this debate by examining the educational strategies of early career financial elites as they seek to use higher education credentials acquired in national contexts to enter more globally orientated elite labour markets.

SITUATING POSITIONAL ADVANTAGE

Work on positional competition provides a valuable starting point for examining the strategies used by educational and occupational elites in order to secure access to the labour markets of professional and business service firms. Brown (2000) defines positional competition as "how one stands relative to others within an implicit or explicit hierarchy" (p. 633). Developing this approach in the context of credential acquisition and labour markets through positional conflict theory, he argues that there has been growing competition in the acquisition of credentials as employers increasingly use them to make shortlisting and recruitment decisions. This reflects the ways in which credentials represent objectified, embodied, and institutionalised forms of cultural capital in a Bourdieuian sense (Bourdieu & Passeron, 1990; Bourdieu, 1990, 1996; Waters, 2009) that continue to be important in selection for entry into elite labour markets (e.g., see Thrift, 1994, on the importance of educational background and the cultural signifiers associated in financial labour markets in the City of London).

Developing this perspective, research has examined how individuals negotiate and strategise within these positional competitions in order to maximise their own labour market outcomes and aspirations. The nature of such competitions has become particularly intense in graduate labour markets following the massification of higher education and wider processes of credential inflation (Collins, 1979). As a result, graduates are increasingly forced to re-evaluate the value of their undergraduate degree on entering labour markets as holding a degree no longer confers the same "positional advantage" (Brooks & Everett, 2009). In response, a range of strategies has been adopted by graduates in an effort to secure entry into elite labour markets. For example, partly in response to the growing number of graduates, individuals are increasingly influenced by the reputation of higher education institutions when choosing where to study. This reflects the ways in which both graduates and recruiters attempt to manage the increase in the number of graduates by using the ranking of the institution studied at as a marker of positional advantage. Research has also highlighted the importance of extra-curricular activities as a way of demonstrating commitment to future career aspirations and thereby enhancing positional advantage (Brown & Hesketh, 2004).

Given the increased number of graduates, obtaining postgraduate qualifications has also become an increasingly common strategy (Bowl, 2003). Building on the significance, historically at least, of the MBA degree (Hall, 2008; Whitley, 1986), postgraduate qualifications are particularly important in elite, service-sector labour markets because they are seen as evidence of the bespoke, specialist knowledge demanded within such workplaces, as well as reflecting the onus placed on individuals to maintain and enhance their skills through investment in their own human capital (Thrift, 2005; Becker, 1993). For example, there is a growing preference to hire individuals with master's and PhD degrees in wholesale finance (Wilmott, 2000; Hall & Appleyard, 2009).

Another strategy used by individuals to secure positional advantage within elite labour markets is to undertake degrees overseas, particularly if they have failed to secure entry into what are perceived to be the elite institutions in their home country (Waters, 2007). This points to the comparatively neglected international dimensions of positional competitions for jobs, particularly in elite occupations. Indeed, as Brown and Hesketh (2004) argue:

> Some occupational elites operate in a global rather than a local context, but they accumulate elite credentials and other cultural assets within national and local contexts. How domestic competitions are organized continue to be important to understanding the fates of eventual winners and losers. (p. 23)

In order to respond to this call, in the rest of this chapter I understand positional advantage as being geographically situated in particular places because *nationally* denominated higher education credentials are valued differently in different national, regional, and local elite labour markets. As a result, I argue that it is important to examine how early career educational and occupational (financial) elites negotiate the resulting spatial mismatch between their positional advantage based on higher education that remains predominately embedded in national socio-economies and the more networked and transnational nature of elite labour markets.

METHODOLOGY

I develop this argument by reporting on an original in-depth empirical study of the ongoing use of postgraduate education amongst early career graduate investment bankers in London's financial district. A total of 102 interviews were conducted with investment bankers working in London to discuss their postgraduate education and training (53 interviews with UK and non-UK nationals); human resource managers in investment banks in London (6 interviews); educators and managers in for-profit financial business education firms in the UK (10 interviews); and business school lecturers and managers (36 interviews). All interviews were transcribed in full and analysed iteratively with theoretical frameworks being used to guide initial coding. Respondents are anonymised in the analysis below. These datasets were triangulated with a desk-based review of investment bank and education providers websites in order to better understand the wider educational landscapes available to investment bankers; business and specialist news providers used to reveal recent developments in postgraduate education and training in elite financial labour markets; policy documents from relevant government departments (e.g., DIUS, HM Treasury); and organisations concerned with graduate employability (e.g., UKCES, HEFCE).

LEARNING TO BE AN INVESTMENT BANKER—POSITIONING FOR-PROFIT EDUCATION

In terms of entry into the City's elite financial labour markets, the types of educational backgrounds considered by financial services employers has broadened to include a larger, although still highly selective, number of universities with particular emphasis placed on select institutions within the Russell Group (Faulconbridge & Hall, 2009) and greater interest being shown in recruiting graduates from elite overseas universities, a point I return to below. However, the increased demand for graduates within financial services has not been accompanied by a decrease in the intensity of positional competitions in terms of securing entry into these labour markets. This is because a larger pool of graduates are being considered at the early stages of recruitment processes and financial services careers remain highly sought after both in terms of the cultural capital they offer and because of the salaries that graduates can hope to achieve in this sector. For example, in 2010, the average annual graduate starting salary in investment banking was £45,000 whilst the equivalent figure for graduates generally was £29,000 (High Fliers, 2012).

Reflecting this competition, a number of strategies are adopted by graduates in order to enhance their initial employability and secure upward career progression within elite financial labour markets. For example—and reflecting extant work on positional competitions within elite labour markets discussed above—undertaking internships whilst studying for a first degree and pursuing postgraduate study through a master's or PhD degree in a scientific discipline are common tactics used in an effort to improve the likelihood of securing entry into elite financial labour markets, as the following examples demonstrate:

> I knew that I wanted to work in the City really before I went to Uni so I went for work experience through my father at the end of my first year and then applied for an internship that I did at the end of my second year. In some ways, getting on that scheme was the most important part of starting my career as I knew if I got an internship and didn't mess up I stood a good chance of being offered a position. (Analyst, UK national, Russell Group University Graduate, City of London)

> I have a 2:1 from a good university but I didn't get on an internship programme so I wasn't surprised when I didn't get any offers (from investment banks or accountancy firms) at the end of my degree. I decided that further study would help so I stayed on to do a master's degree in maths whilst I pursued further work experience options and that's how I got my

> current position. (Analyst, UK national, Russell Group University first and second degree, City of London)

Following entry into these labour markets, further postgraduate education also plays a vital role in maintaining and enhancing individual employability as well as inculcating early career elites into the expected cultural and social norms of both their employing investment bank and the financial centre in which they are working (Hall & Appleyard, 2011; Faulconbridge & Hall, 2009). The role of this type of education can be divided into compulsory and optional education. The most important forms of such postgraduate compulsory education are graduate training schemes run by individual investment banks in conjunction with for-profit education companies. These typically take place in the bank's international headquarters and involve a residential component of up to 6 weeks in which graduates are inculcated into the firms' corporate cultures. These courses also include sessions run by for-profit education companies on particular technical competencies and regulatory issues. The regulatory component of these initial courses overlaps with the second form of compulsory education undertaken by graduates, which is education used to meet the necessary regulatory clearances and practical experience to practice as an investment banker in the city in which they are working. For example, to practice as a financier in London, an individual has to demonstrate that they are 'competent' as defined by the Financial Services Authority. This requirement is met by acquiring credentials from the list of FSA/Financial services Skills Council 'appropriate examinations' as well as demonstrating practical competencies through practical experience and observing more senior colleagues.

Following the successful completion of these compulsory courses, investment bankers move into the optional part of their education and training in their early careers. Optional additional education is either undertaken because of individual motivation or following the recommendation of managers within investment banks. Courses include those related to both technical skills such as higher level mathematical ability associated with the growth of quantitative finance throughout the 2000s as well as education that focuses on the embodied competencies of bankers on topics such as leadership and management. These courses are seen to be particularly important by investment bankers as banks typically hire more analysts (the first level or an investment banking career) than they ultimately need with the expectation that some will leave the bank voluntarily, but others will be made redundant as the following banker summarised:

> You complete your compulsory courses and for a brief moment I thought I could relax. Then I realised that I needed to keep myself up to date and demonstrate commitment by undertaking additional courses as they always hire more analysts than they need and the skills learnt and extra commitment shown by doing courses, often in my free time, means that hopefully I'll be seen as more flexible and committed and therefore less likely to lose

> my job. (Analyst, EU national, European university first degree, UK master's degree, City of London)

This range of educational experiences for early career investment bankers has given rise to a diverse range of education providers. Historically, the gold standard of professional education for elites has been in the form of an MBA degree from a leading business school, particularly in the US where undertaking an MBA is a more well-established part of an investment banking career structure than in the UK (Hall, 2009; Ho, 2009). Indeed, holding an MBA degree from a top-ranked international business school still represents an important career strategy for converting national positional advantage into international positional advantage because of the cultural capital associated with the credential and its close links to financial services (on which see Bernstein, 1992) as the following example demonstrates:

> I'd graduated in Australia and started with an Australian investment bank in Sydney. However, I wanted to get experience in a larger financial centre so transferred with that bank to London. However, to get the position I'm about to start on Wall Street, I needed to do something to make me stand out and that's when I went to INSEAD to get an MBA in order to facilitate that move—I think it just counts much more than a master's from Melbourne [University]. (Associate, Australian National, Australian first and master's degree, US MBA, City of London)

However, the value attached to MBA degrees has been called into question following criticisms that they lack relevance to contemporary commercial life and they have been implicated in financial crises, including the current finance-led recession and the accounting scandals that hit corporate America in the early 2000s (Mintzberg, 2004). In response, a number of for-profit education companies have grown rapidly that focus on the relevance of their curricula to corporate client needs and offer a series of short courses that are seen to fit better with the dynamic operating requirements of investment banks rather than the "two years out of the labour market studying but doing what?" as one analyst said of the MBA degree. These range in size from multinational education companies such as BPP and Kaplan that offer a range of educational services beyond business education but also sell their services to investment banks as well as offering education that leads to particular regulatory clearances being met. These large, global companies are accompanied by a larger number of smaller, more specialist firms that offer education in their own offices as well as being contracted to provide education within investment banks (Hall & Appleyard, 2011). On first impressions the educational services offered by these firms may seem rather distant to discussions of achieving enhanced employability and positional advantage since their credentials are not as well known and not clearly imbued with cultural capital as compared to credentials offered by higher education institutions and business schools. However, in the analysis that follows, I argue that they play an important role in bridging the spatial mismatch between national positional competitions amongst early career educational elites and the globally networked labour market that characterises wholesale financial services.

INTERNATIONAL EMPLOYABILITY AND THE DECISION TO UNDERTAKE FOR-PROFIT EDUCATION

In many ways, individuals seeking work in London's financial district appear to be the 'winners' of the UK education system having typically secured entrance to an elite higher education institution, normally Oxbridge or a Russell Group institution, and graduating with at least an upper second class degree. However, the competition for jobs in financial services is intense. For example, in the 2012 graduate recruitment cycle, it is estimated that, on average, investment banks receive 150 applications for each place on graduate schemes, compared to an average across all graduate schemes of 73.2 (AGR, 2012). This competition is widely recognised by graduates seeking elite financial labour markets with comments such as the following being typical:

> On paper I had everything they [investment banks] wanted. I went to a good school, straight As at A level, 2: I from Cambridge, internships in two banks but I still knew there were no guarantees about getting a job—they [investment banks] can afford to be picky because basically there are more of us [graduates] than they need. (Analyst, UK national, UK undergraduate degree, City of London)

This competition points to the need to locate positional competitions in the context of the labour market demands that individuals are hoping to enter. Locating work on positional competitions with a focus on employability provides a valuable way of doing this. Brown and Hesketh (2004) define employability as "the relative changes of getting and maintaining different kinds of employment" (p. 25). This definition is important because it emphasises what they term the "duality of employability." Such an approach emphasises the relative as well as the absolute nature of employability such that an individual needs not only to negotiate positional competitions for credentials but that their employability will also be a function of the labour market demands for the type of work they wish to undertake. Moreover, in the case of financial services, and elite occupations more generally, this duality of employability is not restricted to the national scale. Rather an individual's employability is also a function of their relative value in more global labour markets.

The duality of employability within increasingly global financial labour markets provides the impetus for early career financial elites to undertake additional education after completion of their university education both before they enter financial labour markets and during the early stages of their financial services career in response to two main features of contemporary elite financial services labour markets. First, the rapid growth of financial services in the economic boom of the 2000s, frequently termed "financialisation" (Froud et al., 2006), was accompanied by a change in the nature of work within investment banks. Prior to this time, investment banking was predominately relationship based with mergers and acquisitions and corporate advisory services dominating their business models (Augar, 2001). This gave rise to a relationship approach to banking such that bankers had to develop longstanding trust-based relationships with clients in order to offer them this advice. However, the financial innovations that underpinned the rapid growth of financial services in the 2000s, notably securitisation, were underpinned by a greater reliance on quantitative finance. In response, investment banks have increasingly demanded high level numeracy and technical skills from new graduate recruits who are able to undertake the technical analysis associated with these products. This is reflected in research conducted by BIS (2011) that estimates that between 40 and 50% of new graduate hires into investment banking in London will hold STEM (science, technology, engineering, and medicine) degrees with the equivalent figure for management consultancy being 30% (BIS, 2011; see also Ho, 2009, on the case of Wall Street, New York).

This preference for quantitative financial skills in investment banking workplaces is having significant impacts on the relative employability of different graduates seeking to enter investment banking labour markets. In part, the changing labour markets demands are reflected in a growing preference to hire individuals with postgraduate qualifications in numerate subjects, particularly maths and physics, who have the necessary skills to undertake the quantitative analysis required (Wilmott, 2000; Hall & Appleyard, 2009). Important for my arguments concerning the situated nature of positional advantage, there has also been a growing concern within investment banking in the City of London that UK graduates are not well placed to provide suitably numerate graduates, reflecting wider concerns voiced by policymakers and employers concerning the skills required by the private sector and the extent to which they perceive these are being met by UK higher education (DIUS, 2009; CBI, 2011). Comments such as the following were common in this regard:

> I guess very generally there has been actually a problem with British students coming into banking. We find that they are just not coming through the interview process of the screening process and I think that's probably true across the board of most banks. (Human Resources Director, Investment bank, City of London)

In response, investment banks have increasingly turned to international early career labour markets to recruit graduates from non-UK institutions who are perceived to have greater numeracy skills and hence enhanced employability compared to their UK counterparts, as the following example demonstrates:

> Because we can't always get the technical skills we want domestically, increasingly we hire international graduates on that basis but then recognise that we might need to invest a little more in their soft skills and their expectations about working in the City. That's not to say we only hire internationally, not at all, but we know that the needs of analysts tend to be different depending on where they studied for their first degree, so, we'll work with talented UK hires to develop their technical skills, using specialist courses and that kind of thing. (Human Resources Director, Investment bank, City of London)

The hiring of international graduates to address the perceived lack of numeracy skills amongst UK graduates clearly reveals the hitherto largely overlooked situated nature of employability and positional advantage. Whilst UK students being interviewed for investment banking graduate schemes in the City are largely seen to have been successful in maximising their positional advantage within UK graduate labour markets, the quantitative skills of their international counterparts means that they are relatively less successful in global positional competitions for access to elite financial jobs in labour markets that are characterised by greater international mobility (on which see Sassen, 2012; Beaverstock, 2005).

In response, an important strategy used to overcome this international positional disadvantage by UK graduates seeking to enter financial labour markets is to undertake additional education after graduation. However, rather than choosing to accumulate credentials imbued with cultural capital, such as MBA degrees from well-regarded international business schools as documented in extant research on graduate employability, graduates engage in covert forms of education in an attempt to address their international positional disadvantage. Specialist courses run by for-profit education firms are a particularly important source of such educational experiences as the following example demonstrates:

> I have a 2:1 degree from a Russell Group University in Physics so I know I'm numerate. But I also know that the online tests they [investment banks] use at interview have the maths in more commercial case studies and although I know the maths, I can't always apply it so I undertook a short course run by [name of company] to improve my skills in a commercial setting. After that, I got through the first round, was fine at interview and am now working here in London. Obviously I didn't tell them that I'd that additional tutoring—it reminded me a bit of school entrance exams. (Analyst, UK national, UK first degree, City of London)

The second important rationale in choosing to undertake for-profit education amongst early career elites is in order to facilitate individual employability in the face of marked changes in the nature of financial services labour markets—particularly in order to move between different wholesale markets. In particular, as the financial crisis unfolded from 2007 onwards, investment bankers faced an increased likelihood of redundancies. It is hard to get accurate data on such redundancies given its commercial sensitivity but estimates suggest that both HSBC and Bank of America/Merrill Lynch have made 30,000 bankers redundant since the start of the financial crisis whilst the equivalent figure for Lloyds Banking group is 15,000 ("Global Bank Job Losses," 2012). For early career investment bankers, job losses are potentially even more significant because investment banks typically hire more analysts (the first stage of an investment banking career) than they require with a number of redundancies and voluntary departures expected before these recruits reach associate level as the following HR manager explained,

> Yes, we do over hire at the analyst level but we know a number of them won't be up to it, some will leave, so it gives us the flexibility to continue to select the most appropriate people for our organisation as they move to associate level. (HR manager, US investment bank, City of London)

In response to this, individuals often pay for for-profit education in order to enhance their employability in different parts of the financial services labour market from their initial specialism, typically responding to labour market demands in making their choice—again pointing to the importance of situating positional advantage within larger labour markets. In the wake of financial crisis and large numbers of investment banking redundancies, one particularly common change of career direction in this respect has been from investment banking to wealth management and private banking, one of the fastest growing areas of financial services activity in the City of London following the 2007–2008 financial crisis. The wealth management industry involves private banks servicing the needs of high net worth individuals, often associated with personal wealth generated outside the UK but managed through private banks in London (see Beaverstock, Hall, & Wainwright, 2013). In order to make this move, individuals again engaged in optional for-profit education but this time through a rapidly growing credential that is recognised globally—the Chartered Financial Analyst (CFA) program as the following example demonstrates:

> I had been made redundant from my initial graduate post in an investment bank and after some time out travelling, I decided I wanted to enter private banking and wealth management. In order to improve my chances of doing this I undertook the CFA [Chartered Financial Analyst] program, which I believe was critical in my getting my current post here. (Analyst, UK National, UK first degree, EU master's degree, City of London)

In a similar way to Waters' work on the second chance at success that studying for an overseas credential at HE level confers on students, the use of for-profit education, whilst already in the labour market, points to the ways in which such education offers early career elites the opportunity of a second chance of success within labour markets when redundancy hits.

Taken together these two rationales for undertaking additional postgraduate education whilst seeking entry into and in the early stages of a financial services career demonstrate the importance of situating understandings of positional advantage within the context of both national and international labour markets and of recognising the duality of employability such that positional advantage is also partly dependent on the changing nature of skills and knowledge demanded by different labour markets. In the case of financial services, the situated nature of the positional advantage of UK graduates is demonstrated first through a perceived lack of numeracy and technical skills as compared to their international counterparts and second through the need for early career elites to adapt to the changing sectoral balance of financial services themselves, particularly in the wake of the financial crisis. This also resonates with work on the duality of employability since positional advantage involves consideration of both the credentials held by individual graduates and the value of these relative to other early career elites and labour market demands. Considering how postgraduate education is used by early career financial elites to not only respond to their situated positional disadvantage but also to enhance it serves to reinforce the need to focus on the situated nature of positional advantage.

FOR-PROFIT EDUCATION AND THE MOBILITY OF EARLY CAREER FINANCIAL ELITES IN TRANS-LOCAL LABOUR MARKETS

In many ways, the relationship between the situated nature of elite financial labour markets in a select number of international financial centres (IFCs) and the global networks that cross-cut these IFCs has become one of the defining features of elite financial services work. For example, the growing number and significance of American banks operating in the City of London following Big Bang initially led to claims of the Wimbledonisation of the City in which, just like in the tennis tournament, the City hosted a range of overseas banks but did not maintain its own domestic culture. However, detailed ethnographies conducted within the US financial centres of New York and Chicago and London demonstrate that whilst there are commonalities, the cultures of work remain geographically distinct (Zaloom, 2006). That said, IFCs act as nodes in a network of more global flows including the mobility of financial elites, the circulation of knowledge through corporate networks between financial centres and the materiality of the technological infrastructure that underpins the international financial system (Beaverstock, 2005; Hall, 2006). Given this interplay between situated working cultures and international flows, elite financial services labour markets are best characterised as being trans-local in nature combining both distinct embedded cultures overlaid with more global sensibilities.

The trans-local nature of these labour markets present opportunities for early career financial elites to enhance their employability as well as the challenges discussed in the previous section, as the following bankers summarised,

> Working in this industry (investment banking) does present you with international opportunities that you have to think about in terms of how you're going to maximise them for your own career. So you've got to get to grips with what's going on where you're currently working but then increasingly having an overseas market, particularly somewhere that's growing fast like Shanghai on your CV really helps in terms of making you stand out for the next promotion. (Associate, UK national, UK undergraduate and master's degree, City of London)

Extant research has examined a range of strategies that individuals engage with in order to facilitate their international mobility between different financial centres, including the role of labour market intermediaries such as executive search companies (Faulconbridge & Hall, 2009) and the ways in which mobility during higher education and postgraduate study relates to future mobility in the labour market. However, less attention has been paid to the ways in which individuals engage with education whilst working in elite labour markets in order to develop their relative positional advantage based around the ability and willingness to render themselves mobile in elite labour markets.

Two strategies are particularly important amongst early career investment bankers in this respect. The first is through in-house graduate training schemes in which investment banks contract a for-profit education company to provide introductory seminars on both the technical and embodied know-how associated with being a financier in London. These courses typically take place in late summer and early autumn and last for between 6 weeks and 3 months. New graduate recruits travel to the bank's headquarters in order to be inculcated into particular corporate cultures and then undertake a series of rations between different departments within the bank aimed at exposing them to a range of different issues and helping them to decide in which area they would like to specialise, as the following example demonstrates:

> There is also quite a lot of time dedicated to them instilling and communicating the values of the company and what is going to be expected of people and giving guidance on the key values, what it means to be professional, what the standards are, and what you are expected to project on a day-to-day basis so yes, quite a lot of time is spent on that in the beginning. (Investment bank vice president, City of London)

Beyond these very early stages of an investment banking career, individuals opt to undertake additional education in order to more explicitly focus on their ability to render themselves mobile. For-profit companies play a key role in facilitating international mobility more explicitly by being part of the global mobility industry that is aimed at supporting companies, often in the business services sector in facilitating the mobility of their staff over a range of time scales from short business trips to longer assignments. This form of elite mobility has been widely studied in terms of more senior levels (Beaverstock, 2005) but less attention has been paid to early career elites and the role of education in particular within this. However, a number of education companies provide training in this area (see Hall & Appleyard, 2011). Much of this focuses on language (which typically isn't that important in financial services where business is conducted in English globally) but also on 'cross-cultural training'—something that is very important in order to tailor the business services offered to different markets.

This form of education and training represents an important element in facilitating the upward career mobility of early career elites and an effort to convert their domestic employability into international employability, as the following example demonstrates:

> When you decide to go for an international secondment you work with HR and your manager to plan the details and part of that was going on training in terms of the commercial and lifestyle factors that would affect my work in Shanghai—what I needed to know both formally and in terms of regulation but also informally in terms of business practice. So that education was crucial in facilitating my secondment and maximising the business and personal benefits. And they are huge because I'll then have an emerging markets on my CV and that will help as I go for promotion etc. (Investment bank associate, City of London)

CONCLUSIONS

This chapter advances understandings of the formation and reproduction of occupational and educational elites by examining the distinct spatiality of positional advantage within these graduate labour markets. In particular, by reporting on empirical research conducted into early career financial services elites working in London's financial district, I have argued that postgraduate education within the workplace, particularly that provided by for-profit education companies, is used by early career elites as a bridge between the predominately geographically situated nature of their higher education credentials and the trans-local financial services labour markets in which they work. In part, these forms of education are used by early career elites to address forms of international positional disadvantage associated with higher education credentials from a select number of UK universities that in a domestic context are seen as conferring significant positional advantage to individuals. This reflects wider concerns surrounding the employability and particularly the numeracy of UK graduates. However, postgraduate education is also used by early career elites to further enhance their employability by explicitly focusing on their ability to move between what remain socio-economically distinct financial centres within the international financial system.

This argument is theoretically and empirically significant for wider research on the intersection between education, work, and employability in strategically important elite labour markets for two main reasons. First, it points to the importance of taking the geographies and spatialities of work and employment seriously as global labour markets continue to contain within them local, national, and regional differences that need to be negotiated by individuals as they seek to maximise their own employability and career progression. In particular, following calls to take the geographies of work and employment seriously (Ward, 2007), there is need to expand both the range of research locations used to explore employability, elite working practices, and education, and the geographical scope of individual work processes in order to capture these processes that are being played out in geographically distinctive ways and cross-cut a range of scales that continue to structure much of our research methodologies. Second, the research highlights the importance of considering the diversity of education providers and experiences that are used in elite labour markets. Whilst research has focused on higher education (in terms of both undergraduate and postgraduate degrees), the literature on the debates about the role of business schools and MBA degrees continues to grow, particularly given the growing intersection between private providers in both business education and in educational landscapes that have previously been the preserve of state providers as seen by the launching of degree awarding powers to private providers in the UK. Taken together, it is therefore important to study both the emerging spatialities and actors in order to advance understandings of the intersection between occupational and educational elite labour markets, employability and work in the contemporary global economy.

REFERENCES

AGR. (2012). *The AGR Graduate Recruitment Survey 2012.* Summer Review, Association of Graduate Recruiters, Warwick.

Augar, P. (2001). *The death of gentlemanly capitalism.* London: Penguin.

Beaverstock, J. V. (2005). Transnational elites in the city: British highly skilled inter-company transferees in New York City's financial distrcit. *Journal of ethnic and migration studies 31*(2) 245–268.

Beaverstock, J. V., & Hall, S. (2012). Competing for talent: Global mobility, immigration and the City of London's labour market. *Cambridge Journal of Regions, Economy and Society, 5*, 271–287.

Beaverstock, J. V., Hall, S., & Wainwright, T. (2013). Servicing the super rich: New financial elites and the rise of the private wealth management retail ecology. *Regional Studies, 47*(6), 834–849.

Beaverstock, J. V., Smith, R. G., & Taylor, P. J. (2000). World city networks: a new metageography. *Annals of the Association of American Geographers, 90*(1), 123–134.

Becker, G. (1993). *Human capital: Theoretical and empirical analysis with special reference to education.* Chicago: Chicago University Press.

Bernstein, P. (1992). *Capital ideas: The improbable origins of modern Wall Street.* New York: Free.

BIS. (2011). *The plan for growth.* Department for Business, Innovation and Skills. London: Crown.

Bourdieu, P. 1990. *The logic of practice*. Stanford, CA: Stanford University Press.

Bourdieu, P. 1996. *The State Nobility: Elite Schools in the Field of Power.* Stanford, CA: Stanford University Press.

Bourdieu, P. and Passeron, J-P. (1990). *Reproduction in education, society and culture*. London: Sage.

Bowl, M. (2003). *Non-traditional entrants to higher education: "They talk about people like ME."* London: Trentham.

Brockmann, M., Clarke, L., & Winch, C. (2011). *Knowledge skills and competence in the European labour market: What's in a vocational qualification?* London: Routledge.

Brooks, R., & Everett, G. (2009). Post-graduate reflections on the value of a degree. *British Educational research journal, 35*(3), 33.

Brown, P. & Hesketh, A. (2004). *The mismanagement of talent: employability and jobs in the knowledge economy*. Oxford: Oxford University Press.

CBI. (2011). *Building for growth: Business priorities for education and skills*. London: CBI.

Clark, G., & Wójcik, D. (2007). *The geography of finance: Corporate governance in the global marketplace*. Oxford: Oxford University Press.

Collins, R. (1979). *The credential society: An historical sociology of education and stratification*. New York: Academic.

DIUS. (2009). *The demand for science, technology, engineering and mathematics skills*. London: Crown.

Engelen, E., Erturk, I., et al. (2010). Reconceptualising financial innovation: Frame, conjecture and bricolage. *Economy and Society, 39*, 33–63.

Faulconbridge, J. (2008). Managing the transnational law firm: a relational analysis of professional systems, embedded actors and time-space sensitive governance. *Economic Geography* 84(2), 185–210.

Faulconbridge, J., Beaverstock, J. V., et al. (2008). New insights into the internationalization of producer services: Organizational strategies and spatial economies for global headhunting firms. *Environment and Planning A, 40*, 210–234.

Faulconbridge, J., & Hall, S. (2009). Educating professionals and professional education in a geographical context. *Geography compass, 3*(1), 171–189.

Faulconbridge, J., & Hall, S. (2014). Reproducing the city of London's institutional landsacpe: The role of education and the learning of situated practices by early career elites. *Environment and Planning A. 46*(7) 1682–1698.

Florida, R. (2002). The geography of talent. *Annals of the Association of American Geographers 92*, 743–755.

Froud, J., Johal, S., et al. (2006). *Financialization and strategy: Narrative and numbers*. London & New York: Routledge.

Global bank job losses rise above 130,000. (2012). *The Guardian*. Retrieved 26 July 2012, from http://www.guardian.co.uk/business/2012/jan/12/investment-bank-job-losses

Hall, S. (2006). What counts? Exploring the production of quantitative financial narratives in London's corporate finance industry. *Journal of Economic Geography, 6*(5), 661–678.

Hall, S. (2008). Geographies of business education: MBA programmes, reflexive business schools and the cultural circuit of capital. *Transactions of the Institute of British Geographers, 33*(1), 27–41.

Hall, S. (2009). Financialized elites and the changing nature of finance capitalism: Investment bankers in London's financial district. *Competition and Change, 13*(2), 175–191.

Hall, S., & Appleyard, L. (2009). "City of London, city of learning"?: Placing business education within the geographies of finance. *Journal of Economic Geography, 9*(5), 597–617.

Hall, S., & Appleyard, L. (2011). Trans-local academic credentials and the (re)production of financial elites. *Globalisation, societies and education, 9*(2), 247–564.

Herod, A., Rainnie, A., and McGrath-Champ, S. (2007). Working space: Why incorporating the geographical is central to theorizing work and employment practices. *Work, Employment and Society, 21*(2), 247–264.

Ho, K. (2009). *Liquidated: An ethnography of Wall Street.* Durham, NC: Duke University Press.

Jones, A. M. (2003). *Management consultancy and banking in an era of globalisation.* Basingstoke, UK: Palgrave Macmillan.

Jones, A. M. (2005). Truly global corporations? Theorizing "organizational globalization" in advanced business-services. *Journal of Economic Geography 5*(2) 177–200.

King, R., Marginson, S., & Naidoo, R. (Eds.). (2011). *Handbook on globalization and higher education.* Cheltenham, UK: Edward Elgar.

Leyshon, A., & Thrift, N. (1997). *Moneyspace. Geographies of monetary transformation.* London: Routledge.

Michaels, E., Handfield-Jones, H., et al. (1997). *The war for talent.* Boston: Harvard Business School.

Mintzberg, H. (2004). *Developing managers not MBA's.* London: Financial Times.

Pryke, M. (1991). An international city going global: Spatial change in the City of London. *Environment and Planning D, 9*, 197–222.

Sassen, S. (2012). *Cities in a world economy.* London: Sage.

Sklair, L. (2001). *The transnational capitalist class.* Oxford: Blackwell.

Thrift, N. (1994). On the social and cultural determinants of international financial centres: The case of the city of London. In Thrift N., Corbridge S., and Martin R. (Eds.). *Money, Power and Space.* Oxford: Blackwell, 327–355.

Thrift, N. (2005). *Knowing capitalism.* London: Sage.

Ward, K. (2007). Thinking geographically about work, employment and society. *Work, Employment and Society, 21*(2), 265–276.

Waters, J. L. (2007). "Roundabout routes and sanctuary schools": the role of situated educational practices and habitus in the creation of transnational professionals. *Global Networks*, 7(4): 477–497.

Waters, J. L. (2009). In pursuit of scarcity: Transnational students, "employability" and the MBA. *Environment and Planning A, 41*, 1865–1883.

Waters, J. (2012). Geographies of international education: Mobilities and the reproduction of social (dis)advantage. *Geography Compass, 6*(3), 123–136.

Whitley, R. (1986). The transformation of business finance into financial economics: The role of academic expansion and changes in UK capital markets. *Accounting, Organizations and Society, 11*, 171–192.

Williams, A. M. (2007). International labour migration and tacit knowledge transactions: A multi level perspective. *Global Networks, 7*(1), 29–50.

Wilmott, P. (2000). The use, misuse and abuse of mathematics in finance. *Philosophical Transactions of the Royal Society London A, 358*, 63–n73.

Zaloom, C. (2006). *Out of the pits: Traders and technology from Chicago to London.* Chicago: Chicago University Press.

CHAPTER FOURTEEN

Education AND THE Crisis This Time

JOHN MORGAN

INTRODUCTION

The financial crash of 2008 and the ensuing global recession have been widely recognised as the most decisive capitalist crisis since the 1973 oil crisis and, before that, the Great Depression of the 1930s. For example, one authoritative commentator, Martin Wolf of the *Financial Times*, asserts,

> The glory days of financial capital are behind it for decades, the hegemonic model of the market economy is past, globalisation may be fatally destabilised by present and future global imbalances, and the prestige of the US is damaged. (Wolf cited in Gough, 2011, p. 49)

In the aftermath of the crisis many commentators pronounced that the particular form of capitalist accumulation that had come to be seen as economic common sense—neoliberalism—was in crisis and dying. There was optimism among those on the 'left' that the tide of history was turning. Six years later, however, it is clear that pronouncements about the death of neoliberalism were premature. Crouch (2011) says that in relation to the question of what remains of neoliberalism after the financial crisis, "the answer must be, 'virtually everything.'" He adds that the combination of economic and political forces behind this agenda is "too powerful for it to be fundamentally dislodged from its predominance." The economist John Quiggin (2010) argues that the post-crisis economic landscape is populated by 'zombie' economic concepts—ones that are to all intents and purposes dead but which refuse to die. Many commentators document how quickly business as usual was restored in terms of returns of income and wealth to the richest sections of societies, and how the crisis was used as a means to impose policies of 'austerity' on sections of society most affected by the economic downturn (Blyth, 2013). As a whole it is hard to avoid the conclusion that neoliberalism has emerged from the crisis even stronger than before. This is the argument of Philip Mirowski's (2013) book *Never Let a Serious Crisis Go to Waste*, which records in detail the response of economists and what he terms the "Neoliberal Thought Collective" to the crisis.

If there has been no crisis of neoliberalism, then it seems to follow that there has been no crisis of neoliberal education. Indeed, it is more the case that the crisis is regarded as an opportunity to intensify the pace of educational reform in ways that are in line with the marketization of schooling. There seems to be no alternative. Commentators such as Brown, Lauder, and Ashton (2011) warn that the promises of increased returns on the investment in education will fail to materialize as a global race to the bottom leads to an over-supply of the high-tech skills required by capital, and nation-states desperately seek to implement system-wide school reforms that will allow them to climb the international league tables in literacy and numeracy, and apologists for capitalism assert that the growing gaps between rich and poor can only be achieved by ensuring that individuals turn themselves into human capitalists, with the skills and dispositions that can make them more attractive to capital (Lindsey, 2013). Levels of student indebtedness are reaching worryingly high levels. But at the current time there are few signs of systematic opposition to the dominate discourses of educational growth.

WHY SO FEW MARXISTS IN UNIVERSITY DEPARTMENTS OF EDUCATION?

Although it seems as if there is no alternative, many of those who work in the field of education do not support these agendas. Many see themselves as committed to working for social justice and equality in education. However, few adopt frameworks and perspectives that would allow them to make analytical sense of the educational inequalities they seek to address. In order to make this point quickly and effectively in the space here, it will be useful to consider a recent text associated with the Faculty of Education in which I currently work. *Twelve Thousand Hours: Education and Poverty in Aotearoa* (Carpenter & Osborne, 2014) is a collection of chapters and shorter contributions that seeks to address the growing concerns about educational inequality. This issue is increasingly recognised at policy and classroom level.

Poverty has become an important issue in New Zealand, not least because of the perception that the country does not have an entrenched class system and that everybody is afforded a 'fair go.' Though there is a tendency to downplay the longstanding division between "rich and poor in New Zealand" (Bedgood, 1980), the effects of thirty years of 'free market' policies have made inequality a recognisable issue, with the OECD noting that the gap between the top and bottom deciles are widening at the fastest rate. This is reflected in educational outcomes, where Maori and Pasifka students suffer from disproportionate underachievement. The role that education can play in dealing with these issues is widely discussed. *Twelve Thousand Hours* on the whole focuses on how schools can make a difference. Whilst there are hints about the way that poverty or social factors can inhibit learning, the focus is largely on area-based and specific interventions designed to prove that schools can make a difference. Poverty is largely untheorised—it is taken for granted that some people live in it, and there is no attention to the fact that the 'failure' of some groups of students is concomitant with the educational overachievement of others. Capitalism—presumably a major factor in the construction of poverty—is not mentioned in the index, and the very title of the book is a reference to Rutter, Maughan, Mortimore, and Ouston's (1979) famous study *Fifteen Thousand Hours*, which is widely seen as inaugurating the whole field of school effects studies enthusiastically embraced by governments to argue that 'poverty is no excuse' for schools failing to help students' achievement. On the whole, the book reflects a stance of well-meaning liberalism, but (with one or two exceptions) offers few analytical insights into the causes of poverty and its impact on educational outcomes.

These comments, though critical, are not intended as criticisms of the authors of *Twelve Thousand Hours*. The point I am making is that, within many Faculty of Education, there is little discussion of the economic and political processes that are the cause of the problem. Instead, there is description and general discussion of socio-cultural factors, along with calls to do better, and policy remedies that effectively promise a technical fix to the problem. As Dale (2014) notes in his foreword to the collection, the book documents examples of the relationship between poverty and education, and the challenge now is to "find ways of addressing the 'whys,' and hence what can be done to bring about greater equality in and through education" (p. 12).

THE CRISIS LAST TIME

In the wake of the Great Depression of the 1930s and Second World War, advanced Western economies adopted relatively state-interventionist forms of capitalism in which the state acted to limit the powers and wealth of corporations and develop forms of state support and wages for workers. The period from 1945 to the late 1960s saw sustained economic growth: between 1952 and 1968 world economic output doubled, and the 1950s and 1960s saw the most rapid and sustained development of production in human history. During this period the gap between the richest and poorest groups narrowed. In the US this was called the 'Great Compression,' and the incomes of the wealthiest declined most rapidly between the 1930s and mid-1950s. In the UK the same process was call the 'Great Levelling,' with one Inland Revenue official claiming that in 1953 there were only 36 millionaires, compared with more than 1,000 in 1939 (Lansley, 2011). This settlement also pertained in Australasia, where it was established earlier and lasted longer. Thus, in Australia the income share of the top 1% of the population fell from 12% to 8% between 1910 and 1950, and then to 5% by 1980. Rubinstein comments that the post-war period constituted an "age of affluence for everyone except the very affluent" (p. 139). New Zealand, too, famously advertised as the 'workingman's paradise,' enjoyed from the mid-1930s to the late 1970s a sustained period of reduced inequality.

In this context, there were moves to include those groups previously excluded from formal education and a general consensus about the desirability of equality of opportunity, aligned with the drive to modernize the curriculum to meet the requirements of a scientific and technological society. 'Expansion' was a key motif of education.

However, as economic growth rates faltered and social tensions emerged, some educators began to question the nature of educational development. From the libertarian left there came arguments about the way that schooling served to institutionalise young people and arguments for de-schooling, and in the context of increased economic pressure, arguments were made about the role of the curriculum in social control. Some on the radical left argued that schooling was effectively preparation for life in a capitalist economy, and the idea that there was a correspondence between the processes of schooling and the requirements of the economic system for labour was proposed. For instance, the Open University Reader *Schooling and Capitalism* (Dale, Esland, & MacDonald, 1976) makes it clear that "schooling is not just one among many of the social institutions which contribute to the perpetuation of the capitalist mode of production, it arguably is the most important" (p. 1). Published at a key moment of political crisis as the UK's Labour government was forced to call in loans from the IMF, the book sought to challenge the 'liberal ideology' that dominated discussions of schooling. This 'liberal ideology' has three characteristics. First, that schooling critically affects the level of economic growth and social progress through its link with technology. Second, that education is an effective means of addressing social inequality, and third, the view that education and the culture it produces and transmits are neutral and autonomous representations of social relations.

A year later, Michael Young and Geoff Whitty (1977) introduced *Society, State and Schooling* with the comment: "One of the most striking features of the world of education in the 1970s, compared with that of only ten years ago, is the sudden disappearance of the overwhelming assumption that schooling is a good thing" (p. 1). These criticisms are not confined to those on the left. Karabel and Halsey (1977) note that "proponents of Human Capital Theory were on the defensive" and that an OECD conference on education "sharply questioned whether increased expenditures on education were an effective means of achieving either economic growth or social equality." However, the text that ignited the debate on the educational left about the relationship between schooling and capitalism was Stanley Bowles and Herb Gintis's (1976) *Schooling in Capitalist America*. Bowles and Gintis argue that schooling reflects the struggles over capitalism. They argue that schooling tends to reflect changes in the nature of the capitalist economy. Their argument is historical. It considers the long-term shifts in the nature of accumulation. Central to their argument is the idea of 'correspondence' between the social relations of formal schooling and those necessitated by the division of labour and its changing requirements, which, in the case of the United States, were the function of a transition from competitive to monopoly capitalism.

Schooling in Capitalist America was the subject of extended debate and critique within the sociology of education, and by the early 1980s a series of "flaws" had been identified in Bowles and Gintis's thesis (see Cole, 1988; Liston, 1988). These included the argument that the correspondence thesis relied on a reductive determinism that saw schooling simply responding to changes in the economy; that Bowles and Gintis did not investigate the processes operating within educational institutions; the thesis neglected the role of lived experience and active agency in the process of cultural reproduction; that the concept of reproduction was too blunt an instrument to capture the complex struggles, resistances, and contradictions in the process of schooling; that there was a failure to adequately theorize the role of the state—which is an active site of struggle; that the focus on capitalism led to a relative neglect of other axes of power, such as gender and ethnicity; that the analysis provided little space for politics—especially educational politics; and that there is much more contingency in the relationship between capitalism and schooling than Bowles and Gintis imagine.

Thus, by the early to mid-1980s it had become common for educators to reject the concept of 'correspondence' in favour of theories that emphasised 'relative autonomy' or the idea that 'the state and education can, given appropriate policies and socially democratic administrations, be relatively free from capitalist domination' (Freeman-Moir 1997, p. 204), Freeman-Moir argues that relative autonomy theory is attractive to educators because its effect is to free educational theory from the explanatory strictures of an historical materialist framework. Whereas the correspondence theory focuses on the limits of capitalism in realizing social quality and points to the need to transcend and transform existing modes of political economy, relative autonomy theories appeal because they offer the hope that something can be done now, and because they allow the study of policy and institutional analysis that focuses on governments without linking the state to its role in capitalist societies.

The preference for ideas about relative autonomy over the concept of correspondence goes a long way to explaining the direction of educational studies in the last two decades. There has been a growing interest in policy studies that are concerned with the discourses that shape and define educational activity, a rejection of ideology, and a concern with forms of governance and performativity. In addition, the study of issues of social class in education has been replaced by the vogue for studies of the relations of gender, sexuality, disability, and ethnicity—with the various axes of difference. At the more conservative end of educational studies these past two decades have seen a growing and burgeoning industry in the field of school effectiveness and school improvement, all of which takes as read that we live in a capitalist economy, and that schools have their own dynamics and organizational forms that exist and can be studied without reference to the operations of capitalism.

However, in the light of the global financial crisis of 2008, there are signs that Bowles and Gintis's work is being re-evaluated, symbolised by its re-publication in 2012. More recent discussions have focused on the historical analysis found in *Schooling in Capitalist America* since, as Freeman-Moir (1997) argues, "The main point of the correspondence thesis is that, over the long-term, education is a social force that tends to harmonise with the requirements of economic activity" (p. 204). This does not mean that in order for the correspondence theory to offer a robust 'scientific' explanation that we should be able to look at any society at a point in time and see a smooth fit between the economy and its education arrangements. There is a time lag, and the important term is 'tends.' Correspondence theory is a "relationship of demonstrable causation over time." A similar argument is made by Sarah Knopp (2012) who stresses that Bowles and Gintis argue that "the economic system is more dynamic—that it changes more quickly—than the educational system, which is notoriously slow to change" (p. 24). This two-speed relationship leads to periods of intense debate when elites seek to 're-purpose' the education to be more in line with current economic forms and needs. Finally, writing in the *Monthly Review*, John Bellamy Foster (2011) recently discussed the way the broad historical analysis offered by *Schooling in Capitalist America* is useful in explaining current moves to mine the public schools for sources of profit.

Given the nature of the global financial crisis and these theoretical ideas, it is therefore instructive to return to Rachel Sharp's (1986) argument in the introduction to *Capitalist Crisis and Schooling* that

> the precondition for developing an understanding of educational systems is via a holistic and historical understanding of the social formations in which they are embedded and the dominant mode of production which is structuring their development. (p. xv)

This requires moving beyond the idea that schools and educational institutions can be studied 'in their own right' without understanding the nature of the capitalist society of which they are a part and are instrument in producing and reproducing. *Capitalist Crisis and Schooling* took the form of a series of studies of how the education systems of nine nation-states were responding to the crisis of accumulation that followed the 1973 recession. These start from the assumption that a "crisis of capital accumulation necessitates a struggle by capital to regenerate the economic, political and ideological conditions for a new wave of growth" (p. 265) and that "schooling institutions cannot be analysed apart from the fundamental processes which derive from the inner logic of capitalist production" (p. 266). I want to suggest that these principles should inform our analysis of the educational response to 'the crisis this time'. Clearly, capitalism evolves and much has changed since the high water mark of these debates about schooling and capitalism. The remainder of this chapter offers some tentative starting points for this work.

WE NEED TO TALK ABOUT CAPITALISM

To recap the argument so far: I have suggested that an educational response to the crisis this time requires us to situate current educational developments within an understanding of capitalism as an economic system. This is no easy task, and there have been literally hundreds of books published on the crisis since 2008. This should be the place where debates about contemporary schooling begin. In this section, I offer an account that draws upon a number of accounts of the crisis.

My account is unapologetically 'capital-centric.' What that means is that in making sense of contemporary education my focus is on the key relationship between capital and labour. This is because it is the central place where 'value' is produced. Like all important concepts, capitalism has been defined and understood differently by different groups and people. Following Wolff (2013), capitalism is characterized by (a) a distinctive set of social relations of production (i.e., who works and for what purpose) and (b) a particular arrangement for distributing the 'surplus' that results from that production.

In terms of the social relations of production, a mass of people—productive workers—interact with nature to fashion both the means of production (e.g., factories, tools, etc.) and final products for consumption. These workers produce a total output larger than the portion (wages) given back to them. The wages sustain the productive workers; it gets them back to work the next week. The rest is the surplus and it accrues to a different group of people, the employers of productive workers. These are capitalists.

Capitalists use the surplus to reproduce the conditions that allow them to keep obtaining surpluses from their productive employees. They hire supervisors and managers to ensure efficient production, or buy new equipment or a plant, they pay taxes to a state apparatus to enforce the law, and they use the surplus to support institutions (e.g., universities, schools, churches, think-tanks, etc.) that persuade workers and their families that this capitalist system is good and unalterable.

Thus, according to this account, workers fall into one of two categories: 'productive' labourers who produce the surplus, and 'unproductive' labourers who are engaged in providing the needed context or 'conditions of existence' for productive workers to produce the surplus. Unproductive labourers have their wages paid out of the surplus that accrues to capitalists. We should note that no moral value is attached to these terms. Both productive and unproductive workers are required to sustain capitalism. For example, it is unproductive labour that keeps people healthy, teaches them to read and write, and maintains welfare and mental health. Schools and universities are clearly part of the unproductive sector that creates the conditions for existence of productive labour.

The implications of this basic arrangement for our understanding of education are profound, since the fact that schooling is funded out of the surplus owned and controlled by capitalists means that schooling is, at base, *capitalist schooling*. This means that it must at some level be supportive of the process of capitalist accumulation (for instance, by producing capable workers or turning out willing consumers), and also that, at times when the overall surplus is reduced, is subject to reduced expenditure or calls to provide greater 'value for money.'

Capitalism is dynamic: it is prone to periodic crises and at those times growth rates fall. There is less value to distribute. At these times, the state, which seeks to present itself as the neutral referee is charged with seeking to provide the conditions for continued accumulation. One way to do this is to seek to reduce spending on social welfare and education. The years following the crisis of 1973–1974 saw a restructuring of the relationship between capital and labour. Labour's share of the surplus was reduced and there followed a period of accumulation by the wealthy. Society was redrawn in lines that favoured the interests of capital and corporations. There are important debates about the exact nature of these shifts. For example, writers such as David Harvey (2005) and Duménil and Lévy (2011) argue that neoliberalism should be seen as a class project—one in which there were deliberately moves to capture the state and pursue pro-market policies. Others see neoliberalism as resulting from longer-term historical forces that lead to a greater reliance on the market (e.g., Howard & King, 2008), and that the crisis can be seen as a crisis of the underlying process of production, which will require large-scale write-off of capital before new rounds of accumulation can resume (e.g., Kliman, 2011; Mattick, 2011).

The central 'law of capitalist accumulation' is that capital must grow. Mainstream economists tend to argue that 3% growth per annum is the 'healthy' rate for economic growth. Anything below that represents 'sluggish' growth and at around 0–1% risks 'recession' or the interruption of accumulation. At the same time as we can see capital as central, there is nothing deterministic about the path it must take, as the 'varieties of capitalism' literature has demonstrated, the arrangements for organizing and realising accumulation are complex and vary from place to place. This suggests that any analysis of capitalism (and thereby the place of education within this) should recognise the 'totality' of social relations. A useful model is provided by Harvey (2010) in *The Enigma of Capital*. Harvey identifies seven 'activity spheres'—production and labour processes, institutional and administrative arrangements, relations to nature, social relations, reproduction of daily life, technological and organisational forms, and mental conceptions—each of which has its own course of evolution but is not independent of the others. No one activity sphere dominates, but at certain times one may spur changes in other activity spheres. The important point is that they are organised so as to achieve capital accumulation of growth.

The idea of 'activity spheres' and their role in the evolution of capitalism has important implications for how we study education. At any one time capitalist schooling is likely to reflect the processes and developments taking place in different 'activity spheres.'

RESPONSES TO THE CRISIS

The immediate aftermath of the crisis has seen an intensification of a number of existing trends. These are: (1) the intensification of 'accumulation by dispossession' as private capital is invited to run the profitable parts of the public school system; (2) the continued drive to innovate in education through technology and creative education; (3) the inducement to realize productivity gains through hyper school improvement; and (4) the continued focus on the problem of educational inequality.

1. *Accumulation by dispossession.* There is a tendency for capitalism to face a long-term decline in the average rate of profit, which leads to moves to seek out new sources of profit through innovation. There are a number of ways in which this can be achieved, for example, the search for new geographical markets, or increase the rate at which goods and services are consumed. Another is to take goods and services that were held in common and turn them into private property. This third option is what is called 'accumulation by dispossession,' and schools, which still retain public ownership and public funding, are a prime site for fresh sources of profit. The period

since 2008 has seen an intensification of moves to privatize schooling or at least usher in new forms of public-private partnerships that allow for the 'unbundling' of aspects of the school's activities to private firms and corporations. Perhaps the most visible example is that of Charter Schools and the role of for-profit schools (with 'chains' of academies running schools).

2. *Cool capitalism.* At a time when many people are suffering the effects of economic decline, a good deal of ideological work is required to persuade people that capitalism remains an exciting and innovative way of organizing economic and social life. Schools play an important part in this process of legitimation, and, if anything, since 2008 the demand for radical change or transformation in schooling has intensified. A strong story has emerged about the need to 're-purpose' schooling. According to this, schools are products of the industrial age. This is reflected in their rigid age and grade divisions, their fragmented subject-based curricula, and their 'one-size-fits-all' mentality. Critics argue that schools are out of kilter with a world that has fundamentally changed. Traditional schools do little to encourage individual initiative or collaborative problem-solving. Learning is cut off from real-world experiences. According to this analysis, schools and teachers need to change. The traditional purpose of schooling—to pass on knowledge and tradition—is no longer relevant. Instead, schools are to become places where children 'learn how to learn.' Teaching is less about the painstaking acquisition of knowledge and more about 'unlocking pupils' minds.' Notions of intelligence need to change too, from being seen as primarily cognitive and individual, to the idea that intelligence is multiple and 'learnable.' Much of this is to be enabled by new forms of digital technology, which are transforming the nature of knowledge. Learning can be personalized or customized, 'anytime, anywhere.' An important aspect of 'cool capitalism' (McGuigan, 2010) are changes in the nature of workplaces. Work revolves around informality, connectivity, flexibility, cooperation, decentralization, creativity, play, and so on, and the same ideas are to be applied to the 're-purposed school.' Many teachers and educators are attracted by the looser forms of schooling promised by 'cool capitalism.' For example, schools are encouraged to be open and informal, have a social conscience through connecting with communities both locally and globally, to be innovative and 'think outside the box,' be responsive to their 'customers,' and, above all, convey the message that learning is fun and playful.
3. *Hyper-school improvement.* As the crisis of capital intensifies, so does the pressure on schools to deliver economic and social goals. School improvement, which was an important growth industry in educational studies from the 1990s, has moved into over-drive. In its 'hyper' mode school

improvement calls for nothing less than 'whole systems change' and a 'Learning Revolution' based on the belief that we have the knowledge to make 'every school a great school.' The goal is to 'scale up' educational innovations, based on ever-growing bodies of evidence about 'what works.' According to Sir Michael Barber—a key broker in this push for school reform—there is now firm knowledge of how to successfully reform education systems based on a science or quasi-science of effective delivery in government or what he calls 'deliver-ology.' Policy circles are awash with reports and manifestos that stress the need for educational transformation and calls for twenty-first-century education.

4. *Social justice and inequality.* Whilst the three developments discussed so far are concerned with the transformation of education in ways that are, consciously or not, about the establishment of market cultures, the final trend, which is supported and articulated by many educationalists, derives from an older tradition of social democracy and is concerned with issues of equality of opportunity and social justice. It accepts the argument that capitalist schooling is a divided schooling, and these divisions reflect wider social relations around axes of social economic grouping, ethnicity, and gender. The social geography of educational success and failure reflects the wider society. The scale of the transfers of public money to bail out the banks and the subsequent adoption of austerity measures has inevitably given rise to a focus on issues of fairness and equality. This is in line with many educators' concern with the stubborn long tail of underachievement, and a set of arguments about the price that societies pay for widening inequality. Critics point out that the distribution of reward and status does not correspond to talent, effort and virtue, but is a function of to whom and where you were born. In addition, the middle and upper classes are becoming increasingly adept at ensuring that their children possess the capabilities and qualifications necessary to populate the upper echelons of the economy and society (Piketty, 2014; Wilkinson & Pickett, 2009)

These four educational responses to the crisis play out in different ways in different places. In the following section, New Zealand is used as a case study to show how a political economic understanding of education can help to make sense of contemporary developments.

EXAMPLE: NEW ZEALAND AND THE CRISIS

This section examines how recent developments in New Zealand education can be seen as responses to the crises of capitalism. Roper (2005) provides a useful periodization of New Zealand's political economic development. The period 1935–1974 saw the rise and entrenchment of Keynesianism. In response to the decade of depression in the 1920s, the 1934 and 1935 conferences of the NZ Labour party endorsed the strengthening of its economic policies and development of a more complete model of the welfare state. This period saw the establishment of the main pillars of New Zealand's welfare state. The economic downturn of the early 1970s and New Zealand's changed economic location with Britain marked a period that Roper describes as a crisis of Keynesian economics. This period saw important debates about the role of welfare in New Zealand's economic development and growing dissatisfaction with the 'interventionist' stance of governments. A broader ideological shift around monetarist economics prepared the ground for the election of a third Labour government committed to radical reform that involved the liberalization of trade and the 'rolling back' of the state. Roper suggests that, by 1999, in the face of growing opposition, the radical changes had run their course and that the period 2000–2008 saw the softening and entrenchment of the neoliberal policy regime.

Freeman-Moir (1986, 1997) provides useful educational detail to this general picture. He notes that in the Keynesian period, economic growth and political consensus allowed for the expansion of schooling and the incorporation of girls and Maori students into secondary education. There was a loose fit between a prosperous economy and the liberal philosophy of schooling. Most New Zealanders were wealthier, healthier, and better educated. The crisis of the 1970s led to a growing disillusionment with schooling on the part of both students and business, who complained that schooling was not equipping students with the appropriate basic skills and attitudes required for the modern workplace. At the same time, arguments about the cost of welfare led to the growth of arguments about the need to shift from a welfare state to a welfare society, and for individuals and communities to take more responsibility. The dramatic shift in the economic culture of New Zealand was reflected in the radical reforms of the Labour government that came to power in 1984. Its major educational legislation, *Tomorrow's Schools* (1988), reflected a desire to reduce the fiscal responsibility of the state and at the same time re-orientate the curriculum to reflect the need for more entrepreneurial and competitive individuals. This was in line with the perceived need to restore New Zealand's competitive advantage by moving away from a reliance on primary industries for export earnings. Education was central to this, and influential reports argued that the New Zealand educational system "is not equipping people with the skills necessary to compete successfully in the global economy" (Crocombe, Enright, & Porter, 1991). The introduction of competency-based curriculum in 1993 and the drive to raise standards for all students reflects this desire to use the education system to raise productivity. Freeman-Moir contrasts the optimism about educational progress that accompanied the economic long-boom with the almost 'total disappearance' of liberal hope as the economic crisis of the 1970s unfolded.

To bring the story up to date, in a recent analysis of the Fifth National (2008–2011) government, Roper (2011) argues that the return of the Fifth National government in 2008 did not mark a substantive 'turning point' but a continuation and entrenchment of the neoliberal policy regime. Roper notes that there has been a sharp reversal in the fortunes of neoliberalism since the onset of the global financial crisis, with New Zealand currently experiencing a low rate of economic growth and continued high levels of unemployment. All this against a backdrop in which the implementation of neoliberal policies has substantially increased socio-economic inequality and where there is little evidence for the 'trickle-down' of wealth from the richest section of the population to the poorest. Indeed, in 2011 an OECD report noted that New Zealand has experienced the fastest rate of growth in inequality over the past decade. For Roper this can be explained by the shift in the balance of class forces from the 1980s onwards. He concludes that the future development of government policymaking in New Zealand will depend crucially on developments within the domestic and global economies, particularly how well the economy recovers from the recession and whether or not New Zealand can avoid a major financial crisis depression (given its ongoing large current account deficits and rising net international liabilities).

The financial crisis was refracted through the lens of national economic policy. The national government acted swiftly to maintain economic stability through an injection of short-term spending into the economy. As Roper suggests, although some commentators regard this as a rejection of neoliberal tenets, in fact it is in line with "actually existing neoliberalism," which is pragmatic and flexible in its operations. However, the government is insistent on the need to maintain international confidence in New Zealand and ensure its ability to borrow on the world's capital markets by maintaining its credit rating. Part of this strategy is the new regional trade agreement, which is designed to provide new and secure markets for New Zealand exports.

In terms of the relations of social forces, class continues to be downgraded in importance in New Zealand society, which befits the claim that, as a small island, 'we are all in this together.' Thus public expenditure reductions are necessary for New Zealand to remain competitive. Within this, there is renewed pressure on those groups who do not contribute sufficiently and who either require discipline (e.g., young mothers, welfare recipients) or support (e.g., Pasifika communities).

In a response to Roper's analysis, Neilson (2011) argues that while the neoliberal project "pulled common sense along" through the 1980s and early 1990s, now "common sense appears to be much more in accord with the neoliberal project." He suggests:

> The natural order is seen to be characterized by intense competition, and New Zealand's competitiveness is seen to be directly dependent on it providing a profitable terrain for firms. In turn, capital's prosperity becomes 'the key to prosperity' of citizens as well. NZ's path to wealth, security and the World Cup becomes obvious: we must compete and win! (p. 70)

New Zealand's crisis (if indeed there is a crisis) is a crisis of growth. The economic growth rates since the mid-1970s are significantly lower than the previous two decades, and the changes in educational policy and practice correspond to the increased need for restructuring that can boost growth. The global economic crisis of 2008 reduced even further these rates of growth, with the influential 'think tank,' the NZIER, arguing in 2012 that New Zealand was back to 2005 levels of economic performance. As Colin Hay (2014) has argued, this can lead to a fiscal crisis for the state, as lower levels of growth lead to lower tax revenues and the need to reduce spending. Much of what has happened in educational policy in the years since the crisis can be understood in these terms, since they are concerned with aligning the goals of the education system with the requirements of the competition state.

Thus, there is evidence of the alleged need to reduce the costs of the public sector through renegotiating the contracts with teachers and challenge the power of trade unions, along with moves to shed the cost of provision and inject private capital into the school sector with the use of charter schools. In addition there is a concerted drive to improve educational attainment through involvement in global education reform and school leadership programmes to address the long tail of underachievement. There is a rejection of the idea that social factors contribute to school failure and to encourage individuals and communities to resolve social problems. New Zealand also seeks to modernize its school system through advances in digital technology and twenty-first-century learning, supported and favoured by large-scale corporations. Most important, there is an incessant urge for New Zealand to innovate, be entrepreneurial, invent, and compete on the world stage in order to 'get off the grass' (a reference to the continued dependency on dairying) and diversify its economy.

CONCLUSION

Perhaps the dominant response to the global financial crisis since 2008 has been the attempt by governments to reassure their citizens that rather than representing a failure of the economic system and ideology that underpins it, the crisis was a temporary aberration, caused by individuals who 'behaved badly,' and that the return to 'business as usual' is not far away. This goes some way to explaining the general failure of educational studies to acknowledge or address the crisis. For the past three decades, schooling has become increasingly geared to preparing young people for lives in the precarious labour markets of fast capitalism, and it might be imagined that a failure of that version of capitalism would prompt questions about the validity of that approach. However, as suggested in this chapter, education is treated as though it has relative autonomy from the economy.

The immediate challenge is to reconnect debates about schooling to the wider discussions about economic futures. The predominant response *so far* has been to see education as serving the needs of an economic system that is seeking to 'return to normal' as soon as possible. However, as many commentators point out, this may not be realistic, and the coming decades may see important shifts in how production and consumption are organized. The challenge for educators is to play a central part in these developments, and to develop theories and practices that understand schooling as unavoidably connected to the totality of capitalist societies.

REFERENCES

Bedgood, D. (1980). *Rich and poor in New Zealand: A critique of class, politics and ideology*. Auckland: Allen & Unwin.

Blyth, M. (2013). *Austerity: The history of a dangerous idea*. Oxford: Oxford University Press.

Bowles, S., & Gintis, H. (1976). *Schooling in capitalist America: Educational reform and the contradictions of economic life*. London: Routledge & Kegan Paul.

Brown, P., Lauder, H., & Ashton, D. (2011). *The global auction: The broken promises of jobs, education and incomes*. New York: Oxford University Press.

Carpenter, V., & Osborne, S. (Eds.). (2014). *Twelve thousand hours: Education and poverty in Aotearoa New Zealand*. Auckland: Dunmore.

Cole, M. (Ed.). (1988). *Bowles and Gintis revisited: Correspondence and contradiction in education theory*. London: Falmer.

Crocombe, G., Enright, M., & Porter, M. (1991). *Upgrading New Zealand's competitive advantage*. Oxford: Oxford University Press.

Crouch, C. (2011). *The strange non-death of neoliberalism*. Cambridge: Polity.

Dale, R. (2014). Foreword. In Carpenter, V., & Osborne, S. (Eds.), *Twelve thousand hours: Education and poverty in Aotearoa New Zealand*. Auckland: Dunmore (pp. 9–12).

Dale, R., Esland, G., & MacDonald, M. (1976). *Schooling and capitalism: A sociological reader*. London: Routledge & Kegan Paul.

Duménil, G., & Lévy, D. (2011). *The crisis of neoliberalism*. Cambridge, MA: Harvard University Press.

Foster, J. B. (2011). Education and the structural crisis of capital: The US case. *The Monthly Review, 61*(3). Available at www.monthlyreview.org

Freeman-Moir, J. (1986). Capital crisis and education in New Zealand. In R. Sharp (Ed.), *Capitalist crisis and schooling: Comparative studies in the politics of education* (pp. 180–211). Melbourne: Macmillan.

Freeman-Moir, J. (1997). State and education across half a century. In C. Rudd and B. Roper (Eds.), *The political economy of New Zealand* (pp. 202–219). Oxford: Oxford University Press.

Gough, I. (2011). From financial crisis to fiscal crisis. In K. Farnsworth and Z. Irving (Eds.), *Social policy in challenging times* (pp. 49–64). Bristol: Polity.
Harvey, D. (2005). *A brief history of neoliberalism.* Oxford: Oxford University Press.
Harvey, D. (2010). *The enigma of capital (and the crises of capitalism).* London: Profile.
Hay, C. (2014). A crisis of politics in the politics of crisis. In D. Richards, M. Smith, & C. Hay (Eds.) *Institutional Crisis in 21st century Britain.* Basingstoke, UK: Palgrave Macmillan (pp. 60–80).
Howard, M., & King, J. (2008). *The rise of neoliberalism in advanced Western economies: A materialist analysis.* Basingstoke, UK: Palgrave Macmillan.
Karabel, J., & Halsey, A. (Eds.). (1977). *Power and ideology in education.* New York: Oxford University Press.
Kliman, A. (2011). *The failure of capitalist production: Underlying causes of the Great Depression.* London: Pluto.
Knopp, S. (2012). Schools, Marxism, and liberation. In J. Bale & S. Knopp (Eds.), *Education and capitalism: Struggles for learning and liberation* (pp. 9–39). Chicago: Haymarket.
Lansley, S. (2011). *The cost of inequality: Three decades of the super-rich and the economy.* London: Gibson Square.
Lindsey, B. (2013). *Human capitalism: How economic growth has made us smarter—and more unequal.* Princeton, NJ: Princeton University Press.
Liston, D. (1988). *Capitalist schools: Explanation and ethics in radical studies of schooling.* New York: Routledge, Chapman & Hall.
Mattick, P. (2011). *Business as usual: The economic crisis and the failure of capitalism.* London: Reaktion.
McGuigan, J. (2010). *Cool capitalism.* London: Pluto.
Mirowski, P. (2013). *Never let a serious crisis go to waste: How neoliberalism survived the financial meltdown.* London: Verso.
Neilson, D. (2011). Making history beyond neoliberalism: A response to Roper. *New Zealand Sociology, 26*(2), 66–76.
Piketty, T. (2014). *Capital in the 21st century.* Cambridge, MA: Harvard University Press.
Quiggin, J. (2010). *Zombie economics: How dead ideas still walk among us.* Princeton, NJ: Princeton University Press.
Roper, B. (2005). *Prosperity for all? Economic, social and political change in New Zealand since 1935.* Southbank, Victoria, Australia: Thomson Dunmore.
Roper, B. (2011). The fifth (key) national government's neoliberal policy agenda: Description, analysis and critical evaluation. *New Zealand Sociology, 26*(1), 12–40.
Rubinstein, W. (2004). *The all-time Australian rich list.* Sydney: Allen and Unwin
Rutter, M., Maughan, B., Mortimore, P., & Ouston, J. (1979). *Fifteen thousand hours: Secondary schools and their effects on children.* London: Open.
Sharp, R. (Ed.). (1986). *Capitalist crisis and schooling: Comparative studies in the politics of education.* Melbourne: Macmillan.
Wilkinson, R., & Pickett, K. (2009). *The spirit level: Why more equal societies always do better.* London: Penguin.
Wolff, R. (2013). Capitalism in deep trouble. In S. Faddo & P. Tridico (Eds.), *Financial crisis. Labour markets and institutions* (pp. 19–39). Abingdon, UK: Routledge.
Young, M., & Whitty, G. (Eds.). (1977). *Society, state and schooling.* Brighton, UK: Falmer.

CHAPTER FIFTEEN

Finance-subjectivity

Thinking through the Consequences of the Global Financial Crisis in Education

DAVID R. COLE

INTRODUCTION

The 2008 Global Financial Crisis (GFC) was an international event that few of us understood at the time in terms of the consequences for education (see Cole, 2012). Subsequent analysis of the GFC has uncovered the complex contemporary workings of capitalism that demonstrate an increasing and yet fully established tendency toward the financialisation of social life. This tendency has tied up international capital flows in escalating forms of inter-related debt and credit structures. These escalating forms of finance had hidden the cause of the GFC—the toxic sub-prime mortgage loans—which had been placed within finance packages, and were openly traded until any connection with grounded modes of exchange was annihilated. This chapter takes the processes of financialisation seriously for education and looks at their impacts in terms of 'finance-subjectivity.' The concept of 'finance-subjectivity' will be developed in this chapter in relation to the work of Félix Guattari, who furnished a useful notion of semio-capitalism. Semio-capitalism analyses the ways in which capitalism works on a semiotic level and reveals the codes and axioms that potentially trap and mould subjectivity. In Guattari's terms "capital is a semiotic operator" that "seizes individuals from the inside" (1996, pp. 200, 212) and has the goal of "controlling the whole of society" (p. 212). The writings of Franco Beradi (Bifo), Christian Marazzi and Maurizio Lazzarato, and others in the autonomous tradition have extended and added to Guattari's sense of semio-capitalism in terms of describing immaterial labour and cognitive capitalism. This chapter will use these ideas to get to the notion of 'finance-subjectivity' and how it now permeates educational practice. A recent (2012–2013) educational research project in the southwest of Sydney with public school teachers will be used to illustrate the idea of 'finance-subjectivity' in this chapter.

SEMIO-CAPITALISM

The workings of semio-capitalism and financialisation were laid bare during the crucial period of the GFC unravelling in October 2008. This event took place during the final months of the Bush regime, through which free market capitalism had been encouraged and promoted in the US and around the world as part of a market solution mentality. The deregulation that went along with the accelerated expansion of the free market was a green light for banks and financial institutions to lend money as mortgages at variable rates of interest to people who couldn't pay off the debt in the long run. The sub-prime mortgage market strategy and financial tactics of the lenders became part of the production of a semi-permanent underclass mired in debt, and alongside this evolving sociological fact, the production of a subjectivity that was desperately, convulsively, and unremittingly directed toward paying off an unsurmountable financial debt. Before the dramatic event of the 2008 GFC, the type of subjectivity produced by the sub-prime mortgage market had been 'normalised' within the Bush-led regime of free-market economics. Such a normalisation had reinforced the clearly predatory and unfavourable exchange conditions of the sub-prime mortgage market through (1) the biased media-reporting of economic events from the capitalised perspective, (2) various governmental bodies involved with the deregulation of lending markets, (3) any learning values and education systems committed to free market economics, and (4) the politics of civil society under the conditions of capitalisation and ownership; and these factors in the normalisation of the sub-prime mortgage market have been variously defined through the rubric of 'neoliberalism' (see Foucault, 2008). Under these conditions, the practice of lending money to individuals without the means to pay off the loans became commonplace and eventually led to market collapse in 2008. One can therefore initially represent the type of 'finance-subjectivity' as a concomitant of neoliberalism and as suitable for this chapter thus:

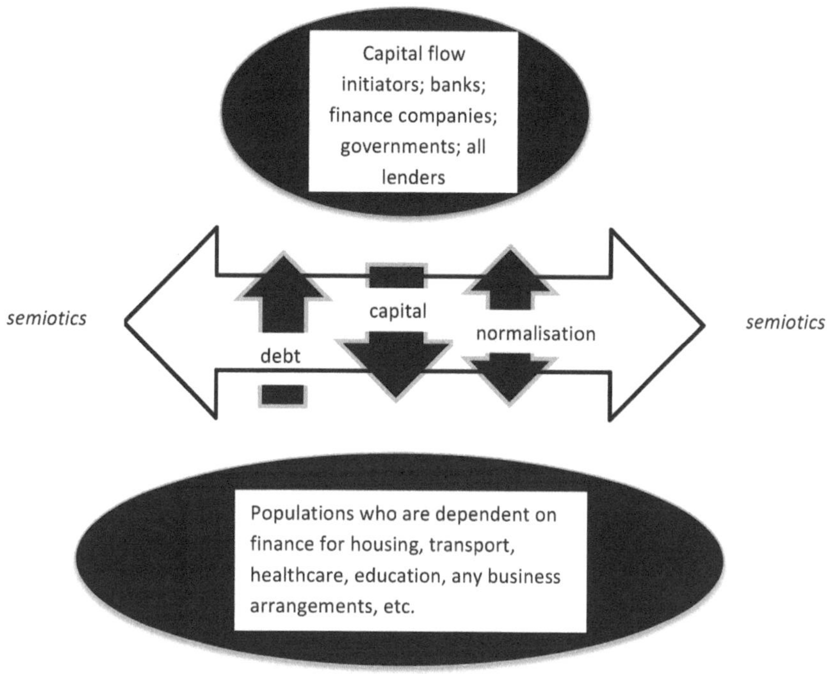

Figure 15.1. Finance-subjectivity as a result of capital lending practises (semio-capitalism).

The subjectivity that is produced through financialisation may be figured as a complex yet reciprocating, time-based, and ubiquitous notion (figure 15.1). The semiotics or exchange of signs that are dependent upon finance-subjectivity and neoliberalism share the flow characteristics as defined by figure 15.1; however, if we exempt the continuation of this model of finance-subjectivity as a form of popularism—the social and economic control of the 'in debt' majority by largely propertied and capitalised bodies through the impersonal imperatives of market forces—implies the de facto subordination of the exercise of state power to the market logic of capital in liberal democratic capitalism (see table 15.1). This logic and exercise of power adds another dimension to the finance-subjectivity of this chapter. As Jessop (2008) points out, "When a normal type of capitalist state is established, political class domination is secured through the dull routines of democratic politics as the state acts on behalf of capital, but not at its direct behest" (p. 418). In effect, finance-subjectivity and the semiotics of capitalism that produces such subjectivity can be enacted through the organs of the state. This custodianship of finance reflects the socially accepted function of the liberal democratic state in defining and enforcing collectively binding decisions on an imaginary political community in the name of an equally imaginary general interest (Jessop, 1990, pp. 240–267; see also Jessop, 2002, p. 40; Gramsci, 1971). In a capitalist society, this imaginary general interest necessarily internalizes a social content concerned with securing "the social conditions in which market forces can operate to maximize capital accumulation in the long-term" (Jessop, 1990, p. 185). Within this context, the production and reinforcement of subjectivity, termed as 'finance-subjectivity' in this chapter and that acts as represented in figure 15.1 is paramount to the normalised social conditions of capital flow and the unequal and potentially debilitating effects of long-term debt. Finance-subjectivity is produced in the interactions of capital, debt, and normalisation as represented in figure 15.1. Furthermore, as Guattari (1995) has argued:

> Considering subjectivity from the point of view of its production does not imply any return to traditional systems of binary determination—material infrastructure/ideological superstructure. The various semiotic registers that combine to engender subjectivity do not maintain obligatory hierarchical relations fixed for all time ... Subjectivity is in fact plural and polyphonic ... It recognizes no dominant or determinant instance guiding all other forms according to a univocal causality. (p. 1)

In other words, Guattari implies the possibility of puncturing, reworking, and the active resistance to finance-subjectivity and semio-capitalism. In Guattari's terms, subjectivity is itself a qualitative multiplicity and not constitutive of a closed or perennially unequal system, as he had argued in detail with Gilles Deleuze (1988). According to Deleuze and Guattari (1988) such a notion of subjectivity as a qualitative multiplicity has the capacity to critically analyse and offer alternatives to the mundane and normalised workings of finance capitalism and semio-capitalism in particular. For example, as Guattari has argued with Éric Alliez:

> Capitalism can be defined as a general function of semiotization of a certain mode of production, circulation and distribution. Capitalism, the 'method' of Capital, will be considered as a specific procedure of valorization of commodities, such as goods, activities and services, founded on index and symbolization systems drawn from a particular syntax and allowing the overcoding and control of the management running it. (1996, p. 233)

Guattari's conception of semio-capitalism draws attention to the forms of valorisation that capitalism attends to, and one could add produces a more subtle picture of this valorisation than orthodox Marxian analysis of value in capitalist relations such as that of Jessop (1990, 2002, 2008). The analysis of value in semio-capitalism extends to a historical framing of capitalism that shows how the various formations of [state-production-market] have been rearranged and ordered through time and geopolitically (table 15.1). The link between these analyses is the semio-capitalism of Guattari that makes the connection between the circulation of signs and value implicit in the functioning of society (table 15.1).

The ordering and valorisation as depicted by table 15.1 shows how the various modes of capitalism have developed a value system central to their control of society.

Table 15.1. The six formulae of structures of capitalistic valorisation (Guattari & Alliez, 1996, p. 239).

Order of priorities	Examples
a) State > production > market	Asiatic mode of production* Nazi-type war economy
b) Market > production > state	Commercial proto-capitalism World economies centred on a network of cities**
c) Market > state > production	Liberal capitalism
d) Production > state > market	Colonial monopoly capitalism
e) Production > market > state	Integrated world capitalism
f) State > market > production	State capitalism

*For instance, China in the second and third centuries BC.

**For instance, Venice, Antwerp, Genoa, Amsterdam, between the thirteenth and seventeenth centuries.

The finance-subjectivity and financial capitalism of this chapter, which still has a basis in the exchange of signs according to Guattari (semio-capitalism)—has effectively merged and augmented the spheres of commercial capitalism, liberal capitalism, and integrated world capitalism (b, c & e) in table 15.1. Furthermore, finance capitalism has benefitted from the use of global computational networks that transmit and communicate data at ever faster and more efficient rates; making the reading, understanding, and investment or disinvestment in international market trends exponentially more powerful and directed. The upshot of recent developments in financial capitalism, is that the hold and reach of the finance-subjectivity of this chapter has deepened and compexified through digital networks. It is therefore worth thinking through the consequences of this development with reference to the finance-subjectivity of this chapter by examining the conceptual work that has emerged from theorists familiar with Guattari's semio-capitalism before moving on to apply these ideas to education.

IMMATERIAL LABOUR AND COGNITIVE CAPITALISM

Direct comprehension of the working of capitalism has become increasingly more opaque given the types of digital and financial cloaking that debt structures and finance packages have been given. This means that, for example, in the run up to the 2008 GFC, traders could deal in financial packages that included the sub-prime toxic loans without directly knowing or disclosing that fact. Perhaps the 'best fit' to comprehend the overall tendencies in contemporary financial capitalism lie in the ways in which the straightforward ownership of the means to production have been replaced by a generalised intellectual endeavour to be productive and to make a profit (at all times and at any cost). Factories and sites of production still exist and many are still directly owned, yet ownership is now often dependent on optimising shareholder and market value. Furthermore, a whole new set of industries have begun to dominate the ways in which value in the market is recognised and understood. With respect to this new sense of value; product development, marketing, product distribution and advertising now have to relate to and deploy social media to be successful and to compete. This process of understanding, crowd sourcing, and reciprocation, and optimal placement in social media implies a new form of mediated value connected to a new form of labour, which has been termed as 'immaterial labour' (Lazzarato, 1997) and the consequent emergence of a new form of capitalism that can be theorised as 'cognitive capitalism' (cf. Marazzi, 2011). The definitions of cognitive capitalism and immaterial labour have been brought together in the following statement, which relates to their value structures:

> Cognitive capitalism theorists believe that it is centered around the accumulation of immaterial assets, especially related to the information core of products, which are protected through Intellectual Property Rights, i.e. legal means such as patents. These patents, as they are used by brands, in sectors such as pharma, agribusiness and software (Microsoft), then allow for the creation of a surplus value resulting from monopolistic rents. The contradiction of cognitive capitalism is that the products themselves are generally cheap to produce (though intellectually strenuous), so they have to be kept in a state of artificial scarcity through IP protection. Cognitive capitalism is associated with the process of a private appropriation of the Information Commons. (P2P, 2009)

This war between the private accumulation of knowledge and the public ownership and circulation of knowledge is played out through finance-subjectivity and debt-credit relations. Financial capitalism will direct investment into anything that can be seen to have growth and profit potential, such as immaterial assets and IP. The question remains as to how one can coherently argue against such a process as imbuing a new sense of value. On the flipside of this tendency, one could suggest that these notions of cognitive capitalism and immaterial labour have coincided perhaps most powerfully in the autonomist tradition and revolt against financial capitalism through the political-aesthetic work of Franco Beradi (e.g., 2012) who tries to set up a counter set of values to financial capitalism. However, as summarized by Paolo Virno (1996), Marx had already identified a future where increasingly the production of value resides not simply in the appropriation of the time of the worker, defined by units of time, but in scientific knowledge incarnated in the system of machines; and in a "mass intellectuality understood as a living articulation of such machines" (Terranova, 2006, p. 29). In the *Grundrisse*, Marx explicitly states that in the capitalist mode of production, the source of wealth is no longer the immediate work of the individual, but a general productivity of the social body—dispersed through technologies and human bodies, connected in new, shifting assemblages (i.e., the general intellect) and defined here through immaterial labour and cognitive capitalism. Furthermore, the general intellect can be directly related to the production of finance-subjectivity through investment strategies, which it could be argued has come to direct all modes of social life under the current regime of financial capitalism.

Of course, one could argue that the characterisations of immaterial labour and cognitive capitalism as currently presented are inadequate to the contemporary social situation (e.g., Caffentzis, 2011, yet for the purposes of this chapter, what is important is that the *tendencies* of immaterial labour and cognitive capitalism are recognised and theorised. Similarly, the way in which the theorisations of cognitive capitalism and immaterial labour have been remapped through Marx's general intellect does show a surprisingly retroactive, contradictory and nineteenth-century approach to understanding contemporary modes of capitalism (e.g., Vercellone, 2007). However, one could argue that it is impossible to map or understand contemporary capitalism without recourse to either Marx or to contradiction. This is because at the heart of the argument of this chapter is the production of 'finance-subjectivity' that is a *tendency with positive and negative attributes*, and is part of the cyclic machinery of financial capitalism. In these terms, rather than only looking at the GFC in 2008 as a terrible calamity of mismanagement and greed gone wild (which it certainly was), the outcome of the analysis from the perspective of the production of finance-subjectivity and financial capitalism in general is that the result of the 2008 GFC was also progressive and assumes increased forms of unassailable debt into the future. In other words, one can argue that the GFC of 2008 was part of the in-built cycles of capitalism that go back to the systemic analysis of value and contradiction taken from Marx and resulting in the 'general intellect' of cognitive capitalism and immaterial labour today. For example, the GFC of 2008 has enabled private financial institutions to increasingly access public funds, putting any free public funding by government under further financial pressure. Contradictorily, banks and financial institutions have been openly bailed out and supported by governments after and beyond the GFC, which has added depth and profundity to the contradictory influence of finance-subjectivity, and has created a new dimension for the control of human subjectivity. As Shaviro (2010) has stated as a concomitant to the 2008 GFC: "The financialization of human life means that market competition, with its calculus of credit and debt, is forcibly built into all situations, and made into a necessary precondition for all potential actions" (p. 8).

The calculus of credit and debt is crucial to understanding how finance-subjectivity works. The relation between credit and debt is understood in neoliberal terms through categories such as 'entrepreneurship,' or in establishing oneself productively in the marketplace through business or personal endeavour. Such endeavour itself rests upon positioning as a 'producer-consumer' in the marketplace, as entrepreneurs have to take account the calculus of credit and debt and profit making with respect to any decisions that they take. Over time, this model of neoliberal selfhood has come to dominate other forms of self and indeed become a collective notion of what it means to be successful in neoliberal or finance-subjective terms. The endgame of finance-subjectivity, that is, to be free from debt, becomes an unrealisable dream and part of a raft of idealisms connected to existing under the regime of financial capitalism—dropping out has been nullified as an option, the unemployed are equally targeted for finance. Again, such normalisation of the processes of financial capitalism is effected socially or through the semiotics of capital flows according to Guattari's semio-capitalism (figure 15.1). The exchange of signs about one's proficiency as an entrepreneur or rights as a consumer can lead to ossified potential dead ends and the closed prospects of bourgeois over-confidence and self-absorption, or, perhaps worse, falling into one of the most conspicuous traps of semio-capitalism, that of 'believing in the hype' instead of developing a questioning attitude and critical practise to the current regime of signs. Such a questioning position was offered by Guattari's philosophical partner Gilles Deleuze in an earlier work, *Difference & Repetition*:

> The more our daily life appears standardised, stereotyped, and subject to an accelerated reproduction of objects of consumption, the more art must be injected into it in order to extract from it that little difference which plays simultaneously between other levels of repetition, and even in order to make the two extremes resonate—namely, the habitual series of consumption and the instinctual series of destruction and death. (1994, p. 293)

The fundamental question for this chapter therefore can be framed through this remark from Deleuze and it is: How can finance-subjectivity be questioned and potentially subverted? Given that the tendency to produce finance-subjectivity has increased and deepened after and due to the 2008 GFC, and this has resulted in a new sense of value that may be characterised through the tendencies to immaterial labour and cognitive capitalism, the only recourse is to go back to habitual practises, beliefs, actions, and thoughts that result due to finance-subjectivity. Such recourse must include the art of which Deleuze speaks and the resonance between levels, in this case figured in terms of finance-subjectivity and semio-capitalism. In many ways, this recourse means going back to the matter of exactly what is immaterial labour and what is the precise cognitive work of cognitive capitalism. To clarify this point, Lazzarato has offered a division between the informational and cultural work of immaterial labour:

> The concept of immaterial labour refers to two different aspects of labour. On one hand, as regards the 'informational content' of the commodity, it refers directly to the changes taking place in workers' labour processes in big companies in the industrial and tertiary sectors, where the skills involved in direct labour are increasingly skills involving cybernetics and computer control (and horizontal and vertical communication). On the other hand, as regards the activity that produces the 'cultural content' of the commodity, immaterial labour involves a series of activities that are not normally recognized as 'work'—in other

> words, the kinds of activities involved in defining and fixing cultural and artistic standards, fashions, tastes, consumer norms, and, more strategically, public opinion. (2014)

As an example to illustrate the distinction between informational and cultural work, if one is hired to explore and report on the market conditions for property development in an area of high environmental value, this is clearly a form of immaterial labour and cognitive work with definite capitalist consequences that would be of interest to financial institutions with respect to its investment prospects. As argued by Lazzarato, this immaterial labour can be divided into two aspects: the first relating to the informational calculation of environmental impacts, costs of construction, labour and materials, current sales pricing, and finance possibilities; the second referring to the qualitative or cultural work around what it means to develop in the area, for example, if there are any indigenous landowners or cultural issues relating to the site. In sum, finance-subjectivity figures these two aspects of the labour as problems to be solved, whereas this chapter figures such work on many levels, both creatively and critically. Guattari's semio-capitalism does not suggest the non-completion of immaterial labour, but the recognition and experimentation with the immaterial aspects of these new forms of labour. Such experimentation happens as a result of the analysis of the immaterial and cognitive functions of work, action, and thought, as well as the material and affective levels of process and form connected to finance-subjectivity, that Guattari terms with reference to psychoanalysis as 'transversality' (see Guattari, 1984). Education could be positioned as playing a vital role in the introduction of the practice of transversality, and this chapter will introduce a connected research study on the teaching of equity in the southwest area of greater western Sydney to the analysis of finance-subjectivity.

TEACHING FOR EQUITY IN TIMES OF FINANCIAL CAPITALISM

Teachers working in the contemporary situation may well be sceptical with respect to the point of the analysis of semio-capitalism and finance-subjectivity in this chapter and unable to think 'transversally' about finance. For example, in Australia, students currently have to study an undergraduate degree before reading for a teaching qualification, which can take six years or more of full-time study. University fees, rent, and a living allowance for these years of study can be borrowed from the government under a university study loan scheme called HECs. This debt has to be paid off over a defined period of time after the student has begun to earn a specific amount of money per year. In total, the average amount of debt accrued for novice teachers entering the profession in 2014 in Australia is $36,000 (before deregulation of the university fee market), whilst the average start wage for teachers in New South Wales, Australia, in 2014 is $59,706. Against this backdrop, two educational researchers (Cole & Ullman)[1] from the University of Western Sydney worked with teachers in state high schools (n = 152) in southwest Sydney, which is an area of high social and economic needs, during 2012–2013 to ascertain how constrained teachers felt by their personal circumstances (finance-subjectivity) in terms of 'teaching for equity.' Whilst the research project did not directly ask teachers about finance-subjectivity, the ubiquitous influence of finance-subjectivity will be synthesised from the results in this section of the chapter. The researchers used a mixed-methods approach to educational research, deploying a 'teaching for equity' survey with teachers and follow up in-depth interviews around issues raised by the survey and more generally with respect to equity in teaching and learning. In the survey, the data analysis was realised through the collapsing of items according to the following 3 constructs:

1. Teacher Self-Efficacy (21 items): (Subscales: "Efficacy to influence decision making," "Instructional Self-efficacy," "Efficacy to create a positive school climate,"—Bandura, 2006) ("Teaching to accommodate diversity"—Chan, 2008)
2. Perceived Influences on Equitable Pedagogies (11 items): (Subscales: "Broad, institutional factors," "Professional development/Support," "Personal responsibility," "Hopelessness/Futility"—modified items from Csikszentmihalyi & Larson, 1987)
3. School Context Evaluation (35 items): (Subscales: "School practice for diverse populations," "Personal teaching practice for diverse populations," "School policy," "Environmental factors," "Overall rating of participants' school")

These three constructs will be manipulated and reported on alongside the thematic analysis of qualitative data in this section. First, it was found that teachers often struggled to articulate what 'teaching for equity' means. One can surmise that this is at least partially in response to the influence of finance-subjectivity, which adds nothing to the definition or articulation of equity in education. On the contrary, finance-subjectivity is about the semiotics, immaterial labour, and cognitive aspects of capitalism as argued above. Being able to define equity in teaching hardly figures in the algorithms of financial planners, yet, along with the first construct for survey data analysis (self-efficiency), can be merged into a general social imperative to 'teach better,' or to 'help improve the learning outcomes' of students in need of greater help. Such improvements in the outcomes of education could be drawn into the capital flows of financial capitalism through the positing and imagination of a 'better life' and increased participation in the mores of civil society, both of which can lead to increased modes of debt-consumption. It was found through the results of the research project (survey + interviews) that teachers in the sample correlated their self-efficiency with factors such as decision making, instructional ability, school climate, and the accommodation of diversity (see table 15.2). The higher Cronbach Alpha (α) scores indicate better internal consistency of the item:

Table 15.2. Efficiency Scales—Teaching for Equity Project.

1) Efficacy to influence decision making (3 items)	Cronbach's Alpha (α) = .64; Bandura (2006)
2) Instructional self-efficacy (8 items)	Cronbach's Alpha (α) = .88; Bandura (2006)
3) Efficacy to create a positive school climate (8 items)	Cronbach's Alpha (α) = .85; Bandura (2006)
4) Efficacy to accommodate diversity (3 items)	Cronbach's Alpha (α) = .84; Chan (2008)

Furthermore, equity domains (table 15.3) were identified on the survey and in the follow-up interviews that show how the teachers conceptualise equity in teaching and could think through the pedagogy for equity to a lesser or greater degree and that adds detail to the efficiency scales above (table 15.2). These equity domains were (1) the school-based resources for equitable delivery; (2) teaching for equity (general); (3) personal equity integration; (4) catering for student sub-groups at the school level; and (5) equity policy (see table 15.3). In terms of the 'finance-subjectivity' of this chapter, the first equity area of school-based resourcing is especially interesting, as this includes the diversion and use of capital funds in a school context. Teachers correlated this area highly with the successful or unsuccessful teaching for equity (comparison of means, $r = 0.50–0.55$, correlation coefficient, $p < 0.01$), as special programmes that enabled equitable teaching and learning had been provided and taken away at the schools according to school policy, government funding and management decisions. Furthermore, teachers who felt supported in their teaching for equity endeavours by the school management were more able to teach for equity in schools ($r = 0.49–0.20$, $p < 0.001$), and where funds had been reallocated and projects that specifically addressed equity needs had been initiated and sustained by the schools.

Table 15.3. The Equity Domains.

1) School-based Resources for Equitable Delivery (4 items; Cronbach's Alpha (α) = .84)	4) Catering to Identified Student Sub-groups at the School Level (6 items; Cronbach's Alpha (α) = .88)
2) Teaching for Equity (General/Student Sub-groups) (8 items; Cronbach's Alpha (α) = .92)	5) Equity Policy (5 items; Cronbach's Alpha (α) = .85)
3) Personal Equity Integration (3 items; Cronbach's Alpha (α) = .78)	

The research project found that there were many teachers drawn to work in schools in areas of high social and economic needs (SEN) such as the three schools in the project but that they were battling with the constant pressure on public funding. As has been suggested in this chapter, 'finance-subjectivity' sets up a contradictory sense of what can be done and what happens. In societies such as Australia, the rhetoric of 'education-for-all' and the subsidising and promotion of free public education makes some teachers in public schools believe that they are 'making a difference' by teaching in schools with children from high SEN backgrounds. However, it was found that according to the demographic element of the survey and follow-up interviews that teachers only felt that they could 'make a difference' at the school level after many years of teaching experience ($r = 0.2–0.24, p < 0.05$). This is because, after the many years of teaching and working in schools, teachers who can prove their efficacy in classroom environments will be able to establish themselves in management positions, and therefore will be party to the divisions of capital entering into the schools and understand how the capital flows are meant to be distributed with respect to equity needs. Teachers with less experience in the job expressed the idea that the capital flows and resourcing of the schools is a process 'done to them' by the management of the schools and government agencies, who may or may not have direct understanding of their specific equity needs, and they may feel as a consequence that resourcing for equity is usually 'out of synch' with their specific classroom and school experience. However, teachers with less teaching experience did feel that they could make more of a difference on the personal and pedagogic level by introducing specific strategies into their classrooms that could address equity needs, by, for example, the adaptation and tailoring of curriculum for specific cohorts ($r = 0.3–0.45, p < 0.001$).

The project found that there were teachers in the schools who had taken it on themselves to 'make a difference' through political-educational activism. For example, a teacher had found that LTGB (lesbian-transsexual-gay-bisexual) students at the school were being discriminated against and that the school was doing nothing to accommodate their needs. This teacher made an effort to initiate a social club for LTGB identifying students at the school, and had found hostility and little support for this club from fellow teachers and the school management: "I did some work … this year we've … some kids were identified as same sex attracted, who, because I do too, so and they know that, so they approached me, and they set up a … some Year 12 kids they set up a Gay Straight Alliance, which was difficult to do" (Teacher 1 from transcript). Such an uncertain tale is common under the auspices of financial capitalism because the LTGB club was clearly not profitable and can be marked out 'as other' by the normalising processes of heterosexual majority in a liberal democracy. According to Guattari's semio-capitalism, the circulation of signs happens in accordance with capital flows and debt and the resulting finance-subjectivity of this chapter. Such semiotics can produce what

Deleuze and Guattari call 'order-words' (see Cole, 2013), which circulate around society and pick up new meanings as a form of indirect discourse. An example relevant to the LTGB club would be the word 'gay,' which can be used as a normalised, derogatory term apart from its specific reference to sexual orientation or its earlier reference to joy or happiness.

In another example taken from the qualitative interviews of this project, a teacher had questioned the funding model for equity matters right up to the Australian federal level: "There are many equity funding initiatives that come from federal-state partnerships but do not get translated into school policy because of the uncertainty of these partnerships lasting into the future and beyond the current voting cycle" (Teacher 2 from transcript). The finance-subjectivity of this chapter is complicated in Australia by the different spheres of government, all of which could have an influence on teaching for equity. At the federal level a recent report into teaching for equity and equitable funding for all schools called the Gonski Report (Gonski et al., 2011) has been largely ignored by the current Coalition right-leaning government. At the state government level, where most educational budgetary matters for schools get decided, many special funding arrangements for equity needs in New South Wales (NSW) have been recently cancelled under the umbrella of the budget crisis, itself stemming back to the 2008 GFC. At the local level, councils have very little extra funding for schools though will 'work together' with schools on projects of specific local interest. This teacher lamented the non-introduction of the specifics of the Gonski Report, which would have had the effect of introducing greater funding for students with special needs. One could state that this teacher was aware of and could critically analyse 'finance-subjectivity' beyond the personal or pedagogic level and as a matter of general governance. The sometimes obscure and complicated matter of exactly how the capital flows for education are divided in Australian state schools makes this type of understanding rare.

Several teachers in the study compared the ways in which equity matters are dealt with in private and state schools in NSW. Private schools usually have better resources and more specific capabilities for dealing with equity matters that can be placated through resourcing. Extra helpers in the classroom and better library resources were given as examples of the ways in which private schools in NSW could better deal with diversity and special learning needs. In general, the move toward local school fund raising was noted and teachers were becoming voluntary workers at weekend school fêtes to help the schools to fund extra school activities connected to high equity needs. This tendency, to make schools fund-raising as well as fund-receiving entities, sits well with the analysis of finance-subjectivity of the chapter, and the idea that schools could become self-directing corporate structures in line with US and WA models (Charter schools). These models for school financing introduce entrepreneurship into every level of school life and present the lifting of monetary ring-fencing and guarantees that have occurred up until now in free Australian schools. One wonders if the endpoint of such a tendency isn't a system of schooling heavily dependent on fees and with schools competing with one another over every asset including students, capital flows, academic results, teachers, high-quality resourcing including ICT provision, and leadership.

CONCLUSION

This chapter has asserted that Guattari's model of semio-capitalism is a 'good fit' with respect to the reality of education and schooling in the contemporary situation. Of course, the choice of schools (n = 3) in the research project in the catchment of southwest Sydney are not meant to be exemplary or ideal examples, but show how the trickle-down effects of finance-subjectivity work in the different levels of education. On the personal level, teachers might feel as if they are able to defy and question the unequal and destabilising effects of finance-subjectivity through their creativity and commitment to the specific needs of their students through pedagogy. On an institutional and governmental level, teachers might question how funding decisions for equity happen and how the 'logic of the market' seems to be being imposed on all schools, whereas evidence from educational research (see Cole, 2014) clearly points to the opposite; that is, the ring-fencing of school funding away from market forces as having the greatest educational benefit. Furthermore, the tendency of the encroachment of market forces on schooling, education, and learning, speaks to another concern that the characterisation of semio-capitalism might have with respect to the imposition of the work-model on life, or

> impose the Work-model upon every activity, translate every act into possible or virtual work, discipline free action, or else (which amounts to the same thing) relegate it to 'leisure,' which exists only by reference to work. We now understand why the Work-model, in both its physical and social aspects, is a fundamental part of the state apparatus. (Deleuze & Guattari, 1988, p. 490)

The suggestion of this chapter that education is dominated by semio- and cognitive capitalism and immaterial labour speaks to the pervasiveness of capitalism in our everyday lives. Guattari was an activist and campaigner against the ways in which life was being conformed and suppressed by the current manipulations in capital flows and financial decision making that chooses the profit motive over any other form of thinking. The question for teachers, students, researchers, and activists alike is whether the thinking and writing strategies that Guattari suggests, which one may term as "cartography" (see Masny & Cole, 2012), have any relevance or impact on finance-subjectivity as an enveloping shell that directs anything that we do.

The example of this chapter of teachers working in state schools sets up the contradictory and paradoxical situation of these teachers potentially questioning the very grounds upon which their pay depends, that is, the remodelling of education in neoliberal terms, and their work as being factored into a cost-benefit analysis of public finance. Once that has happened, and teaching in free public schools is understood as immaterial labour and as a part of cognitive capitalism, the finance-subjectivity of this chapter be unthinkable, as it would have been folded into the very thought processes of learning itself (i.e., non-transversal). The 2008 GFC was an event that has solidified and cemented the tendency toward finance-subjectivity throughout society and into the fabric of educational practice, thought, and research.

REFERENCES

Bandura, A. (2006). Guide for constructing self-efficacy scales. In F. Pajares & T. Urdan (Eds.), *Self-efficacy beliefs of adolescents* (Vol. 5., pp. 307–337). Greenwich, CT: Information Age.

Beradi, F. (2012). *The uprising: On poetry and finance*. Los Angeles: Semiotext(e).

Caffentzis, G. (2011). A Critique of "Cognitive Capitalism." In M. A. Peters & E. Bulut (Eds.), *Cognitive Capitalism, Education and Digital Labor* (pp. 23–57). New York: Peter Lang.

Chan, D. W. (2008). Teacher self efficacy and successful intelligence among Chinese secondary school teachers in Hong Kong. *Educational Psychology: An International Journal of Experimental Educational Psychology, 28*(7), 735–746. doi: 10.1080/01443410802259246

Cole, D. R. (Ed.). (2012). *Surviving economic crises through education*. New York: Peter Lang.

Cole, D. R. (2013). Affective literacies: Deleuze, discipline and power. In I. Semetsky & D. Masny (Eds.), *Deleuze and education* (pp. 94–112). Edinburgh: Edinburgh University Press.

Cole, D. R. (2014). Inter-collapse ... educational nomadology for a future generation. In M. Carlin & J. Wallin (Eds.), *Deleuze & Guattari, politics and education: For a people-yet-to-come* (pp. 77–95). London & New York: Bloomsbury.

Csikszentmihalyi, M., & Larson, R. (1987). Validity and reliability of the experience sampling method. *Journal of Nervous and Mental Disease, 175*, 526–536.

Deleuze, G. (1994). *Difference & repetition* (P. Patton, Trans.). New York: Columbia University Press.

Deleuze, G., & Guattari, F. (1988). *A thousand plateaus: Capitalism and schizophrenia II* (B. Massumi, Trans.). London: Athlone.

Foucault, M. (2008). *The birth of biopolitics*. Lectures at the College De France. (G. Burchell, Trans.). New York: Palgrave Macmillan.

Gonski, D., Boston, K., Greiner, K., Lawrence, C., Scales, B., & Tannock, P. (2011). Review of funding for schooling: Final report. Canberra: Department of Education, Employment and Workplace Relations. Retrieved July 10, 2014, from www.schoolfunding.gov.au

Gramsci, A. (1971). *Selections from the prison notebooks*. London: Lawrence & Wishart.

Guattari, F. (1984). *Molecular revolution: Psychiatry and politics*. Harmondsworth, UK: Penguin.

Guattari, F. (1995). *Chaosmosis: An ethico-aesthetic paradigm*. Sydney: Power.

Guattari, F. (1996). *Soft subversions*. New York: Semiotext(e).

Guattari, F., & Alliez, E. (1996). Capitalistic systems, structures and processes. In G. Genosoko (Ed.), *The Guattari reader: Pierre-Félix Guattari* (B. Darling, Trans., pp. 233–247). Oxford: Blackwell.

Jessop, B. (1990). *State theory: Putting the capitalist state in its place*. Cambridge: Polity.

Jessop, B. (2002). *The future of the capitalist state*. Cambridge: Polity.

Jessop, B. (2008). States, state power, and state theory. In J. Bidet & S. Kouvelakis (Eds.), *Critical companion to contemporary Marxism* (pp. 404–431). Leiden, The Netherlands: Brill.

Lazzarato, M. (1997). *Lavoro immateriale* [Immaterial labor]. Verona: Ombre corte.

Lazzarato, M. (2014). Immaterial labor (P. Colilli & E. Emery, Trans.). Retrieved January 10, 2014, from http://www.generation-online.org/c/fcimmateriallabour3.htm

Marazzi, C. (2011). *The violence of financial capitalism* (K. Lebedeva & J. M. McGimsey, Trans.). Los Angeles: Semiotext(e).

Masny, D., & Cole, D. R. (2012). *Mapping multiple literacies: An introduction to Deleuzian literacy studies*. London & New York: Continuum.

P2P. (2009). Cognitive Capitalism. Definition retrieved January 10, 2014, from http://www.p2pfoundation.net/Cognitive_Capitalism

Shaviro, S. (2010). The "bitter necessity" of debt: Neoliberal finance and the society of control. Retrieved September 27, 2014, from http://www.shaviro.com

Terranova, T. (2006). Of sense and sensibility: Immaterial labour in open systems. In J. Krysa (Ed.), *Curating immateriality: The work of the curator in the age of network systems* (pp. 27–37). London: Pluto.

Vercellone, C. (2007). From formal subsumption to general intellect: Elements for a Marxist reading of the thesis of cognitive capitalism. *Historical Materialism, 15*, 13–36.

Virno, P. (1996). Notes on the general intellect. In S. Makdisi, C. Casarino, & R. E. Karl (Eds.), *Marxism beyond Marxism* (pp. 265–272). London: Routledge.

NOTE

1. Associate Professor David R. Cole and Dr Jacqueline Ullman from the Centre for Educational Research (CER) at the University of Western Sydney, Australia.

Contributors

Jacob Assa (New School for Social Research) Jacob is currently a PhD candidate in economics at the New School for Social Research in New York, specializing in labor economics and economic methodology. He holds an M.Phil. in economics from the New School for Social Research, and is currently completing his doctoral dissertation on the political economy of national accounting. Jacob's most recent publications include "Financialization and Its Consequences: The OECD Experience" (*Finance Research*, Vol. 1, No. 1, January 2012) and "Inequality and Growth Re-examined" (*Technology and Investment*, Vol. 3, No. 1, February 2012).

Clyde W. Barrow (University of Texas-Pan American) Clyde is a policy analyst and since August 2014, Chair, Department of Political Science, University of Texas-Pan American, having spent 27 years at University of Massachusetts Dartmouth, and was Director of the Center for Policy Analysis. He specializes in public policy research and analysis. His areas of expertise include feasibility analysis, economic impact analysis, regional economic development, survey development and implementation, and policy analysis. He has provided consulting services to private companies, business and trade associations, governments, nonprofit organizations, and educational institutions. His work has involved a wide variety of industries, including casino gaming, retail trade, science and technology, textiles and apparel, national defence, education, health care, and arts and crafts. He has studied the economic, fiscal, and social impacts of casino gaming, including commercial casinos, racinos, and Indian gaming, existing and proposed gaming around the United States. He is project manager for the New England Gaming Research Project, which annually conducts research and analysis of New England and Northeastern casino gaming. He has delivered expert testimony to Illinois, Massachusetts, Michigan, New Hampshire, and Rhode Island. Clyde has published many books, book chapters, applied policy monographs, book reviews, and articles in trade publications, magazines, and newspapers and in various scholarly journals such as *Gaming Law Review and Economics*, the *Journal of Travel Research*, and *MassBenchmarks*.

Tina Besley (University of Waikato, New Zealand) Tina is Professor of Education and Director of the Centre for Global Studies in Education, University of Waikato. She has held academic posts at the University of Glasgow, California State University-San Bernardino, and the University of Illinois at Urbana-Champaign, where she remains Adjunct Professor. Tina's research interests encompass philosophy of education, school counselling, educational policy, subjectivity, youth studies, interculturalism, and global knowledge economy. Tina has written some 10 books and monographs and is Associate Editor of *Educational Philosophy and Theory* (EPAT), co-editor of *E-Learning and Digital Media* and sits on many editorial boards. Tina is Vice-President of the Philosophy of Education Society of Australasia (PESA), a long-standing member of the New Zealand Association of Counsellors (MNZAC). Her recent books include *Interculturalism, Education and Dialogue (2012), The Creative University* (2013), and *Re-imagining the Creative University in the 21st Century* (2013).

David R. Cole (University of Western Sydney) David is Associate Professor in Literacies, English, and ESL. Before becoming a university lecturer in 2004, David was an international English teacher for eleven years, working in Egypt, Colombia, and the UK. Since 2004, he has held teacher education positions at the University of Tasmania and the University of Technology, Sydney. In that time he has directed Bachelor of Teaching courses, been responsible for the Honours course, led doctoral writing groups, and initiated distance-learning programs. At UWS, he is currently a member of the Centre for Educational Research.

Shanti Daellenbach (University of Auckland, New Zealand) Shanti researches and teaches sociology of finance and political economy in the Department of Sociology at the University of Auckland, Aotearoa (New Zealand). Her work is concerned with the interface of pedagogy, financialisation, and politics. Her current research seeks to develop a theory of financial literacy from below through the documentation of collective and egalitarian social relations that contain possibilities for emancipatory politics within the world of finance.

Howard Gibson (Bath Spa University, UK) Howard is Programme Director of the Masters in Education Studies at Bath Spa University. He has a PhD in Political Philosophy, works in a School of Education and is interested by the field betwixt. He has most recently published in *Oxford Review of Education* on the rise of juridification and contractualism in English schools, in the *Journal of Curriculum Studies* on the nature of economic well-being, and his essay "The Teaching of Democracy" is to be republished in Routledge's Major Works series, *Philosophy of Education*. He currently writes on the augmentation of law-based forms of interactions in educational institutions and on the nature of government directives on early reading instruction in English schools.

Sarah Hall (University of Nottingham, UK) Sarah is currently Associate Professor and Reader in Economic Geography in the School of Geography at the University of Nottingham, UK. She holds a PhD in Geography from the University of Bristol. She is currently undertaking research into the reproduction of economic elites in London's financial district with the support of a British Academy Mid Career Fellowship. She has published widely with recent papers appearing in *Environment and Planning A* and the *Journal of Economic Geography*. She is co-author with Jonathan Beaverstock (University of Bristol) and James Faulconbridge (Lancaster University) of *The Globalization of Executive Search* (Routledge, 2014).

Campbell Jones (University of Auckland, New Zealand) Campbell is Associate Professor of Sociology at the University of Auckland, where he teaches critical theory, political economy and a senior undergraduate course on the Fantasies of Finance. His most recent book is *Can the Market Speak?* (Zero, 2013).

Costas Lapavitsas (School of Oriental and African Studies (SOAS) University of London) Costas is an Associate Dean (Research) at the Faculty of Law and Social Science and a Professor of Economics at the School of Oriental and African Studies (SOAS) University of London. His main research interests include the relationship of finance and development, the structure of financial systems, and the evolution and functioning of the Japanese financial system. He has recently started work on the interaction between market and non-market relations in the financial system. He has authored numerous books and articles exploring finance in the North East Asia region.

Emanuele Leonardi (University of Bergamo, Italy) Emanuele received his interdisciplinary PhD in Theory & Criticism from the University of Western Ontario (Canada), in November 2012. He is currently post-doc researcher at the Centre for Social Studies, University of Coimbra (Portugal). His research interests include theories of political ecology, the financialization of nature, and the relationships between social movements and institutional change. Recently published articles include "Carbon Trading Dogma: *teoria e pratica dei mercati globali di emissioni di anidride carbonica*," *Culture della Sostenibilità*, *13*: 107–120 [2014] and "Foucault in the Susa Valley: The No TAV Movement and Struggles for Subjectification," *Capitalism Nature Socialism*, *24*(2): 27–40 [2013].

Stefano Lucarelli (University of Bergamo, Italy) Stefano (Marsciano 1975) is Tenured Assistant Professor in Political Economy at University of Bergamo, where he teaches International Monetary Economics and Economic and Business Ethics. He obtained his PhD in Political Economy at the Università Politecnica delle Marche in Ancona (2008). Also he is Membre Associé at Centre d'Economie de la Sorbonne. His research projects include institutional economics, cognitive capitalism, monetary theory of production, financialization, stock-flow consistent models and complementary currencies. On these issues he published in a wide variety of journals including the *Journal of Evolutionary Economics* (2014), *Metroeconomica* (2014), *Forum for Social Economics* (2014), *International Journal of Political Economy* (2011 and 2012), *International Journal of Pluralism and Economics Education* (2012), *Review of Social Economy* (2008), *Theory Culture and Society* (forthcoming). Also he edited in 2008, with Andrea Fumagalli, the special issue of the *European Journal of Economic and Social Systems* (EJESS) on "Money and Technological Change," and in 2012, with Marco Passarella, *New Research Perspectives in the Monetary Theory of Production* (Sestante-Bergamo University Press). He is a researcher in the D-CENT European Project (http://dcentproject.eu/).

Sheila L. Macrine (University of Massachusetts Dartmouth, USA) Sheila is an Associate Professor at the Department of STEM and Teacher Development at the University of Massachusetts Dartmouth. Macrine's interests focus on Reading/Special Education, Education Reform, and Critical-Feminist Theory. She is the current Program Chair of the Marxian Analysis of Society, Schools and Education SIG at AERA. Macrine's latest work includes *Critical Pedagogy in Uncertain Times*, *Class in Education*, and *Revolutionizing Pedagogy*. Awarded by the Qatar National Research Fund she is currently doing research on how to adapt a U.S.-based assessment tool to serve blind and visually impaired preschool children who speak Arabic in Qatar.

John Morgan (University of Auckland, New Zealand) John is Professor of Education at the University of Auckland. Prior to that he held posts at the Institute of Education (London) and the University of Bristol. His research interests include curriculum theory, geographical education and sustainability, and digital cultures. He is currently researching the educational implications of the global financial crisis.

João M. Paraskeva (University of Massachusetts Dartmouth, USA) João is Full Professor at the University of Massachusetts, Dartmouth. He was born in Maputo, then People's Republic of Mozambique. He concluded the middle and secondary education under the Marxist-Leninist state. He graduated in Humanities (Ancient Greek, Latin, and Portuguese); Masters in Education, major in Curriculum Studies; and a PhD in Education, major in Curriculum Studies. A former middle school and high school teacher in the southern Africa region he was also a Professor at the University of Minho Portugal; Honorary Fellow of the University of Wisconsin Madison; Visiting Professor at the University of La Coruna, Spain; Visiting Professor at Federal University of Pelotas, Brazil; Visiting Professor at the University of Florence, Italy; visiting Professor at Miami University, Oxford, Ohio. He is currently the founder and Chair of the Department of Educational Leadership and Program Director of the EdD PhD in Educational Leadership and Policy Studies at UMass Dartmouth. Founder of the journal *Curriculum Sem Fronteiras*, editor of *Itinerarios*, and member of several editorial boards of academic peer-reviewed journals. He is the Chair of the AERA SIG Marxian Analysis of Society, Schools and Education. He was recently appointed Ambassador of the European Union PhD programs in the U.S. A prolific scholar with nearly fifty books, numerous articles, and critical reviews, he is also responsible for translating into Portuguese the works of many intellectuals from the U.S., UK, Slovenia, Spain, Argentina, and New Zealand. His latest books are *Conflicts in Curriculum Theories: Challenging Hegemonic Epistemologies* (Palgrave, 2014) and *Globalisms and Power: Iberian Education and Curriculum Policies* (Peter Lang, 2012) (co-edited with Jurjo Torres Santome).

Michael A. Peters (University of Waikato, New Zealand) Michael is currently Professor of Education, WMIER, University of Waikato. He held a Personal Chair at the University of Auckland, was Professor at the University of Glasgow and the University of Illinois at Urbana-Champaign (now Emeritus Professor). Michael is an international scholar with interests in education, philosophy, and social policy, who has published more than 65 books and is Editor-in Chief of *Educational Philosophy and Theory* (EPAT), editor of *Policy Futures in Education* and *E-Learning and Digital Media*. Some recent books: *Education Philosophy and Politics: Selected Works of Michael A. Peters* (2011);

Education, Cognitive Capitalism and Digital Labour (2011), with Ergin Bulut; *Neoliberalism and After? Education, Social Policy and the Crisis of Capitalism* (2011); *The Last Book of Postmodernism: Apocalyptic Thinking, Philosophy and Education in the Twenty-First Century* (2011); *The Virtues of Openness: Education, Science and Scholarship in a Digital Age* (2011) with Peter Roberts; *Education in the Creative Economy* (2010) with D. Araya; a trilogy on Creativity, all with Simon Marginson and Peter Murphy (2009–2010); *Subjectivity and Truth: Foucault, Education and the Culture of the Self* (2008) (AESA Critics Book Award 2009); and *Building Knowledge Cultures: Educational and Development in the Age of Knowledge Capitalism* (2006), *The Creative University* (2013), *Re-imagining the Creative University for the 21st Century* (2013) with Tina Besley.

James Reveley (University of Wollongong, Australia) James is Associate Professor in the Faculty of Business at the University of Wollongong (NSW, Australia). He undertook his PhD at the University of Canterbury (Christchurch, New Zealand). His research interests broadly centre on the changing nature of education, work, and organisation in financialised capitalism. His work has been published in journals such as *Educational Philosophy and Theory*, *Science and Society*, *Human Relations*, *Culture and Organization*, and *Policy Futures in Education*. His most recent publication is an article, co-authored with John Singleton and published by *Enterprise and Society*, about the public relations techniques used by London's commercial banks in the period 1950–1980. Currently he is working on a Marxian-Foucauldian critique of positive education.

Sharon Rider (Uppsala University, Sweden) Sharon is Professor of Philosophy at Uppsala University where, from 2008–2014, she was Vice-Dean of the Faculty of Arts. She is currently heading a research project funded by the Swedish Research Council that examines the conceptualization of the goals of education in Sweden, especially HE. Together with Michael Peters, she is series editor for the Springer book series Evaluating Education: Normative Systems and Educational Practices. Recent publications in English include *Transformations in Research, Higher Education and the Academic Market: The Breakdown of Scientific Thought*, eds. Sharon Rider, Ylva Hasselberg, and Alexandra Waluszewski (Springer, 2013) and "The Meaning of Higher Education: Vocation of Man or Vocational Training?" in *The Humboldtian Tradition*, eds. Thomas Karlsohn, Peter Josephson, and Johan Östling (Brill, 2014).

John Singleton (Sheffield Hallam University, UK) John is Professor of Economic and Business History at Sheffield Hallam University, UK. His research interests include the parallels between financial disasters and other types of disaster and the history of the interaction between banks and the social and political spheres. His most recent book is *Central Banking in the Twentieth Century* (Cambridge University Press, 2011). He has also written intensively on aspects of British and New Zealand economic and business history and previously worked for many years at Victoria University of Wellington, New Zealand.

Alexandra Waluszewski (Uppsala University, Sweden) Alexandra is Professor of Business Studies, Department of Economic History, Uppsala University and Research Director, Uppsala University's Centre for Science and Technology Studies (Uppsala STS). Alexandra's research concerns are innovation, technological development, and industrial renewal and a special interest is the relation among publicly funded university research and production/use of knowledge in a business setting as well as how these processes are construed in economic theory and policy. She has presented her research in these issues in a number of books, published by Routledge, Wiley, and Springer Verlag among others and in journals such as *Research Policy*, *Industrial Marketing Management*, and *The IMP Journal*.

Slavoj Žižek (University of Ljubljana) Slavoj is a Slovenian Marxist philosopher, psychoanalyst, and cultural critic, and a senior researcher at the Institute for Sociology and Philosophy, University of Ljubljana, Slovenia, Global Distinguished Professor of German at New York University, international director of the Birkbeck Institute for the Humanities, UK. He was recently appointed Eminent Scholar at Kyung Hee University, South Korea. He writes widely on a diverse range of topics, including political theory, film theory, cultural studies, theology, and psychoanalysis. Žižek's work was chronicled in a 2005 documentary film entitled *Zizek!* A scholarly journal, the *International Journal of Žižek Studies*, has been founded to engage his work.

Name Index

C

D

E

N

O

Y

Z

GLOBAL STUDIES IN EDUCATION

A.C. (Tina) Besley, Michael A. Peters,
Cameron McCarthy, Fazal Rizvi
General Editors

Global Studies in Education is a book series that addresses the implications of the powerful dynamics associated with globalization for re-conceptualizing educational theory, policy and practice. The general orientation of the series is interdisciplinary. It welcomes conceptual, empirical and critical studies that explore the dynamics of the rapidly changing global processes, connectivities and imagination, and how these are reshaping issues of knowledge creation and management and economic and political institutions, leading to new social identities and cultural formations associated with education.

We are particularly interested in manuscripts that offer: a) new theoretical, and methodological, approaches to the study of globalization and its impact on education; b) ethnographic case studies or textual/discourse based analyses that examine the cultural identity experiences of youth and educators inside and outside of educational institutions; c) studies of education policy processes that address the impact and operation of global agencies and networks; d) analyses of the nature and scope of transnational flows of capital, people and ideas and how these are affecting educational processes; e) studies of shifts in knowledge and media formations, and how these point to new conceptions of educational processes; f) exploration of global economic, social and educational inequalities and social movements promoting ethical renewal.

For additional information about this series or for the submission of manuscripts, please contact one of the series editors:

A.C. (Tina) Besley: t.besley@waikato.ac.nz
Cameron McCarthy: cmccart1@illinois.edu
Michael A. Peters: mpeters@waikato.ac.nz
Fazal Rizvi: frizvi@unimelb.edu.au

To order other books in this series, please contact our Customer Service Department:
(800) 770-LANG (within the U.S.)
(212) 647-7706 (outside the U.S.)
(212) 647-7707 FAX

Or browse online by series:
www.peterlang.com